ALIX AND NICKY

ALSO BY VIRGINIA ROUNDING

Catherine the Great: Love, Sex, and Power

Grandes Horizontales: The Lives and Legends of Four Nineteenth-Century Courtesans

ALIX AND NICKY

The Passion of the Last Tsar and Tsarina

VIRGINIA ROUNDING

 ST. MARTIN'S GRIFFIN ✉ NEW YORK

www.stmartins.com

The Library of Congress has cataloged the hardcover edition as follows:

Rounding, Virginia.
Alix and Nicky: the passion of the last tsar and tsarina / Virginia Rounding.—1st ed.
p. cm.
Includes bibliographical references and index.
ISBN 978-0-312-38100-4 (hardcover)
ISBN 978-1-4299-4090-0 (e-book)
1. Nicholas II, Emperor of Russia, 1868–1918. 2. Alexandra, Empress, consort of Nicholas II, Emperor of Russia, 1872–1918. 3. Russia—Kings and rulers—Biography. 4. Russia—History—Nicholas II, 1894–1917. 5. Emperors—Russia—Biography. 6. Empresses—Russia—Biography. 7. Nicholas II, Emperor of Russia, 1868–1918—Marriage. 8. Alexandra, Empress, consort of Nicholas II, Emperor of Russia, 1872–1918—Marriage. 9. Married people—Russia—Biography. 10. Love—Russia—Case studies. I. Title.
DK258.R68 2012
947.08'30922—dc23
[B]

2011033222

ISBN 978-1-250-02219-6 (trade paperback)

First St. Martin's Griffin Edition: January 2013

10 9 8 7 6 5 4 3 2 1

For Shir Aloni Yaari

CONTENTS

LIST OF ILLUSTRATIONS

INTRODUCTION

"Most noble and sublime was your life and death, O Sovereigns; wise Nicholas and blest Alexandra, we praise you, acclaiming your piety, meekness, faith, and humility, whereby ye attained to crowns of glory in Christ our God, with your five renowned and godly children of blest fame. Martyrs decked in purple, intercede for us." —*Tropar (dismissal hymn) of the Royal Martyrs*

"[The Russian Empire] was ruled from the top by a sovereign who had but one idea of government—to preserve intact the absolute monarchy bequeathed to him by his father—and who, lacking the intellect, energy or training for his job, fell back on personal favorites, whim, simple mulishness, and other devices of the empty-headed autocrat . . . the impression of imperturbability he conveyed was in reality apathy—the indifference of a mind so shallow as to be all surface."

—Barbara W. Tuchman, *The Guns of August,* 1962

"I have no hesitation in saying that I have seldom in the course of 30 years met any man so quick in the uptake, so bright in his mental perception, so sympathetic in his understanding, or one possessing a wider range of intellectual interest." —W. T. Stead, *The Times,* 1905

"It is, generally speaking, hard to penetrate the Emperor's soul. He was reserved, shut up in himself, mistrustful; knew well how to hide his feelings and, without showing it, to take everything in and forget nothing. What he thought after his abdication, observing the results of his unhappy reign, he confided to no one, not even to his diary. For all his simplicity, graciousness, capacity to charm, he was profoundly alone; the only person close to him, the only one he trusted wholeheartedly, was the Empress, a pure and passionate woman, boundlessly devoted to him, but thanks to her nature, his real evil genius."

—Boris Maklakov, "On the Fall of Tsardom," *SEER,* 1939

THE FOUR QUOTATIONS above, chosen more or less at random, illustrate only a very small part of the range of opinions about the last Tsar of All the Russias, Nicholas II, and his wife, Alexandra Fyodorovna, and show something of the contradictory nature of many of those opinions—from saint to "evil genius" where Alexandra is concerned, from dim-witted dunce to agile and well-informed thinker in the case of her husband. So which of these opinions, if any, is right? This book is an attempt to answer that question—and I choose the indefinite article advisedly. So many books have already been written about the life, love, and death of Nicholas and Alexandra that one might reasonably wonder what else there is to say. Indeed, during the course of researching and writing this book, I have often been asked that very thing. Conversely, I have also been told what I "ought" to say, as many people have very strong opinions about the last Romanovs, and their own clear ideas on what should be included in a book about them. It is only necessary to read some of the contributions to the discussion forum at the popular and comprehensive Web site "The Alexander Palace Time Machine" (http://www.alexanderpalace.org/palace/) to realize that, in engaging with Nicky, Alix, and their family, one is entering a minefield.

THE ANALOGY THAT comes most readily to mind when writing a new book about such apparently well-known yet still controversial figures is that of curating an exhibition of some already famous artist. Just as the curator endeavors to present a different view, through judicious, sometimes idiosyncratic, selection, juxtaposition, ordering, and even omission, so the biographer must select, consider, compare, and above all look with a fresh eye at what is already "known" as well as seek out the previously "unknown." In so doing, curator and biographer may respectively light upon something that previous exhibitions and books have missed, some detail or a new way of seeing that may alter earlier perceptions. Through engaging closely with a number of texts, particularly diaries and letters—and sometimes looking at what is unsaid as much as what is said—I have aspired to come as close as possible to "penetrating the souls" of these two complex characters, while presenting the story of their "passion" (taken in both senses, of love and of suffering) in a way that I hope will pique the interest of both the Romanov expert and the general reader. At the same time—and again bearing in mind the curating analogy—mine is only one way of seeing, of arranging the material to allow the characters to appear, of "telling the same story differently." It may be almost as impossible to find the historical Nicholas and Alexandra as to find the historical Jesus, so much being dependent on the attitudes and beliefs of witnesses. There may be as many Nickys and Alixes as there are theories about them, their images distorted by the parts they are assigned in other people's mythologies. During their lifetime they were constantly surrounded by gossip, and sometimes it may seem that it has not yet died down. They were in addition extremely private people, only really known to one another—and maybe too shy even for such private knowledge to be complete. Nicky's own account of himself, in his diary, is designed to give little away; he was always restrained, rarely given to obvious self-expression (though at times his silence speaks volumes). And, as if misleading gossip on the one hand and considerable reticence on the other did not present sufficient obstacles to knowledge, Nicholas and Alexandra have now vanished even further from our sight, into the reflective surface of an icon—where the image as instrument of devotion is meant always to point beyond itself, to be seen *through* rather than stared *at*, the portal to a different sort of knowledge. As saints—if that is what they are, or might be—they have moved literally beyond our understanding.

A few practical points: As Simon Dixon said in his book on Catherine the Great, "There is no universally satisfactory system of transliteration for the Cyrillic alphabet." My aim has been to keep it as simple as possible, and therefore to use the most familiar and easily recognizable form for proper names. In particular, where Nicky and Alix themselves use certain versions of people's names (for they wrote to one another in English), they are the ones I have used, too (unless their versions are overly idiosyncratic). I refer to the Tsar as "Nicholas" in order to distinguish him from other "Nikolai"s, and as "Nicky" despite the fact that the actual spelling used by his family was "Niki." I usually use "x" rather than "ks" in words such as "Alexandra," "Alexei," and "Alexandrovich." For the sake of simplicity I have decided to dispense, wherever possible, with the patronymic—so, Ivan Goremykin, for instance, rather than Ivan Logginovich Goremykin. The main exception to this is in relation to the imperial family, the various Grand Dukes and Duchesses generally being referred to by first name and patronymic. I have also taken the decision, on the whole, to refer to varying degrees of cousin (there being many such within the imperial family) simply as "cousin." Otherwise it could become unbearably complicated, and the different terminology used in English and Russian could also create confusion: For instance, Nicholas's cousin Grand Duke Alexander—technically, his first cousin once removed—mentions in his memoirs that this relationship is known in Russian as "second uncle." (This may explain why Grand Duke Nikolai Nikolaevich, Commander-in-Chief during the first months of World War I and another of Nicholas's first cousins once removed, is sometimes mistakenly referred to as his uncle.)

The other source of potential confusion concerns dates. Throughout the Tsarist period and for some months after the Revolution, the Julian (or Old Style) calendar was still in use in Russia, with the effect that during the nineteenth century the "Old Style" date is 12 days, and in the twentieth century 13 days, behind the Gregorian or "New Style" used throughout most of the Western world. I will be using Old Style dates throughout, except when I indicate to the contrary; in Nicholas and Alexandra's last months, when the New Style had been introduced into Russia, they used both dates and so shall I.

DRAMATIS PERSONAE

Alexander III, *Tsar*	Nicky's father.
Alexander Mikhailovich, *Grand Duke (also known as Sandro)*	Nicky's cousin and brother-in-law (the husband of Xenia Alexandrovna).
Alexandra Fyodorovna, *Empress (known in the family as Alix or Alicky)*	Fourth daughter and sixth child of Louis IV, Grand Duke of Hesse and Princess Alice of the United Kingdom; a granddaughter of Queen Victoria; married to Tsar Nicholas II.
Alexeev, *Admiral Evgeny*	Viceroy of Far East and commander of Russian forces at Port Arthur and in Manchuria during the first year of the Russo-Japanese War.
Alexeev, *General Mikhail*	Commander in World War I and the Tsar's Chief of Staff from 1915 to 1917.
Alexei Alexandrovich, *Grand Duke*	Nicky's uncle. As General Admiral nominally commanded the Russian Navy from 1882 to1905, when the rank was abolished.
Alexei Nikolaevich, *Tsarevich*	Alix and Nicky's son.
Alia	See Pistohlkors, Alexandra.

Alice, *Princess of the United Kingdom, Grand Duchess of Hesse*	Alix's mother, and second daughter of Queen Victoria.
Alix	See Alexandra Fyodorovna, Empress.
Anastasia Nikolaevna, *Grand Duchess*	Youngest daughter of Nicky and Alix.
Anastasia Nikolaevna, *Princess of Montenegro and Grand Duchess (also known as Stana)*	Sister of Militsa Nikolaevna, married first to the 6th Duke of Leuchtenberg and then to Grand Duke Nikolai Nikolaevich.
Ania	See Vyrubova, Anna.
Aprak	See Obolenskaya, Princess.
Benckendorff, *Count Paul von*	Grand Marshal of the Imperial Court. Aide-de-Camp General of Emperor.
Bertie	See Edward, Prince of Wales.
Botkin, *Dr. Evgeny*	Head Physician-in-Ordinary to His Majesty the Emperor, and Alix's personal physician.
Buchanan, *Sir George*	British Ambassador to St. Petersburg from 1910.
Dediulin, *Vladimir*	Palace Commandant from 1906 until his death in 1913.
Derevenko, *Andrei*	Sailor whose task it was to look after Alexei.
Derevenko, *Dr. Vladimir*	Assistant to Professor Fyodorov, and Alexei's personal doctor.
Dmitry Pavlovich, *Grand Duke*	Nicky's young cousin, son of his Uncle Pavel (by his first wife Princess Alexandra of Greece), brother of Maria Pavlovna (the younger).
Ducky	See Victoria Melita.
Dzhunkovsky, *Major-General Vladimir*	Assistant Minister of Internal Affairs and Commander of the Corps of Gendarmes from 1913 to 1915.
Edward, *Prince of Wales, later King Edward VII (also known as Bertie)*	Uncle of both Alix and Nicky (he was the brother of Alix's mother Alice, and the husband of Nicky's mother's sister Alexandra of Denmark).
Elisabeth, *Grand Duchess (also known as Ella)*	Alix's sister, married to Grand Duke Sergei Alexandrovich. After his death, she became Abbess of her own order of nuns.

Elisabeth, *Princess (also known as Ella)*	Alix's niece, the daughter of her brother Ernie and his first wife Ducky.
Ella	See both Grand Duchess Elisabeth and Princess Elisabeth.
Ernest Louis, *Grand Duke of Hesse (also known as Ernie)*	Alix's brother, the last Grand Duke of Hesse and by Rhine.
Ernie	See Ernest Louis.
Fredericks, *Baron (later Count)*	Assistant Minister of Imperial Court from 1893, and Minister of Imperial Court from 1897 to 1917; received title of Count in 1913.
Fyodorov, *Professor*	Court surgeon.
George, *Duke of York (later King George V of Great Britain and Ireland, also known as Georgie)*	Nicky and Alix's English cousin, son of King Edward VII.
George, *Prince*	Nephew of Militsa and Stana, son of Peter I of Serbia.
George, *Prince of Greece and Denmark*	Nicky's cousin.
Georgy Alexandrovich, *Grand Duke*	Nicky's brother.
Georgy Mikhailovich, *Grand Duke*	Nicky's cousin, brother of Sandro.
Gilliard, Pierre	One of the tutors of the imperial children.
Goremykin, *Ivan*	Prime Minister for a brief period in 1906, and again from 1914 to 1916.
Guchkov, *Alexander*	Chairman of Third Duma, March 1910; resigned March 1911. Chairman of Central War Industries Committee during World War I and member of State Council; first Minister of War and Navy in Provisional Government 1917.
Hanbury-Williams, *Sir John*	Head of British Military Mission at Russian Army GHQ in World War I.
Hendrikova, *Countess Anastasia*	Lady-in-waiting to Alix.

Kerensky, *Alexander* — Member of Third and Fourth Dumas; Vice Chairman of Petrograd Soviet 1917; Minister of Justice, of War and Navy, and Prime Minister in Provisional Government 1917.

Khvostov, *Alexei* — Served in Ministry of Justice; later Vice-Governor and Governor of Nizhny Novgorod; member of Fourth Duma in extreme Right group; Minister of Interior from 1915 to 1916.

Kirill Vladimirovich, *Grand Duke* — Nicky's cousin.

Kokovtsov, *Vladimir* — Minister of Finance from 1904 (with a break when Sergei Witte was Prime Minister), and also Prime Minister from 1911 to 1914.

Konstantin Konstantinovich, *Grand Duke (also known as KR)* — Nicky's cousin, and a poet.

KR — See Konstantin Konstantinovich, Grand Duke.

Kshessinskaya, *Mathilde* — Ballerina, and Nicky's mistress before his marriage.

Kuropatkin, *General Alexei* — Minister of War from 1898; in 1904 given command of Russian Army then mobilizing in Manchuria for war with Japan. Resigned command after Russian defeat at Mukden. Served in World War I on the Russian western front.

Lamsdorf, *Count Vladimir* — Foreign Minister from 1900 to 1906.

Louis IV, *Grand Duke of Hesse* — Alix's father, married to Princess Alice of the United Kingdom.

Louis of Battenberg, *Prince* — Husband of Alix's eldest sister, Victoria.

Makarov, *Alexander* — Minister of Internal Affairs after death of Stolypin in 1911. Late in 1916 appointed Minister of Justice.

Maklakov, *Nikolai*	Minister of Internal Affairs from 1912 to 1915.
Maria Fyodorovna, *Empress (known in the family as Minnie, before marriage Princess Dagmar of Denmark)*	Nicky's mother, Dowager Empress after death of Alexander III, second daughter of Christian IX of Denmark; sister-in-law of King Edward VII.
Maria Nikolaevna, *Grand Duchess*	Third daughter of Nicky and Alix.
Maria Pavlovna (the elder), *Grand Duchess (also known as Aunt Michen)*	Wife of Grand Duke Vladimir Alexandrovich.
Maria Pavlovna (the younger), *Grand Duchess*	Nicky's young cousin, daughter of his Uncle Pavel (by his first wife Princess Alexandra of Greece); sister of Dmitry Pavlovich.
Michen	See Maria Pavlovna (the elder).
Mikhail Alexandrovich, *Grand Duke (also known as Misha)*	Nicky's brother.
Militsa Nikolaevna, *Princess of Montenegro and Grand Duchess*	Daughter of the King of Montenegro and wife of Nicky's cousin, Grand Duke Pyotr Nikolaevich. Sister of Stana.
Minnie	See Maria Fyodorovna, Empress.
Misha	See Mikhail Alexandrovich, Grand Duke.
Mosolov, *Alexander*	Head of the Court Chancellery.
Muravyov, *Count Mikhail*	Minister of Foreign Affairs from 1897 to his death in 1900.
Nicholas II, *Tsar (known in the family as Nicky)*	Eldest son of Tsar Alexander III and Empress Maria Fyodorovna.
Nicky	See Nicholas II, Tsar.
Nikolai Mikhailovich, *Grand Duke*	Nicky's cousin, Sandro's brother, a historian.
Nikolai Nikolaevich, *Grand Duke (also known as Nik Nik or Nikolasha)*	Nicky's cousin, second husband of Grand Duchess Anastasia (Stana) Nikolaevna and brother-in-law of Grand Duchess Militsa Nikolaevna. Commander-in-Chief of the Russian armies on the main front in the first year of World War I. Subsequently appointed Viceroy of the Caucasus.

Nilov, *Admiral Konstantin* — Occupied honorary post of Flag Captain, which made him member of the Tsar's personal suite.

Nostitz, *Countess* — American actress married to a Russian Count.

NP — See Sablin, Nikolai Pavlovich.

Obolenskaya, *Princess (also known as Aprak)* — Close friend of Nicky's sister, Xenia.

Oldenburg, *Duke Peter of* — First husband of Nicky's sister Olga.

Olga Alexandrovna, *Grand Duchess* — Nicky's sister, married first to Duke Peter Alexandrovich of Oldenburg and subsequently to Nikolai Kulikovsky.

Olga Nikolaevna, *Grand Duchess* — Eldest daughter of Nicky and Alix.

Orbeliani, *Princess Sonia* — Maid of honor to Alix.

Orlov, *General Alexander* — Great friend of Nicky's, commander of regiment of Uhlans.

Orlov, *Prince Vladimir* — Assistant Chief, and subsequently Chief, of Military Secretariat of Emperor, from 1906 to 1915; Secretary for Civil Affairs to Viceroy of the Caucasus, Grand Duke Nikolai Nikolaevich, former Commander-in-Chief, 1915. Often referred to by Nicky and Alix as "fat Orlov."

Ott, *Dr. Dmitry* — Imperial obstetrician.

Pavel Alexandrovich, *Grand Duke* — Nicky's uncle. Married first to Princess Alexandra of Greece, and later to Olga Pistohlkors. Father of Grand Duke Dmitry Pavlovich and Grand Duchess Maria Pavlovna (the younger).

Philippe, *Monsieur or Doctor* — Abbreviated name of Nizier Anthelme Philippe Vachot, from Lyon; Alix and Nicky's first "Friend," variously regarded as a mystic or a charlatan.

Pistohlkors, *Alexandra (known as Alia)* — Sister of Anna Vyrubova, married to Alexander Pistohlkors, the son of Grand Duke Pavel's second (morganatic) wife.

Pistohlkors, *Olga (later Countess of Hohenfelsen and then Princess Paley)*	Second wife of Grand Duke Pavel Alexandrovich.
Plehve, *Vyacheslav*	Minister of Internal Affairs from 1902 until his assassination in 1904.
Pobedonostsev, *Konstantin*	Chief Procurator of the Holy Synod from 1880 to 1905.
Polivanov, *Alexei*	Minister of War from 1915 to 1916.
Protopopov, *Alexander*	Deputy Speaker of State Duma from 1914 to 1916 and Minister of the Interior from September 1916 to end of February 1917.
Rasputin, *Grigory*	The Empress's "Friend," a so-called "starets" or "elder."
Rodzianko, *Mikhail*	Elected to First Duma and all subsequent Dumas; elected Chairman of Third Duma in March 1911, and Chairman of Fourth Duma; Chairman of Provisional Committee of Duma after Revolution.
Sabler, *Vladimir*	Chief Procurator of the Holy Synod from 1911 to 1915.
Sablin, *Nikolai Pavlovich*	Senior officer on imperial yacht *Standart* from 1906, eventually becoming its Commander. A great friend of the imperial family, generally referred to by them as "NP."
Sandro	See Alexander Mikhailovich, Grand Duke.
Sazonov, *Sergei*	Foreign Minister from 1910 to 1916. Appointed Russian Ambassador in London in 1916, but February Revolution occurred before he could take up post.
Sergei Alexandrovich, *Grand Duke*	Nicky's uncle, married to Alix's sister Ella. Governor General of Moscow until his assassination in the Kremlin in 1905.
Sipyagin, *Dmitry*	Minister of Internal Affairs from 1900 to 1902, when he was assassinated.
Spiridovich, *Major-General Alexander*	Head of Emperor's personal security police.

Stana — See Anastasia Nikolaevna, Princess of Montenegro and Grand Duchess.

Stead, W. T. — English journalist (died on the *Titanic*).

Stolypin, *Pyotr* — Prime Minister from 1906 until his assassination in Kiev in 1911.

Stürmer, *Boris* — Prime Minister from February to November 1916, as well as Minister of Internal Affairs from March to July and Minister of Foreign Affairs from July to November of the same year.

Sukhomlinov, *Vladimir* — Minister of War from 1909 until his dismissal in June 1915. Blamed for some of the problems facing the Russian Army, but commission investigating the charges against him terminated, partly through the influence of Alix and Rasputin.

Svyatopolk-Mirsky, *Prince Pyotr* — Minister of Internal Affairs from 1904 to 1905.

Taneev, *Alexander* — Chief Steward to His Majesty's Chancellery, and father of Anna Vyrubova.

Tatiana Nikolaevna, *Grand Duchess* — Second daughter of Nicky and Alix.

Trepov, *Alexander* — Brother of Dmitry and Fyodor Trepov. Prime Minister from November 1916 to January 1917.

Trepov, *Dmitry* — Brother of Alexander and Fyodor Trepov. Head of Moscow police from 1896 to 1905, and close collaborator of Grand Duke Sergei Alexandrovich. Appointed Commandant at Imperial Court in October 1905. Died of angina in 1906.

Trepov, *Fyodor* — Brother of Alexander and Dmitry Trepov. Governor General of Kiev at time of Stolypin's assassination in 1911.

Tyutcheva, *Sofia Ivanovna* — Governess of imperial children. Dismissed from court service 1912 for opposing Rasputin. Granddaughter of the poet Fyodor Tyutchev.

Victoria Melita, *Princess of Saxe-Coburg and Gotha (also known as Ducky)*	Ernie's ex-wife, daughter of Alfred, Duke of Edinburgh, a granddaughter of Queen Victoria.
Vishnyakova, *Maria*	Nurse of imperial children.
Vladimir Alexandrovich, *Grand Duke*	Nicky's eldest uncle, married to Grand Duchess Maria Pavlovna (the elder).
Voeikov, *General Vladimir*	Appointed Commandant of the Imperial Palace in 1913. Son-in-law of Count Fredericks.
Vyrubov, *Lieutenant Alexander*	Ania Vyrubova's ex-husband.
Vyrubova, *Anna (also known as Ania)*	Daughter of Alexander Taneev, and close friend of Nicky and Alix.
Wilhelm II, *Kaiser*	Last German Emperor and King of Prussia. Cousin of both Nicky and Alix; a grandson of Queen Victoria.
Witte, *Count Sergei*	Minister of Finance from 1893 to 1903, when became Chairman of Committee of Ministers. Prime Minister from 1905 to 1906.
Wulfert, *Natalia (later given the title of Countess Brasova)*	Mother of Misha's (Mikhail Alexandrovich's) child, and eventually his wife.
Xenia Alexandrovna, *Grand Duchess*	Nicky's sister, and wife of Sandro (Alexander Mikhailovich).
Yusupov, *Felix*	Husband of Nicky's niece and Xenia's daughter, Irina.

FAMILY TREE

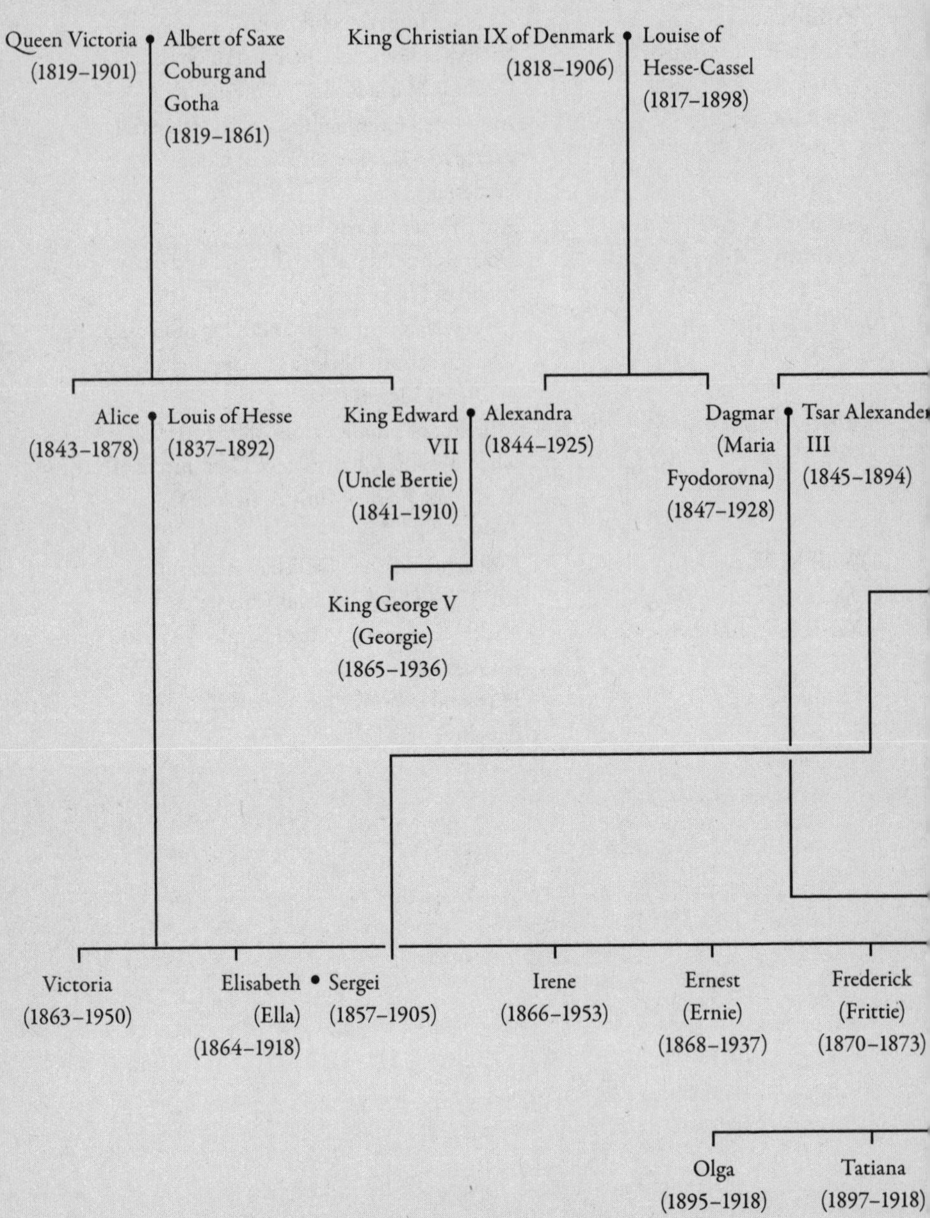

Queen Victoria (1819–1901)
Albert of Saxe Coburg and Gotha (1819–1861)
King Christian IX of Denmark (1818–1906)
Louise of Hesse-Cassel (1817–1898)
Alice (1843–1878)
Louis of Hesse (1837–1892)
King Edward VII (Uncle Bertie) (1841–1910)
Alexandra (1844–1925)
Dagmar (Maria Fyodorovna) (1847–1928)
Tsar Alexande
III (1845–1894)
King George V (Georgie) (1865–1936)
Victoria (1863–1950)
Elisabeth (Ella) (1864–1918)
Sergei (1857–1905)
Irene (1866–1953)
Ernest (Ernie) (1868–1937)
Frederick (Frittie) (1870–1873)
Olga (1895–1918)
Tatiana (1897–1918)

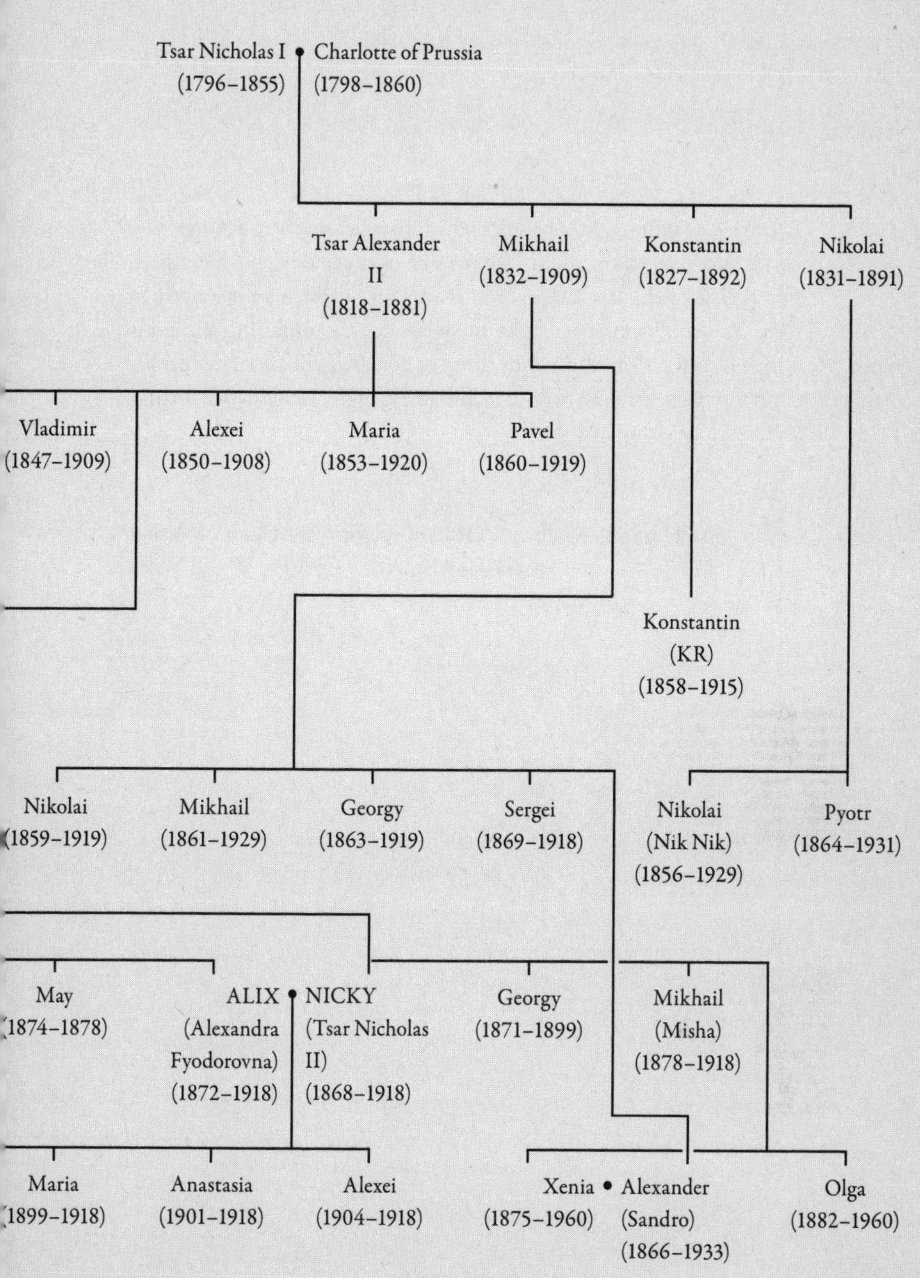

Tsar Nicholas I (1796–1855)
Charlotte of Prussia (1798–1860)
Tsar Alexander II (1818–1881)
Mikhail (1832–1909)
Konstantin (1827–1892)
Nikolai (1831–1891)
Vladimir (1847–1909)
Alexei (1850–1908)
Maria (1853–1920)
Pavel (1860–1919)
Konstantin (KR) (1858–1915)
Nikolai (1859–1919)
Mikhail (1861–1929)
Georgy (1863–1919)
Sergei (1869–1918)
Nikolai (Nik Nik) (1856–1929)
Pyotr (1864–1931)
May (1874–1878)
ALIX (Alexandra Fyodorovna) (1872–1918)
NICKY (Tsar Nicholas II) (1868–1918)
Georgy (1871–1899)
Mikhail (Misha) (1878–1918)
Maria (1899–1918)
Anastasia (1901–1918)
Alexei (1904–1918)
Xenia (1875–1960)
Alexander (Sandro) (1866–1933)
Olga (1882–1960)

Everyone, I suppose, has shadows which pass before them at times like "ships that pass in the night." To me one of the darkest of these shadows is that of the late Emperor of Russia and those who belonged to him. The sunbeams that light them up are the unfailing kindness which he always showed me in times of personal or other trouble, his sunny and cheerful nature, and his unfailing courage when things seemed to be going badly.

—Sir John Hanbury-Williams, Head of the British Military Mission
at the Russian Army GHQ in World War I

CHAPTER ONE

Setting the Scene: The Romanov Tercentenary

1913

The final curtain is about to drop,
Some fool in the gallery still clasps his hands;
Around their bonfires, cabmen stamp and hop.
Somebody's carriage! Off they go. The end.

—Osip Mandelstam, 1913 (tr. Robert Tracy)

At nine o'clock on the morning of May 19, 1913, the firing of cannon, the clashing of cathedral bells, and the cheering of expectant crowds welcomed the stately appearance of the steamship *Mezhen,* flying the imperial flag with its double-headed eagle, steaming up the Volga to the city of Kostroma, birthplace of the three-hundred-year-old Romanov dynasty. As the *Mezhen* slowly approached the specially constructed landing stage, a procession bearing the wonder-working icon of the Fyodorovsky Virgin emerged from the Cathedral of the Assumption, golden vestments glinting in the occasional rays of morning sun breaking through the clouds. Everyone on the imperial ship crossed themselves, as both procession and ship advanced slowly toward the Ipatyev Monastery, the very place from which Mikhail Romanov was summoned in 1613 to become the Tsar of Russia.

At a quarter to ten the imperial family—Tsar (or Emperor) Nicholas II; his wife the Tsarina (or Empress) Alexandra; their four daughters, the Grand

Duchesses Olga, Tatiana, Maria, and Anastasia; and their son, the Tsarevich, Alexei—disembarked, to be greeted by the city's official delegation and offered bread and salt, traditional symbols of hospitality. They then climbed into the waiting cars and were driven the short distance to the monastery, the road flanked by a double line of soldiers, holding back the dense crowds.

At the monastery, the Emperor was greeted by another procession, this one headed by Tikhon, the Archbishop of Kostroma and Galich. Here were also gathered representatives of the local peasantry and descendants of those who had come to beg Mikhail Romanov to accept the throne, at the end of the "Time of Troubles," three hundred years earlier. They carried objects dating from that momentous occasion, including a cross and an icon that the Emperor and his family duly kissed. They then followed the procession into the grounds of the monastery and toward the Cathedral of the Trinity, in front of which they found other members of the wider imperial family, the array of tall, imposing, and bearded Grand Dukes, most in military uniform, with their assorted wives, mothers, and children. The Empress and her son, both afflicted with physical ailments and unable to stand for long periods, went straight inside the cathedral, while all the other members of the family and their retinue set off again, this time to meet the procession coming from the town with the wonder-working icon, followed by a crowd of thousands. Absolute silence fell as Tsar and procession came face-to-face, broken only by the discordant clashing of the ancient monastery bells.

The Emperor crossed himself, right to left in the Orthodox fashion, and kissed the holy icon, as did his daughters. Then all entered the cathedral to hear the liturgy, followed by a Te Deum. After the lengthy service Nicholas and his daughters went to visit the house of Tsar Mikhail, which had been turned into a museum for the occasion, and where many objects that had belonged to the first Tsar were on display. The Empress was not feeling well enough to go to the museum, and remained in the cathedral with her sister, the Grand Duchess Elisabeth (known to the family as Ella), dressed as usual in her elegant grey habit, as the abbess of her own order of nuns. After a series of farewells, the immediate family returned on board the *Mezhen,* where they lunched in private.

This brief glimpse of the imperial family afforded to the citizenry and ecclesiastical dignitaries of Kostroma, when the last in the line of Romanov tsars came to venerate the memory of the first, can be examined, like a photograph, to reveal much about the apparently straightforward scene. Central to it is the figure of the forty-five-year-old Tsar himself. Slighter than many of his Romanov uncles and cousins, of medium height, his brown beard and moustache carefully tended, his face lined—sometimes he could look very weary, though the creases around his eyes also came from laughter—nearly always in military uniform and often with a cigarette in his hand, he presented a picture of affable dignity. Very conscious of his own status as autocrat, anointed by God, he nevertheless appeared modest and—overwhelmingly—charming. So many people who met Nicholas (or Nicky, as he was known within the family), whether friend or foe, testify to that charm. "With his usual simplicity and friendliness," wrote his Prime Minister, Vladimir Kokovtsov. "A rare kindness of heart," commented Foreign Minister Sergei Sazonov. "A charm that attracted all who came near him," wrote British Ambassador Sir George Buchanan, who added that he always felt he was talking "with a friend and not the Emperor." "Charming in the kindly simplicity of his ways," said his niece's husband, Felix Yusupov. Nicholas's eyes, in particular, attracted people to him. His cousin, Grand Duke Konstantin Konstantinovich (a poet, also known by his initials "KR") wrote of "that clear, deep, expressive look [that] cannot fail but charm and enchant." Yet the color of these attractive eyes seems to be in dispute. His early biographer Sergei Oldenburg refers to his "large radiant grey eyes" which "peered directly into one's soul and lent power to his words"; Hélène Vacaresco, who met Nicky when he was still Tsarevich, also wrote of his "large grey eyes." The English historian and scholar Sir Bernard Pares, on the other hand, who also met the Tsar, refers to the "beauty of his frank blue eyes." More strangely, Kokovtsov, who had the chance to stare into those eyes many times, writes that they were "usually of a velvety dark brown." In Serov's famous portrait, painted in 1900, the eyes are a grey-blue, matching the color of his uniform.

Charm—the art of pleasing other people, and the desire to please—seems never to have been a characteristic of Empress Alexandra Fyodorovna (Alix or Alicky to friends and family). Though possessed of many fine qualities (the chief of which consisted in wholeheartedness and utter loyalty toward any cause, or person, in which she believed), she was also afflicted by self-consciousness and an extreme shyness, which led her to hold herself aloof. Footage that has survived of her at public ceremonies shows her repeatedly bowing her head at the crowds—but stiffly, like a puppet, and only from the neck. Even taking into account the jerky nature of early film, she looks strained, unnatural, ill at ease—quite unlike her genial husband. An attractive woman with fine features and auburn-tinged hair, she was too tense, her mouth too set, her gait too rigid, for her natural endowments to be fully appreciated. And at intervals throughout her life—almost constantly from 1908—Alix had been an invalid, spending much of her time lying down (as can be seen in the family photograph albums) and frequently absent from public occasions. The Romanov tercentenary was important enough for her to make an effort to overcome her physical debility and participate, but even here she could not do so fully. And so, despite her great attachment both to her husband and to the Russian people, she remains at a distance, detached, in her own private space.

As is so often the case, Nicholas and Alexandra's strengths were also their weaknesses. Alix's wholeheartedness and loyalty made her inflexible, unable to adapt to changing circumstances, and tenacious in clinging to those in whom she put her faith, unwilling even to consider opinions contrary to the ones she had decided to adopt. Conversely, it was Nicky's desire to please, to charm, that contributed to his reputation for indecision, so anxious was he to make each person he received feel that he had treated them well and listened to them attentively. It was not until after a person had left his presence that he could act in opposition to what he had just heard—and had appeared to agree with. On August 15, 1905 the English journalist W. T. Stead met with Nicky's mother, Dowager Empress Maria Fyodorovna, and rather daringly told her a story that had been going the rounds:

> Once two Ministers came to see the Emperor. He received first one and then the other in the presence of his wife. Minister No. 1 brought a long elaborate report, full of all the wearisome platitudes of such official documents. ("Yes, indeed," said [Maria Fyodorovna].) He read it to the close and finished up setting forth definite recommendations that this, that and the other should be done. The Tsar listened attentively and then said: "Thank you so much for your excellent report. I have heard it with much pleasure and your recommendations are exactly in accord with my conclusions." Exit Minister No.1 in high glee. Enter Minister No. 2. Another long wearisome report concluding with definite recommendations to do this, that and the other which are exactly opposed to the recommendations of Minister No. 1. The Tsar listened attentively and then said: "Thank you so much ('Oh, how wicked,' [Maria Fyodorovna] cried.) for your admirable paper. I have heard it with much pleasure and your recommendations are exactly in accord with my own conclusions." Exit Minister No. 2 in high glee. Then the Empress said to her husband: "But this is nonsense. These two Ministers have proposed exactly opposite things and you know it is impossible to agree with both of them." And the Emperor said: "My dear. You are quite right. I absolutely agree with you." And then they both burst out laughing.

Having to negotiate the claims represented by both parents were their five children. Olga, Tatiana, and Maria, and to a lesser extent Anastasia and Alexei, all shared something of their father's need to please, and both parents had inculcated in them a strong sense of duty. This conflicted with a natural desire to assert their own feelings and sense of independence, and as a result their relationship with their mother could be both stifling and, at times, stormy. Of the five, the youngest girl, Anastasia (who, at the time of the visit to Kostroma, was almost twelve years old), seemed the most free of their mother's rather repressive influence. She adored her father (so did they all, but Anastasia's letters to her "golden, good, darling Papa" are among the most effusive; "Love you always, everywhere," she writes in a letter dated May 8, 1913), and she seems largely to have avoided the fate shared by her sisters of being the one to keep her mother company when she was not feeling well enough to join in family activities. She was a mischievous, tomboyish child, often to be found up a tree or hiding in a cupboard. She still enjoyed playing with toys, taking particular delight in a variety of little flasks and pots given to her and her brother by one of the imperial doctors. She had no trace of her mother's shyness; "If you happened to be sitting next to her at table," recorded one court official, "you had constantly to be ready for some unexpected question. She was bolder than her sisters and very witty." She was also, according to one of the tutors of the imperial children, Pierre Gilliard, "extremely idle, though with the idleness of a gifted child." The sister nearest to her in age and her usual companion, Maria, was far less sure of herself. A very sweet and loving girl, with something of the devotion of an affectionate family dog (her sisters rather cruelly dubbed her "fat little bowwow"), she was sturdy and pretty, with "large and beautiful grey eyes" and "a happy Russian face." She had a very good memory and whenever the girls needed to remember something, they allotted the task to her. The oldest sister, Olga, was, at seventeen, a complex character, less amenable and tractable than at first appeared, more than capable of holding her own in conversation. Pierre Gilliard considered her very gifted intellectually—far more so than her sisters—and was disappointed that she did not make the most of these gifts. She was also a very talented musician—a talent inherited from her mother—and possessed the ability to play the piano by ear. She showed little inclination to move from girlhood into adulthood, and took no particular trouble over her appearance. The daughter most attentive toward Alix was the second oldest, the sixteen-year-old Tatiana. She was in many ways most like her mother (in appearance she resembled her maternal grandmother, Princess Alice of Hesse)—reserved, sensitive, her self-restraint rather ineffectively concealing a desire to take the lead, to control others as she controlled herself. Her sisters recognized this controlling tendency in her by nicknaming her "the governess."

In Kostroma, as throughout the tercentenary celebrations, the girls' duty lay in accompanying their father as much as possible, bolstering the idealized image of the imperial family, rather than tending their invalid mother, which task was relegated on this occasion to their aunt, the Grand Duchess Elisabeth. Alix herself, in a letter written a few months earlier to her old friend Bishop William Boyd Carpenter, formerly a chaplain to Queen Victoria, alludes to the public role her daughters are beginning to assume on her behalf: "My children are growing up so fast and are such real little comforters to us—the elder ones often replace me at functions and go about a great deal with their Father—they are all five touching in their care for me—my family life is one blessed ray of sunshine excepting the anxiety for our Boy." The four girls were dressed in their trademark identical white dresses and picture hats (though they did take care to personalize their outfits through the judicious addition of a ribbon or other minor detail); it was chilly enough on the visit to Kostroma, however, for them to need to cover their summer dresses with warm dark coats for at least part of the time. The two eldest were now considered old enough to wear their hair up, though Tatiana had recently had hers cut off after she had contracted typhoid fever as a result of drinking contaminated water at the Winter Palace in St. Petersburg.

Also staying behind with Alix, rather than engaging in all the activities at Kostroma, was the boy about whom she was so anxious, the eight-year-old heir to the throne, Alexei. A boisterous and energetic child when well—a fact that in itself caused his mother endless anxiety—he already had a strong sense of himself as the future Tsar, and his natural inclination would have been to be alongside his father. But, a sufferer from hemophilia, he had nearly died following a series of minor accidents the previous autumn, and was still not able to walk normally. So although he did his best to keep up with his siblings, he had to spend part of his time lying or sitting next to his mother. In some ways this was no hardship, as each enjoyed the other's company. Despite his illness and the constraints it placed upon him, the little boy was of a very sunny temperament and loved by all. "Alexei Nikolaevich was the centre of this united family," recalled Pierre Gilliard, "the focus of all its hopes and affections. His sisters worshipped him and he was his parents' pride and joy. When he was well the palace was, as it were, transformed."

Curiosity, at least as much as adulation, had brought the crowds to the landing stage at Kostroma (this was one of the few places on the triumphal progress that year where the crowds seemed genuinely enthusiastic and of a good size), for the chance to glimpse the Tsar and his family in the flesh was rare. Portraits and photographs of the imperial family abounded, but the images were carefully controlled (this being one aspect of public relations in which the Empress took an active interest—particularly as it did not involve actually having to meet anyone). The family had spent the earlier part of 1913 at Tsarskoe Selo, fifteen miles outside St. Petersburg, in the intimacy of their own apartments in the Alexander Palace. Existence at Tsarskoe Selo, and at the other royal palaces, was highly ordered. For the children, it was dominated by lessons and outdoor activities; for the Tsar it was similar, except that for lessons was substituted work. The children's lessons generally began at nine o'clock in the morning and continued for two hours, before a break of one hour that usually involved a walk, ride, or drive (depending on the time of year and the weather). More lessons followed, until lunch at one. Two hours of every afternoon were spent outside, the Tsar joining in his children's exercise and play whenever he had time—which was not, in fact, very often, for he was extremely conscientious over his work and his ministers tended to deluge him with reports; he also insisted on performing quite menial tasks himself and refused to employ a personal secretary. When the girls were not undertaking physical activity or lessons, they would be engaged in reading, needlework, or some other improving pastime—for their mother, a Victorian by conviction as well as by descent, believed in the adage "The devil makes work for idle hands," and hated to see her daughters sitting around doing nothing. Except when prevented by ill health, she applied the same stricture to herself; even when lying on her sofa, she would be busy writing letters, stitching, or reading. The girls also drew and painted, and loved amateur dramatics. Anastasia was given to more original occupations; in 1913 she was preoccupied with breeding worms.

This period, this year in particular, was a vibrant one in Russia; both the economy and the arts were flourishing, new ideas were in the air, and there was a sense that anything could happen. Against this background—when one looks beyond the palace gates to see something of what was going on in the two Russian capitals—the private life of the imperial family can appear remarkably circumscribed and insular. Many of Olga and Tatiana's contemporaries were desperately trying to achieve the perfect physique and (imaginary) flawless complexion of the famous ballerinas, such as Tamara Karsavina and Anna Pavlova, by applying the cold creams, scents, and soaps constantly advertized in Russian middle-class magazines of the period, such as *Field* and *Town and Country*. And, rather than amateur dramatics and needlework, it was the tango that fascinated the fashionable young ladies of Moscow. "Our faces are like the screech of the streetcar warning the hurrying passersby, like the drunken sounds of the great tango," declared the cubo-futurist manifesto of 1913 called *Why We Paint Ourselves*. Several avant-garde artists (including David Burliuk, Natalia Goncharova, and Mikhail Larionov) had taken to painting the jagged, geometric forms of so-called rayonist art on their faces and other body parts and then walking around the city streets, in an attempt to shock and make (literal) exhibitions of themselves. Late in the year the futurist film *Drama in the Futurists' Cabaret No. 13* was made, and December saw the production of the cubo-futurist antiopera, *Victory over the Sun,* in St. Petersburg's Luna Park. The libretto of this notorious piece was written by the radical Futurist poet Alexei Kruchenykh with a prologue by fellow Futurist Velimir Khlebnikov; the music was by avant-garde composer Mikhail Matushin and the costumes and sets designed by the artist Kasimir Malevich. "Some actors spoke only with vowels, others only with consonants, while blinding lights and ear-splitting sounds rocked through the theatre in an effort to give man 'victory over the sun': freedom from all dependence on the traditional order of the world." The performances were sponsored by the Union of Youth and, along with Mayakovsky's tragedy *Vladimir Mayakovsky,* were the sensation of the season, selling out despite the extremely high prices. All this was indeed worlds away from the domestic entertainments at Tsarskoe Selo, where the girls performed extracts from the French classics for their own close circle where "traditional order" reigned supreme, and where the reading matter of even the seventeen-year-old Olga was carefully censored by her tutor. In Paris *The Rite of Spring* was premiered by the Ballets Russes, featuring the legendary Vaslav Nijinsky, while in Russia Leon Bakst designed the costumes for the ballet *Jeux,* which concerned a flirtation during a game of tennis. Late in 1913 Vsevolod Meyerhold opened a new studio in St. Petersburg, where actors and students of drama explored experimental theater and where Meyerhold adopted his alternative persona of "Doctor Dapertutto" to distinguish his experimental from his official self as director of the imperial theater. In the field of literature, notable events of 1913 included the publication in book form (it had previously appeared as a newspaper serialization) of Andrei Bely's symbolist novel *Petersburg,* and of Osip Mandelstam's first collection of verse, *Stone.* The journal *Argus,* which specialized in accounts of exotic and far-flung adventures (including that of Captain Scott's to the Antarctic) appeared for the first time. And during that year the writer Maxim Gorky returned to St. Petersburg from exile.

1913 was also a year marked by technological progress and vision; to name but three examples, experimental shafts were dug in Moscow to explore the feasibility of an underground railway, the Romanov irrigation canal was opened in the steppe of Samarkand, and Captain Boris A. Vilkitsky took two icebreakers on the Arctic Ocean Hydrographic Expedition, during which a huge uncharted archipelago was discovered, which he named Nicholas II Land. (It is now known as Severnaya Zemlya, or Northern Land.) The economy was buoyant, there had been bumper harvests in the previous two years, and the state treasury was in very good shape. Five years earlier, the then prime minister Pyotr Stolypin had said: "Give us twenty years of peace, domestic and foreign, and you will not recognize contemporary Russia," and it looked as though his prediction was on the way to being fulfilled. On the other side of the coin, however, there were over twenty-five thousand homeless people in St. Petersburg, the populations of both the capital and of Moscow, the old capital, having nearly doubled since the beginning of the century.

The use of modern publicity methods had reached its height during the tercentenary celebrations. Pictures of the Tsar and his family had appeared on postage stamps, commemorative coins, and other souvenirs, including written accounts of the Tsar's everyday habits. Unfortunately, such publicity could in itself be a double-sided coin, running the danger of associating the lofty image of the Tsar with the commonplace. As Richard Wortman has pointed out, "Descriptions of the tsar's personal life gave him an aspect of the ordinary that was devastating to the worshipful admiration the tsar still hoped to command." The imperial couple themselves, however, remained oblivious to such ambivalences.

As many as one and a half million commemorative roubles were issued on the occasion of the tercentenary, making them accessible to a far wider public than had been the case for any previous imperial celebration. But unfortunately the rise in production brought a concomitant decline in quality. The coins portrayed a bust of Nicholas in the uniform of the Imperial Rifles, with his brother, Grand Duke Mikhail Alexandrovich (known to the family as Misha) on the obverse, wearing the Monomakh Cap, the crown of the Russian Grand Princes and Tsars from Dmitry Donskoy to Peter the Great. A breakdown of the die after the minting of the first fifty thousand resulted in Misha's image being flattened, giving him a ghostly look. The tercentenary medal, which also bore images of Nicholas and Mikhail, was judged by at least one commentator, Alexander Spiridovich, the chief of palace security, to be "as ugly as possible."

The issue of postage stamps on January 1, 1913, bearing portraits of the tsars was a first for the Russian Empire, though faces of monarchs had begun to be printed on stamps in other countries in the middle of the previous century. Nicholas, a keen philatelist, had happily given his consent to the practice being introduced in Russia. A problem emerged with the fact that the stamps had to be postmarked when used on an envelope, and many postmasters felt this would be a desecration of the face of the Tsar and so left the stamps uncanceled. The newspaper *Zemshchina* (Populace) the organ of the extreme right-wing Union of the Russian People, even pointed out that the law specified sentences of penal servitude for anyone defiling the imperial image. In response, the government suspended the series in February 1913, but resumed printing later that year.

Similar problems were connected with other artifacts. Permission was granted, for instance, for the production of scarves bearing a portrait of the Tsar, but only with the proviso that the scarves should not be of the right size to be used as handkerchiefs—there should be no blowing of noses on the Tsar!

Nicholas was particularly attracted to the medium of film, as through it he was able to establish direct visual contact with a mass audience without jeopardizing either privacy or security. Between 1911 and 1914 the censors approved more than a hundred requests submitted by firms such as Pathé, Khanzhonkov, Drankov, and Gaumont to screen newsreels of the Tsar. The films showed the Tsar at various ceremonial occasions, including the tercentenary celebrations in St. Petersburg and Moscow, military reviews, launching of ships, and receptions of foreign dignitaries.

The censors wanted to ensure that the screening of such films should take place with appropriate dignity, and therefore prescribed that newsreels of the Emperor and his family should be presented separately from other films and without musical accompaniment. The curtain should be lowered before and after a showing of the imperial family and the films should be projected by hand, at a speed that ensured the characters did not look comical in their movements.

The danger for the Tsar was that all these modern genres of publicity held the possibility of demeaning his image and associating him with the everyday and the ordinary. Again, as Richard Wortman has pointed out, such devices may have been appropriate in helping to popularize Queen Victoria's "homey grandmotherly character," but she was not, like Nicholas, seeking to uphold an absolute autocracy.

The tercentenary celebrations had opened in St. Petersburg on February 21, Jubilee Day, with a twenty-one-gun salute being fired from the Peter and Paul Fortress at eight o'clock in the morning. On the day before, the imperial family had left Tsarskoe Selo to install themselves in the Winter Palace. The main public event of February 21 was a procession along the Nevsky Prospekt from Palace Square to the Kazan Cathedral. The whole processional route was festooned with triumphal decorations, the Winter Palace and Admiralty being adorned with vast double-headed eagles and portraits of the Romanov tsars. The side façade of the Admiralty had been entirely draped in imperial purple displaying the Romanov coat of arms, topped by a huge crown. These decorations had been put in place on the previous evening, but almost immediately a fierce storm had blown up and dislodged the Admiralty drapings. On Jubilee Day the wind continued to play havoc with the decorations along the processional route, which was lined with troops, with the populace behind. Nicholas traveled in an open car, with Alexei next to him, both in military uniform. The two Empresses, Alexandra and her mother-in-law, followed in another car. Next came the four daughters, then the suite and the maids-of-honor.

Outside the Kazan Cathedral, a semicircle of flags and banners of the Union of the Russian People, a right-wing and strongly anti-Semitic organization founded in the wake of the 1905 revolution, was flamboyant in its display. Members of the Union had come from all over Russia, several thousand of them having processed early that morning from the Alexander Nevsky Monastery, at the far end of the Nevsky Prospekt, to the cathedral. All sorts of other people had joined the procession en route and were massed outside the cathedral to await the Tsar and his immediate family. The rest of the imperial family was already assembled inside, along with military and civic dignitaries, the diplomatic corps, and selected members of the public. According to Major-General Alexander Spiridovich, the head of the Emperor's personal security police, the main focus of the expectant congregation was the rumor that the Empress's "Friend," the so-called "*starets*" or "elder," Grigory Rasputin, was in their midst. Everyone was looking round, trying to identify him, in a scene reminiscent of a story by Nikolai Gogol, the senators and other bigwigs quite as indignant at seeing the peasant "elder" in the cathedral as they would be at meeting their own nose dressed in the uniform of a state councilor. His actual attire, according to the Chairman of the State Duma, Mikhail Rodzianko, consisted of "a dark raspberry silk peasant shirt, high patent-leather boots, wide black trousers, and a black peasant's coat." Having located the interloper, Rodzianko furiously ordered him out, accompanying him to the door to ensure his departure. Three months later Rasputin turned up for the celebrations in Kostroma, where he was admitted to the cathedral on the Empress's orders, despite the fact that he had officially been refused a ticket. He was also seen walking around the town, in the company of a bishop.

For the liturgy at the Kazan Cathedral, the Patriarch of Antioch officiated, at the head of many other clergy. The proceedings included the reading out of an imperial manifesto, granting amnesties to prisoners and the cancellation of tax arrears owed by the peasantry. Two days later there was a ball at the Hall of Nobles, attended by Nicky, Alix, Olga, and Tatiana and most of their adult relatives. Alix made an enormous effort to overcome her debility and managed to participate in the opening polonaise. The imperial couple and their daughters left before supper was served. The Petersburg celebrations concluded three days later with a state banquet at the Winter Palace.

Despite all the effort that had gone into devising and organizing these celebrations, it was felt by some of the participants, including General Spiridovich and Prime Minister Kokovtsov, that there had been something rather lackluster about them (symbolized by the weather wrecking the decorations) and that there had been a disappointing lack of enthusiasm from the onlookers. Nicholas and Alexandra themselves were not unaware of this, and attributed it to the disagreeable and cynical nature of the capital and its inhabitants. For this is where there is some unexpected congruence between the attitudes of the imperial couple and of some of the avant-garde artists of the time, particularly Malevich—in the tendency to conceive of the "real" Russia as existing not in the sophisticated circles of the two capitals (and especially not in the western-influenced, "unnatural," and artificially constructed St. Petersburg) but as residing in "the people," the rural peasantry, dedicated—or so it was imagined—to orthodoxy, autocracy, and fatherland. It was partly this belief that led to the Tsar's insistence that the tercentenary celebrations should extend beyond the main urban centers and into southern Russia, and to the imperial journey down the Volga.

Prior to the arrival at Kostroma, however, even this journey seemed rather disappointing, with the numbers turning out to see their sovereign being rather less than expected. The imperial family set out from Tsarskoe Selo on May 15, and, traveling by rail and road, visited Vladimir and Nizhny Novgorod, where they embarked on the *Mezhen* and set off along the Volga. The weather had again proved unconducive to a festive atmosphere; a bitingly cold wind had been blowing along the river, and the imperial family had kept out of sight on the steamship, not making any attempt to greet the groups of peasants gathered hopefully at various points along the bank. Late in the evening of May 18, the *Mezhen* arrived at Krasnoe, twenty-six miles downstream from Kostroma, and there it spent the night, in preparation for the celebrations described at the beginning of this chapter.

After Kostroma, the family traveled on to Yaroslavl and Pereslavl, where the Empress, feeling unwell all the time, was reunited with her close friend Ania Vyrubova, who, having no official position at court, had been unable to join in the tour until that point; she had, however, been invited to Pereslavl by the local nobility. The tour culminated in Moscow, with a triumphal entry (the imperial family having arrived by train at the Brest station in the afternoon, there to be greeted by their relatives, suite, officials, and courtiers) on May 24. After the official reception at the station and despite worries over security, the Tsar mounted a horse—he was an excellent horseman—to ride at the head of the procession. No one watching could have been unaware of the risk Nicholas was taking in being so exposed; a terrorist bomb or bullet could easily have turned the celebration into a catastrophe. But he was determined that his people should see their Tsar. Bernard Pares, who was among the onlookers, wrote subsequently: "The Emperor showed his personal courage when he rode into Moscow some twenty yards in front of his escort, followed by his family in an open carriage. There was an anxious hush till the outbreak of bells announced that he had reached the Kremlin." As he rode along, the Tsar constantly raised his hand to his cap in greeting, while the Empress and the girls bowed left and right, and the Tsarevich happily saluted everybody. There was a mixture of jubilation, the crowds ceaselessly cheering, and fear on the part of the authorities, as evinced by Pares's "anxious hush" and Spiridovich's recollection that "nerves were tense in the extreme." Spiridovich himself walked on the left of the Emperor, alert to every movement of the crowd, while the prefect of Moscow was on the Emperor's right. Fortunately no untoward incidents occurred and Nicky's sister Grand Duchess Xenia Alexandrovna was able to write in her diary: "It was magnificent, a mass of people, and everything, thank God, went off splendidly." When the cortege arrived at the Kremlin's Iversky Gate, with all the bells of Moscow's "forty-times-forty" churches resounding in the air, the Tsar dismounted, the Empress and the children descended from their carriage, and all followed the time-honored custom of going first into the chapel in front of the gate, the shrine of the miraculous icon of the Iversky Virgin, to venerate the icon and to pray, before proceeding to the Cathedral of the Archangel to pay their respects at the tomb of Tsar Mikhail. Rasputin, it seems, was haunting these celebrations, too. "Rasputin was standing by the entrance, everyone saw him, except for me!" reported Xenia.

Apart from when he was sitting in a carriage, little Alexei had to be carried by one of the Cossack bodyguards; there were those in the crowd who reacted to this sight by exclaiming with pity and making the sign of the cross. Alix was also visibly unwell, her face covered with red blotches. She nevertheless managed to take part in the ball held two days later at the Moscow Hall of Nobles, where, in a dazzling ballroom filled with flowers and greenery, she looked both beautiful and majestic as she danced the polonaise (or, rather, walked it, this traditional formal opening to a ball consisting of a stately progress through all the rooms) with Alexander Samarin, the leader of the Moscow nobility. Olga and Tatiana wore their customary white dresses and modest pearl necklaces, Tatiana's newly growing hair tied up with a velvet ribbon. The sisters opened the ball with a waltz, at which they acquitted themselves admirably. More virtuosic and flamboyant were the children of Nicky's Uncle Pavel, Dmitry and Maria, who danced the newly fashionable Boston. Alix struggled on for as long as she was able but departed after an hour, using a lift that had been specially constructed for her, while her husband and daughters remained until nearly two o'clock in the morning. Later that day the family left Moscow, convinced after their experiences in the old capital and especially in the towns along the Volga of the popularity of the monarchy among "the people." As Spiridovich recalled,

> Back home, the imperial family lived for a long time on memories of this journey. They would recount delightful and touching episodes to everyone. And such episodes were numerous. The people, foreign to politics, uncontaminated by revolutionary propaganda, had everywhere received the Emperor cordially, lovingly, with cross and prayers, as the Lord's Anointed.
>
> Was this not evidence that people such as these really loved their Tsar?
>
> "The people love us," the Empress said frequently, after this journey.

The rest of the year took its usual pattern, with a trip to the Norwegian fjords on board the imperial yacht *Standart* in early summer, followed by some weeks spent at Peterhof on the Gulf of Finland, before the annual removal to the palace at Livadia, near Yalta, for the late summer and early autumn. The trip to the fjords, though enjoyable, was marred by Alexei's continuing ill health and the fact that he had to wear a special contraption to help straighten his leg. He was only allowed to have this contraption removed when the weather became very hot, and then he had to hop about on one leg; most of the time he played quietly in the sand, a shadow of the lively child he had been in earlier years. Yet even now, when his movements were necessarily limited, he was unable to prevent further injury to himself, developing when back at Peterhof in July a hemorrhage "from waving his arms around too much" while playing. A visit from Grigory Rasputin had its usual calming effect, however, the pain in his elbow beginning to ease after Grigory had talked with him for a while. At Livadia in the autumn, just as he was finally recovering from the aftereffects of the previous year's illness, he had yet another accident, falling off a chair on which he had been standing in the schoolroom and banging his right knee. As ever, this resulted in a hemorrhage under the skin and a swelling that spread from below his knee to his calf and ankle. He was soon unable to walk, and the swelling pressed on the nerves of his leg, giving rise to excruciating, shooting pains. In addition to the usual bed rest, the child was subjected to a course of high-temperature mud baths in an attempt to aid his recovery.

The wider Romanov family was plagued by marital difficulties and irregularities throughout Nicholas's reign, and the tercentenary year presented no exception. In January Nicky's younger brother Misha had, as one of the consequences of his morganatic marriage to a divorcée, been relieved of the duty of becoming Regent in the event of the Tsar dying before Alexei had attained his majority. In the autumn it became clear that the marriage of the young Maria Pavlovna (who in May had danced the Boston with her brother) was a disaster, and she had taken refuge with her father, Grand Duke Pavel Alexandrovich, in France. Pavel himself, "the nicest of the four uncles of the Tsar," according to Nicky's cousin and brother-in-law, Grand Duke Alexander Mikhailovich (known as Sandro), had for several years lived in exile, being another member of the imperial family to have disgraced himself by marrying a divorced commoner; Dmitry and Maria, his children by his first, deceased wife had been brought up mainly by Alix's sister Ella. Pavel now wrote to Nicky, asking permission to be allowed to begin negotiating his daughter's divorce. The Empress was also disapproving of the engagement announced in October of Nicky's niece Irina (the daughter of his sister Xenia) to Felix Yusupov, who had a reputation for fast living and amorous adventure; she would never have let one of her own daughters marry him, Alix declared to her sister-in-law. Nicky's other sister, Grand Duchess Olga Alexandrovna, looked back on the checkered marital history of the Romanovs with despair. "What example could we give to the nation?" she asked in her memoirs. "Little wonder that poor Nicky, lacking support on all sides, became a fatalist. He would often put his arms round me and say, 'I was born on Job's day—I am ready to accept my fate.' "

Alexei's illness meant that the family stayed longer in Livadia than usual, not returning to Tsarskoe Selo until December. On Christmas Eve Nicky and his daughters traveled to St. Petersburg to spend the evening with his mother, his sister Xenia, and her children at the Anichkov Palace. Even a "simple" family outing such as this involved hours of police preparation and tight security. For a number of years after the revolution of 1905, when assassinations of public figures were a frequent occurrence, it was considered too unsafe for the Emperor to travel into the capital unless absolutely necessary. It was not until 1910 that restrictions on his travel had begun to be relaxed, the information gathered by the security forces and secret police suggesting that terrorists posed no immediate threat to his life. But this did not mean that General Spiridovich and his team could relax their vigilance.

The agreed procedure was for the Tsar to announce his intention of making a journey to St. Petersburg to the Palace Commandant, who would in turn inform Spiridovich. The latter would then travel into the city himself, either early in the morning if the imperial visit was to take place later in the day, or the night before. There he would meet with the prefect of the city to discuss the required security arrangements; he was able to request more men from the city's police to back up his imperial security team, in order to monitor the whole route and to keep under observation any characters deemed suspicious. Any disputes between the two forces were referred to the Palace Commandant, who had the final say. These arrangements were working well by 1913, though it had taken some time to get them right. When Nicholas first began to make these occasional forays into the city in 1910, the conflicting priorities of the two police forces had the potential for disaster. While the imperial security police were concerned above all else with keeping the Emperor's specific route as secret as possible, the city police were keen to demonstrate their zeal by preparing that route meticulously—by, for example, spreading sand along the roads to be traversed by the imperial vehicle—and thus inadvertently advertising the route to all and sundry, including any would-be assassins. To overcome this problem, the security police would inform the city authorities of one route and then send the Emperor by another. Clearly that could only be a short-term solution; eventually communications were improved and a coordinated response to the Tsar's travel plans developed.

In the first section of her *Poem Without a Hero,* Anna Akhmatova envisages characters from the Petersburg of 1913 returning as shades wearing carnival masks; the atmosphere is frivolous yet filled with foreboding. During the autumn of that year, when the imperial family was at Livadia, Prime Minister (or Chairman of the Council of Ministers) Kokovtsov made two visits there to present his report to the Tsar. On neither occasion did the Empress emerge from her rooms; whether she was indisposed or whether she wished to avoid Kokovtsov, who had fallen out of her favor by being insufficiently pliable, the minister could not tell. He did make a perceptive comment about such visits in general: "I felt that though the ministers were received as guests their hosts were most cordial at the moment of their departure." Kokovtsov had recently returned from a visit to Berlin, where he had concluded that preparations were being made to "let loose a war upon Europe." He reported these observations to Nicholas, who had himself been in Berlin in May to attend the wedding of Kaiser Wilhelm's daughter; this was the last time he ever saw his cousin Willy. "His Majesty never interrupted me during my report," wrote Kokovtsov, "and kept looking straight into my eyes as if to probe the sincerity of my words. Later, turning to the window near which we were sitting, he looked for a long time over the spreading sea before us; then, seeming to awaken from a reverie and again looking steadily into my eyes, he said simply: 'God's will be done.'"

CHAPTER TWO

The Empress's Illness, and Her Friend Ania

To me she was everything that was good and kind, and into my heart there was born a great emotion of love and loyalty that made me determine that I would devote my whole life to the service of my Sovereigns.

—Ania Vyrubova, *Memories of the Russian Court,* 1923

WHAT WAS THE NATURE of the Empress's illness, this state of debility that had such an influence on her behavior, on her relationship with her family, and on how she was perceived by court and public? It has tended not to be taken seriously, her constant complaints about an "enlarged heart," or neuralgia, or headache, and the frequent retreats to her bed or her sofa being seen either as reaction to the strains of her life, particularly the anxiety about her son, as an attempt to avoid having to perform the public duties she found so taxing, or as evidence of hypochondria. Alhough stress and anxiety did play their part in exacerbating Alix's feelings of ill health, there is also, I would contend, plenty of evidence to suggest that her symptoms were by no means imaginary or self-induced but that she was, for most of her life, genuinely ill.

When Alix and Nicky first encountered one another in May 1884—he a teenager, she practically still a child—there was nothing immediately to suggest she was anything other than healthy. She joined in all the "romping" and "jumping about" that went on among this group of boisterous cousins, gathered in Russia to celebrate the wedding of Alix's elder sister Ella to Nicky's uncle, Grand Duke Sergei Alexandrovich. At their next meeting five years later, when Alix, accompanied by her father and brother, came to stay in Russia for several weeks, there was again no indication that she was in anything other than robust health, as she happily joined in the winter activities of skating and—that perennial Russian favorite—sliding down ice-hills. She found the ball she attended at the Winter Palace "quite delightful" (though there may be a hint of her shyness in company in the further approving comment that it "did not last very long"), and at a less formal ball hosted by Ella and Sergei the young people "danced until [they] dropped," Alix dancing the mazurka with Nicky.

By her late teens, however, Alix is being stalked by bouts of ill health, and her letters to and from Nicky include many references to her various ailments. On October 31, 1893, Nicky alludes to her recent earache, expressing the hope that "that awful pain has not come back." On April 30, 1894, by which time the couple was engaged, Alix refers to the problems she has with her legs, expressing the fear that this will make life difficult for her husband-to-be, who so much enjoys walking. All we know is that her legs were "painful" (Nicky refers to "those awful pains in the legs"), and it was in the hope of a cure for this pain that Alix's grandmother, Queen Victoria, sent her to the spa town of Harrogate, to take a course of sulphur baths, known to be beneficial to sufferers from rheumatism. Alix remarks to Nicky that the first of these sulphur baths turned her silver bracelet quite black, but does not mention any other effect it might have had (other than that it smelt rather unpleasant). Even so, despite the intermittent aches and pains and when not being subjected to treatment, Alix was still prepared to undertake strenuous activity, writing to her fiancé from the Isle of Wight: "we went into the boat and I rowed with heavy oars in the broiling sun—the result is that I look like a vulgar poppy and have big blisters on my hands which stick out like a red lump." The next day she had a swimming lesson, and was delighted to discover that she could almost swim unaided. After some more rowing, she experienced what sounds like perfectly normal tiredness, telling Nicky: "Now I am going to rest on the sofa till breakfast, as I feel somewhat exhausted. You will have to teach me some day to swim properly." But in the background of this healthy, happy activity lurked the figure of the anxious and watchful Queen, no foreigner herself to ill health and constantly on guard, instilling in her young charge the idea that she must be "careful," and demanding reports that she was indeed so.

The influence of Queen Victoria, the encouragement she wittingly or unwittingly gave her granddaughter to view herself as an invalid, should not be underestimated. Particularly during the period before her marriage, when she was staying in England, her royal grandmother (who, since the early death of Princess Alice, had viewed herself as "in loco parentis" for the Hesse-Darmstadt children and now, after the death of their father in 1892, she felt herself doubly responsible) encouraged Alix to perceive herself as someone who needed to take special care of her health, and fostered the belief that the way to do this was through rest and seclusion. The Queen made a point of writing to Nicky to instruct him on how his future wife should be treated—"She has to lie down a great deal," she insisted. Indeed, according to Victoria, Alix should have been doing all this lying down long before, but the Hesse family doctor had been "stupid" and would not insist on the correct course of action. Victoria does not suggest any physical reason for Alix's poor health, but ascribes her granddaughter's ailments to her nerves and is characteristically emphatic in her strictures: "Her dear father's death, her anxiety about her brother, and the struggle about her future have all tried her *nerves very* much. You will I hope, therefore *not* hurry on the marriage as she *ought* for *your* as well as *her* sake to be strong and *well before* that." Later in the year, when Alix was back in Darmstadt with her brother and his wife, the Queen wrote to Nicky: "Darling Alixey [sic] is, I am glad to hear, careful and doesn't ride or play at lawn tennis." The subtext of such letters was an instruction to Alix's future husband to ensure such "care" would continue.

Thus the idea of Alix as an invalid is introduced before the marriage, and a particular set of behaviors is expected from the beginning, though at the same time the Queen seems to foresee trouble if Alix enters the marriage in less than good health. She appears to imagine that by taking great care of her health now—spending much of her engagement lying down, or taking cures—Alix will make a full recovery, undoing the damage inflicted by the "stupid" Hessian doctor, and be enabled to lead a normal life once married. Yet the particular nature of the treatment on which she insisted unfortunately had its own addictive quality; it could too easily become a habit, a way of life, rather than a short-term remedy.

Nicky joined Alix in England for a few weeks in June 1894, and during this holiday he had his first taste of what it would be like to live with a semi-invalid. It was a prospect about which he seemed perfectly cheerful; he had, in fact, rather relished the time he was able to spend with his fiancée when she was feeling unwell. "I suffered so for you, poor sweety," he wrote afterward, "when you had those awful pains in the legs and still were so good and patient to let me remain with you. No! those delightful evenings with my girly-dear, were too divine for words." Alix herself seems to have been fairly stoic at this stage in her life, submitting to treatment because she was instructed to do so, but not expecting to be defined by illness or allowing herself to be cast down by it. She draws a contrast between her own experience of pain and that of her grandmother—though some of the symptoms were clearly shared. "I have just returned from a solitary drive with Granny," she told Nicky a few days after his departure. "She was talkative till a dreadful spasm of pain came on, which made her pale, and cry. She says she can't help it, it gets on her nerves when the pain is so great. I rubbed her leg for a quarter of an hour and then it got better by degrees. Poor dear, it is horrid to see her suffer so. I am young so it does not matter so, suffering pain, I daresay it is even good to have to bear pain—but she, an old lady, that is hard, and it makes one sad to see it, and it frightens me."

In the end, the Queen's wish that the wedding be deferred until the bride was quite well could not be fulfilled, even had it been possible, as the sudden death of her fiancé's father, Tsar Alexander III, precipitated Nicky both onto the throne and into marriage. Alix's less than robust health was a matter for comment among the wider Romanov family from the start, KR noting as early as November 2 (she had only arrived in Russia in October) that she had lumbago and had fainted, and that this was not a one-off incident. "This happens to her," he noted in his diary, "her heart is not strong."

In addition to lumbago and fainting, headaches were a constant feature of the new young Empress's life, as was her preferred cure for them—bed rest. This, after all, was what she had learned from her grandmother. If these headaches were at least partly the result of stress—a stress caused by anxiety over her new life in Russian society, her fears of not belonging, not knowing how to behave, not being accepted—then the retreat to bed can hardly have helped. That suddenly being thrown into the center of the Russian imperial family—with its plethora of Grand Dukes and Duchesses, all vying with one another for favor and precedence, argumentative and self-important—would be sufficient cause for major stress on the part of a young, shy girl from a small German court can be adduced from the effect a first meeting with that family *en masse* could have even on one of its own. Nicky's cousin and brother-in-law Sandro was horrified when, as a thirteen-year-old boy, he first met all his grand ducal relatives at a Sunday family luncheon in the Winter Palace. He had already met Nicky and his brother Georgy and had taken to them, but as for the rest of them—"Looking at the proud faces of my cousins," he recorded in his memoirs, "I realized that the choice lay between becoming popular or keeping my personality intact." Alix also chose the path of trying to "keep her personality intact," but unfortunately one of the ways by which she attempted to do so—fleeing to her bedroom—only made the problem worse. The symptoms of stress (the headaches and the subsequent retreat) served to exacerbate the causes of that stress (the fear of court, family, and society, the difficulty of making a place for herself within those daunting groups), leading to a vicious circle: The more the Empress absented herself from society and court, the less she felt that she belonged there, and the more frightening her new life became. Nicky's diary for the early months of 1895 contains a litany of headaches and bed rest: "Dear Alix woke up with a headache, and therefore stayed in bed until 2 o'clock" (January 29); "Poor Alix got a bad headache at tea time—she went to bed until dinner" (February 1); "Alix did not feel too well all day, and lay on the sofa in her room" (March 13); "Poor Alix developed a headache and was forced to go and lie down" (April 8); "Unfortunately dear Alix's headache continued all day. She did not go upstairs at all—neither to church, nor to luncheon" (April 9). Mindful of Queen Victoria's strictures, and already developing the pattern of keeping his wife happy by acceding to her every wish, Nicky colluded with Alix in her invalidism: "Dear Alix still has an unbearable pain in the temples, and she was forced to remain in bed, on my advice."

Apart from the headaches, Alix's main health complaints up until 1909, when her condition seemed suddenly to deteriorate, most frequently concerned her recurrent leg problem. A few months after the birth of her third child, Maria, in June 1899, the family enjoyed a relaxing holiday with Alix's relatives at the hunting lodge of Schloss Wolfsgarten, and Nicky was able to report to his sister Xenia that the rest had completely cured Alix's leg pains. His only fear was that her duties back in St. Petersburg—of having to stand through receptions and other official occasions—would bring them on again. Is there perhaps a suggestion here that Alix became ill when faced with things she did not want to do? In the autumn of 1901 she took a course of mud baths, but was by no means always an invalid at this stage, writing to Xenia during this treatment: "I was good and only began riding now—one has to be reasonable when one has four Children and has not been well"—an indication that she did still enjoy engaging in active pursuits when able. She was back in the wheelchair in the summer of 1905—"my old legs hurt too much to walk," she told her eldest daughter—and she had a long bout of illness in the autumn of 1907, which again seems to have been leg related. "Doctor just made an injection again—today in the right leg," she wrote to her daughter Tatiana on December 30. "Today it is the 49th day that I am ill, tomorrow begins the 8th week."

As Alix struggled with, or succumbed to, recurrent health problems over the years, her own explanations for them tended toward Victoria's early diagnosis of "nerves"—that is, that her state of debility had to do with what we would term "life events," and particularly with the anxiety caused her by the ill health of her precious last child and only son, the Tsarevich Alexei. She noted in a letter to William Boyd Carpenter, for instance, that "the months of physical and moral strain" during the child's severe hemophiliac attack in 1912 (not that she referred by name to Alexei's condition) had "brought on a collapse." According to her sister-in-law Xenia, Alix said something similar (again in 1912) to Nicky's other sister, Olga: "For the first time she admitted that the poor little one has that terrible illness and that she herself has become ill because of this and will never fully recover." Though the nature of Alexei's illness and the round-the-clock care he required whenever he was going through a crisis were certainly enough to induce severe physical and mental strain in a loving mother, to attribute all—or even most—of Alix's own symptoms to this cause would be to ignore the fact that she was herself unwell, at least periodically, for many years prior to Alexei's birth in 1904. And it was in 1908 and 1909, rather than 1912, that Alix's condition noticeably deteriorated.

A very different diagnosis from mere "nerves" and stress has been suggested, at least tentatively, by historian John C. G. Röhl and molecular geneticists Martin Warren and David Hunt in their book *Purple Secret,* published in 1998. This trio was building on the work of an earlier pair of researchers, the mother and son team of psychiatrists Ida Macalpine and Richard Hunter, and hoped by their own work to establish once and for all whether the hereditary disease of porphyria had not only been the cause of George III's famed "madness" but had also afflicted a number of other members of the royal houses of Britain and Germany. Porphyria, a relatively rare condition, is the name given to a group of largely inherited disorders that interfere with the ability of the body to make red pigment in the blood. Symptoms may include attacks of severe abdominal pain, skin sensitivity, temporary mental disturbance, sensitivity to sunlight, the production of discolored urine, general muscle weakness, numbness, constipation, difficulty in breathing and swallowing, profuse sweating, an increased heart rate (tachycardia), and high blood pressure. That it was not only George III who suffered from such symptoms but that the disease was indeed transmitted to many of his descendants is convincingly attested to by Röhl, Warren, and Hunt, who write:

> Our brief survey of the medical history of George III's thirteen surviving children has produced a startling result . . . What we have discovered is that all, or very nearly all, of his children suffered severely from

> porphyria-like symptoms such as spasms, colic and cramps, sharp headaches, lameness and brachial weakness, pain in the chest, back and side, biliousness, vomiting and constipation, breathlessness, irregularity of the pulse, inflammation and fragility of the skin, mental disturbance and, in one or two cases, discoloured urine.

Porphyria, further categorized in George III's case as variegate porphyria, is caused by a faulty gene, and Alix, as a direct descendant of the unfortunate king, would have been in line to inherit it. Röhl, Warren, and Hunt note that the physical symptoms of variegate porphyria are often accompanied by psychological ones: "Patients can become hypersensitive, anxious, restless, insomniac, paranoiac or depressed and, in some cases, have been labelled hysterical." All these adjectives were applied to Alix at various stages of her life.

General Spiridovich notes that, on the family's return to Peterhof from the Norwegian fjords at the end of July 1909, the Empress was feeling exhausted and ill. She had been unwell toward the end of the previous year, KR noting in his diary on January 1: "The [Empress] is still feeling weak, avoids getting tired and is being careful. For this reason, the Emperor received the congratulations of the diplomatic corps without her." It is in 1909 that the references to Alix suffering from some sort of nervous complaint begin. "The Tsar said that the Empress is very unwilling to receive," wrote KR, "and is fearful of people, especially in crowds." In the late summer her personal physician Dr. Botkin was making daily visits, and rumors were spreading around the court that the Empress was seriously ill, with some undefined, unnameable illness. She was beginning to grow stout, red patches were appearing on her face, her legs were swollen, and from time to time she had what were referred to as "heart attacks." Spiridovich comments that the Hesse family was known for its hereditary diseases, and that both Alix's father and paternal grandfather had been ill for most of their lives (there is no evidence to suggest this was more than a rumor, and Spiridovich does not identify the more likely culprit—that is, the maternal side of Alix's genetic inheritance) and that her brothers and sisters had also inherited the family illness (whatever that might be). Spiridovich quotes a certain "M.X.," whom he identifies only as a famous Russian professor, well acquainted with the Empress's condition; the most striking of the symptoms listed by this professor, in light of a possible diagnosis of porphyria, are the "periodic changes in the coloration of the skin (dermographism) and in the appearance on the face of more or less extensive red blotches." Furthermore, the "psychic disorders (loss of psychic equilibrium)" identified by the professor—and manifested in the Empress, according to him, "mainly by a state of strong depression, by a great indifference to everything around her and by a tendency to religious reverie"—could be read as the "mental disturbance" sometimes associated with porphyria. Dr. Botkin advised bed rest, advice that Alix was happy to accept, since this had long been her preferred treatment for any illness. There were those in the imperial retinue who felt Botkin did not know what he was talking about and that a specialist in nervous diseases should be consulted, but Alix had infinite trust in Botkin and insisted on following his prescriptions. On a visit to Riga in 1910 she was again very ill. She was unable to accompany Nicky on his official engagements, and instead received the ladies of the town on the imperial yacht. Spiridovich noted that she was doing her best to be agreeable and welcoming, but was hardly able to do so. She was visibly struggling and her face was covered with thick red blotches. She also continued to be plagued by headaches, neuralgia in her face, and aches all over her body—which she attributed partly to the weather. The climate of Russia's northern capital—so often shrouded in mist, cold, and damp, and with little light for much of the year—may well have exacerbated any tendency to rheumatism and general aches and pains, and to depression. Kokovtsov noted in 1911 that the Empress had difficulty standing for any length of time, while KR commented: "I asked [the Emperor] about the Empress's health. She is still unwell, sometimes better, then worse again. The Emperor is so patient, and doesn't complain, but he admits it is tiresome and depressing."

A particularly close match with many of Alix's symptoms, and identified by Röhl, Warren, and Hunt as a very likely instance of porphyria, is found in the case of her aunt Vicky, her mother's eldest sister and the mother of Kaiser Wilhelm II. Vicky's symptoms are recorded in her husband Fritz's diary and in the letters she wrote several times a week to Queen Victoria. They included excruciating pain in her head, neck, arms, shoulders, back, side, abdomen, legs and feet, a pain she described variously (as would Alix) as "rheumatism," "neuralgia," "colic," "lumbago," or "sciatica." The attacks occurred several times a year and could last for anything between a few days and several weeks (Alix's pattern of affliction was similar). She, too, often suffered from dark red blotches appearing on her skin, and from biliousness, giddiness, and vomiting, hot and cold flushes and sweating, and sometimes inflammation of the eyes. In short, Röhl, Warren, and Hunt suspect Queen Victoria of having passed the mutant porphyria gene to her daughter Vicky (symptoms also appeared in Vicky's eldest daughter, Charlotte), with a 50 percent chance that each of the Queen's other children (including Alix's mother Alice, who was also prone to rheumatism, neuralgia, severe headaches, eyestrain, and exhaustion) would also have inherited the disorder.

Throughout their work, however, Röhl, Warren, and Hunt make clear that what they are presenting is necessarily only a hypothesis, and a recent article in the *History of Psychiatry* by Timothy J. Peters and D. Wilkinson concludes that the porphyria claim does not stand up to rigorous analysis.

There is, however, another possible physical cause for Alix's ill health. Some of the headaches she experienced in her early months in Russia—and the advice she was given to stay in bed—may have been associated with pregnancy, for the couple's first child, Olga, was born in November 1895, barely a year after their marriage. This first birth was extremely difficult, labor was exhausting and protracted, and the baby—weighing in at an enormous ten pounds—had to be removed with forceps. Xenia described Olga at one year old as a "splendid, huge little girl" and, in fact, at least three of Alix's babies were "macrosomic"—that is, much larger than average. Tatiana and Maria were both on the large side but not enough to give rise to comment, but Anastasia outdid all her siblings at a massive eleven and a half pounds while Alexei weighed ten and a quarter pounds. The size of her babies certainly helps to explain why Alix found walking difficult during her pregnancies and often had to maneuver herself around in a wheelchair. As for what this may tell us about her condition in general, one of the major factors behind a woman giving birth to macrosomic babies is genetic; a form of congenital heart disease may be the explanation both for Alix's large babies and for many of her reported symptoms.

Specifically, a congenital abnormality that can be a determining factor for mothers giving birth to macrosomic babies is transposition of the great vessels, which involves an abnormal spatial arrangement of some of the primary blood vessels. It is a condition first described in the 1790s by Matthew Baillie in his *The Morbid Anatomy of Some of the Most Important Parts of the Human Body* and is often accompanied by other heart defects, the most common being atrial septal defect, which may lead to an "intracardic shunt." This defect means that blood is enabled to flow between the left and right atria via the tissue, or septum, which normally separates the two sides of the heart. In a left-to-right shunt, extra blood from the left atrium may cause a volume overload of both the right atrium and the right ventricle, which, if left untreated, can result in enlargement of the right side of the heart and ultimately heart failure. Over time various causes, including hypertension, may worsen the left-to-right shunt, and the constant overload of the right side of the heart will cause an overload of the entire pulmonary vasculature, which may then develop pulmonary hypertension in order to divert the extra blood volume away from the lungs. The pulmonary hypertension will increase pressure in the right side of the heart and eventually a reverse, right-to-left, shunt may occur.

Most people with an atrial septal defect may be unaware of it throughout early adulthood, the symptoms starting to appear as they approach their forties. These symptoms usually include becoming very easily tired, shortness of breath from minimal exercise, palpitations, and fainting. As the condition progresses, the person may experience pulmonary hypertension, congestive heart failure, and atrial fibrillation (a form of abnormal heart rhythm). Though it is of course impossible to make a retrospective diagnosis of the heart condition of somebody long dead, and may be unwise to attempt to do so, many of these symptoms sound very familiar to the reader of the last Empress of Russia's letters and diaries, as she reached the age when they were most likely to manifest.

Though Spiridovich's medical informant, Professor "M.X.," refers to Alix's symptoms as "neurasthenic," he does talk specifically of a weakness "of the cardiac muscle in particular, with painful sensations in the pericardial area." Connected to this weakness, he opines, is the Empress's poor circulation, which has given rise to edema of the legs. Alix herself, in addition to attributing her condition to anxiety over Alexei, believed that the nature of her illness was primarily heart related and this was known by members of the family. Xenia commented in her diary in January 1910: "poor Nicky is preoccupied and upset by Alix's health. She has again had severe pains in the heart and is very much weaker. They say it's on the nerve lining—the nerves or the heart valves." Alix consistently talked of her heart being "enlarged" and of feeling pressure in her heart area. She sometimes used a numerical code for her condition; in December 1912, for instance, her daughter Maria wrote in a note to her: "I am so sorry that your heart is still No. 2."

Unfortunately for her and for perceptions of her, Alix never received an accurate diagnosis of her condition during her lifetime. Porphyria was not recognized as a specific metabolic disorder until the 1920s and 30s so, though there seems to have been some awareness of a family illness, or at least of shared symptoms, the sufferers would not have known its name. And the theory that Alix suffered from a congenital heart disease, even if suspected and discussed by the imperial physicians, was never given broad currency. Instead, her worsening state of health tended to be attributed, if not to hypochondria, then to that term so favored in the nineteenth and early twentieth centuries for labeling troublesome women—"hysteria." Spiridovich's Professor M.X. is explicit in his diagnosis:

> In the case of the Empress Alexandra Fyodorovna the heredity [of the house of Hesse] has manifested itself, since her youth, in a great vulnerability of the nervous system and by a great impressionability; later,

> as a result of the unfavourable conditions presented by life at Court, the nervous system began to present definite alterations: hystero-neurasthenic symptoms and various psychic disorders.
>
> Proof of the hysterical nature of the nervous symptoms is provided by the ease with which the Empress submits to the positive suggestions of some and the negative suggestions of others.

In addition, it was the belief of the learned professor—as of many of his contemporaries—that these "hysterical" symptoms became particularly acute with the onset of the menopause. Alix's many references to her periods in her wartime letters to Nicky demonstrate that she was far from menopausal in 1908, at the age of thirty-six, when her physical condition took a marked turn for the worse, but that did not trouble most of her male observers. She was a woman approaching middle age and frequently ill with what appeared to be "hysterical" symptoms; it therefore stood to reason that she must be menopausal or at least rapidly approaching menopause. Moreover, according to our informative professor, the menopause further impairs the functions of such a woman's brain, making her even more "illogical": "The neuro-vascular phenomena which are concerned here (dilation or constriction of the vessels) become more pronounced with the approach of the menopause. They are then complicated by a feeling of anguish, by a weakening of the centres of inhibition and by intellectual disorders bearing mainly on the logical progress of intellectual operations." With such a diagnosis attached to her, it is unlikely that anything the Empress said would ever be taken seriously; all her utterances would be dismissed as the illogical ramblings of a hysterical, menopausal woman. Count Sergei Witte referred to her as "our neurasthenic Empress," and Spiridovich considered the case proven: "It was this hystero-neurasthenic illness which was the reason for the Empress's exaggerated sympathies and antipathies, for the bizarre nature of her way of thinking and acting, for her religious exaltation, for her belief in the miraculous in general, and her faith in Rasputin in particular." It was no wonder if Alix felt lonely and misunderstood, and the more she tried to express herself, the more she appeared to justify the diagnosis. As in her early days at the Russian court, she was trapped in a vicious circle, but one from which it was even more difficult to escape.

Whatever the interpretation to be put upon Alix's symptoms, they did not make for a happy atmosphere around her. As Spiridovich puts it, when describing life at Livadia in the autumn of 1909: "The presence of someone afflicted with a nervous illness made itself felt in the house." A note Alix wrote to Nicky in October, on the eve of his departure for Italy, gives an indication of her state of mind at this time. She was feeling very fragile, both physically and emotionally:

> My heart aches so these days from the sorrow of parting—I try not to break down, but there are moments when all tears inside. It's silly being so, but I cannot help—we are so rarely separated and when one feels ill, all seems harder to bear and the loneliness gets greater . . . I dread the moment of goodbye and yet I want to come with you to the last, I hope God will give me strength to behave well, formerly I could always master myself, now I have less strength and it's my despair.

Ania Vyrubova's memoirs provide further evidence of Alix's mental state: "The last part of our stay in the Crimea that year was not very gay. The Emperor left us for an official visit to the King of Italy, and on the day of his departure the Empress, greatly depressed, shut herself up in her own room refusing to see anyone, even the children."

Even when their mother was not depressed, her children had often had to accustom themselves to not being able to see her, the little bulletins which passed back and forth indicating that, though the family might all be under the same roof, access to the ailing Alix was strictly limited. A letter from the eleven-year-old Tatiana, in hesitant misspelled English, poignantly expresses how difficult this could be for the children. The little girl is struggling so hard to be brave, wanting to support her mother during her illness and encouraging her to rest, while at the same time missing her very much. "I am always so awfuy sorry when you are tied and when you cant get up," she writes. "Please sleep well and dont get tied. . . . It is very nice that you didnt go to church yesterday els I am shore you would be much more tied." The letter also contains hints at the central presence of Ania Vyrubova—that she, unlike the imperial daughters, is admitted to Alix's presence during her illness ("Was it nice to [dine] yesterday with Ania in your little room"). Who, then, was this woman—this imperial "favorite"—whose company was preferred, or at least tolerated, by the Empress when even her own daughters were not welcome?

Anna (known familiarly as Ania) Alexandrovna Vyrubova was the daughter of Alexander Taneev, Chief Steward to His Majesty's Chancellery for about twenty years, a very intelligent man, a composer, and a consummate courtier. Ania was therefore initiated early in the ways of the Russian court and was unlikely to have been as naïve and dim-witted as has sometimes been suggested. According to Ania herself, she was only a child and staying at her family's estate near Moscow, where they were neighbors of Ella and Grand Duke Sergei, when she encountered the Empress for the first time; her recollection of this event has a fairy-tale quality: "My childish impression of her was of a tall, slender, graceful woman, lovely beyond description, with a wealth of golden hair and eyes like stars, the very picture of what an Empress should be." In 1903, at the age of nineteen, Ania was appointed as one of the Empress's maids-of-honor and by 1905 Alix was showing a marked affection for the girl, whom she regarded as innocent and morally unspoiled (having been brought up in a home-loving family, of the type of which the Empress approved). Ania in turn developed something of a crush on the Empress. The two women shared a love of music and spent much time playing piano duets together. They both took singing lessons, the Empress boasting "a lovely contralto voice" while Ania was a soprano. Sometimes they were joined by a violinist-friend of Alix's and by Ania's sister Alia (short for Alexandra), another singer. According to Ania, Nicky "for some strange reason" did not like hearing his wife sing, so they had to make sure their music-making was out of earshot of the Tsar. Spiridovich backs up these observations, both about Alix's musical talents and the rumor that Nicky did not like her to sing. He recalls her being able to play at sight parts of Rachmaninov's opera *The Covetous Knight* (first performed in 1906) and that she had studied singing with Madame Natalia Iretskaya of the St. Petersburg Conservatoire, a formidable lady and the teacher of several professional singers. On one occasion at Peterhof the Empress had sung a duet from Tchaikovsky's *The Queen of Spades* with the famous Polish singer and prima donna of the Mariinsky Theatre, Adela Bolska, at a gathering organized by the Master of the Court's Music, Baron Stackelberg. The Empress had "charmed all those present," relates Spiridovich, but "It was said that the Emperor was displeased when the Empress sang."

By the summer of 1906, Ania had become the semiofficial "favorite" of the Empress, and this raised as much jealousy and backbiting in court circles as such favoritism has always done. Some of the innuendoes were inevitably of a sexual nature. Ania was taken along with the imperial family on their summer expeditions to the Norwegian fjords, she and the Empress becoming particularly close during the expedition of autumn 1906. Ania was now accepted as one of the family; even the children, according to Spiridovich, adored her. The Emperor enjoyed teasing her, and his bons mots were picked up and repeated by various courtiers.

Ania's memoirs, which one must approach with caution as written by someone to whom lying came naturally, do nevertheless offer some clues as to why this relationship was, at least initially, approved by some members of the imperial entourage and encouraged by Nicky. Ania's company made the Empress more relaxed, happier, and less reserved, and thus easier for everyone around her to deal with. Ania relates that the commander of the imperial yacht told her that she had "broken down the wall of ice that seemed to surround Her Majesty." Alix, in common with other shy people who yet have a high opinion of themselves, felt happier in the presence of people who were no threat to her own self-image, whom she could view, however affectionately, as inferior in both status and quality. Ania fitted this bill perfectly, intelligent enough for conversation but of no dazzling wit, presentable in appearance but plain. Countess Nostitz, an American actress married to a Russian Count, has provided a memorable description: "Ania, although she had a sweet, fresh face, was a stout, ungraceful woman, not attractive to men, and invariably badly dressed. Her only evening gown was a tomato red plush in which she looked like an armchair."

The relationship between Ania and the Empress provided endless grist for the Petersburg gossip mill. What gave added piquancy to the gossip was that Ania was unmarried, whereas it was known that the Empress was a firm believer in woman finding her only true destiny as wife and mother. (And here one cannot help wondering whether some of Alix's physical symptoms resulted partly from the frustration of a highly talented and capable woman forcing herself to accept, indeed to make a virtue of, this restricting view.) And so Alix set about finding a husband for her favorite. Her first choice was the Emperor's great friend, General Alexander Orlov, commander of the Uhlan Regiment (light cavalry armed with lances, sabers, and pistols) and a frequent visitor to Tsarskoe Selo. But Orlov, a widower with a long-term mistress, proved resistant to the idea of marrying Ania.

The eventual fiancé, Lieutenant Alexander Vyrubov, was encouraged to propose to Ania by his parents, seasoned courtiers who realized the potential advantages to be gained from marrying off their son to an imperial favorite. (Such machinations would not have been out of place in the Russian court of the eighteenth century, when families vied with one another to supply the Empresses—particularly Catherine the Great—with young men.) Vyrubov duly proposed and was accepted, Ania presenting him to the Emperor and Empress on February 4, 1907. Ania herself seems to have felt that she became engaged almost by accident, merely because it was expected of her. The Empress gave her blessing to the union, and the wedding took place in the church of the Catherine Palace at Tsarskoe Selo, with disproportionate pomp and ceremony, on April 30, 1907. The young couple moved into a small one-story white house—it came to be known as Ania's "little house"—in the town of Tsarskoe Selo, only three minutes walk from the Alexander Palace. The little house was modestly furnished but Ania's delusions of grandeur, and her tendency to imitate the style of her beloved Empress, were apparent in the photographs "signed by important people" that covered the walls and cluttered up the shelves and occasional tables, along with masses of flowers and many ornaments. It was, despite all attempts to make it cozy, very cold in winter. A telephone was installed in the house, as part of the palace network, so that there need be no interruption in communication between the Empress and her favorite.

Some of Ania's ornaments and furniture, including six embroidered antique chairs, were gifts from the Empress, but Alix did not make a habit of showering her friend with presents. In fact, it does not seem to have occurred to her that Ania might be short of money, and she was resistant to the idea of her being given a court appointment (Ania having necessarily ceased to be a "maid" of honor on her marriage). Eventually she was persuaded to make a contribution to Ania's living expenses, but she kept strictly to the sum she thought Ania needed, rather than giving her any extra for luxuries. What Alix desired was a friend, and not someone paid to be her friend.

It had been during her engagement to Lieutenant Vyrubov that Grigory Rasputin had entered Ania's life, when she was introduced to him by Grand Duchess Militsa Nikolaevna, the Montenegrin wife of Nicky's cousin, Grand Duke Pyotr Nikolaevich. Ania, to whom Militsa had been singing Grigory's praises as a holy man, asked him to predict what her marriage would be like. He replied that it would be unhappy; on this first occasion of Ania's receiving one of Grigory's prophecies, she disregarded it and went ahead with the wedding. The marriage was short-lived, its failure being ascribed by Ania, as one might expect, entirely to her husband, whom she writes off in her memoirs as a lunatic: "It is a hard thing for a woman to tell of a marriage which from the first proved to be a complete mistake, and I shall say only of my husband that he was the victim of family abnormalities which in more than one instance manifested themselves in madness." The truth is rather more nuanced. The marriage was one of those which had little chance from the start, because of the presence of a third party; Vyrubov might with justification have said that his marriage was, to quote the late Diana Princess of Wales, "a bit crowded." There was a rather public row in August, when Vyrubov returned home one evening to find the Empress there yet again and had gone storming off, returning later to berate his wife—loudly enough for the police stationed opposite to hear. Ania summarizes the outcome of the experiment thus: "After a year of intense suffering and humiliation my unhappy marriage, with the full approval of their Majesties and of my parents, was dissolved."

Intense gossip swirled around the intimate friendship of Ania and the Empress, exacerbated by the failure of the Vyrubov marriage and by the introduction of Grigory Rasputin into the potent mix. Ania's "little house" became infamous as a meeting place for Grigory and the imperial family, and yet what is strange about this choice is how very public it was. There could be no chance of concealing a visit to Ania's establishment—rather, it would be advertised far and wide, as is made very clear by General Spiridovich: "Positioned in the angle between two streets, with all its windows looking outwards, it resembled a real glass-house, open to every gaze. Opposite, a three-storied building, the offices of the Palace police, seemed to stare at it from all its windows. The proprietress could not take one step, or receive anyone at all, without being seen and noticed by hundreds of people." When she was well, the Empress, accompanied by one or other of her daughters, would frequently come to call during the afternoon. More rarely, the Emperor would pay a visit. More rarely still, the imperial couple would come to see Ania together, after dinner, when the other company might include officers from the imperial yacht, the *Standart.* All visitors were observed, both officially and unofficially, by the imperial security police. Neither Alix nor Nicky can have meant such meetings to be secret, whatever the gossips may have said.

As for Grigory Rasputin and what he meant to the imperial couple, that will be examined in detail at a later stage. Suffice it to say here that Nicholas and Alexandra both took their religion very seriously—the kissing of icons and the attendance at the divine liturgy evident in the descriptions of the tercentenary celebrations being no empty show for them, but undertaken with the utmost seriousness—and the tradition within Russian Orthodoxy, particularly prevalent in the nineteenth century, of God's word being mediated to individuals through a *starets* or elder, to whom the individual should be subservient, was familiar to them. As far as they were concerned, Grigory was such an elder, and he had been sent to them by God. Many would see such a belief as yet more evidence of Alix's "hysteria" and Nicky's gullibility. The truth, again, may be rather more nuanced.

CHAPTER THREE

Mystical Circles, and the Struggle to Produce an Heir

1901–1905

Precious is a true friend who shares our joys and sorrows. But such friends are as rare as are all precious things. Therefore the Holy Fathers have bidden us to be very careful how we choose our friends, especially the people to whom we confide our souls.

—Father Pimen, *Spiritual Poems* (1875), *The Journey to Russia of Macarius, Patriarch of Antioch,* and other works

"A GREAT AND UNFORGETTABLE day for us," wrote Nicky in his diary on July 30, 1904, "during which we were clearly visited by the grace of God. At 1:15 in the afternoon Alix gave birth to a son, whom we named Alexei." How much lay behind that simple phrase: "Alix gave birth to a son."

Three years earlier, with the birth of a fourth daughter on June 5, 1901, there appears for the first time in Nicky's diary the merest hint of hidden anguish over the lack of a son. He expressed no overt disappointment—that was never his way. It is merely that the habitual taciturnity of his writing is even more marked than usual; the sense of rejoicing that marked the births of his first three children is less evident. He is thankful that labor was quick and without complications (notwithstanding the baby's size), but otherwise he merely reports the facts: "At about 3 o'clock in the morning, Alix started to have strong pains. At 4 o'clock I got up, went to my room and dressed. At exactly 6 o'clock in the morning *a little daughter—*

Anastasia—was born." Nicky's laconic report of what he then had to do—"After that I sat down to write telegrams to relatives and friends in various parts of the world"—glosses over the heavy task with which he was confronted, for he well knew the reaction his news would provoke. The very brief impersonal mention of his mother's visit, with no reference to any conversation or to any remark she may have made, suggests, between the staccato phrases, emotion held in check, too painful or dangerous to admit: "Mama arrived from Gatchina. Went for a short walk. After tea, Mama left." And then another giveaway sentence, intended to give away nothing at all: "Luckily Alix felt quite cheerful." The unspoken implication is that she had cause not to feel cheerful, and the visit of her mother-in-law might have been expected to remove whatever cheerfulness she had. The "luckily" hints at how difficult life could be when Alix was miserable. And even with this luck, she was still only "quite" cheerful. In counterbalance to Nicky's restraint, the entry in Xenia's diary conveys the full force of the family's—and particularly of the Dowager Empress's—despair: "Alix feels splendid—but my God! What a disappointment! . . . a fourth girl! They have named her Anastasia. Mama sent me a telegram about it, and writes 'Alix has again given birth to a daughter!'" Eighteen months later, Nicky and Alix's English cousin George, Duke of York, alluded sympathetically to the problem, after his wife Mary (or May, as she was called within the family) had just given birth. "May is making a capital recovery," he wrote to his "dear old Nicky"—"fancy we have now got four sons, I wish one of them was yours."

Had Emperor Paul I not introduced strict laws of succession in 1797, the situation would not have seemed so desperate. If a woman could have inherited the Russian throne in the twentieth century, any one of Olga, Tatiana, Maria, and Anastasia would probably have proved at least as adequate to the task as any of their male relatives, and the pressure would have been taken off their mother to produce a male heir. Throughout the eighteenth century there had been a number of very capable and dynamic women on the Russian throne, culminating in Catherine the Great; it was largely in reaction against her that her son Paul had taken steps to ensure there would not be a repeat performance, by determining that in the future the succession should be according to male primogeniture. According to these rules, if Alix did not bear a son, then the next Tsar after Nicky would be his brother Misha. As Misha also had no sons, the next in line after him was Nicky's eldest uncle, Grand Duke Vladimir Alexandrovich, and subsequently Vladimir's sons, of whom there were several.

Grand Duke Vladimir's wife, Grand Duchess Maria Pavlovna (known in the family as Aunt Michen), a patroness of the arts and an accomplished hostess, was far more at her ease in court and society circles than was Alix, and the latter seems to have felt rather threatened by the Grand Duchess's popularity. The fact that Maria Pavlovna's sons were so close in line of succession to the throne only exacerbated this sense of threat, and increased the pressure Alix felt to produce an heir. She knew it was her duty and, despite the fact that no amount of will-power could do the job unaided, she could not help but feel herself a failure until the task was completed. All eyes were upon her; each time she was pregnant the pressure increased.

There was more to it, however, than mere expectations of a patriarchal society, bound by gender-biased laws of succession. Alix and Nicky had no doubt that the Tsar of All the Russias was divinely anointed and called to his great task by God. This is what had been affirmed at Nicky's coronation in 1896, and the couple believed it implicitly. In line with this and reflecting attitudes they had imbibed from their understanding of pre-Petrine Russia (before Peter the Great set out to "westernize" his Empire), they believed in the God-given nature of an heir. If, therefore, God intended them to have an heir, then He would provide. The long wait was a test of their patience, fortitude, and faith. Their response to that test included prayer and supplication—and not just praying directly to God but, as was normal Orthodox custom, making an appeal to various saints, the intermediaries between God and humankind. This is not to say that they put all their trust in the saints, without taking the more normal practical measures; despite Alix's intermittent invalidism, the couple enjoyed an active sex life, their physical love for one another being very strong and enduring.

It is in the weeks following Anastasia's birth that the mysterious character referred to by the Tsar as "Monsieur Philippe" or "our friend" begins to make frequent appearances in Nicky's diary, though he received his first mention on March 26, 1901. Those performing the introduction were the two Montenegrin sisters (daughters of the King of Montenegro), Militsa and Anastasia (or Stana), jointly known by their denigrators in St. Petersburg as "the black peril," both on account of their dark coloring and their reputed interest in mysticism and the occult. Militsa was married to Nicky's cousin, Grand Duke Pyotr Nikolaevich; his brother, the tall, lean, and excitable Grand Duke Nikolai Nikolaevich, known within the family as "Nik Nik" or "Nikolasha," was also often to be found in their company. Something of the strength of Militsa's personality can be gauged from her photograph in an album of the entire House of Romanov, published in St. Petersburg in 1902. She is the only woman to be photographed in profile, her long luxuriant black hair, piled on top of her head, shown to full advantage. Her sister Stana was at that time married to the 6th Duke of Leuchtenberg (who was not, however, part of this intimate group).

Nicky and Alix spent the evening of July 10, with this small mystically inclined circle, attentively listening to Monsieur Philippe during what Nicky described as "a wonderful few hours"; this was but one of several such evenings. The fact that the imperial couple consistently referred to Philippe as "our friend" is suggestive of a number of meanings. First, there is the implication that there were very few others they might call "friend," the phrase "our friend," with its singularity, carrying a very different weight from "one of our friends," for instance. Secondly, there is the unspoken opposite: To call one person "our friend" creates the possibility of another category—"our enemy." Though it is not until much later that Alix starts to use such language overtly (by which time some former "friends" have become the "enemy"), the opposition between "them" and "us" is set up during these weeks and months of belonging to a tightly closed mystical circle. That it is so tight, so private and protected—the group usually consisting only of seven adherents (Nicky, Alix, Militsa, Stana, their nephew George, Grand Dukes Pyotr and Nikolai Nikolaevich) in addition to the master, the "friend"—suggests both the desire to keep something very special to themselves and the fear that others will misunderstand, spoil, and ultimately destroy that special something. For Nicky and Alix there was also a great sense of novelty in all this, both in having someone who could be termed a "friend," and in what that friendship involved: "We showed him our daughters and prayed together with him in the bedroom!"—the exclamation mark suggesting delight at such unexpected and unusual informality. The imperial couple were very quick to trust this man whom they barely knew, letting him into their intimate family life without hesitation.

Monsieur, or Doctor, Philippe (whose actual name was Nizier Anthelme Philippe Vachot) was from Lyon, and was reputed to be able to cure nervous diseases by hypnosis. General Spiridovich had an informant who told him what was known about the man's background; if his description is accurate (and Spiridovich certainly believed it was, preferring to trust his informant rather than give credence to the somewhat lurid and melodramatic report allegedly copied from the French newspaper *Le Temps* by a Russian secret police agent, Rachkovsky, whose usual job was to collect information on political exiles), Nicky and Alix's attraction to him is understandable. "The Frenchman Philippe was known in Lyon, during the 1890s, as a gentle, good and very pious man," wrote Spiridovich, "able to heal, through prayer, a large number of illnesses. Philippe's apartment in Lyon attracted a crowd of people who came in search of healing. Philippe would carefully question each sick person, after which he would begin to pray and to recite aloud the *Our Father;* this done, he would place his hand on the sick person and order him, in the name of the Saviour, to be healed. And the sick person would be healed. A duty doctor would register the healing. But the medical fraternity had opened a whole campaign against Philippe, and the Jesuits, from their side, had declared war on him."

During a short but intense period in the summer of 1901, while Nicky, Alix, and their children were living at Peterhof, they spent a great deal of time with Philippe, usually visiting him at Znamenka, the home of Militsa and Grand Duke Pyotr, where they would be joined by the rest of the seven. These sessions with Philippe—which took place most days, sometimes more than once a day—often carried on until the early hours of the morning. (These, it must be remembered, were the "white nights" when St. Petersburg and its environs are suffused in a beautiful transparent light for most of the night; staying out until the early hours at this time of year was not so very unusual.) There are occasional intimations that Philippe was present at court, or in a wider circle; Nicky mentions his presence, for instance, at a military parade that took place on July 17. KR once met him after attending a dance class at Znamenka and subsequently described him as "a man of about fifty, small, with black hair and a black moustache, very unsightly in appearance, with an ugly southern-French accent. He talked about the decline of religion in France and in the West in general." But these were the exceptions; Philippe was usually to be found in the small circle of his intimates, and it seems that Nicky and Alix could not get enough of their new friend, Nicky recording on July 19: "Immediately after dinner, we hurried over to Znamenka. We sat upstairs, as Militsa was feeling unwell. We listened to 'our friend' all evening. It was a wonderful moonlit night as we returned home; and quite fresh." Sometimes, in addition to listening to Philippe, the group prayed together. It seems partly to have been the sense of equality, of not having to be the isolated, unapproachable autocrat, which Nicky so much enjoyed about these gatherings; one gets a sense that he was at last able to relax, and that this came as a revelation to him. Neither, for once, did he have any difficult decisions to make and he could give himself over to the luxury of having someone else tell him what to do.

Curiosity among the wider Romanov family and among Petersburg high society bred manifold rumors. "During his stays in Russia," recalled Spiridovich, "Philippe saw no one outside the family of the Grand Duke and the people in his immediate entourage. And it was this mystery with which he seemed to be surrounded that greatly intrigued Petersburg high society. Without knowing him, people talked of him as a hypnotist, a spirit who did table-turning and indulged in other experiences of this kind." Felix Yusupov reproduced a typical anecdote in his memoirs: "One day as my father was walking by the seaside in the Crimea, he met the Grand Duchess Militsa driving with a stranger. My father bowed, but she did not respond. Meeting her by chance a few days later, he asked her why she had cut him. 'You couldn't have seen me,' said the Grand Duchess, 'for I was with Doctor Philippe, and when he wears a hat he is invisible and so are those who are with him.'" Sergei Witte, who did not share his cousin Madame Blavatsky's interest in theosophy, paid heed to those who believed that Philippe was "on the whole a clever man with some sort of mystic power over people with weak or disturbed personalities." According to the prevailing gossip, Philippe's techniques for gaining submission over his aristocratic followers included verbal abuse. Nothing could have been less likely to win over the imperial couple, and there is no evidence to suggest he engaged in any such behavior with them.

Philippe left for Lyon on the afternoon of July 21, Nicky and Alix managing to spend a last hour with him that day and saying good-bye "with great sadness." The parting was only temporary, however, and in any case Philippe was a source of mental and spiritual support even in his absence. "How rich life is since we know him," Alix commented in a letter to her husband in late August, when Nicky had left on a visit to inspect the German fleet, "and everything seems easier to bear." A year later this sense of invisible support had become even stronger, particularly as far as Alix was concerned, Philippe having acquired for her the abilities of a spirit-guide. "Our dear Friend will be near you," she assures her husband in July 1902, when he was once more on his way to visit his cousin Kaiser Wilhelm, "and help you answering William's questions." Philippe, now more than a mere spiritual mentor, has made the rather disturbing transition in Alix's mind from "friend" to "Friend." This is where she seems to part company with the Orthodox Church, in according to Philippe the kind of honor that legitimately belongs only to God and to the saints recognized by the Church. At this point the imperial couple's secrecy about Philippe—and about a subsequent, even more significant "Friend"—changes from an innocent desire to keep something special for themselves to the consciousness that they have something to hide (even if that something is only that they have taken it upon themselves to determine who or what is sacred, in the knowledge that, in so doing, they have moved beyond the bounds of orthodoxy, in all its senses).

The couple's boundless faith in Philippe coexisted with the knowledge that he had no official sanction to warrant it. However well-meaning and blessed with gifts of insight, understanding, and healing, he was in the eyes of the world technically a charlatan, having been in trouble with the French police for practicing as an unqualified physician. This situation was remedied by his friend the Tsar obtaining a medical degree for him from the Petersburg Military Medical

Academy, speedily followed by Nikolasha buying him the full-dress uniform of a military doctor.

The imperial couple's intimacy with Monsieur Philippe not only piqued the curiosity of the wider family but also annoyed and upset those who felt excluded by it—particularly Nicky's mother, Maria Fyodorovna, who was acutely aware that this new friendship threatened her own influence over her son, which, in the early years of his reign, had been considerable. She largely blamed Militsa and Stana for having brought the situation about. Unable to make satisfactory contact with Nicky, Maria Fyodorovna had been unburdening herself to Xenia, who, in March 1902, took it upon herself to write to her brother about the situation. "You talk to Mama so seldom, I know it upsets her," she told him. "It seems to her that you avoid all conversation with her, so what happens is that she remains silent and takes everything, until finally she can't stand it any more and she tells you everything she has had on her chest for a long time—she's in such a rush she doesn't manage to say everything. This does not satisfy her, so she waits for the next time." Xenia suggested to Nicky that the tension would be eased if he took the initiative himself to talk to his mother more. Her exhortation seems to have fallen on deaf ears.

Alix's sister Ella was also becoming increasingly concerned over the imperial couple's isolation and the strange rumors about Philippe. In July, while Nicky was away visiting the Kaiser, she decided to tackle her sister, as the latter subsequently related to her husband. Alix seems to have been expecting this cross-examination and to have had her answers ready. "We drove round the Alexander Park," she wrote, "and during that time Ella assailed me about our Friend. I remained very quiet and gave dull answers. . . . She has heard many very unfavourable things about Him and that He is not to be trusted. I did not ask what one said—I explained that all came from jealousy and inquisitiveness." Ella's accusation centered on the secrecy surrounding the imperial friendship with this man, but Alix denied there was anything secret about it. How could there be? she protested, as in their positions "there can never be anything hidden," living as they did "under the eyes of the whole world." All the inhabitants of Znamenka knew him, he ate with everyone else, there was no secret, Alix insisted. Ella asked if they saw him often. Alix replied they had seen him "several times." She then intriguingly remarks: "I stuck to the story of the remedy." Whatever "the story of the remedy" may have been, Ella found it "funny a foreigner doing such a thing." There was also some controversy surrounding Grand Duke Nikolai Nikolaevich's involvement in all this, and about "spiritism," but Alix managed to evade these questions. What this letter most clearly expresses is Alix's determination to divulge as little as possible about her private, mystical life to her sister, someone she had formerly trusted; she did not expect Ella to be sympathetic to whatever was happening, and she feared her interference. Did she at heart suspect something was not quite right herself? Or did she fear that any publicity—even only within the wider Romanov family—would result in Nicky and herself being deprived of their "Friend"? "I am sure my answers are most unsatisfactory to her," Alix concluded, "let's hope that she won't begin again."

The "remedy" to which Alix so intriguingly referred may have been connected with the wonderful development that had occurred that year. On April 4, 1902, Alix told Xenia that she (like Xenia) was again pregnant—in fact, well advanced in pregnancy—and that she was expecting a child in August. What she did not say, but believed, was that the child would be male. "I know by your looks you have been thinking it was so," she wrote, "but I on purpose did not tell you, so as that when others asked, you can honestly say that you did not know. Now it begins to be difficult to hide." She asked Xenia not to tell "Motherdear," as she wanted to tell her herself in person. She also tells Xenia how well she is feeling, and comments: "My broad waist all winter must have struck you."

By late summer everyone in the family was anxiously awaiting the birth. But then catastrophe struck. Alix, apparently nine months pregnant and expecting to give birth any day, suddenly had a normal period. The imperial obstetrician, Dr. Ott, was finally allowed in to see her (that Alix had been under the sway of a fantasy that she did not fully, consciously believe herself is suggested by this refusal to allow a medical examination during the course of her "pregnancy"), and he confirmed that there had never been any such pregnancy but that "luckily everything internally was all right." Such cases did happen, Dr. Ott assured the family, explaining that they were "caused by anaemia." Xenia, detailing this denouement in a letter to her close friend Princess Obolenskaya (known by her maiden nickname of "Aprak") is both sympathetic and horrified: "It's so awful, we can't think about anything else, how terrible for them, painful and sad." She is also aware that the gossipmongers could now have a field day: "I can just imagine what they will start saying, when it becomes known, and in order to avoid all the false rumours, I decided to write to you so that you should know the truth."

When it became clear that Alix had suffered a false pregnancy, the walls of privacy that she and Nicky had been so painstakingly building around themselves were seriously breached—though the couple continued to be very protective of their relationship with Philippe. Alix was courageous in her return to reality, bravely telling her mother-in-law herself about what had happened, though she "cried terribly" when she did so. When Xenia went to see her, the day after she had told Maria Fyodorovna, she found her "in a very sad mood, although she talks about it with great acceptance." Maria Fyodorovna seized the opportunity to remonstrate with her son about Philippe, but she got no further than had Ella with Alix: "she told him everything she had on her heart," recounted Xenia, "but unfortunately only received rather vague explanations, although he said all the rumours were very much exaggerated, and so on. I am glad for Mama that she at last spoke out, but the result of their conversation was not satisfactory!"

The official version of what had happened, given some credence by Alix experiencing pain and heavy bleeding, was that she had suffered a miscarriage, and this was the information given to the press. As far as the outside world was concerned, Nicky maintained his usual inscrutability, concealing whatever stress he must have undergone both during the false pregnancy, supporting his wife in her delusion, and afterward, when she must have needed his support even more. At the end of August he wrote to his "own beloved Wify" from Rishkovo, on his way to attend maneuvers at Kursk (the largest peacetime maneuvers in Russian history, including over four thousand officers and nearly ninety thousand men and lasting a fortnight), and talks of how hard it was to say good-bye on the previous day: "Knowing that I was leaving you all alone (except the children) after such trying circumstances and with Ella, too, made me more miserable than ever—I mean this separation is the most painful one we have had." His own attitude seems to have been that of religious acceptance; there is more than mere resignation to fate in his declaration that "God knows what is good for us, we must bow down our heads and repeat the sacred words 'Thy will be done.' " No element of doubt has crept into his mystical outlook or practice: "I tried to pray very fervently last night and this morning and that has also brought comfort to the soul." And then he reverts to the matter-of-fact concerns with which he is always most at ease: "After dinner it rained yesterday, but now it is lovely, quite warm and sunny. If it is so for the manoeuvres it will be simply delicious." Yet perhaps Nicky was more stressed than he cared to admit—or realized—for he experienced uncharacteristic difficulty that evening in fulfilling his duties. "The first speech went off very well," he told his wife at the end of the evening, "but in the beginning one I stuck and could not for the life remember what I wanted to say." From Alix's reply to this letter, it is clear that her ability to endure suffering came in large measure from the—reciprocated—love she had for her husband. After four children and a phantom pregnancy, Alix remained as besotted as a young girl: "Your precious letter and telegrams I've put on our bed so that when I wake up in the night I can touch something of yours. Fancy an old married woman speaking so—'old-fashioned' many would say. But what would life be without love—what would become of Wify without you?"

Both Xenia and Maria Fyodorovna continued trying to pry information out of Nicky and Alix about Philippe, but were again politely stonewalled, as Xenia related to Aprak: "Mama and I talked to them both today about Ph., I felt very much relieved but unfortunately they once again failed to explain anything and were only surprised that everyone seems to think they are trying to conceal their friendship with Ph., when they never had any intention of keeping it a secret. Nevertheless the mystery remains—we still haven't found out exactly what he is! They said he is a very modest man and says 'things which do one good'! All the same it's good at least that *la glace est rompue*!" But if Xenia thought that the ice being broken meant that the subject of Monsieur Philippe could be discussed in greater detail later, she was mistaken. KR's attitude was perspicacious; he could see that the position adopted by Nicky and Alix was having the reverse effect from that which they intended—that these two private people who hated being surrounded by idle talk were actually behaving in such a way as to encourage, rather than defuse, such gossip: "My personal opinion is that if their Majesties really have got carried away with mysticism or mystical states, it's really more funny than dangerous; what is bad, however, is that they shroud their visits to Znamenka in mystery. There is no way they can hide—the Cossacks and the secret police are everywhere—and you cannot suppress or conceal what has been seen by many. They are only giving fuel to the gossip and rumours, which increase and spread the whole time." KR was himself no stranger to secrecy. He was, however, markedly more successful than Nicky and Alix in maintaining it.

By the end of the summer Xenia had reached the conclusion that the false pregnancy had come about as a result of "suggestion"—in other words, that Philippe had hypnotized Alix into believing she was pregnant. In fact, hypnosis was probably unnecessary, false pregnancy or "pseudocyesis" being known sometimes to occur in women with a very strong desire to conceive. Alix's desperate longing for a son, combined with her fervent belief in Philippe as someone whose prayers were efficacious and advice sound, was all that was needed.

The fact that Alix survived this crisis with no long-lasting ill effects suggests that she was more psychologically robust than she was sometimes believed to have been, and attests to the support she received both from her husband and from the unshakeable faith she had placed in Philippe as a mediator of the divine. If he had predicted she was going to bear a son, then bear him she would; she just had to pray harder and wait longer. On September 1, Nicky was confident enough of his wife's mental state to tell her of the looks that had passed between himself and the ladies at the Hall of Nobles in Kursk. He and Misha had been taking tea surrounded by "a wall" of ladies, some of whom were "rather good looking with fatal eyes," who spent the whole time "smiling sweetly" at the imperial brothers. He had not misjudged Alix in telling her this, for she responded with great good humor and teasing: "I can see you drinking tea, surrounded by a band of languishing ladies, and I know the adorable expression of shyness which creeps over you and makes your sweet eyes all the more dangerous. I am sure many hearts have beaten faster ever since then, you old sinner."

Nicky had also told Alix of the miracle-working icon of "The Mother of God of the Sign," which he had kissed in Kursk's Znamensky Monastery; she had been delighted to hear about this, she told him, as "the image of the Virgin is the one Serafim loved and which cured him as a boy." The Serafim to whom she referred was Serafim of Sarov, an obscure hieromonk (a monk who is also a priest) born in 1754. Serafim had become a hermit, living alone in a timber cell about three miles away from his monastery. There, so the legend went, he had accomplished a superhuman feat of prayer and asceticism, kneeling on a rock in prayer before an icon of the Madonna for a thousand days and nights. After fifteen years of living alone in the forest, he was compelled by the church authorities to return to the monastery, where he observed a vow of total silence for a further five years. All this prepared him to be an elder or *starets,* able to transcend all social barriers and counsel laymen of every rank. He was also famed for having exercised the particular virtues of humility and "*smirenie*"—a serene acceptance of suffering. One autumn, it was said, three thieves "aroused by malice and enmity" arrived at Serafim's cell, demanding money with threats of violence. Very strong after his feats of endurance, Serafim could have dispatched the thieves with ease, but instead he chose to submit. Putting aside his axe, he folded his arms, and said, "Do what you need." Such an attitude would be bound to resonate with the Tsar, born on Job's day and temperamentally inclined toward accepting whatever happened to him as the ineluctable workings of fate, or the will of God.

Monsieur Philippe was aware of the attraction Serafim held for both Nicky and Alix—after all the late-night conversations they had shared on such subjects, he could hardly have been unaware—and he now encouraged them to enlist Serafim's aid in seeking the birth of a son. This aid would be particularly effective, he suggested, if they were able to bring about the canonization of Serafim as a saint. In deciding to take this advice, the Emperor and Empress were aligning themselves with the tradition of the Muscovite Grand Princes, particularly with some of the stories related in Russia's first narrative history, the *Stepennaya Kniga* or Book of Degrees of the Royal Genealogy, written between 1555 and 1563 in the reign of Ivan the Terrible. This book was an account of the "enlightened God-ordained sceptre-holders who ruled in piety the Russian land," its authors tracing the descent of the tsars to the Roman emperors and portraying their successive reigns as the history of the nation's salvation. One of the "histories" it contains is that of Sofiya Paleologue, the wife of Ivan III, the Great, first Sovereign of All Russia, who gave birth to the future Vasily III in 1479 through, it was said, the intercession of St. Sergius of Radonezh. This story would have held particular resonance for Alix and Nicky, as until this time Sofiya had produced only daughters (Elena in 1474, Feodosia in 1475, and another Elena in 1476); desperately needing to provide her husband with a male heir, Sofiya had made a pilgrimage on foot to the Trinity-Sergius Monastery to implore the help of the saint. Not only was her predicament the same as Alix's; her choice of saint was also significant. Both the imperial couple and Serafim of Sarov had a particular devotion to St. Sergius, a fourteenth-century ascetic, founder not only of the Trinity-Sergius Monastery but also, through his followers, of many dozens more monasteries throughout central and northern Russia. Images of this saint (who, like Serafim, was particularly popular with the Orthodox faithful, the "common people") featured prominently among the large collection of icons that covered the wall of the imperial bedroom, in the old Russian fashion, while Serafim was reputed to have had such a reverence for his own icon of St. Sergius that he had requested to be buried with it placed upon his chest. For Alix and Nicky to have chosen Serafim as "their" saint in their quest for a son would have made perfect sense to them, linking them, through him, to St. Sergius of Radonezh and his attested role in providing divinely ordained tsars for Russia.

Pilgrims had been visiting Serafim's remains at the Sarov Monastery since his death in 1833, but the Holy Synod had initially dismissed the validity of miracles ascribed to him as they could not be verified (and verifiable miracles were needed before anyone could be proclaimed a saint). An official inquiry into Serafim's sanctity had begun in 1892, and three years later the Bishop of Tambov reported that the commission had examined ninety-four incidents of miracles. The Synod was still not convinced, however, and directed the Abbot of Sarov to collect more evidence. In 1897, after a further report compiled by the Bishop of Tambov, the Synod decided the moment was still not right to proceed, being wary of acceding to the "superstitious ignorance of the masses" as well as suspicious of local clergy with a vested interest in sacred relics. After the imperial couple's intervention—according to the then finance minister Sergei Witte, they invited the Chief Procurator of the Holy Synod to lunch expressly in order to tell him to speed up the canonization (and to the Procurator's protestations that the Synod had to follow correct procedures, Alix is reputed to have declared "but the Tsar can do anything!")—the Synod reluctantly had to abandon its delaying tactics. The ceremony of canonization (also known in the Orthodox church as "glorification") was duly set for July 1903.

On the 17th of that month the Tsar, Tsarina, and their entourage arrived in Arzamas in the province of Nizhny Novgorod, having traveled by imperial train from St. Petersburg. Unlike the meetings with Philippe, this pilgrimage was shared with other members of the imperial family, including Maria Fyodorovna; Ella and Grand Duke Sergei were also enthusiastic partisans of Serafim's glorification. The imperial party was welcomed on the platform by representatives of the local nobility, townsfolk, and peasants, and then transferred into carriages for the forty-mile journey to Sarov. Nicholas gave a detailed account of events in his diary: "There was something very special," he wrote, "about going into the cathedral of the Assumption and then into the church of St. Zosima and St. Savvaty, where we were able to pray to the relics of the holy father Serafim." He noted with satisfaction the "huge crowd of pilgrims" thronging the courtyard.

At the beginning of the service of glorification, Serafim's remains were carried in a coffin out of the church of Sts. Zosima and Savvaty and borne in procession to the cathedral of the Assumption, the Tsar himself among the pallbearers. Peasants scattered pieces of linen and thread on the path, so that they could gather them up afterward and take them home, impregnated with sanctity. There were prolonged prayers at the western gates of the cathedral, before the coffin was carried inside and placed on a special plinth. Bishop Innocent of Tambov gave an address, and then Metropolitan Anthony of St. Petersburg slowly lifted the cover from the coffin. "It was a very solemn moment when the glorification began," wrote Nicholas, "and then the kissing of the casket."

The sense of sharing in this momentous occasion with the "common people" increased its significance for Nicholas and Alexandra. In addition to their very personal reasons for supporting the glorification of Serafim, the imperial couple also believed that there could be political benefits from their involvement with this popular figure of veneration, at a period of increasing turbulence in Russia. It was Nicky's belief that making direct contact with "the people," the Orthodox faithful in the towns and villages of Russia, far from the machinations of St. Petersburg and the court, would help strengthen the autocracy at this critical time. A letter Alix wrote to her old friend William Boyd Carpenter on December 29, 1902, demonstrates that she shared this sense of a dichotomy between the Russian "people," toward whom (or, rather, toward the idea of whom) she is patronizingly affectionate, and those she by implication marks out as separate from the people—that is, the "bad elements and influences," presumably including within this category intellectuals, members of high society, revolutionaries—in short, everyone who does not evince a "boundless love" for the Tsar. "My new country is so vast that there is no lack of work to be done," she writes. "Thank God the *people* are very religious, *simple*-minded, childlike and with boundless love for their Sovereign and faith in him; so that bad elements and influences take a time before rooting amongst them." To some extent, however, the close bond between the "common people" and the Tsar at Serafim's glorification was illusory. The security arrangements considered necessary to protect the imperial family had entailed the issuing of admission tickets for the actual ceremony, which could only be obtained by the elite. The ordinary pilgrims, including many parish priests, had to stay outside. Furthermore, as the existing facilities at the monastery could accommodate few visitors, luxurious new quarters had been built for the court and the elites, while the common people were to be housed in simple barracks, also constructed specially for the event. The official estimate of the numbers likely to attend had been 100,000, but, in the event, nearly three times that number of pilgrims arrived, including many sick hoping for a miracle as well as poor people desirous of alms. Unfortunately, therefore, the barracks proved insufficient, and most of the pilgrims had to seek refuge in makeshift huts or sleep in the open air. More disastrously, there was a serious shortage of provisions. On the day of Serafim's glorification—the day after the arrival of the imperial party—the official state telegraph agency reported from Sarov that "bread is nowhere to be bought, and everyone is begging for bread, not money."

On the following day there was another lengthy service, during which the newly consecrated relics were exposed. "One felt an enormous lift," wrote Nicholas, "both from the event itself and the extraordinary mood of the crowd." In the evening came the most significant event of all for the imperial couple—bathing, as Philippe had instructed, in the stream reputed to have been blessed by Serafim himself. At this point they even managed to evade police protection, only their personal guards being in attendance. Nicholas was deeply moved by the experience: "Then we went in twos and threes down to the source, where we bathed with a particular emotion in the stream of icy water. We got back safely, in the darkness no one recognised us. We heard of many people being cured today and yesterday. Another cure happened in the cathedral, while the holy relics were being carried round the altar. God is miraculous through his saints. Great is his mercy towards dear Russia; there is inexpressible comfort in the evidence of this new manifestation of the Lord's grace towards us all; let us put our hope in the Lord for ever and ever. Amen!"

For the first few months after Serafim's glorification, there was no sign of anything that could be ascribed as miraculous having happened in the lives of the imperial couple. In fact, the reverse was the case—a tragedy had taken place which deeply affected Alix. In the autumn her brother Ernie (Ernest Louis, Grand Duke of Hesse) had come to join the imperial family at Skierniewice in Poland (from where the men in the party went off to Spała on hunting expeditions), bringing with him his eight-year-old daughter Elisabeth, also (like her aunt) known as Ella, whom he adored. Two years earlier he and Ella's mother, Victoria Melita or "Ducky," had divorced, to Alix's consternation, and Ella lived for part of the year with each parent. She was a very bright little girl, sweet and attentive, and loved playing with her Romanov cousins, especially the "baby," two-year-old Anastasia. Early one morning, during her stay at Skierniewice, Ella complained of a sore throat. No one thought she was seriously ill; she was put to bed and it was assumed that she would soon sleep off whatever was ailing her. But instead she grew rapidly worse, and by the time specialist doctors were summoned, it was already too late—Ella had contracted typhoid fever, and her heart was failing.

The night after the doctors arrived, as Ella lay with weakening pulse in an adjoining room, little Anastasia and Maria suddenly began to scream. Their nurse hurried in to find the children standing on their beds, rigid with fear; they had seen, they claimed, a horrible man, and nothing would console them. To the explanation that this must have been the new doctor, they insisted it was not; Maria eventually went back to bed, but Anastasia clung, trembling, to the nurse. Then the child seemed to see something the adult could not see; the "horrible man" had returned, but this time he went into her cousin's room. "Poor Princess Elisabeth, poor Ella," whispered Anastasia. Ella, who realized she was dying, insisted a telegram be sent at once to her mother, but by the time Ducky received it, her daughter was dead.

Alix had intended to accompany Ernie to the funeral in Darmstadt, but, weakened by grief and guilt (for her niece had been in her charge), she first caught cold and then succumbed to an ear infection. She and Nicky therefore remained for a further six weeks in Skierniewice. The children had been dispatched back to Tsarskoe Selo immediately, without their parents, on the evening of the day Ella died, so that their rooms at Skierniewice could be disinfected and fumigated. The gossips got to work at once, a rumor spreading that the little girl had died of eating poisoned food intended for the Tsar, next to whom she always used to sit at mealtimes. When Nicky and Alix finally returned to Tsarskoe Selo, Alix contracted flu. Xenia was horrified when she went to see her. "She has become terribly thin and has an air of suffering," she wrote, "her temperature keeps rising every day and she is very weak. She stays in bed all day, hardly eats anything, and is so sad that it's simply awful and too painful to see!" In fact, though she did not yet know it, Alix was in the early stages of pregnancy, her son having most probably been conceived during those awful days at Skierniewice, when she and Nicky were mourning the loss of little Ella.

Monsieur Philippe now begins to fade from the picture, having apparently told his followers that "soon he will die and will reappear afterwards to the circle of friends in the guise of another man." KR, to whom this claim was related by his sister, who in turn had heard it from Stana and Militsa's nephew George, understandably dismissed it as "nonsense," but this was a prediction that was to play an influential part in future events. Philippe did indeed die in 1905, so at least that part of his prediction was accurate. (The nephew George's involvement with the mysterious doctor seems to have had little good effect on his character; he was forced to renounce his succession rights to the throne of Serbia after kicking his servant to death in 1909.)

Once Alix became aware of her pregnancy, she was careful to keep it hidden as long as she could, understandably fearful after the trauma of the pseudocyesis that had preceded it. Xenia only found out, from Maria Fyodorovna, when Alix was already six months pregnant—by which time she was transformed, feeling very well and, though much thinner in the face, looking "wonderfully beautiful."

KR, who made this observation about Alix's beauty, was himself in the grip of his addiction to casual sexual encounters with men. On several occasions in 1904 he succumbed to temptation in public bathhouses with what he termed "simple men" and also indulged himself in his *banya* (bathhouse) at home (either with one of his own servants or with an attendant brought in from a commercial bathhouse). All this was while his wife was in the early stages of pregnancy with their eighth child. It was by no means unusual in turn-of-the-century Petersburg for men to have sex with other men in bathhouses, some of which were run rather like brothels, with private rooms for hire and male prostitutes available. It was a recognized, if undercover, part of life in the "little homosexual world" of St. Petersburg; it was, nevertheless, unusual for a Grand Duke to partake in such pleasures, and KR's family, including his cousin the Tsar, would have found any such revelations about him horrifyingly shocking. Discovery would also have led to a prison sentence. There was a masochistic streak in KR, for, in the wake of each incident, he wallowed in torments of conscience—while knowing perfectly well that he would "fall" again at the earliest opportunity.

By the time Alix was admitting her pregnancy, Russia was at war with Japan. It has been suggested that the assertive policy Nicholas pursued in the Far East in the months leading up to the war was influenced by what he believed he had experienced and witnessed during the ceremonies to glorify St. Serafim. The apparent unity of tsar and people, inspired by the power of this saint, had given him the confidence and courage to carry forward Russia's religious and imperial mission in Asia. This argument is bolstered by the timing. It was on July 30, 1903, shortly after Serafim's glorification and contrary to the advice of Sergei Witte, Minister of War General Alexei Kuropatkin, and Foreign Minister Count Lamsdorf that the Russian government suddenly announced the formation of a "Viceroyalty of the Far East," including Port Arthur and northern Manchuria. Nicholas appointed Admiral Evgeny Alexeev as Viceroy, with authority over all military and naval forces and the civil administration in the area. Nicholas resolutely refused to believe in any real threat from Japan, despite dire warnings issued by his cousin and brother-in-law, Grand Duke Alexander (Sandro), among others.

When war did break out, with Japanese torpedo boats attacking Russian warships at Port Arthur on the night of January 26–27, 1904, there was great indignation and anger in the Russian capital, but little anxiety. "Contemptuous nicknames, such as 'macaques,' were applied to the Japanese," recalled Kokovtsov, "and everyone was supremely confident that there would be a speedy termination of the 'adventure'." The artist Alexandre Benois used similar language: "The attitude of almost everybody to it was extraordinarily frivolous, as if it were a minor adventure in which Russia would certainly be the victor."

Soon after the declaration of war, Kokovtsov (later to be Prime Minister) was appointed Minister of Finance. His account of being received by the Tsar to mark this appointment gives something of the flavor of what it was like to serve an anointed autocrat—the "confirmation" the Tsar bestows is almost episcopal. Kokovtsov was summoned by telephone to the Winter Palace at under two hours' notice and, being dressed at the time in his ordinary business attire, had to get his wife to dispatch his white tie and decoration to him in a carriage. At the time specified by Nicholas (a quarter past two in the afternoon), he was in the Tsar's waiting room. After confirming Kokovtsov's appointment, telling him "I have known you for a long time and do not at all suppose that you will refuse this appointment at such a critical moment," the Tsar made the sign of the cross over his new minister, then embraced and kissed him. Next he sent him to see the Empress, adding, "She wishes very much to make your acquaintance and is much pleased to know that I have chosen you, as we have often talked about you." Kokovtsov duly went to meet Alix, in the drawing room next to the Malachite Hall, where they had a brief conversation in French. She congratulated him, adding that she, too, was sure he would not have refused "to help the Emperor" at such a difficult time. She also, according to Kokovtsov, stipulated that he should never be afraid to tell the truth to herself and the Tsar, "not hesitating lest it be unpleasant for us. Believe me, even if it be so at first, we shall be grateful to you for it later." Then she, like Nicky, blessed the new minister.

After such tumultuous years—a fourth daughter, a new "friend," a false pregnancy, an unexpected war, and, at last, the arrival of a son—no wonder Nicky described July 30, 1904, as a "great and unforgettable day." Alexei's birth was greeted with a 301-gun salute and, at his baptism in the palace church at Peterhof 12 days later (at which his two eldest sisters, Olga and Tatiana, were present, dressed in blue sarafans), the baby was awarded a plethora of godfathers, including Kaiser Wilhelm II and all the Russian soldiers on active service. How cheered the hard-pressed troops felt by this honor can only be imagined; it must have had about as much or as little meaning—depending on individual attitudes and beliefs—as being blessed with an icon of St. Serafim before being sent off to fight for tsar and fatherland. General Kuropatkin held a parade at Anshan in Manchuria to celebrate the Tsarevich's birth, heavy rain forcing the men to wade rather than march past. Reuters' special correspondent commented dryly: "A band did its best to make us merry, and the Commander-in-Chief in an appropriate little speech told the men that he hoped soon to lead them to victory. And thus we showed our loyalty to the Little Father, and our sympathy in the joys of the Imperial House."

Alix and Nicky were convinced that God had sent their baby son to them at precisely this time of troubles in order to comfort and sustain them for, as Alix commented, "God never forgets one" and Alexei had "come as a real Sunbeam." The fact that God, through the agency of St. Serafim, appeared to have heard the prayers of the imperial couple—in accordance with the tradition, as related in the tales of old Muscovy, of Russian saints blessing the Tsarina's womb—could only have reinforced their already firm belief that the Tsar of Russia was anointed and appointed by God, a divinely blessed leader of the Orthodox world. This seemed further to validate Nicholas's mission to extend Russian—and specifically Orthodox—influence farther east.

There can at first have been no reason for anything other than rejoicing, for baby Alexei was a picture of health. Xenia wrote of him when he was just over a fortnight old: "He's an amazingly hefty baby, with a chest like a barrel and generally has the air of a warrior knight." But Alix cannot have been unaware, even if she did her best to hide the awareness from herself, of the possibility that he might have inherited what Xenia called "the terrible illness of the English family." This "terrible illness" had led to the death, only a few months earlier, of Alix's little nephew Henry, the four-year-old son of her sister Irene. Henry had died after falling and bumping his head; Alix had wept on hearing the news. Her own earliest childhood had been marked—and marred—by the death of her two-year-old brother, Frittie, who had fallen from a window in their mother's bedroom. And her uncle, Prince Leopold, had died in 1884 at the age of thirty as a result of the same "terrible illness." It was hardly a secret that the curse of hemophilia had a tendency to afflict the male descendents of Queen Victoria. (In October 2009 four scientists published the results of genotype analysis on historical specimens from the Romanov branch of the royal families descended from Victoria, which identified the genetic mutation that caused this disease. They concluded from their research that the "royal disease" was indeed the severe form of hemophilia, also known as hemophilia B or Christmas disease.)

Anxiety that Alexei might have inherited the dreaded disease began when the baby was only about six weeks old; on September 8, he started bleeding from the navel and the bleeding continued on and off all day. When it ceased the next day, his parents allowed themselves to feel reassured "by his healthy appearance," as Nicky put it in his diary, and for some weeks they continued in this state of denial, while hiding their anxieties from those around them. A week after this first episode of bleeding, Alix wrote to Nicky (as he was about to leave on one of his visits to the troops) that she was sure "our dear Friend" had been watching over "tiny," as she called the baby, and recalls, "oh, what anguish it was, and not to let others see the knife digging in one." Then she repeated the reassuring mantra: "Thank God he is so well now!" But they were hoping against hope, and soon there was no possibility of ignoring the truth, when doctors confirmed the diagnosis. The imperial couple did all they could to conceal Alexei's condition from the eyes of the world, and even from their retinue and the wider Romanov family—but with little success. This merely added to their reputation for unsociability and secrecy, and provided further grist for the rumor mill, while increasing their own distress. The poor parents would never now be free from terrible anxiety, and the mother also had to bear a burden of guilt—even if largely repressed—for having passed on, however inadvertently, the "terrible illness" to the heir to the Russian throne. Nicky's young cousin Maria, the daughter of Grand Duke Pavel, asserted in her memoirs: "Nobody ever knew what emotions were aroused in them by this horrible certainty, but from that moment, troubled and apprehensive, the Empress's character underwent a change, and her health, physical as well as moral, altered."

As for the war, as defeat followed defeat the earlier Russian sangfroid evaporated, to be replaced by a sense of impending catastrophe. In October, the correspondent of *The Times* tried to gauge the attitude of ordinary Russians. "It does not require a very long stay in the country," he wrote, "or a very deep insight into its life, to realize how unpopular the war is among all classes save the officials . . . The bulk of the Russian Press did its best for a long time to keep up the illusion [that the war would be over in a few months], and repeated daily that all is for the best in the best of all possible Russias, Manchuria included: but few sensible persons paid any attention to it." He referred to the kind of mood also evoked by Benois—of rebellion and simmering revolution—remarking that "some go so far as to wish that Russia may be defeated as quickly as possible, so that she may at last obtain real reforms. It is extraordinary indeed how openly some people express themselves on the subject, even people of wealth and position." The Russian press, asserts the English journalist, is not to be trusted, and this is realized by "all the more intelligent people": "They will add up the totals of Japanese losses, on which subject the Russian Press is so liberal, and, on realizing the wonderful results obtained, ask themselves how it is there are any Japanese left!" Enthusiasm for the war, he concludes, was there none: "To be called out to serve at the front is regarded as a most appalling misfortune, and the number of deserters is very large. All means are resorted to, including suicide, to avoid military service."

In the same month as Alexei's birth the Minister of Internal Affairs, Vyacheslav Plehve, had been blown up by a terrorist bomb, and by the end of the year it was clear to everyone that serious internal troubles were brewing in Russia. On the anniversary of the Decembrists' revolt of 1825, December 14, a banquet was held in the Pavlov Hall in St. Petersburg, attended by a thousand "liberals," including such intellectual and literary luminaries as Dmitry Merezhkovsky, Zinaida Hippius, Dmitry Filosofov, and Nikolai Berdyaev, and many professors. They had used the excuse of a banquet in order to assemble together to protest, primarily, against the war. The police took no action, though they watched carefully and, reported *The Times*, the Petersburg press contained no mention of the event. The weather also appears to have been, for the time being, on the side of law and order: "A blizzard and intense cold during the past week have militated against any outdoor gatherings. Last night some students tried to sing revolutionary songs but were overruled." The prescient KR confided to his diary: "The disturbance is increasing, and one senses ahead something unknown, but inescapable and terrible."

CHAPTER FOUR

Autocracy in Crisis

1905–1907

Thus are reputations made; and even Kings are apt to be fashioned into the image of them which rumour makes.

—*The Times*, August 18, 1906

THREE DAYS AFTER the event which came to be known as Bloody Sunday, *The Times* printed the report of a conversation that a French journalist claimed to have had in St. Petersburg with "a working man in the crowd." "Well, what do you think of all this?" the journalist had asked his representative man. The latter had answered unhappily that there was no longer a Tsar, and continued: "the Tsar was our father, the defender of his people against the bureaucracy. Yesterday he betrayed us. He caused us to be fired upon. While we came with crucifixes and with ikons to ask him to intercede for us, to help us out of the misery in which we live, we were shot down. I threw myself on my knees with many others to entreat them not to kill us. They fired again twice. We had not come to do any harm, but to entreat our Little Father, the Tsar, to help us. We were told that he was waiting at the Winter Palace, and we tried to go there."

This has become the popular image of January 9, 1905: the crowd of loyal, God-fearing workers, processing through the snowy streets of the Russian capital, bearing aloft sacred icons and banners, led by a fervent and well-meaning, if mysterious, priest, Father Georgy Gapon, in the belief that a kindly Tsar would welcome them as his beloved people and listen to their requests, only to be gunned down in cold blood on the orders of that Tsar, thereby justifying his sobriquet of Nicholas the Bloody and leading to the bitterness of *The Times*'s "workman" and all like him. If we examine this picture a little, however, we will discover that image and reality do not entirely coalesce.

To begin with, Father Gapon was not only a well-meaning priest shepherding his flock; neither was he entirely in control of events. Up until a few weeks before the demonstration he had not been in favor of it, arguing against the presentation of a petition. The Assembly of Russian Workers, of which Gapon was the self-appointed leader, had been formed as a "Zubatovist" organization—that is, a type of pro-government trade union devised by Sergei Zubatov, a police administrator. Urban workers were to come together for the purposes of socializing, education, and, within limits acceptable to the government and with the knowledge of the police, requesting improved conditions. Such organizations were seen by the revolutionaries as an attempt to infiltrate and subvert their movement, and by the authorities—or most of them—as a means of defusing revolutionary agitation by providing the workers with a legitimate alternative. On this basis, Gapon and his Assembly enjoyed the approval of the Governor-General of St. Petersburg, General Fullon. What the authorities did not appreciate, however, was the extent to which the organization had in recent months been subverted by more revolutionary influences, Gapon himself becoming more of a figurehead than a genuine leader. As a priest, he was useful to the more revolutionary elements within the organization in that he provided reassurance to many nonradical, nonpoliticized workers who would be prepared to follow him in a demonstration; he also continued to enjoy the confidence of the authorities. With the strikes now taking place in St. Petersburg, particularly at the Putilov factory (provoked partly by opposition on the part of the factory management to the Assembly), Gapon, in addition to being manipulated by activists more radical than himself, had also become radicalized. As a result of all this, a situation had developed that the authorities imagined they had under control but that had in fact become an unknown quantity.

Finance Minister Kokovtsov, summoned on the eve of the demonstration to an emergency meeting by Prince Svyatopolk-Mirsky, the Minister of Internal Affairs who had replaced the assassinated Plehve, to discuss "some aspects of the labor movement," claims never to have heard of Gapon before that meeting. Neither did he detect any anxiety in his fellow attendees: General Fullon; Dmitry Trepov, the Assistant Minister of Internal Affairs; and General Meshetich, Chief of Staff of the Guards and of the troops of the Petersburg District. They knew a procession had been planned, but seemed to be of the opinion that it would be canceled.

Contrary to what the anonymous "working man" had professed to believe, the Tsar was not waiting for the demonstrators that Sunday morning or sitting at a window in the Winter Palace, observing his loyal subjects being fired upon in the great square below. He was at Gatchina, the palace on the outskirts of St. Petersburg that had been his father's favorite residence and where he had spent much of his own childhood. Though the removal to Gatchina had been considered wise in light of the planned procession, Nicholas had been assured by Prince Svyatopolk-Mirsky that there was nothing to worry about and that "measures" had been taken. (The "measures," it appears, comprised a decision that the police should inform the workers of the Tsar's absence from the city, so that they would realize there was no point in processing to the Winter Palace and attempting to present a petition.) Given that Nicky was dependent on information supplied to him by his ministers, it is not altogether surprising if, as averred by KR, "when the disturbances were in preparation, he was not inclined to take them seriously and thought that they had been greatly exaggerated." His only knowledge of Gapon was that he was "some priest at the head of the workers' union" and a "socialist." (He later spoke of him in far less anodyne terms, clearly blaming him for what had happened, referring to him in a conversation with W. T. Stead as "that pig Gapon.")

On that fateful Sunday morning, Kokovtsov was working in his study when he heard volleys of gunfire from near the palace and observed crowds of people running along the side of the Moika Canal. He was all set to go out and investigate but found his front door was locked, the police having called and instructed the doorman not to let anyone leave the house until the crowd had been dispersed from Palace Square and removed from the district. The firing ceased at around noon, and after lunch Kokovtsov went out and walked along to Palace Square. Most of the city now seemed deserted, some infantry patrols stationed in the square, and the police urging any people standing about to move on. Kokovtsov picked up what information he could: "From the conversations of those about me and the words of a police officer whom I knew I learned that part of the crowd headed for the Palace Square . . . had broken through the military and police guard and had been fired upon. Just how many persons had been killed and wounded was uncertain, but the general opinion was that the number was small." In fact, though unofficial estimates at the time ranged from a few hundred to several thousand, about one thousand people had been killed or injured.

Nicky himself wrote in his diary on January 9: "A terrible day! There were serious disturbances in Petersburg as a result of the workers wishing to reach the Winter Palace. The troops were forced to open fire in several parts of the town, there were many killed and wounded. Lord, how painful and how sad!" Yet despite the pain the news evoked in Nicky, there is a sense of distance here—not only the physical distance (a matter of a few miles) between Petersburg and Gatchina, but also a distance engendered through an apparent lack of responsibility or involvement. Somehow this is all at one remove from the Tsar, who, in the afternoon, went for a walk with his brother. It may be that this sense of distance between the Tsar and his suffering people is only imaginary, a perception generated in today's reader by the paucity and restraint of Nicky's recorded words, just as it was generated in the direct participants and observers of Bloody Sunday by the lack of communication and of reliable information at the time.

As far as Kokovtsov was concerned, the events of Bloody Sunday had two major repercussions. One was that they made it harder for him to negotiate loans in Paris and Berlin, as Russia's standing abroad was very low after press reports of the violence and killings. The second was the pressure put upon the Tsar, in particular by General Dmitry Trepov who now replaced General Fullon as Governor-General of St. Petersburg, to address the workers personally, in order to demonstrate that "he did take their interests to heart and that he would extend to them his personal protection." According to Kokovtsov, Nicky had some sympathy with Trepov's suggestion, "believing that he personally ought to try to pacify the working classes and even to call into his presence representatives of the factory workers of the capital." Kokovtsov himself had severe doubts about both the wisdom and effectiveness of this move, realizing that it was open to all kinds of negative propaganda. Trepov, however, got his way and set about devising a scheme to select a number of factory workers to meet the Tsar. The workers showed little enthusiasm for the proposal. When Kokovtsov reported to the Tsar that revolutionary propaganda leaflets making fun of the idea of the deputation were being pasted on the walls of factory buildings, the Tsar merely responded: "If this is so, no one can reproach me for being indifferent to the needs of the workers; they are to blame for having refused to come to me with confidence."

Nicholas duly received a deputation of thirty-four workmen on January 26, the deputation being accompanied by Kokovtsov and Trepov. They traveled on the imperial railway to Tsarskoe Selo and then by carriage to the Alexander Palace. There was a special train line that ran between St. Petersburg and Tsarskoe Selo. This branch line, constructed specifically for the imperial train, ran alongside the main track from the city, before turning off to the right. It was kept under the surveillance of its own detachment of police, with guards stationed at every hundred feet along the track, and ended at a private station called the Imperial Pavilion. The Tsar, attended by his cousin, Grand Duke Georgy Mikhailovich, and by the Palace Commandant, met them at three o'clock in the afternoon, and the usual formulaic greetings were exchanged. The Tsar then addressed the workers, assuring them that he understood the difficulties of their lives but insisting that they must be patient and that "strikes and revolutionary demonstrations" were the wrong method to use in seeking to overcome those difficulties. He very much took the tone of the archetypal headmaster, speaking "more in sorrow than in anger," remonstrating with his misguided, but fundamentally good and loyal pupils, for having allowed themselves to be led astray by "traitors and enemies of the Fatherland." Strikes and demonstrations inevitably led to disorders, continued the Tsar, which in turn would force the authorities to call in the troops. He promised that the workers' legitimate grievances would be examined (always provided that they had obediently gone back to work) and he "pardoned their transgression." No concession was given to the idea that it might be for the workers to "pardon the transgression" of those who had commanded troops to fire on them, no acceptance whatsoever of culpability on the part of the government. After respectfully listening to the Tsar's address, the deputation went to church to pray, light candles, and kiss the icons, and then refreshments were served. Cheering, the men drank to the Tsar's health. At half past four they were driven back to the Imperial Pavilion station. Kokovtsov was dismissive of the whole event: "The workers expressed no particular wishes. The Tsar spoke very kindly with nearly every one of them, asking questions as to where they came from, what their former occupation had been before entering factory work, and what their family circumstances were. The delegates were served tea and sandwiches and went home." Trepov was very pleased with how it had all gone, while the chief factory inspector was relieved that there had been no "incidents."

What impression did the men carry away with them from their rather pleasant jaunt? The Tsar had worked his usual charm, and at least he had listened to them. He had indicated that their requests for improved working conditions would be considered, but the clearest indication of all was that the status quo would be preserved. The working class was not to step outside the place allocated to it, and the message that any further demonstrations were forbidden and would be met again with force was unmistakable. Nicholas might be charming, he might insist he had the interests of the workers at heart, but he was inflexible. The people were his children—his naughty children, of late—and they must be taught to obey their loving father.

Part of the Tsar's remonstrance to these representatives of his formerly rebellious, now presumed repentant, subjects touched on the war with Japan. How could they have rebelled against the Fatherland by withdrawing their labor at a time when they should have been joining in the struggle to overcome the foreign enemy? The war was not going well, though Nicholas continued to maintain that Russia would be victorious—until Saturday, May 15, when news reached St. Petersburg of the disaster at Tsushima, in which two thirds of the Russian fleet was destroyed by the Japanese. When Kokovtsov presented his report on the following Friday, he found the Tsar "greatly depressed; evidently for the first time he had abandoned his customary hopes for a speedy and glorious termination of the war. He did not mention the catastrophe itself." He was no more forthcoming in an interview a few weeks later with the American ambassador, who had been instructed by his President, Theodore Roosevelt, to offer America's aid in brokering a peace agreement with Japan. Once negotiations got under way, led on the Russian side by Chairman of the Committee of Ministers Sergei Witte, Nicky played a significant, if not always obvious, role. Kokovtsov was convinced that it was the Tsar's personal determination, rather than anything Witte said, that assured Russia's coming out unexpectedly well from the peace terms, Japan relinquishing both an indemnity and half of the island of Sakhalin. Russia lost Korea and the southern half of Manchuria, including Port Arthur, but it had been anticipated they would lose far more. Nicky made his position clear at the outset, annotating a report drawn up by Count Lamsdorf with the words, "I am ready to terminate by peace a war which I did not start, provided the conditions offered us befit the dignity of Russia. I do not consider that we are beaten; our army is still intact, and I have faith in it." He was prepared to make concessions over Korea, but was absolutely determined to pay no indemnity, underlining the word "never" three times. Unfortunately, the Tsar's firm stand and the unexpectedly favorable peace settlement did him little good in terms of public opinion—partly because Witte took all the credit and partly because the public was tired of the whole business anyway, just wanting the war to be over. They were more concerned with the developing turmoil at home.

Neither did the conclusion of peace bring any joy to the Tsar himself. As his sister Xenia recorded on August 18, "Mama asked Nicky to cheer up and at least look as if he considered the peace a necessity"—to which Nicky had replied, "Yes, *faire bonne mine à mauvais jeu.*" The talk among the family was that Nicky's insistence on paying no indemnity had been calculated to provoke the Japanese into not accepting, thereby providing Russia with an excuse for continuing the war. But then, when the Japanese conceded and accepted the terms, the Russians had no alternative but to do the same. "And so," as KR put it, "the Emperor was caught out unexpectedly and has, in the words of Olia [KR's sister], who saw him and the Empress at Peterhof, been dropped in at the deep end." Nicky's visible grumpiness at this outcome demonstrates that, at least within the safe confines of his family, his usually impenetrable mask could on occasion slip.

During the years of turmoil this habitual impenetrability took an outward form. It was especially on account of the terrorist threat of assassination that, from 1905, the Tsar and his family largely disappeared from view, retreating into a private life in a variety of suburban palaces and other refuges. Though in many ways this secluded life was to their taste, it should be remembered that it was undertaken for reasons of security, and on police advice, rather than entirely through personal preference; as for the constant surveillance that was deemed necessary for their protection, they did not enjoy that at all. It was at this time that General Spiridovich was appointed to the newly created post of head of the Emperor's personal security detachment, a post that he held for the next ten and a half years.

The retreat into private life can be seen as having begun in earnest on February 4, 1905, when Nicky's uncle and Alix's brother-in-law, Grand Duke Sergei, was killed in Moscow by a terrorist bomb. Those of the imperial family who were in St. Petersburg gathered at Tsarskoe Selo in grief and shock. Alix wanted to travel at once to Moscow to be with her bereaved sister Ella, as did other members of the family, but General Trepov, fearing further assassination attempts, advised strongly against this. Nicky, who had initially thought of attending the funeral himself, reluctantly accepted Trepov's advice. Only KR was allowed to represent the Emperor at the funeral, all the other Grand Dukes being informed by letter that, not only were they not to travel to Moscow, but they were also forbidden to attend the requiems at the Kazan and St. Isaac cathedrals in St. Petersburg. This was not an easy decision to make; according to KR, the Tsar, his mother, and his wife were all "inconsolable" at not being able to pay their last respects to the deceased. Neither was it necessarily the right decision, at least not as far as public opinion was concerned. KR noted that "in Moscow, the absence of close relatives creates a strange and painful impression," while V. F. Djunkovsky, Grand Duke Sergei's aide-de-camp, opined: "I think that if the Emperor had not listened to Trepov, and had come to Moscow—it would have made a colossal impression and would have increased the Tsar's standing with his people."

Instead, the Tsar and his immediate family remained sequestered in the Alexander Palace at Tsarskoe Selo. Their living quarters comprised one wing of this palace originally commissioned from Quarenghi by Catherine the Great for her grandson, the future Alexander I. The wing had been redesigned as a family home for Nicky and Alix shortly after their marriage, the rooms being decorated by the fashionable St. Petersburg designer Roman (or Robert) Meltzer, and they had always enjoyed spending time there. Their rooms were on the ground floor, the children being housed above. (In 1899 a hydraulic lift was installed between the two floors, which was particularly useful for Alix.) The domestic servants were also accommodated in this wing, the other one being occupied by various members of the retinue and by the Dowager Empress when she was in residence, while the central block contained the state apartments. In an alteration to the eighteenth-century design, the rooms of the Emperor and Empress were arranged along either side of a long corridor. On the Tsar's side a reception room led into his official study, where he both received his ministers and worked alone. His mahogany desk was illuminated by an electric lamp with a large green lampshade, and comfortable leather chairs were spread around the room. Nicky was very particular, to the point of obsession, about the objects on his desk; each thing—his pens, paper, cigarette box, photographs—had its own allotted space and had to be kept in it. Prior to departure for one of the other imperial palaces, a plan would be drawn so that anything removed could be returned to precisely the same place on its return. His rationale for such behavior was that he wanted no time wasted in looking for things.

Another important room for the Tsar was his bathroom, next door to his study and containing a large heated swimming bath. Occasionally the children would be allowed to use this bath, to their great delight. Then came the cloakroom, the domain of the Emperor's valet. This led on to a gallery and into Nicky's second study, where he received private delegations, family members, and friends. He also used to play billiards here with the young Dmitry Pavlovich, son of his Uncle Pavel, and would relax here (briefly) in the evenings, often with the rest of his family. On the other side, the gallery led into a small room occupied by Alix's head chambermaid, Madame Zanotti, a tall, pretty woman hardly known outside the close circle of the imperial family, who had known Alix since her childhood in Darmstadt and had accompanied her to Russia.

At the far end of the Empress's apartments a staircase led up to the children's schoolroom, from a dressing room adjacent to Nicky and Alix's bedroom. This latter was a large three-windowed room, the walls decorated in light cretonne. A large silk canopy was raised above two metal-framed twin beds, and behind the beds was an alcove filled with icons. The furnishings were of light-colored wood, upholstered in cretonne. Many photographs and small pictures filled the walls, pride of place being given to portraits of Alix's father (the late

Louis IV, Grand Duke of Hesse) and of Alix and Nicky themselves, hung at high level. Light came from three electric lamps suspended from the ceiling.

Next to the bedroom was the Mauve Boudoir, Alix's private domain and her favorite room. Its principal feature was a very large corner divan, on the left of which was a desk and on the right a table covered with newspapers and magazines. A piano was adjacent to one wall, a sofa or daybed to another, partitioned off by a screen. On a low table next to the sofa were photographs, flowers, and a telephone. This was the room in which Alix spent most of her time, particularly in later years; here she would read and receive her few friends (an armchair was provided for Nicky). Five o'clock tea was taken in here; on occasion the family would lunch and dine here as well.

Then came the Rosewood Drawing Room (sometimes known as the Palisander Room), which was also connected by a door to the gallery; its name came from the rosewood furnishings, upholstered in dark red silk. This was the usual family dining room. It led into the Maple Room, designed in art nouveau style under the guidance of Alix's brother Ernie, known for his patronage of art nouveau artists in Darmstadt. The Maple Room's cream-colored chairs were upholstered in a greenish-mauve material. It was connected by the gallery to Nicky's study, all this space having originally comprised the Palace's great two-storied concert hall and ballroom. Behind Nicky's study and next to what was known as the Corner Room was his library, which contained mahogany furniture from the time of Nicholas I. A number of equestrian statuettes of cavalry officers were placed atop the tall bookcases lining the walls. In the middle of the room were display cases containing rare editions, coins, and prints. Alix would sometimes set up her easel in here and paint. Once a week the bookseller Shcheglov would leave all the newly published Russian books as well as many foreign works on the table, for the Tsar to choose which he wanted to buy. In the evenings he would nearly always read aloud to his family, his favorite books including Turgenev's *A Huntsman's Sketches* and the works of Nikolai Leskov. Of one of Leskov's stories, *The Sealed Angel*, Nicky was so fond that he took it with him on all his journeys. These were popular rather than high-brow works, Nicky's tastes reflecting those of a large proportion of his literate subjects. The avant-garde would have characterized them as "bourgeois."

The children's rooms were on the floor above, as described by their young relative Maria Pavlovna, who, along with her billiard-playing brother, was a frequent visitor to the Alexander Palace: "These rooms, light and spacious, were hung with flowered cretonne and furnished throughout with polished lemonwood. The effect was luxurious, yet peaceful and comfortable. Through the windows you could see the palace gardens and guardhouses and a little beyond, through the grille of a high iron gate, a street corner." In overall charge of the imperial daughters was an English nurse, managing a team of Russian nurses and chambermaids, all dressed in white uniforms—apart from two of the Russian nurses who were allowed to wear traditional peasant dress. A maid-of-honor called Princess Sonia Orbeliani, who was a particular friend of the Empress's, also lived in this wing. She was afflicted by a hereditary disease, a form of progressive paralysis, and was by 1905 confined to a wheelchair. Alix used to visit her every day, unless she was unwell herself, in which case she would send a note and flowers.

The Tsar could not be faulted on the amount of time he dedicated to work while at Tsarskoe Selo, though one might legitimately question the nature of that work. His daily routine was unchanging. Each morning he got out of bed between seven and eight o'clock. After saying his prayers, he would leave the bedroom quietly, so as not to wake Alix, go into his bathroom, and dive into his swimming bath. At half past eight he had breakfast, consisting of tea and bread rolls, in the Rosewood Drawing Room, though if Alix was already awake, they would drink their tea together in the bedroom. Then Nicky would go to his study to begin the process of receiving reports. The first people to arrive would usually be the duty aide-de-camp and the Grand Marshal of the Imperial Court, Count Paul von Benckendorff, whose brief concerned ceremonial matters and court finances. Next would come the Palace Commandant, to discuss matters of security or those of wider political concern. He would be followed by various ministers or other people whom the Tsar had ordered to report to him. These receptions lasted until half-past eleven, at which point Nicky would break for half an hour to take a walk in the gardens, accompanied by some of his dogs. More visitors would be received between noon and lunchtime.

In these years, before Alix's health took a serious turn for the worse, there were nearly always guests for luncheon in the Rosewood Drawing Room. The menus would be drafted by von Benckendorff for three days at a time and submitted to Alix during evening tea for her to make any desired adjustments. Then each morning the menu for the day would be re-presented to her, for final approval. Luncheon generally consisted of four courses preceded by *zakuski* (hors d'oeuvres); dinner consisted of five courses. Nicky always preferred Russian dishes, especially *shchi* (cabbage soup), *kasha* (a form of porridge), and suckling pig. He was so fond of the latter that he would often order a slice of it seasoned with horseradish just for himself.

After lunch Nicky would carry on working—reading official papers and minuting his remarks in the margin—until half-past three, when he would take a complete break and go for a walk until tea at five. If there were any urgent matters to discuss, the Palace Commandant would intercept him on his way out. Five o'clock tea was taken in Alix's Mauve Boudoir, Nicky making use of this time to leaf through the Russian newspapers, while Alix skimmed the English ones. Audiences would resume between six and eight o'clock, which was the usual hour for dinner. Then from half-past nine until eleven, Nicky would work alone or occasionally receive a minister. He would join Alix for tea at eleven, which was also the time when the couple read aloud to one another. Even then the day was not over; Nicky would return to his study until a quarter-past midnight in order to finish off his day's work. He would then write up his diary (exhaustion may partly explain why the entries were often very brief, more like notes than narrative) and, finally, go to bed. No chances were taken with security during the night, a platoon of the interior guard being stationed, from midnight, in the lower gallery leading to Nicky and Alix's apartments. Sentries guarded access to all the rooms.

The next morning it would all begin again, in an endless procession of reports to receive and documents to consider. As the British journalist W. T. Stead described it, "from day to day and from hour to hour the Emperor grinds on, unhasting and unresting, in the prison-house of Empire, and long before his allotted stint of work is done, his strength and time are exhausted, and he has neither leisure nor energy in which to grasp his sceptre." It was Stead's belief that there was an element of deliberation on the part of the bureaucrats in thus keeping the Tsar chained to his desk—that they feared that, left to his own devices, he might start to take the initiative and try to implement ideas that would be inconvenient to the working of the "huge unwieldy machine" that was the Russian Empire. But it should also be noted that this routine was not dissimilar to that of the Emperor of Austria, Franz Joseph I, who perceived himself as his Empire's "first public servant." Endless paperwork and bureaucracy seem to have become the curse of the latter-day autocrat; they do not in themselves imply that Nicholas II was unfit for the task, though they may be symptomatic of the defects of the system.

It was in 1905 that Pierre Gilliard first came to know the imperial family, being taken on as tutor to Olga and Tatiana. He did not find his first lesson with the girls very easy. They were not as advanced as he had expected, so that the lesson he had prepared was of no use; furthermore, he felt he was under examination by the Empress, who stayed throughout, paying close attention to the proceedings. Alix continued to attend the girls' lessons for several months, and impressed

Gilliard by her views on the teaching of modern languages. He was also impressed by her appearance, finding her to be "still a beautiful woman. . . . She was tall and slender and carried herself superbly." Spiridovich's impressions were similar: "At that time the Empress Alexandra Fyodorovna was a very pretty woman. Tall, imposing, she had a really queenly bearing. She had a reputation for being intelligent and extremely cultured. She was then only 34 years old, but lived only for her family and children." Eventually, the Empress decided that Gilliard knew what he was doing and relaxed her surveillance of him, handing over the duty of being present at the lessons to one of her ladies-in-waiting.

The eldest girl, Olga, was always a favorite with Gilliard, the imperial daughter of whom he had the most hope intellectually. He described her at ten years old as "very fair . . . with sparkling, mischievous eyes and a slightly retroussé nose." She seemed to be searching for "the weak point in [his] armour," but there was something so "pure and frank" about her that he liked her immediately. The auburn-haired Tatiana was, he thought, prettier than Olga but also "less transparent, frank, and spontaneous." In due course Gilliard was also introduced to the baby of the family, the little Alexei: "one of the handsomest babies one could imagine, with his lovely fair curls and his great blue-grey eyes under their fringe of long curling lashes. He had the fresh pink colour of a healthy child, and when he smiled there were two little dimples in his chubby cheeks." When Gilliard approached him, "a solemn, frightened look came into his eyes, and it took a great deal to induce him to hold out a tiny hand."

Every year, in early summer, Nicky, Alix, and the children (with their numerous attendants) would transfer to Peterhof, by the edge of the sea. Here they principally occupied the Lower Palace in the Alexandria estate. (Sometimes referred to as the Lower Dacha, or the Alexandria villa, or the New Palace, it was badly shelled during the Second World War and subsequently obliterated by the orders of Nikita Khrushchev.) Built during the reign of Alexander III, it incorporated a stone tower, originally made of wood, one of a number of signal towers used for observation and communication during the Crimean War. On his accession Nicholas had had this palace enlarged, by the construction of a new two-story main building, joined by a covered vaulted arcade to the tower; later, kitchens and outbuildings were added. The tower was crowned by a small glazed platform, above which floated the Alexandria flag—bearing an azure shield, a sword with a crown of roses, and the motto "For Tsar, Faith and Fatherland."

The Emperor's study was on the second floor of what had been the tower and featured a glazed, semicircular veranda with a view east toward the port of Kronstadt. Another window faced north, toward the sea. A small walnut desk was placed at right angles to this window; the chairs were upholstered in dark green morocco and the walls were wainscoted with walnut panels. Here Nicky received his ministers when they came to report, and held other private audiences. For larger delegations another building at Peterhof, the Farm Palace, was used. Nicky and Alix's bedroom was on the floor above the study, while the Empress's other apartments and the children's quarters were located in the new main building. Much of the Peterhof complex of palaces, fountains, and gardens had already become a tourist attraction, a museum open to the public, during the reign of Nicholas's father. As Spiridovich described it, "A court valet, clean-shaven, imposing, in livery and tights, friendly but dignified, gave explanations on all the historic treasures."

Life at Peterhof, though viewed partly as holiday, had its own routine for this very ordered family. Walks for the children began at ten o'clock in the morning. Alix, who liked to spend time in the English garden designed and planted during the reign of Catherine the Great, would set out for her dose of fresh air after lunch, often driving herself in a small horse-drawn charabanc, usually accompanied by one of her daughters. At half-past two Nicky went riding, always accompanied at this period by his close friend General Orlov—and followed, invariably, by a Cossack bodyguard. They would ride cross-country and pass through various villages, where the Tsar would sometimes get into conversation with the locals, asking them about the harvest or other village concerns. In the evening, after dinner, Nicky and Alix would go for a drive together, in a two-horse carriage under the direction of their coachman, Konkov. Before long the itineraries for these drives became fixed—to the extent that the security agents would be able to work out the precise route to be taken, depending on which gate they had left by.

While on the one hand, such regular habits made life easy for those in charge of imperial security, they also created problems—for if the security guards could work out which way the Tsar would go, so could anybody else. Quite apart from potential terrorists, there were many people wanting to waylay the Tsar in order to present petitions, and an unofficial protocol developed to deal with this. Usually a petitioner would kneel as the imperial carriage approached, holding the petition above his head. The vehicle would carry on, but the escorting Cossack would take the petition and hand it to the Emperor. When the petitioners became particularly numerous, Spiridovich's men grew adept at recognizing them in advance and would arrest them before the imperial carriage appeared, taking them off to the duty aide-de-camp. If they were genuine, they would come to no harm and would get their petitions read but, as there was always the fear that a terrorist might be masquerading as a petitioner, no leniency was shown to those on duty if they allowed a petitioner to get through the net. "If, despite everything, a petitioner succeeded in approaching the vehicle and actually handing his petition to the Emperor, that was too bad for the guard on whose patch the incident happened. He was discharged on the spot for not having fulfilled his duty, for not having succeeded in preventing an unknown individual from approaching the imperial vehicle." As for petitioners who had been arrested, or who tried to present themselves at the palace, they were taken to the guardroom where the duty aide-de-camp received them every day, between the hours of three and five in the afternoon. He would examine them to find out the details of their individual circumstances as well as the nature of their petitions, and then classify the requests and record the substance of them in a book kept especially for this purpose. This book would then be handed over to a gentleman of the bedchamber to be given to the Tsar. Nicky would read through the book and annotate each entry, sometimes specifying a financial sum to be given in assistance, or ordering a report to be carried out.

After the weeks spent every year at Peterhof, the family would enjoy part of their summer as a real holiday, cruising in the Finnish fjords on the imperial yacht *Standart*. The word *yacht* hardly does justice to the *Standart,* conjuring up in the mind's eye a rather modest vessel. The *Standart,* with its three masts and two funnels and a water displacement of over five thousand tons, was in fact enormous, a floating palace—which is certainly how the imperial family viewed it. The officers were as carefully chosen as were the staff of the palaces on dry land, and their appointments had to be agreed upon by the Emperor and Empress. At this period the yacht's commandant was the elderly bachelor and cavalier of the Order of St. George, Admiral Ivan Chagin, one of the Emperor's aides-de-camp and very popular with both officers and men. The yacht's 350-man crew included a brass band and a balalaika orchestra. Whenever the *Standart* had members of the imperial family on board, it was accompanied by a number of destroyers and, as ever, the security police were in attendance, Spiridovich and his men occupying a separate ship. The whole fleet fell under the command of His Imperial Majesty's flag captain, Admiral Konstantin Nilov, who had previously served as aide-de-camp to Nicky's uncle, Grand Duke Alexei Alexandrovich. During that time Nilov was said to have acquired a taste for whisky and soda that he drank to an immoderate degree even for a sailor.

The Tsar was not entirely free from paperwork even during his summer cruises, his cabins on the *Standart* including both a private and an official study, in addition to his bedroom and bathroom. Alix also had a study-boudoir, bedroom, bathroom, and dressing room, while the children had their usual allocation of bedrooms, the two younger daughters sharing. A particular feature of many of the family's cabins on this, their favorite yacht, was the amount of light and air they enjoyed, through specially designed long windows, rather than conventional portholes. Otherwise, the cabins replicated many aspects of the domestic arrangements of the family elsewhere. Photographs covered the walls, and the mahogany salon, which communicated with both Nicky's and Alix's quarters, boasted many objects given to them by foreign heads of state, including a portrait of Kaiser Wilhelm in his Russian naval uniform, given and signed by "Willy" himself specifically to hang there. Above the family's cabins were those of the retinue and the maids-of-honor, while underneath were those of the servants and junior-ranking officers. This whole part of the yacht was under the supervision of a designated officer responsible for its maintenance and safety in the case of fire or other emergency. The officer fulfilling this role in 1907 was Lieutenant Nikolai Sablin, who was to become a great friend of the family. On the bridge there was an immense "deck-house," containing the Emperor's official study, a reception room, and dining room that could seat up to eighty people. The interior of this room was of light maple, the seats upholstered in blue leather. Embossed leather medallions framing watercolors of the Russian fleet adorned the panels between the windows. This room was also filled with light from large windows and a skylight.

An unfortunate incident occurred during the summer cruise of 1907. The *Standart,* surrounded by destroyers, was advancing through an untroubled sea, passing between several small islets, when suddenly the great yacht shuddered to a halt and was thrown forward. The imperial family were at tea when they heard a frightful noise, crockery and windowpanes were smashed, and the alarm bells rang out. The yacht was heeling over on one side. Derevenko, the sailor whose task it was to look after Alexei and prevent any harm from coming to him, was seized with panic and began running, shouting, toward the bow with the child in his arms. The Emperor told him to be quiet at once and brought him to his senses. The crew meanwhile got on with the emergency routine, letting down the lifeboats and putting the watertight bulkheads in place. The imperial family, the children first, were taken on board the yacht *Eyleken.* The Finnish admiral in charge of this craft, overawed at the presence of the Tsar, greeted him with the customary formula, assuring him that "no untoward incident had taken place within the radius of his pilotage." "So this doesn't count?" asked the Emperor, pointing to the *Standart* aground on a rock. The Admiral was lost for words.

It was inevitable that the first thing to cross Spiridovich's mind—and no doubt the minds of many others in the party—was that this might have been a deliberate attack on the *Standart,* an assassination attempt, perhaps caused by a mine. Spiridovich's detachment made a minute search of the area, but nothing was discovered. What in fact had happened was that the *Standart,* traveling at fifteen knots, had hit one of the sharp underwater rocks that the sailors called "sugar loaves." The rock had slit the yacht's hull, beneath the second heating chamber, and immobilized it.

In the first instance the imperial family and all their entourage were transferred onto the *Asia,* where Prince Putyatin managed to get dinner served to everyone that evening, albeit rather late. It was an uncomfortable meal for all present—which included the officers of both ships, as well as Spiridovich and his men—for, although Nicky seemed calm, Alix was very upset and did not say a word. And, despite his outward demeanor, Nicky was also on edge, as became clear during the flag officer Osten Sachen's valiant attempt at making conversation. In an attempt to distract the Tsar, Osten Sachen remarked that the court photographer had managed to get a shot of the damaged *Standart.* Nicky finally lost his temper at this, and replied sharply: "The man's an imbecile. He always does the wrong thing." Everyone fell silent again, Osten Sachen wishing the floor would swallow him up. "I myself sat glued to my chair," recalled Spiridovich, "for my conscience was far from clear: when the destroyer I was on had been circling the *Standart,* I had also taken the opportunity to get a picture of the yacht."

That the terrorist threat was not imaginary had been amply demonstrated during the second half of 1906, when the Socialist Revolutionaries' Combat Organisation was particularly active. On the afternoon of August 12, a Saturday, suicide bombers made an attempt on the life of the then prime minister Pyotr Stolypin. Two terrorists dressed as policemen arrived at his villa on Apothecary Island in the outskirts of St. Petersburg, at the time when he normally received petitioners, and detonated two bombs. Over thirty people were killed, including servants and people waiting to see Stolypin, as well as the bombers themselves, and about the same number were wounded; among the lightly wounded was Stolypin's three-year-old son, while his fourteen-year-old daughter sustained a serious leg injury. Stolypin himself was unhurt—though splattered with ink, as he had been seated at his writing desk at the time of the explosion. On the following day there was another assassination attempt, this time successful. The victim was General Min, who had been in charge of crushing the Moscow uprising in December 1905. He was killed by a female terrorist who shot him at the Novy Peterhof railway station. In total, 768 officials and government agents were killed by terrorists over the course of the year, and 820 were wounded. Intelligence was constantly being gathered concerning threats to the Tsar's life, and Spiridovich's detachment lived in a permanent state of vigilance. At one point news came through, via the head of the St. Petersburg department of security, Gerasimov, of a plot hatched by a group of "maximalists" (a faction of the Socialist Revolutionary Party, or SRs) to blow up the Tsar during one of his journeys across Tsarskoe Selo. These maximalists were already installed in a house on one of the routes habitually used by Nicky. The police initiated a program of "verification" of the locals, thereby making it clear to the maximalists that they had been routed; they hurried back to St. Petersburg, where, reported a satisfied Spiridovich, they were placed under the surveillance of the secret police, or Okhrana.

The end of the year saw two major terrorist attacks. On December 21, the Prefect of St. Petersburg, Vladimir von der Launitz, was assassinated during the consecration of the new church of the Institute of Experimental Medicine. What particularly alarmed the authorities about this incident was that admission to the service had been by ticket only and limited to 150 people—among whom had been Nicky's sister Olga and her husband the Duke of Oldenburg. It was thought that the terrorists must have received inside information even to have known that Launitz (accompanied by his usual posse of secret police bodyguards) would be present, as he had been privately invited by the Duke. The assassin, wearing the same formal attire as the rest of the congregation, walked quietly up behind his target and shot him in the back of the head. Launitz's bodyguards fell upon the murderer, a young man called Kudryavtsev, and began hacking at him with their swords—but he had already turned his gun on himself. Five days later, General Pavlov, the Chief Military Prosecutor, was murdered. He had been walking in his garden when he was approached by a man wearing the uniform of a secretary of the Military Tribunal. The man turned out to be a revolutionary activist, a former sailor, and he fired several shots at the general. On the report given to him concerning the murder of General Pavlov, Nicky wrote: "an irreparable loss."

One of the few occasions during these turbulent years when the Tsar, with many members of the wider imperial family, appeared in public was at the official inauguration of the first State Duma in April 1906. The path leading to this day had been long. More than a year before, imperial announcements had been issued concerning the creation of a representative assembly. In June 1905 details began to emerge in the press of the form this assembly was to take: It was to have consultative powers and to be called the State Duma. The same month saw the mutiny on the *Potemkin,* a battleship belonging to the Black Sea Fleet. Xenia encapsulated the horror felt by the imperial family at this event, involving as it did the murder of the ship's commander and several officers. "It's terrible, terrible what we have lived to see!" she wrote in her diary on June 16. "This news has simply killed us, we have been wandering around in a daze all day—what a nightmare, it's too awful." The *Potemkin* held out for several days, cruising the Black Sea but unable to dock to take on necessary supplies. Eventually, on June 24, the mutinous crew disembarked at the Romanian port of Constanza, having obtained a guarantee from the Romanian government that they would not be repatriated. The Romanians returned the ship to Russia, while its crew divided up the ship's cash and made off for various parts of Europe.

On July 10, the Tsar set off from Peterhof on the *Polar Star* toward Björkö in the Gulf of Finland, where he was to meet his cousin, Kaiser Wilhelm. Meeting on board the yacht on the following day, the two emperors signed a secret treaty (the signatures witnessed by Wilhelm's adjutant, and by Admiral Birilev, who was asked not to read the text) by which the two powers agreed to come to one another's assistance if either were to be attacked in Europe. The treaty was to come into effect once peace had been concluded between Russia and Japan. Accordingly the Tsar informed his foreign minister, Count Lamsdorf, of the existence of the Björkö Treaty after the Portsmouth Treaty had duly been signed, but Lamsdorf was unimpressed, pointing out that France, with whom Russia was already allied, would never agree to join a triple alliance involving Germany. Neither was Witte in favor. In the end, the Björkö Treaty died a natural death, much to Kaiser Wilhelm's chagrin.

On July 18, deliberations on the organization of the State Duma, presided over by the Emperor and attended by the Grand Dukes, ministers, and various members of the State Council and the Senate, began at Peterhof and lasted for just over a week. The procedure that was followed involved full discussion of each clause, after which the Tsar would announce whether or not he approved. There was no voting. The legislation agreed upon was published on August 6. It established a consultative assembly elected by (some of) the people and empowered to debate projected legislation and official reports. The existing State Council was to be kept alongside the new assembly. The Emperor retained the power to promulgate laws contrary to the recommendations of both Duma and Council, but it was considered unlikely he would do this without a compelling reason. Deputies to the Duma were to be chosen by electors, themselves elected by those eligible to vote—the latter including every peasant and landowner, but far fewer urban dwellers (who had to be householders paying substantial property taxes to be eligible). A belief in the loyalty of the peasantry—and the disloyalty of urban workers and intellectuals—to the autocracy lay behind this choice of electors. As the Duma was to be only consultative, and almost the whole of the professional class and other very large sections of the population were ineligible to vote, this legislation did very little to satisfy the public. As a result, disorders continued and increased throughout the summer.

These discussions had been going on at the same time as the peace negotiations with Japan. Russia's chief negotiator Sergei Witte arrived back home in mid-September 1905, in the middle of a general strike. The capital's transport system was paralyzed and the only way ministers could visit the Tsar at Peterhof was by water. Witte (who was made a Count on conclusion of the peace with Japan) strongly advised the Tsar to take one of two alternatives if he wanted to avoid a revolution: Either he should set up a military dictatorship, or change the proposed nature of the Duma to make it legislative rather than merely consultative. This second alternative would in effect be tantamount to granting a constitution. Nicky consulted his advisers, including Grand Duke Nikolai Nikolaevich, considered by many a suitable choice for military dictator. (His cousin Sandro was not among these; he, along with his brother, the historian Grand Duke Nikolai Mikhailovich, had never been able to bear the excitable Nikolasha: "Looking back at the twenty-three years of the reign of Nicholas II, I can find no logical explanation why, in the name of God, the Czar should have sought Nicholasha's advice on any matters of state importance. Like all army men accustomed to tackling clearly defined tasks, Nicholasha felt dizzy when confronted with a complicated political situation where his habit of raising his voice and threatening punishment failed to produce the desired effect.") Whether or not Nik Nik "felt dizzy" in this instance, it was alleged (by Alexander Mosolov, Head of the Court Chancellery, who claimed he had heard it from Baron Fredericks, Minister of the Imperial Court) that he threatened to shoot himself if such a task were imposed on him, demanding that Nicky adopt the other of Witte's alternatives. Nicky seems to have felt he had no option other than to acquiesce.

Nicky signed the manifesto granting the legislative assembly on the morning of October 17, 1905, at Peterhof, in the presence of Grand Duke Nikolai Nikolaevich, Baron Fredericks, and Count Witte, who had been instrumental in drawing it up. This document, which became known as the Manifesto of 17th October (its full title being "Manifesto on the Improvement of State Order"), guaranteed fundamental civil liberties, including freedom of opinion, of press, of assembly, and of association. Among its fine-sounding phrases was, "The welfare of the Russian Sovereign cannot be separated from the welfare of His people, and the people's sorrow is His sorrow." After the promulgation of the Manifesto, the Tsar retained only the departments of war, navy, and foreign affairs under his personal control. Everything else became the responsibility of a Council of Ministers, and particularly of its Chairman, also known as the Prime Minister. This was the change that the Tsar found the hardest to accept, the first holder of this office being Count Witte himself. The Manifesto came as a great surprise to the revolutionary parties, who felt they had lost the initiative. Nicky's own overriding concern was the restoration of order, and the Manifesto concluded with a rallying cry to his people: "We call upon all loyal sons of Russia to remember their duties to their country, to assist in terminating this unprecedented turmoil, and together with Us to make every effort to restore peace and tranquillity to our native land."

In the immediate aftermath of the proclamation of the Manifesto there was no restoration of order, but rather the reverse. Even before the proclamation, fighting had erupted in Moscow between striking workers and their right-wing opponents (who classified the strikers as "students and Jews"). These right-wing rioters became known by the opponents of the autocracy as the "Black Hundreds"—a reference to medieval Russia, when the term had been used to denote the violent, illiterate, and conservative lower-class population living outside the town walls. The term was nevertheless embraced by the new right-wing factions, as indicative of their connection with the "Black millions" of simple Russians whom they presumed to be in agreement with their attitudes. The authorities stood by and did not intervene. And then the situation took a dramatic turn for the worse. As Xenia noted in her diary on October 21, "Telegrams are arriving from all over Russia about attacks on the Jews—it's simply terrible, how will it all end." Though the Tsar was not personally involved in any of the pogroms visited on the Jewish population of many towns throughout Russia, his image was everywhere. *The Times* noted, for instance, under the headline ANTI-JEWISH EXCESSES that "At Kherson the mob, carrying a portrait of the Emperor and national flags and singing the National Anthem, proceeded this morning to pillage the Jewish shops, and afterwards went to the cathedral to attend a thanksgiving service in connexion with the Tsar's Manifesto." The apparent connection between the anti-Jewish mobs and supporters of the government—and what should have been the forces of law and order—was not lost on the reporter: "in many parts of [Rostov on the Don] the disorders were witnessed by the police, who made no effort to interfere. Cossacks who were sent to protect the shops themselves joined in the looting. The owners of five shops fired on the pillagers, whereupon the troops sided with the latter and fired on the shopkeepers." The popular perception seems to have been that the Jews were on the side of the revolution, and hence it was only patriotic to attack them. The anti-Jewish riots were particularly virulent in Odessa; hundreds were killed, the faces of many victims so battered with hammers that they were unidentifiable. An "officer of high rank" in that town told the *Times*'s reporter: "The disturbances were the result of the insolent behaviour of the Jews themselves, which constituted a rude offence to Russian patriotic feeling. By their boisterous celebration of Tuesday's Manifesto they abused the freedom which had been granted to them. . . . They openly insulted the Emperor by their impertinent boasting that they alone had conquered and won freedom for Russia. The people could not endure such insults. The vengeance taken on these fellows may have been too severe, but excesses always produce excesses." There is no evidence that the Tsar himself did anything to provoke the pogroms or that he supported them in any way; unfortunately, however, his prejudiced attitude toward the Jews also did little to prevent them and may even have been interpreted, by some participants, as assent.

The first meeting of the Union of the Russian People took place in St. Petersburg on November 21 and attracted several thousand people. Other right-wing organizations were formed around the same time, including the Union of Landowners, who met in Moscow and appealed to the Tsar to replace the present government with another one, more able to establish firm authority and quell rebellion. On November 24, more restrictive "provisional rules" were promulgated, weakening some of the freedoms granted by the October Manifesto. Nevertheless, at a meeting between the Tsar and representatives of the various newly formed right-wing organizations on December 1, Nicholas showed no inclination to accede to their demands, stating that "The manifesto that I issued on October 17th is a complete and conscientious expression of my inflexible will; it is an act not subject to change." A more positive reception by the Tsar was afforded a delegation of the Union of the Russian People on December 23, when the Union's founder, Alexander Dubrovin, spoke of their hope of being able to elect like-minded people to the State Duma, and Nicky agreed to accept the emblem of the Union on behalf of himself and the Tsarevich. After the formation of these various right-wing parties, the Tsar began to be deluged with telegrams and letters from their supporters, telling him that Jews and other agitators—but particularly Jews—were behind the revolutionary turmoil. Nicky was inclined to take these telegrams at face value as the honest outpourings of his loyal subjects, concerned only to bring important matters to his attention. Never devious himself, he frequently failed to notice the ulterior motives of others.

W. T. Stead had cheerfully predicted of the official inauguration of the State Duma: "When Nicholas II comes face to face with the elected representatives of all the Russias it will be a day of pleasant surprises on both sides." Once again, the reality was rather different. The elections to the First Duma had not turned out as planned, the government's faith in the peasantry having been apparently misplaced. The peasant electors, rather than showing themselves devoted to the autocracy, had been seduced by their age-old hope of receiving land and so had elected either peasant deputies or candidates from the revolutionary parties who appeared to be promising to fulfill this hope. In March 1906 Nicky was putting his faith in "common sense" and hoping that, despite his justifiable worries over the likely composition of the Duma, the members would "settle down to work and everything would turn out for the best." The official opening of the Duma took place in the St. George's Hall (the Great Throne Room) of the Winter Palace on April 27, 1906.

For security reasons, particularly as there had just been an assassination attempt on the Governor-General of Moscow (he had been wounded but not killed), it was decided that the Tsar should travel to the Winter Palace by water from Peterhof, rather than by road or rail from Tsarskoe Selo. Even with this precaution in place, the security forces were on full alert. General Trepov (now Palace Commandant and in overall charge of the personal safety of the Emperor and his family) had issued instructions as to what should happen to the Tsarevich in the event of the Emperor not returning alive from the capital. He had also warned the operator of the imperial telephone system not to transmit any order received in his name or appearing to be given in his voice. And so, on that bright spring morning, the Emperor, Empress, and Dowager Empress arrived in St. Petersburg on board the yacht *Alexandria.* They then transferred to a steam launch to visit the Peter and Paul Cathedral, where they prayed at the tombs of the Tsar's ancestors, before crossing back over the Neva to the Winter Palace. There they assembled with the rest of the imperial family, moving off in procession at a quarter to two in the afternoon. Nicholas, wearing the uniform of the Preobrazhensky Regiment and preceded by the symbols of his autocratic power—the diamond-encrusted imperial crown, the state seal, the sword of state, the orb and scepter—walked alone and, once arrived in the St. George's Hall, took up his position before the throne, on which was spread an ermine mantle. The throne was surmounted by a canopy of red velvet emblazoned with the imperial crown, and with the armorial bearings of the Russian Empire embroidered on its rear panel. One step lower than the Tsar and to his left stood Adjutant-General Count Ignatyev bearing aloft the imperial banner, while to his right another adjutant-general stood holding the imperial sword. The rest of the imperial family, including the two Empresses, both in ceremonial dress of white gown and pearl-studded headdress, stood on a platform to the right of the throne. The proceedings began with the singing of the Te Deum.

Many of those present have left their impressions of that strange and momentous occasion, on which the two "sides" faced each other across the huge St. George's Hall. The right-hand side was filled with dignitaries resplendent in their embroidered parade uniforms, members of the State Council and of the imperial retinue. Opposite stood the newly elected members of the Duma, a small number of them in formal frock coats but most dressed rather ostentatiously in workers' blouses and shirts, while the peasant representatives were a motley crowd, some in colorful national costume. A large number of cassocked clergy added to the variety of the assembly. Kokovtsov's attention was particularly drawn to a tall man, "dressed in a worker's blouse and high, oiled boots, who examined the throne and those about it with a derisive and insolent air," whom he identified as F. M. Onipko, who later became renowned for his revolutionary opinions and actions. Stolypin was also struck by this man's demeanor, and half-jokingly wondered to Kokovtsov whether he might be about to throw a bomb. What the ladies of the imperial party found most difficult to accept were the looks of hatred they perceived on the faces of some of the Duma members. For the Dowager Empress, such apparent hatred was very hard to bear and beyond her comprehension.

At the conclusion of the Te Deum Nicholas climbed the steps leading to the throne and read aloud, while standing, the speech that Baron Fredericks handed him, "in a loud steady voice." Xenia seems to have been almost overcome by this "great historic moment, unforgettable for those who witnessed it. He spoke so well, saying just what was needed, asking everyone to come to his aid. When he finished, a cheer broke out, which was taken up by everyone including in the other halls—it sounded magnificent. The choir sang the anthem (it was all terribly emotional!)." By the end, as the procession returned in the order in which it had arrived, several members of the imperial family were in tears, including both Maria Fyodorovna and Alix and even, most unusually, Nicholas himself, "his self-control finally overcome."

The reaction of the crowds gathered outside the Winter Palace to watch the imperial family embark for Peterhof, amid cheers, suggested that the popular mood was positive. None of the feared disturbances or terrorist attacks had occurred; the only "demonstration" was staged by the common criminals incarcerated in the Kresty prison on the far bank of the Neva, who waved handkerchiefs and rags out of their cell windows as the members of the Duma were transported along the river to the Tauride Palace, where the Parliament was to be housed.

Some of the deputies, seeing the criminals waving, imagined they were political prisoners and waved their hats and handkerchiefs in return.

In order for the sessions of the Duma to take place in the Tauride Palace (originally built by Catherine the Great for her favorite, the great General Grigory Potemkin), an exhibition supervised by Sergei Diaghilev had had to be brought to a premature close. The Tsar himself had attended the opening ceremony of the "Historical and Artistic Exhibition of Russian Portraits," for which the colonnaded Potemkin Hall had been decorated by Leon Bakst, using fabric backdrops in order to create the atmosphere of an eighteenth-century park. Nicky had spent two hours at the exhibition, which included large portraits of former Russian Emperors and Empresses, being shown around by Diaghilev, the historian Grand Duke Nikolai Mikhailovich, and Prince Dashkov. Nicky had been courteous but inscrutable, saying little and expressing no particular preferences. Six days later KR was also shown around by Diaghilev; the bisexual Grand Duke found it "unpleasant" to meet the homosexual impresario because "he knew something about him." According to Alexandre Benois, Nicky had also "taken a personal dislike" to Diaghilev, who instead enjoyed the support of the so-called "Small Court"—that of Grand Duke Vladimir Alexandrovich and his wife Grand Duchess Maria Pavlovna. But now the Potemkin Hall had been stripped of its artistic backdrops and turned into a debating chamber.

Back at Peterhof on that April day, the family had tea and exchanged their impressions. Their principal feeling was one of relief that the ordeal was over; perhaps now life could resume a more normal course. "Nicky was delighted that he would at last be able to sleep properly," wrote his sister. "Last night he couldn't sleep—he kept lying there, waking every few minutes with a feeling of sadness and melancholy in his heart!"

The charge most frequently leveled against Nicholas, by friends as well as enemies, by those who worked for him as well as those who sought to bring him down, even at times by his nearest and dearest, and by many later commentators, has been that of "indecisiveness," not being able to make up his mind, changing his opinion every time he heard someone else expressing theirs, usually taking the advice of the person to speak to him last. Can this charge be proven, or is it a reflection of the disappointment felt by those whose advice he did not take, despite appearing to agree with them when they were giving it? Is it that he kept his counsel so close, giving away so little of himself, being so reserved, so controlled, that it was next to impossible to tell what he was thinking? If this was the case, his decisions might indeed have come as a surprise to those around him, but that does not necessarily imply that he had wavered when making them, merely that he had not kept everyone apprised of his thought processes. It certainly seems likely that what appeared to be lack of decision-making was at least in part a lack of communication. This was a man who expressed annoyance, even anger, by studying his fingernails, playing with his pencils, adjusting his belt, or staring out of the window. Reading the Tsar was notoriously difficult, but his closest officials learned how to interpret these small signs.

On October 20, 1905, Kokovtsov had resigned as Finance Minister, having irretrievably fallen out with Count Witte. The Tsar's immediate response was to suggest Kokovtsov become Chairman of the Department of Economy of the State Council, in place of Count Solsky. But Witte proved vehemently opposed to this, declaring himself unable to work with Kokovtsov in any capacity, and Nicky had been forced to back down—to his great displeasure. "I have been forced to renounce my decision and to destroy my signature. I shall never forget this," he told Kokovtsov. Just as when he was appointed, so when he resigned, Kokovtsov was asked by Nicky to present himself to Alix. "When I had explained the reasons for my retirement," wrote Kokovtsov in his recollections of this moment, "she said that she was not surprised, that 'when views changed (*quand les idées sont devenues toutes autres*) one could not ask people to submit to such changes and alter their own views accordingly.' After a few more words I departed, uncertain whether the Empress was pleased or sorry at my retirement or whether, in the face of the trying conditions of the time, she was altogether indifferent." Alix's reaction was very telling; she could have been speaking of herself, as she found it next to impossible to change her views just because other people had changed theirs—it could take her a long time to make up her mind about something, but once it was made up, it remained immutably fixed.

On November 10, Nicky wrote in some consternation to his mother that the government, despite the changes he had introduced, seemed unable to quell the disturbances in the country by taking decisive action. "I keep trying to force them," he told the Dowager Empress, "even Witte himself—to act more energetically. . . . I cannot conceal from you some disappointment in Witte. Everyone thought he was a terribly energetic and authoritative man and that he would begin at once to establish order." This gives a clear indication as to why the Tsar had acted as he had; what he valued above all else was "order." By the spring of 1906 Witte had been dismissed as Prime Minister and Ivan Goremykin appointed in his place (described memorably by Nicky's cousin Sandro as "an old courtier with carefully washed wrinkles who looked like an upright corpse supported by a pair of invisible hands"). The main reason for this choice (misguided, in Kokovtsov's opinion) was that Nicholas could rely on Goremykin not to act behind his back.

With Goremykin, he could feel confident that there would be no surprises or decisions taken without imperial authority. With Witte, so the implication was, this had not been the case.

Kokovtsov was summoned to see the Tsar again on December 15, in connection with a request for his assistance in securing a further foreign loan. "He received me with his habitual simplicity and kindness," recalled the former Finance Minister, "in the study I had visited so many times, and his first words were, 'Here you are with me again and I am very glad it is so.'" Kokovtsov's account of this interview also sheds some light on Nicholas's way of dealing with his ministers and suggests one of the difficulties of being an autocrat—how to have a genuine discussion when one's every word is taken immediately as an instruction and one's interlocutor is fearful of engaging in argument. Nicky told Kokovtsov that his successor, Ivan Shipov, a protégé of Witte's, was no doubt "a fine man" but that he could not get used to his way of reporting. "He tries to explain every little detail," complained the Tsar, "and as soon as I do not agree with a suggestion he abandons it and adopts my idea, although I sometimes express it quite casually just to hear his opinion." Other conversations the Tsar had with Kokovtsov in June 1906, concerning the possible makeup of a new cabinet suggested by the Palace Commandant, give further insight into how Nicholas conducted business with his advisers. He often appeared noncommittal in conversation, neither accepting nor rejecting proposals put forward, because he wished to take further advice from people he trusted before coming to a decision. This refusal to commit himself at once, his tendency to listen politely to proposals and appear to acquiesce without actually doing so, was frequently interpreted by those subjected to this treatment as "wavering," "weakness," an inability to make up his mind. It would come as a shock to an interviewee to receive a message some time after the interview to the effect that the Tsar had not, after all, accepted their proposal, and that he might even—very politely, of course—have sacked them. Not only his officials but also Alix grew increasingly impatient over the years with how long it could take Nicky to come to a decision, for the Empress reached her conclusions in a very different, entirely intuitive, way. Nicky's decision-making was complicated not only by his attempt to consider various opinions but also by the promptings of his own "inner voice," which he listened to as well as, and sometimes in opposition to, the voices of his ministers. The "inner voice" came into play over a particularly tricky question, that of whether certain restrictions on the Empire's Jewish population should be relaxed. The Council of Ministers had decided in December 1906 that there should indeed be some relaxation, but the Tsar refused to ratify the decision, telling

Stolypin: "Despite most convincing arguments in favor of adopting a positive decision in this matter, an inner voice keeps on insisting more and more that I do not accept responsibility for it. So far my conscience has not deceived me. Therefore I intend in this case also to follow its dictates. I know that you, too, believe that 'A Tsar's heart is in God's hand.' Let it be so. For all laws established by me I bear a great responsibility before God, and I am ready to answer for this decision at any time." Given that in this instance Nicky's inner voice was anti-Semitic, one can only conclude that he had some difficulty distinguishing between the promptings of conscience and of prejudice. "Inner voices" always need to be tested against some other authority or objective measure, but unfortunately, if one believes that one's inner voice comes from God—precisely because one is the anointed Tsar—then any other authority appears superfluous.

A conversation Kokovtsov reports as having taken place between himself and the Tsar at the beginning of 1906, on the former's return from having successfully negotiated a loan with France, gives an indication of the inherently contradictory position Nicholas was trying to maintain—in attempting to embrace limited reform while simultaneously clinging to his prerogatives as autocrat. He imagined that somehow he could hold together irreconcilable opposites. "I wish to stand honourably by my promise given in the Manifesto of October 17," Kokovtsov records him as saying, "and shall give my people legislative rights within established limits, but should the Duma demand that I be deprived of my historical authority, am I supposed to grant everything without protest?" Alix, on the other hand, had no such inner conflict, for she could see nothing wrong with the system as it had existed before October 17, and refused to believe there had been any need for change. Discussion of a new code of Fundamental Laws had begun at Tsarskoe Selo in April 1906, with the most difficult discussions focusing on the meaning of the word *autocratic* and whether the sovereign's autocratic power was to continue to be defined as "unlimited." Nicky felt the decision had to be his alone, and eventually he determined that the word *unlimited* should be omitted. Again his attitude appears inherently contradictory: He exercises his unlimited power in order to place limits upon it.

It quickly became apparent that the attitudes and behavior of the members of the First Duma were not proving satisfactory to the Tsar and his ministers, and it could only be a matter of time before it was dissolved. Once the Tsar had made up his mind, he was ready to take firm and decisive action. Convinced by the summer that the composition of this Duma was only aggravating the revolutionary tendencies in the country and militating against the "order" he so much valued, he was sure that its dissolution had become a matter of urgent necessity and could not be postponed any longer. He signed the manifesto proroguing the Duma on Sunday, July 9, having held a long discussion with Goremykin and Stolypin, and having been assured by the Prefect of St. Petersburg that this would create no serious disturbance in the capital. The Tauride Palace was locked and surrounded by troops. On the following day Stolypin became Prime Minister, while also retaining his existing office as Minister of Internal Affairs.

Later that month *The Times* published an article entitled "Russia Revisited" by "an occasional correspondent" who had not visited St. Petersburg for several years. He particularly commented on current attitudes toward and perceptions of the Tsar: "The freedom with which the Emperor is discussed is a new and ominous sign . . . he and his deeds alike are the subject of such comment, criticism, aspersion, ridicule, and condemnation as fill with amazement one who, after but a few years' absence, returns to this country which, nominally at least, is still under autocratic sway." The old charge of indecision could, the correspondent felt, be justified and "not even his stoutest apologist has ventured to suggest that [the Tsar] is a man of inflexible will." He considered, however, that the Tsar's errors were often merely the result of poor advice, and that his main fault here lay in his tendency to keep the purveyors of that poor advice in post: "Too frequently he discovers that information and advice which had been given to him by a Minister had led him into an unwise course of action; but he discriminates between an error of judgment and a breach of faith and continues his *bienveillance* towards those who have led him astray if only their fidelity has been proved." The correspondent went on to suggest that the Emperor's famed "indecisiveness" may have been at least in part a result of disappointed expectations on the part of various Duma representatives rather than a fixed personality trait. The Tsar had, for instance, been quite determined to prorogue the First Duma, whatever his opponents may have thought or however they may have interpreted any delay: "the Tsar is not quite as 'shapeless' as he is sometimes made to appear. His evil reputation in that particular has been, perhaps, unduly enhanced by members of the *Duma* who, having confidently attributed to him intentions which he never entertained, have afterwards asserted that he had changed his mind, and denounced not their own miscalculations but his feebleness and indecision." In fact, whatever may have been thought of the decision itself—and the *Times*'s correspondent believed it was "an irreparable mistake . . . yet one which any man of intelligence, probity, and character, with the traditions and training of the Tsar, might have made"—the Tsar had never wavered in believing it was the right one, and seeing that it was carried through. It was a matter of rumor and speculation that " 'Peterhof' [as the Tsar was referred to by some] changed his mind many times every day," while in fact he had done nothing of the sort. The correspondent went on to suggest that this unjust reputation for indecisiveness may have actually served to protect the Tsar, as the terrorists when drawing up their list of targets had assumed he was not personally responsible for the acts they deplored: "Whenever resolution and persistence are displayed, some energetic Minister is blamed; and when these slacken, the change is attributed to the changeful Tsar."

The Second Duma convened on February 20, 1907, with far less ceremonial than had attended the opening of the First. No untoward incidents took place; there was some marching about and singing of revolutionary songs outside the Tauride Palace but the crowd was soon dispersed. The government had decided in advance that, if this Duma did not succeed in accomplishing anything, it would be prorogued and the electoral law amended. Its membership included more semiliterate peasants and pseudointellectuals than the First Duma, it being dubbed by Count Vladimir Bobrinsky "the Duma of national ignorance." It lasted for only three and a half months before it, too, was dissolved, and there was indeed a new electoral law published at the same time, in June 1907, abolishing any pretense of universal suffrage. In addition, the majority of members of the Second Duma belonging to the Social Democratic grouping were arrested (troops having been brought into St. Petersburg), and it was announced that, after new elections, the Third Duma would be convened on November 1. Most of the public did not appear very interested in any of this; they seemed to have lost their appetite for demonstration and upheaval. The imperial manifesto accompanying the dissolution of the Second Duma reasserted the Tsar's authority as the foundation of the Russian state, restoring to him the right to promulgate whatever laws were necessary for its good order and survival. KR wrote with relief in his diary: "So—it's a coup-d'état. In truth the Russian people can now breathe more easily." Nicky's own diary entry was even more cheerful; he wrote that, following the dissolution, his mood was as "luminous" as the weather.

Throughout these stressful months in Russian politics, the internal wranglings of the Romanov family had been no less stressful. Nicky's cousin Grand Duke Kirill Vladimirovich could not have chosen a worse time to incur imperial displeasure—and deep upset on Alix's part—by marrying (on September 25, 1905, in Bavaria)—Ducky, the ex-wife of Alix's brother Ernie. In addition to being extremely tactless, the union was doubly forbidden, as Ducky was both a divorcée and Kirill's first cousin. Having committed the forbidden act, Kirill confessed it, hoping to be treated leniently. In this he was disappointed; not only did the Tsar mete out the maximum possible punishment, stripping his cousin of the title of Grand Duke, of his income from the "appanages" (funds granted by the state to members of the imperial family) and of his position in the services, he also refused to receive him, dispatching Baron Fredericks to intercept him en route to Peterhof and order him to return abroad at once. Though he had been forewarned of the likely consequences of his action, Kirill was deeply offended by this treatment, as was his father, the oldest of Nicky's uncles, Grand Duke Vladimir. The latter resigned in protest from all his own administrative duties.

Despite his anger, both on his own behalf and on that of his wife, Nicky showed himself more than usually aware on this occasion of the effect his actions might have on public opinion. It was important, he realized, not to make too much of a public spectacle of his cousin's disgrace, as this could risk attracting further negative publicity about the imperial family as a whole, at a time when, as he put it in a letter to his mother, people were "generally ill-disposed" toward them. And so he reflected further on what to do—to the extent of giving himself a headache—and decided to make use of the occasion of little Alexei's name day (October 5) to grant a partial pardon to Kirill by restoring his title of Grand Duke. The other penalties, less public in their nature, would remain in force.

In the summer of 1906 another irregular relationship arose to trouble Nicky, this time involving his younger brother Misha, who requested permission to marry the woman he had long been in love with, one of his sister Olga's ladies-in-waiting, Dina Kossikovskaya. Misha was insistent that he could wait no longer, but Nicky was adamant in his refusal to allow the match, forbidden for a member of the imperial family—and particularly for one so close in line to the throne—because Dina was a commoner. Nicky wrote to his mother: "I feel with all my being that dear Papa would have acted in exactly the same way. To change the law in *this* instance and in such dangerous times, I consider completely impossible." He was determined to leave no room for doubt, continuing: "It would be so much easier to agree, rather than to refuse, but in this I will NEVER give my consent." He wanted to enlist his mother's help in dissuading Misha from pursuing the matter, and hoped there would be no dissent among the wider imperial family. "Even without that," he wrote, "I hardly have the strength to bear all the trials which we are called to live through." The Dowager Empress found herself in a very difficult position, with neither son prepared to give way and both appealing to her for support; the arguments Nicky brought to bear, however, that such a match was against the law and that, moreover, his father would never have consented to it, would be the most powerful for her, however unhappy her youngest son might be.

After celebrating Alexei's second birthday on July 30, Nicky, Alix, the children, and the two Montenegrin princesses set off for Krasnoe Selo, traveling for the first time by motorcar—Nicky, his three eldest daughters, and Stana in one car, with Alix, Anastasia, Alexei, and Militsa in another. The courtiers made the journey by train. They spent a week at Krasnoe Selo, watching the military maneuvers and theatrical entertainments, both the Emperor and Empress in excellent humor. On their return to Peterhof, they again spent many evenings with their friends at Znamenka. Alix was particularly close at this time to Militsa and again the Petersburg gossip-mill was grinding away for this friendship was considered, even by a sympathetic observer such as Spiridovich, to be "of a far more serious character than the kind of friendship that generally exists between women." Alix's close friendships with a few women seem frequently to have given rise to gossip and to the accusation, despite her being the mother of five children, that these relationships were "unnatural." Jealousy among the other women at court played its part in spawning these rumors, but what these few relationships most clearly indicate is Alix's wholeheartedness: She loved rarely but, when she loved, she did so with her whole being, holding nothing back. Thus when she felt "betrayed" by a friend, the experience hurt her profoundly.

The strict line taken by Nicky over the marital irregularities of his uncle Grand Duke Pavel, his cousin Grand Duke Kirill, and his own brother were particularly resented by the family in light of the very different attitude he demonstrated toward the irregular marriage of another of his cousins, Grand Duke Nikolai Nikolaevich. For some time there had been talk in the family about the relationship between Nikolasha and Stana. She had married Duke George of Leuchtenburg (known within the family as "Yuri," the Russian equivalent of "George") at Peterhof in 1889, and in the autumn of 1906 it was being said that the couple were on the point of divorcing so that Stana could marry Nikolasha instead. What alarmed, confused, and annoyed the wider imperial family was the deduction that the Tsar must have given his consent to the match, which was inconsistent with the stand he had taken in all previous cases. KR was horrified to learn of the impending divorce and remarriage, and concluded that it could only be happening because of the couple's close personal relationship with Nicky and Alix—that, in other words, the Tsar was prepared to bend the rules for his particular friends, when he would not do so for his other relatives. (This whole episode also shows that the imperial couple were still friendly toward Nikolasha, despite the way in which he had helped force the Emperor's hand into signing the manifesto of October 17.) Not only was Stana about to be a divorcée, but she and Nikolasha were, at least by marriage, first cousins, and so the case appeared to be parallel with that of Kirill Vladimirovich and his cousin, the divorced Ducky. Even closer to home, as far as the Emperor was concerned, was the history of his younger brother, for all Misha's troubles over women arguably stemmed from his early mutual love for Ducky's younger sister, Princess Beatrice of Saxe-Coburg and Gotha. Misha and Beatrice (whom Misha nicknamed "Sima") had fallen in love in 1902 but, being first cousins, they had been forced to break off their relationship a year later. In light of the different treatment accorded to Stana and Nikolasha (against whom no sanctions of any kind were proposed), all the resentment against and suspicion of the tight "mystical" circle formed by the Emperor, Empress, the "black princesses," and Nikolasha himself inevitably resurfaced. What was more, so the gossip went (KR heard it from Grand Duke Andrei Vladimirovich), Nikolasha maintained that his impending marriage was the result of miraculous intervention, that it had all been inspired through Monsieur Philippe's influence from beyond the grave.

Nikolasha and Stana were married, in Livadia, on April 29, 1907. Nicky's brother-in-law, Grand Duke Alexander Mikhailovich, "absolutely refused to send a telegram," while the Dowager Empress was "beside herself—and so upset that she had to take tranquillizing drops." (Alix was involved in other wedding preparations at the time, as it was on the next day that the wedding of her favorite, Ania Taneeva, to Lieutenant Vyrubov was celebrated at Tsarskoe Selo.) Nicky's Uncle Pavel was not slow in pointing out the inconsistencies in the Tsar's attitude, writing to him on May 12 about the continued ban on Pavel's wife accompanying him on his occasional trips back to Russia. "If it's because she has been divorced, or rather she divorced because of me," he wrote, "then Nikolasha's recent marriage, to which you gave your permission and blessing, has once and for all broken all the existing impediments in this respect. I know in your heart you are just and kind and that you realize I am right." Pavel's forthcoming trip to Russia (without his wife) was in connection with yet another wedding—this time of his young daughter Maria Pavlovna to the second son of King Gustav of Sweden. He had severe doubts about the wisdom of this arranged marriage (doubts that turned out later to be fully justified) but, on account of the position the Tsar (and the Empress) had taken toward his own marital circumstances, he had no say whatsoever in his daughter's future and no official standing at her wedding, a situation he found intolerable. His letter to his nephew was a real *cri de coeur:* "I have suffered greatly, yet continued to hope that in the end, seeing how we live, you would understand and forgive me. Alas! I was bitterly mistaken. It's terribly painful to write all this to you, whom I love as fondly as before, but you will feel the truth echoed in my every word!" If Nicky did "feel the truth" of what his uncle wrote, he gave no sign of doing so.

The wider family's consternation in this case is understandable, given the very great disparity between Nicky and Alix's usual approach to such questions and their apparent acceptance, even welcoming, of the marriage between Nikolasha and Stana. Reading between the lines, what seems most likely is that Nikolasha and Stana managed to persuade the imperial couple that their match was indeed "made in heaven," that Monsieur Philippe was somehow influencing events, and that this was meant to be. Given that Nicky and Alix were entirely used to the opposition of the rest of the family toward their involvement with Monsieur Philippe and his ideas, their opposition now would have come as no surprise and would have had no effect—if anything, it would only have strengthened their belief that they should support Nikolasha and Stana, as the rest of the family could not be expected to understand. The subsequent, and severe, falling-out between Alix and the Montenegrin sisters, and Nikolasha, suggests that she and Nicky came to believe they had been duped in this regard—and that the person who convinced them of the deception was Grigory Rasputin.

It was in November 1905 that Nicky and Alix had first encountered Rasputin, Nicky recording in his diary for November 1: "We had tea with Militsa and Stana. We made the acquaintance of a man of God—Grigory, from the Tobolsk region." This first meeting seems not to have made a deep impression, however, as nearly a year later, Nicky told Stolypin that he had met this "peasant from the Tobolsk district, Grigory Rasputin" only a few days ago. He was writing to Stolypin in the aftermath of the explosion at the latter's villa to suggest—almost to insist—that the minister receive Rasputin, who would like to bless his injured daughter with an icon. "I very much hope that you will find a minute to receive him this week," writes the Tsar. Rasputin had made a far stronger impression on the imperial couple at this most recent meeting—they had talked together for upwards of an hour—but at this point Grigory was far better known to Militsa and Stana, Nicky recording in his diary on December 19, 1906, that "Stana and Militsa came to dinner, and spent the whole evening telling us about Grigory." This frequent visitor to the Montenegrin princesses had already come to the attention of Spiridovich's men, who had noticed his frequent appearances at church; wearing a blue shirt and strong peasant boots, he was clearly not a monk or a priest, though he was staying with a priest and seemed on familiar terms with several of the clergy. None of the information gathered about him threw up anything suspect, however, and as he was known to be connected in some way to the household of Militsa and her husband, Grand Duke Pyotr Nikolaevich, the police decided to leave him alone. Nevertheless, Spiridovich observed, "the Grand Duke's servants used to tell all sorts of strange stories about him." Nicky and

Alix seem to have accepted him at once as one of the "men of God" who emerged from time to time from among the Russian people; a combination of pilgrim and prophet, such a person might journey from monastery to monastery, learning the ways of God and communicating his message to those able and willing to listen. The fact that Monsieur Philippe had prophesied he would return to them in the guise of another "friend" also ensured that Rasputin's words fell on fertile ground.

According to Kokovtsov, it was Rasputin's ability to tell the imperial couple, and particularly Alix, what they wanted to hear—indeed, what they already believed—that endeared him to them and made them receptive to what he had to say, despite Alix's alleged initial difficulty in understanding Grigory's "broken speech, his short, almost unintelligible sentences, his quick shifting of subjects." What he told them seemed an accurate reflection of their experience and provided reassurance that they had no need to worry or to change anything in either their actions or attitudes: "He began to tell her that she and the Tsar were surrounded with difficulties; that they would never learn the truth, surrounded as they were by flatterers and selfish climbers who would never show how to make the people's lot easier; only by searching their own hearts and by supporting each other could the Imperial couple learn the truth. When in doubt, they must pray and ask God to instruct and enlighten them. If they put their faith in God, everything would be right, as God would never abandon those he had set to rule over the people." Rasputin also confirmed the imperial couple's prejudice against the Petersburg elite as opposed to "the people": "Here he struck another note, pleasing to the Tsarina's ears. He advised closer contact with and closer study of the people, who deserved to be trusted more, as they would never deceive those they considered almost equal to God himself. The people would tell the real truth, the exact opposite of what was told by ministers and officials, who were not concerned over the tears and wants of the people." Here Kokovtsov's frustration is discernible; how difficult such an attitude must have made the lives of those "ministers and officials" who attempted to present the Tsar with honest advice. On the other hand, Rasputin's advice does not sound so very far removed from the remarks of the *Times*'s "occasional correspondent"—or indeed from some of the comments made by W. T. Stead when he blamed the "bureaucrats" for smothering the Tsar with endless paperwork.

The conclusion the "occasional correspondent" reached about Nicholas's character was that he most resembled a fictional character from Tolstoy's *War and Peace:* "He openly yet simply and sincerely proclaims his faith that he is in the hands of God. He believes also that the destinies of the Empire are in the Divine care; and therefore even the wild revolution that seems to threaten the stability of his Throne leaves him calm. He is blamed for his insensibility by some, praised for his faith by others, and called a fatalist by most. But by one who knows him well I heard him called a Karatayev; and perhaps that was nearest the mark." The character to whom the correspondent refers is Platon Karatayev, a peasant whom Tolstoy portrays as exemplifying the peculiarly Russian virtue of acceptance, neither searching for happiness nor seeking to avoid suffering, and finding peace and Christian joy in living thus. If Nicky himself took Karatayev as an exemplar—and he never explicitly said that he did—his so-called "indecisiveness" could even be seen as a virtue: "[Karatayev] would often say the exact opposite of what he had said on a previous occasion, yet both would be right." Tolstoy himself, at least in his later years, would have been horrified at the idea that the Tsar might resemble a character he had meant to portray as positive, for he had famously declared, in a diatribe published by *The Times* in August 1905: "about Nicholas II do I know that he is a most commonplace man, standing lower than the average level, coarsely superstitious and unenlightened . . . a man in every respect standing lower than the intellectual and moral average level of all those who are perishing, as it seems by his will." W. T. Stead was quick to contradict the great writer, declaring in the same paper a few weeks later: "If Count Tolstoy had ever met the Emperor to talk with him as man with man, he would never have made so false an assertion." Stead's experience demonstrates the usual gulf between rumor and reality, even taking into account the journalist's known enthusiasm for the Tsar. "I have been assured," writes Stead, "that the Emperor was a very stupid, ignorant, even half-witted man, who reads nothing, knows nothing, and spends his life in terror. I have been told that he was a nervous wreck, that his hair had turned grey, and that his face was haggard with wrinkles." On the contrary, he declared, the Tsar had hardly changed at all in six years, despite all the pressures of those years: "when he greeted me at Peterhof a fortnight since he did not seem to have aged a day since I bade him good-bye at Tsarskoe Selo on the eve of The Hague Conference in 1899. His step was as light, his carriage as erect, his expression as alert. His brow bore no lines of haggard care. I could not see a grey hair on his head. His spirits were as high, his courage as calm, and his outlook as cheerful as ever." As for the slurs on the Emperor's intelligence, nothing, according to Stead, could be further from the truth: "I have no hesitation in saying that I have seldom in the course of 30 years met any man so quick in the uptake, so bright in his mental perception, so sympathetic in his understanding, or one possessing a wider range of intellectual interest. Neither have I ever met any one man or woman who impressed me more with the crystalline sincerity of his soul."

So what conclusions, after all this, can we reach about Tsar Nicholas II—Nicky—at this period of his life? We have seen him holding himself at one remove from the events of Bloody Sunday, talking like a stern but loving father to his erring subjects, disappointed at the end of the war with Japan, working day in, day out at his desk to fulfill what he saw to be his duty, enjoying quiet family occupations during his limited time off, appearing with all his accoutrements as Tsar to address the elected members of the Duma, attempting to hold two contradictory concepts at once—until giving up and reverting as far as possible to the status quo ante. He has told us little about himself directly, and those who observed him have given us varied opinions. We have seen something of his anti-Semitism, of his anger at unacceptable behavior within the family, but also of his patience and willingness to listen and his sincere attempts to do what he thought was right. He still seems almost like a blank sheet of paper, on which one can write one's own interpretations. He has a tendency to keep disappearing from view, even when he is ostensibly center stage.

It may be idle speculation to wonder whether Nicky's penchant for mysticism and for the intimacy of a small group of initiates might have led him, in other circumstances and at a slightly later date, to investigate theories of personality. But one can easily imagine him being drawn to the theories of Carl Jung and maybe even being persuaded to take a Myers-Briggs Type Indicator assessment. Be that as it may, I decided to carry out such an experiment on his behalf, to see what might be learned in the process. I answered five online personality tests "as" Nicky, one each at personalitypathways.com, teamtechnology.co.uk, humanmetrics.com, similarminds.com, and sminds.com. Many of the questions were fairly easy to answer, particularly those relating to ways of working, and the more I answered questions about how "I" made decisions, the clearer it became that feelings predominated over logic and analysis—those feelings that, for the Tsar, mediated the voice of God. The results were gratifyingly consistent: In four of the tests, the result came out as ISFJ ("Introverted, Sensing, Feeling, Judging"), and in the fifth as ISTJ ("Introverted, Sensing, Thinking, Judging")—but with a rather weak emphasis on Thinking. So from that I concluded that Nicky's personality might reasonably be identified as belonging to the ISFJ type, sometimes referred to as the "Conservator."

Many of the descriptions of and comments about this personality type seem to corroborate such an identification. Typical adjectives are "polite," "dutiful," "private," "organized," "modest," "not spontaneous," "responsible," "guarded," and "cautious." Observations about the ISFJ personality that seem applicable to Nicky include the following:

"ISFJs bring an aura of quiet warmth [compare this with the "charm" so consistently attributed to Nicky], caring, and dependability to all that they do; they take their work seriously and believe others should do so as well." [Nicky was always most annoyed with people who did not seem to be doing their duty, whereas he could more easily forgive a genuine mistake.]

"They feel useful when their roles and responsibilities are clearly established and they can monitor their activities and productivity in tangible ways." [Hence Nicky's preference for clearing papers on his desk to the less measurable, strategic thinking that might actually have been more useful and appropriate to his role.]

"They tend to be rather modest, traditional and conventional [consider Nicky's tastes in art and literature], to like sensible clothing [his preference for wearing military uniform at all times], to be thrifty, careful and wise with both money and possessions." [Within the framework of the Romanov imperial family, where tradition and protocol demanded the expenditure of extravagant sums, Nicky was nevertheless relatively simple in his own tastes and not naturally profligate.]

"They tend to like to stay in one neighbourhood, often choosing to live close to where they were themselves raised." [This chimes with Nicky's preference for the palaces of his boyhood, particularly in Livadia and at Peterhof, and his love of the summer cruises on the *Standart,* exactly the same holidays as those enjoyed by his father.]

"They tend to shy away from surprises and what is perceived as unnecessary change." [Nicky would greatly have preferred everything in the Russian Empire to have stayed just the way it was under the reign of Alexander III.]

ISFJs direct their energy "primarily toward the inner world of thoughts and emotions." [Nicky's attraction to the "inner world" was apparent in his response to mysticism and spirituality.]

"They are notoriously bad at delegation." [Think of Nicky's refusal to employ a personal secretary, preferring to do trivial work himself.]

"While their work ethic is high on the ISFJ priority list, their families are the centers of their lives" [this was often asserted about Nicky]; they are "more interested in relationships and family than intellectual pursuits."

"ISFJs are extremely warm and demonstrative within the family circle" [Nicky's wife and children would certainly have corroborated this].

"If any of their nearest and dearest depart from the straight and narrow, it causes the ISFJ major embarrassment: the closer the relationship and the more public the act, the more intense the embarrassment." [Think of Nicky's horror at the marital misadventures of family members.]

"ISFJs have a few, close friends."

"They hate confrontation." [Nicky habitually avoided it, preferring to speak nicely to his ministers and sack them by letter.]

Unfortunately, many of these qualities are not ideal for an autocrat—"ISFJs make pleasant and reliable co-workers and exemplary employees, but tend to be harried and uncomfortable in supervisory roles." Modern career advice recommends that ISFJs become office workers, administrative assistants, teachers, and librarians rather than CEOs or entrepreneurs. A particularly poignant summary is given at sminds.com—by replacing "ISFJ" with "Nicholas" and "they" with "he," one would not be far off the mark: "ISFJs are traditional, loyal, quiet and kind. They are very sensitive to other people's needs because they are very observant. They have rich inner thoughts and emotions. They value stability and cultural norms. They are very adept at giving attention to detail. They do not seek positions of authority."

CHAPTER FIVE

Beginnings

to 1896

As there is no power higher, so there is no power on earth more arduous than the power of the Tsar, no burden so wearisome as the duty of Tsar.

—The Metropolitan of Moscow to the Tsar before his coronation, May 14, 1896

THE PRINCIPAL FEELING among both family and onlookers at the accession of Nicholas II in October 1894, at the age of twenty-six, had been one of shock. No one, least of all Nicky himself, had expected the apparently robust and bull-like Alexander III to fall ill and die at the relatively young age of forty-nine. Prior to the winter of 1894 he had only ever been ill once. According to Nicky's cousin, Grand Duke Alexander Mikhailovich (Sandro), the former's first response on the death of his father was to weep, his second to panic: " 'Sandro, what am I going to do,' he exclaimed pathetically. 'What is going to happen to me, to you, to Xenia, to Alix, to mother, to all of Russia? I am not prepared to be a Tsar. I have never wanted to become one. I know nothing of the business of ruling. I have no idea of even how to talk to the ministers.' "

Nicky's sister Olga blamed their father for this alleged lack of preparedness, attributable in part to Alexander's desire not to allow affairs of state to "encroach" on family life. In fact the heir was not quite as ill-prepared as has often been asserted. Sandro's account makes for a good story, but Nicky knew perfectly well that he would one day become Tsar, as did his father—the problem was with the timing, not with any innate or perceived inability on Nicky's part. As Tsarevich he had served as chairman of the commission for the construction of the Great Siberian Railway (an enduring interest), and he had headed the famine committee in 1891–92. He had also been a member of the State Military Council. During his father's initial bout of illness in early 1894, Nicky had noted in his diary (January 24) that he had read a navy report "as Papa is still not back at work" and that he had looked through the post and papers of the Siberian Committee. But such activities were interspersed with more entertaining pastimes; later on the same day Nicky, Sandro, and the duty aide-de-camp played hide-and-seek "like little children." The Tsarevich also loved spending time with his fellow guards officers, staying out late, singing "Hungarian songs" in the company of "the very best ladies of the capital," and frequently drinking too much. On at least one day that month he felt unable to face lunch, but had nevertheless to turn up at an official reception—after which he spent the afternoon sleeping off his hangover. This was entirely normal behavior for a young Russian guards officer and, until his father became ill, there seemed no reason why Nicky should not continue to enjoy it for several years; further initiation into the nature of his future duties, it was imagined, could wait.

Sandro had first encountered Nicky during a family holiday in Livadia when they were ten and eight years old respectively. The cousins had immediately taken to one another, embarking on a friendship that would endure until the last time they met, in 1917. "I frequently disagreed with his policies and wished he had shown better judgment in choosing his counselors and more determination in some of his decisions," Sandro wrote in his memoirs, "but all this concerned Emperor Nicholas II and did not in the least affect my relations with 'Cousin Nicky.' Nothing could have altered in my mind the image of the cheerful boy in a little pink shirt, who stood on the marble steps of the long stairs in Livadia pointing at the sailing ships on the horizon and squinting his dreamy, curiously shaped eyes at the sunset."

It was in his cousin Sandro's company five years later that Nicky witnessed the last minutes of his grandfather, Tsar Alexander II, brought back to die in the Winter Palace after an assassin's bomb had torn off his right leg and covered him with wounds. Nicky, remembered Sandro, looked on in horror, "deathly pale in his blue sailor's suit." The fear of assassination had been a constant in the lives of the Russian imperial family for generations—"autocracy tempered by assassination," as the old saw goes—and Nicky's generation was no exception, despite Alexander III and Maria Fyodorovna's best efforts to ensure their children had a "normal," secure childhood. What is remarkable is how successful they were in concealing their burden of anxiety from their children—as is evident from the predominantly lighthearted attitude of their eldest son during his adolescence. In this, as in so many other aspects of his life, Nicky would follow his father's example, giving his own children as carefree an existence as possible. The constant terrorist threat against the imperial family was remarked upon by the artist Alexandre Benois, who, as a teenager (he was two years younger than Nicky), watched the wedding procession of Grand Duke Pavel and Princess Alexandra of Greece from an upper floor in the house of the Society for the Encouragement of the Arts. It was summer and the room was very stuffy, the police having forbidden any windows to be opened on account of "the usual fear of assassination." The young artist found himself wondering what effect such fear must have on the likely targets; he felt he had noticed something "stern and also harassed" in the eyes of the Tsar: "The glance of a man standing high above everyone, but who bears a monstrous burden and must every moment fear for his life and for the lives of his nearest and dearest."

One tactic for infusing a sense of normality into the lives of the imperial children was to keep them very busy, too occupied to dwell on anything except the immediate day-to-day requirements of their parents and tutors. From the age of nine and until his middle teens, Nicky's education was directed by the former head of the infantry college, Adjutant-General Danilovich, known at court as "the Jesuit," and its program was comprehensive. It included the study of English, French, and German (Nicky became adept at the first two of these languages, his written English reading like that of a native speaker), political history, and Russian literature, along with the fundamentals of mineralogy, botany, zoology, anatomy, and physiology. The study of Latin and Ancient Greek, usual components of contemporary schoolboys' education, was not considered necessary. The imperial children (Nicky's siblings and the majority of his cousins) led an ordered, rather austere existence, sleeping on army-style camp beds (another tradition that Nicholas would pass on to his own offspring) and getting up most days at six o'clock. The keeping of a diary was thought a necessary part of this routine—considered more as a means of self-improvement and a guard against wasting time than as an exercise in "creative writing" or a resource for future historians—and Nicky conscientiously adhered to this task until almost the last days of his life. Again, his children would be taught to do the same.

Pierre Gilliard, the future tutor of Nicky's son Alexei, reflected in his memoirs on the education of the heir to the Romanov throne, and his reflections are as pertinent to Nicky's experience as to that of his son. Gilliard commented particularly on the isolation of the royal student (Nicky's brother Georgy followed the same course of studies, but in a separate room) and of the effect this was likely to have both on teachers and pupil: "the education of a prince tends to make him an incomplete being who finds himself outside life if only because he has not been subject to the common lot in his youth. Such teaching as he receives can only be artificial, tendencious [sic], and dogmatic. It often has the absolute and uncompromising character of a catechism." He argued that there were several reasons for this artificiality and dogmatism: "the restricted choice of teachers, the fact that their liberty of expression is limited by the conventions of their official life and their regard for the exalted position of their pupil, and, finally, that they have to get through a vast programme in a very few years. It inevitably means that they have to resort to mere formulae. They proceed by assertion, and think less of rousing the spirit of enquiry and analysis and stimulating the faculty of comparison in their pupils than of avoiding everything which might awaken an untimely curiosity and a taste for unofficial lines of study." Gilliard also thought that isolation had a further damaging effect: "a child brought up in such conditions is deprived of something which plays a vital part in the formation of judgment. He is deprived of the knowledge which is acquired out of the schoolroom, knowledge such as comes from life itself, unhampered contact with other children, the diverse and sometimes conflicting influences of environment, direct observation and simple experience of men and affairs—in a word, everything which in the course of years develops the critical faculty and a sense of reality." In short, the odds were stacked against anyone who had undergone such an upbringing and education: "Under such circumstances an individual must be endowed with exceptional gifts to be able to see things as they are, think clearly, and desire the right things."

Nicky's education entered its second phase when he was seventeen (by which time he had been the heir apparent for four years), a number of eminent statesmen, military experts, and academics from the General Staff Academy and the university faculties of economics and law being summoned to the imperial palace of Gatchina, where the family spent most of the year, to lecture him on a wide range of subjects. These tutors included the Chief Procurator of the Holy Synod, Konstantin Pobedonostsev (who as Alexander III's most trusted adviser and erstwhile tutor was given general oversight of the Tsarevich's education, as well as personally teaching him jurisprudence and public, civil, and criminal law), Nikolai Bunge (Russian Minister of Finance from 1881 to 1886 and a leading economist, who taught Nicky statistics and political economics), and Yegor Zamyslovsky (who lectured on political history). Father John Yanyshev (later entrusted with the responsibility of preparing Alix for her reception into the Orthodox Church) lectured him on canon law, theology, and church history, while Nikolai Beketov, an academician and founder of the Russian school of physical chemistry (and grandfather of the symbolist poet Alexander Blok) gave him a course on general chemistry. A number of eminent generals undertook the military side of his education: General Genrikh Leyer, a military theoretician and infantry general, taught him strategy and military history; General César Cui, an outstanding musician and composer (one of the group of Russian composers known as "The Five") as well as a military engineer, gave him lessons on fortifications; General Nikolai Obruchev, a professor at the General Staff Academy and an honorary member of the St. Petersburg Academy of Sciences, contributed a course on military statistics; and General Mikhail Dragomirov, the head of the General Staff Academy, a divisional commander in the last Russo-Turkish War, and a renowned military tactician, taught him about the training of troops for battle. In addition, Nicky received a series of lectures on the art of warfare, military administration, surveying, and topography.

This was a demanding and exhaustive program of studies, designed originally to last four years and then extended by one further year; the only components missing from it were fellow students and examinations. These were not insignificant lacunae. The tutors were not permitted to ask the heir any questions; they were to lecture him and that was all. This prohibition necessarily limited their ability to check whether he was understanding what he was being taught and it meant that their pupil had little chance to put theory into practice, to develop and apply the knowledge he was acquiring. He was supposed to be a "sponge"—and he was a very able one, with an excellent memory for factual information. He was a diligent and intelligent student, and would have benefited greatly from the company and input of other intelligent students, from an opportunity to debate and engage with his contemporaries and his teachers. It became clear later in life, for instance, that though Nicky had been taught *about* strategy, he had not learned how to think strategically, having never been given the necessary practice in doing so. Even more disastrously, because of the lack both of fellow pupils and of examinations, he never attained an accurate understanding of his own strengths and weaknesses, particularly in military matters.

When Nicky did meet his contemporaries it was in the context of military service, his military education including serving with the household troops of the Preobrazhensky Regiment and the Horse Artillery and spending two summers with the Life-Guards Hussar Regiment—an experience in which he reveled. But here, too, practical education in strategy and command was lacking, life in a Russian Guards regiment having always been more concerned with parades and reviews than field exercises. And, in common with many of his Romanov forebears, Nicky found a particular delight in dressing up and parades. The fact that he imagined he understood how to command an army, having acquired a romantic idea of leading his troops into battle without any experience of warfare or even simulated warfare, goes some way to explain why he took the decision, regarded by many as unwise if not plain disastrous, to appoint himself Commander-in-Chief in 1915.

But all that lay far in an unimaginable future when, in the summer of 1894, Nicky conveyed the news of his father's illness to his fiancée Alix. Initially he was reassuring, believing himself that "there is nothing to be anxious about. It is the fatigue from having worked all these years far into the night. The old doctor from Moscow says he must rest for a couple of months and change air for some time." But from his letter of only a couple of days later, it is clear that Nicky—even though he could hardly bring himself to admit it—knew deep down that his father's symptoms were ominous. "I don't know, but I feel so frightfully low today and this evening especially," he wrote to Alix from Peterhof on August 13, "I don't like my dear Papa's look at all, he coughs so much, they say it's an irritation of the throat." Alexander was unable to sleep at night, with the consequence that he was exhausted by day. He had also gone off some of his favorite foods, including fruit, and could not stomach tea or coffee, though he was still eating heartily at lunch and dinner. He was not in pain, but was very weak; it was this weakness that particularly troubled his son, though the doctors kept assuring him that all Alexander needed was rest and sleep. But in fact the Tsar needed rather more than this, for he was dying of kidney failure. He nevertheless insisted on taking part in the family's habitual summer hunting expedition to Spała in Poland before finally, in mid-September, accepting the doctors' recommendations to head for the Crimea, there to recuperate, or so it was hoped, at the imperial palace at Livadia. By now, although his wife and family were trying to convince themselves that the air in Spała had been beneficial, they had sent for a specialist doctor—a Dr. Leyden from Berlin, who was "very nice and comforting—he said he found Papa's condition better than he had thought, and that except for the illness (something in the kidneys), his weakness came from the nerves!" Nicky had been hoping to join his fiancée in Darmstadt for a few weeks, but had reluctantly decided his duty lay with his ailing father. His letter to Alix of September 15 again conveys a barely admitted realization of the reality of the situation, and of its probable consequences for himself as heir apparent: "Of course, it is too hard, not to be able to fly (not to be taken literally!) over to you.

I could not do otherwise than this, my decision that I had taken after a whole day's violent struggle, as a devoted son and my Father's first faithful servant—I have to be with him wherever he needs me."

By the end of September Nicky was with his parents in Livadia, everyone still trying to believe that rest and the Crimean climate would lead to Alexander's recovery. But then events began to move quickly. Nicky was given permission to summon Alix from Darmstadt; she would travel to Moscow and then on to the Crimea with Ella and Grand Duke Sergei. This seems to have been presented on one level as Alix coming to join her fiancé for a short period, to make up for the fact that he was unable to leave the country to spend time with her. But there was also an awareness that she might be coming to stay—certainly on Alix's own part, as she announced her intention of being received into the Orthodox faith as soon as possible after her arrival. Now, as later, Alix showed her ability to respond well in a crisis.

Alix arrived at Livadia on October 10; the Tsar continued to decline, losing strength daily. Father John of Kronstadt, the famous healer and spiritual adviser, had also been summoned; Nicky notes in his diary that the effort expended in talking to Father John and then in greeting Alix had worn Alexander out. In Livadia Alix continued the practice she had begun earlier that year of writing messages to Nicky in his diary, and on October 15, she wrote the first of what would be many exhortations to her beloved. So much of the pattern of their future relationship is contained in this note—assurances of love combined with a slightly hectoring tone, a determination even at this early stage to bolster her man, to give him added strength (with the implicit criticism that, on his own, he is not quite strong enough), a firm belief that those around him must be made to recognize who he is (the future autocrat), and, at the end, the note of apology ("Forgive me, lovy"), suggesting an awareness that Nicky might not actually wish to be spoken, or written, to in this manner. Alix is nevertheless quite sure that she is right, recognizes her own strength, and is determined to advise her man, whether he likes it or not. These characteristics were unchanging facets of Alix's personality and of the nature of her relationship with Nicky; they grew stronger with the years, but are already present in the twenty-two-year-old "little girly." On this occasion her advice is very sensible and demonstrates that she has quickly sized up the situation. "Darling Boysy," she begins in the baby talk the couple liked to employ, "me loves you, oh so very tenderly and deep. Be firm and make the Drs Leyden or the other Z[akharin] come alone to you every day and tell you how they find him, and exactly, what they wish him to do, so that you are always the first to know. You can help persuading him then too, to do what is right. And if the Dr has any wishes or needs anything, make him come direct to you. Don't let others be put first and you left out. You are Father dear's son and must be told all and be asked about everything. Show your own mind and don't let others forget who you are. Forgive me lovy." While the crisis continued, Alix's own health seemed better, the pains in her legs only returning after the Tsar's death.

By October 18, the family was expecting the end; Nicky did not dare to leave the house for any length of time, and at one point they were all called to the side of the patient as he seemed on the verge of expiring. The dying Tsar did what he could, at this late stage, to complete his son's preparation for rule, instructing him to continue the policies he had himself pursued. Nicky would take these instructions, conveyed in such emotional circumstances, very much to heart. The death finally came on October 20, in the presence of the family and of Father John of Kronstadt. "I felt as if I were dead also," Nicky wrote in his diary.

On the very next day Alix was received into the Orthodox Church. Thus from the beginning, Orthodoxy, though also a source of great comfort, was associated for her with death, mourning, and the acceptance of suffering, all contributing to her conception of her sacred duty as consort of the Emperor of Russia. Her embracing of that sacred duty, as she perceived it, was all the more ardent for having been hard-won.

In 1872 Alix had been born Victoria Alix Helena Louise Beatrice on June 6 (May 25, in the Old Style calendar, hence this was the day she always celebrated her birthday in Russia), the third daughter and fifth child of Princess Alice (Queen Victoria's second eldest daughter) and Louis, the Heir Presumptive to the Grand Duchy of Hesse. Princess Alice had married Prince Louis, a man best described as "amiable," in 1862, while her mother was still in deepest mourning for Prince Albert. The family lived in the New Palace in Darmstadt, built in the English style, with English decorations and gardens, and complete with an English governess, Mary Anne Orchard, who had been brought to Hesse to help Princess Alice bring up her children. Alice described her third daughter at ten weeks old, in a letter to her mother, as "a sweet, merry little person, always laughing, with a deep dimple in one cheek." Alix kept this sunny disposition, so much so that she was known in the family as "Sunny," throughout her early childhood—until the shadow of death fell upon her as upon the rest of the family.

In May 1873, when Alix was still a baby, a terrible accident occurred in the New Palace: Her two-and-a-half-year-old brother Frittie fell out of the open window of their mother's bedroom during a game with his elder brother Ernie, while Princess Alice's attention was momentarily elsewhere. The child survived the initial fall, but he was a hemophiliac and the accident set off a brain hemorrhage. He died several hours later. The grief and guilt his death inspired in Alice, who had adored the little boy, and in his poor four-year-old brother Ernie, who could not stop thinking how only the day before he had run away from Frittie when he had wanted to play with him, were unspeakable.

For many years Princess Alice had been regarded as unusual for her time, position, and gender on account of the openly agnostic position she took toward religion. Widely read and with an inquiring mind, she had become a good friend of the philosopher David Friedrich Strauss, famed for his book *The Life of Jesus Critically Examined,* and in 1870 she accepted the dedication of Strauss's collection of essays on Voltaire, which he had read to her in manuscript. Frittie's death changed all that, the grieving mother seeking consolation in a conventional piety that promised freedom from suffering in a future life and the strength to endure its inevitability in this one. Ten days after the accident, she wrote to her mother: "The horror of my Darling's sudden death at times torments me too much, particularly waking of a morning; but when I think he is at rest, free from the sorrow we are suffering, and from every evil to come, I feel quite resigned." And there was indeed more evil to come for this family. Five years later there was an epidemic of diphtheria in Darmstadt, and all the children—and their father—caught the disease. The exhausted mother, having nursed all but her youngest child through the crisis, and having witnessed the death of that last child, the four-year-old May, finally succumbed herself and died within days.

Queen Victoria now took charge of her Darmstadt grandchildren from afar, supervising their education and ensuring that they spent long holidays with her in England. Their father Louis was never a match for the Queen—and never less so than when he attempted to marry again, five and a half years after Alice's death. His intended was Alexandrine von Kolemine, the thirty-year-old Polish ex-wife of the Russian chargé d'affaires in Darmstadt, and the wedding took place in secret, just an hour or two after that of his eldest daughter Victoria and Prince Louis of Battenberg, the father of the bride slipping out of the wedding banquet to go and get married himself. Both the Prince's new son-in-law and his son-in-law-to-be, Grand Duke Sergei, were horrified by the match, while his own children seemed broadly in favor of it, Princess Victoria recalling, "We others quite liked the lady, who was full of attentions towards us, and I hoped my father would feel less lonely when married to a woman he was much in love with." But Louis had reckoned without the Queen, who was in Darmstadt for his daughter's wedding. He had made sure she did not know about his own wedding in advance, and appears to have imagined that once it was a fait accompli, she would accept it, or at least be unable to do anything about it. It was not so. Gradually the news had spread among the visiting British party, and they realized they needed to tell the Queen before she found out by some other means. One of her ladies-in-waiting, Lady Ely, drew the short straw and was deputed to tell Victoria, whose reaction behind closed doors was explosive. She acted quickly and decisively, instructing the Prince of Wales to interview the new wife and then to arrange for the marriage to be declared null and void. Her wishes were fulfilled. The marriage was never consummated and was annulled within a year.

It was shortly after her father's abortive wedding that the twelve-year-old Alix met Nicky for the first time as, a month later, she traveled to Russia for the wedding of her next eldest sister, Ella, to Grand Duke Sergei. After their first meeting, Nicky noted in his diary that he liked Alix very much; nevertheless, at that point he preferred her sister. Their interaction on this first visit consisted mainly of "romping" and "jumping about," along with all the other young cousins (Nicky and Alix, sharing a great-grandmother in Princess Wilhelmine of Baden, were second cousins). Yet despite the childishness of this family boisterousness, just a few days after the first meeting the sixteen-year-old Nicky was referring to "pretty little Alix" and asserting that they loved one another. In between jumping and romping, they told one another secrets, and Nicky was sad to see her leave. But as yet he was in no hurry to think seriously of a future wife, recording in his diary a few months later, "The desire to get married lasted until luncheon, and then went away."

The two young people met again five years later, in January 1889, when Alix, her brother Ernie, and her father (who made no further attempt to secure a second wife) came to visit Ella for several weeks. Nicky was struck by how much more grown up and pretty Alix now was. At sixteen, going on seventeen, she had grown into a beautiful young woman, tall and slender with golden-red hair and grey eyes. The twenty-year-old Nicky now fell seriously in love with her. After this visit the two young people began to correspond (in English, as would always be the case), discussing such things as the operas of Wagner (Nicky liked *Siegfried* "so awfully especially the melody of the bird and the fire!"), Nicky's service with the Hussars, and the recent engagement of his cousin, Grand Duke Pyotr Nikolaevich, to the elder of the two Montenegrin princesses, Militsa. They had already begun to use nicknames for each other, "Pelly I" referring to Alix and "Pelly II" to Nicky. Why they chose these particular names remains obscure, the only other instances of "Pelly I" and "Pelly II" referring to two fur-trading posts constructed in Saskatchewan for the Hudson's Bay Company in the mid–nineteenth century. Whatever the origin of the names, their use served to alleviate some of the shyness the two young people felt in writing to one another.

In June Nicky confided his feelings for Alix to Ella (who told her husband, but promised that "nobody else will know a word of it"), and she took up the idea of their eventual marriage with enthusiasm, undertaking to sound out her sister. At around the same time, Nicky also told his father of his hopes. There were other possible suitors for Alix's hand, including the Duke of Clarence, Prince Albert Victor, the elder son of the Prince of Wales and known to the family as "Eddy." Eddy proposed to Alix in 1889, with Queen Victoria's consent, but was turned down—Alix showing that she already had a will of her own and was not afraid to exercise it. By the end of 1891, Nicky was almost sure that his feelings for Alix were mutual, but he was also aware that he now had to contend with more than an earthly rival. "My dream," he confided to his diary, is "one day to marry Alix H[esse]. I have loved her for a long time, but more deeply and strongly since 1889 when she spent six weeks in Petersburg during the winter! For a long time I resisted my feelings, and tried to deceive myself about the impossibility of achieving my most cherished wish! But now that Eddy has withdrawn or been rejected, the only obstacle or gulf between us—is the question of religion!" His mother, meanwhile, was trying to divert him from this fixation on Alix, hinting about the availability of a daughter of Louis Philippe d'Orléans, but he was not to be deflected—demonstrating now as throughout this pursuit that, at least when it came to personal issues, he could very definitely make a decision and abide by it, whatever the opposition. Nevertheless, his determination one day to make Alix his bride by no means prevented him from indulging in a healthy young man's interest in girls—and having younger sisters afforded certain opportunities: "After tea I crept into Xenia's room," Nicky confessed in his diary in January 1892, "and watched from behind the curtain as she had her gymnastic lesson with a certain young and attractive person." Neither did he confine himself to looking. For some months he considered himself in love with Princess Olga Dolgorukaya, and also enjoyed a more long-standing relationship with the ballerina Mathilde Kshessinskaya. This latter affair had begun in 1891, at the Imperial Ballet School's graduation ball, and had been encouraged by his father (presumably as part of Nicky's "education"). The young man himself was rather puzzled by his ability to love more than one person at a time, asking himself: "Would it be right to conclude from all this that I am very amorous?" He concluded that he probably was, while also being "a severe judge and very choosy!"

Eighteen ninety-one was a significant year for Nicky, as he also undertook an extended journey to the Far East, at his father's instigation—again largely with the intention of broadening his education. The expedition was led by Prince Vladimir Baryatinsky, and was to have included Nicky's younger brother Georgy. As it turned out, however, Georgy's ill health (he suffered from tuberculosis of the lungs) meant that he had to abandon the trip, returning to Russia after the party reached India. Another George, Nicky's cousin Prince George of Greece, accompanied the Tsarevich throughout the expedition.

The Russian party arrived at Nagasaki on four warships on April 15, 1891. As it was Orthodox Holy Week and Nicky and his companions were observing the fast, the official landing did not take place for a week, though there were in the meantime various unofficial forays to shop for souvenirs—and to meet some former procuresses of Japanese women for visiting Russian officers. After the two-day state visit to Nagasaki, Nicky and George spent a further two days on Kagoshima Island, as guests of Prince Shimazu Tadayoshi of Satsuma. The ships then set off for Kobe Harbor and, after having visited the famous Nunobiki Waterfalls, the party traveled on to Kyoto by special train. Nicholas's entourage included the Russian minister to Japan, Dmitry Shevich, and Japanese officials assigned as guides by the Japanese Emperor, Meiji. At the Tsarevich's request, the party was traveling "incognito," or in civilian clothes, in order to be able to see more of the country and avoid numerous official receptions. On arrival in Kyoto, Nicky did all he could to act like a "normal" tourist, shunning the official carriage for a hired rickshaw, avoiding the Western-style wing prepared for him at the hotel in favor of the Japanese style, and wearing Japanese clothes. According to Sandro, who, in the course of his naval duties, intersected with Nicky during the trip, such attempts to escape from the prescribed protocol met with only limited success: "'My trip is senseless,' [Nicky] said with a great deal of bitterness; 'palaces and generals are the same the world over, and that's all I am permitted to see. I could just as well have stayed at home.'" On April 30, he and his retinue went to visit Otsu, a nearby resort, traveling there by train.

It was in Otsu that Nicky was the victim of an assassination attempt, or at least of an attempt to inflict physical harm on him, and he bore the scar from this incident for the rest of his life. He had been riding near the front of a procession of about fifty rickshaws, his vehicle being pulled by one rickshaw man and pushed by two others. Suddenly a Japanese policeman, who had ostensibly been standing guard, rushed up to the imperial visitor and struck him over the head with his sword. Nicky was saved by his quick reaction—he had ducked so that the sword missed his neck—and by his grey bowler hat, which protected his head from the full force of the blow. He leaped out of the rickshaw and ran toward the head of the procession, while his assailant was tackled by two of the rickshaw men and by Prince George, who set about him with a bamboo cane. The Governor of Otsu took Nicky into a shop, where the doctor traveling with him tended to his wounds and bandaged his head. After lunch and a rest, though he felt shaken and blood was seeping through the bandage, Nicky managed to make light of the attack as he traveled back to Kyoto by train. He had sustained two cuts to the crown of his head, neither particularly serious but both requiring stitches. Thousands of Japanese, horribly embarrassed by such an attack on an esteemed guest, left visiting cards at Nicky's hotel, and he also received thousands of telegrams and letters of sympathy from all over Japan. The ruling family was mortified, Emperor Meiji setting off for Kyoto to see the victim for himself.

Nicky's would-be assassin turned out to be a thirty-six-year-old ex-samurai called Tsuda Sanzo; he had apparently acted from motives of patriotism, considering that the Tsarevich had shown discourtesy to the Japanese Emperor by setting out to tour Japan without first paying his respects. He was also under the impression that the Russians intended to invade Japan, an impression strengthened by Nicky's arrival in a fleet of warships. Nishi Tokujiro, the Japanese minister in St. Petersburg, had the unenviable task of reporting the incident to the Russian Minister of Foreign Affairs, Nikolai de Giers. The latter, on hearing the news, "slapped his own forehead and . . . exclaimed that he felt as if he had been struck by lightning, that nothing worse could have happened!" Nicky's parents were understandably greatly upset, but somewhat reassured on receiving a telegram from their son, in which he told them the injury was not serious and that he was feeling all right. In the absence of accurate information, the censors of the Russian Telegraph Department having suppressed the official reports and foreign news dispatches, the wildest rumors began to circulate in Russia. According to some, the attacker was a Russian terrorist in disguise, while others asserted that Nicky had provoked the attack by a variety of foolish actions, such as entering a Buddhist temple without first removing his boots.

Tsar Alexander decided to take no chances and issued orders that his son was to be transferred at once onto one of the Russian warships. Nicky, pale, slightly unsteady, and still wearing civilian clothes and a blue silken skullcap that concealed his bandage, was accompanied back to Kobe by Emperor Meiji himself, who expressed the hope that the Tsarevich would resume his tour once he was recovered. The Tsar was unwilling to allow this, however, particularly in light of two anonymous death threats that had been received, and he sent instructions that Nicky was to recuperate in Vladivostok before journeying home through Siberia. And so Nicky left Japan early, despite the attendant loss of face for the Japanese and his own desire to complete the expedition. Before leaving, he celebrated his twenty-third birthday on board the warship the *Memory of Azov,* with the cannons of Russian, Japanese, and foreign warships being fired in salute. He was given a twelve-foot-square piece of embroidery from Emperor Meiji and a gold-lacquer cabinet from the Empress, as well as other gifts from Osaka manufacturers (including twenty barrels of saki). The celebrations concluded with a brilliant firework display.

Nicky reached Vladivostok on May 11, where he laid the first track at this eastern terminus of the Great Siberian Railway and from where he sent messages of thanks to the Japanese Emperor. Tsuda was eventually sentenced to life imprisonment with hard labor. The two rickshaw men who had tackled him were awarded pensions by both the Japanese and Russian authorities and also received a personal reward from Nicky of twenty-five hundred yen each. Another sequel to the story was that of a young woman called Hatakeyama Yuko, who felt so upset by the shame brought upon her country by the attack that she committed suicide in an attempt to restore its honor. The trip had certainly broadened Nicky's experience, though perhaps not quite in the way his father had intended.

Nearly two years later, during which time Nicky's resolve one day to marry Alix had shown no sign of diminishing, Tsar Alexander and Maria Fyodorovna finally gave him permission to begin making inquiries (of a more official nature than the messages he had been sending via Ella) as to whether Alix might be prepared to accept him. Nicky was shortly to travel to Berlin for another family wedding—this time of his cousin "Mossy" (Margaret of Prussia, the youngest sister of Kaiser Wilhelm) to Prince Frederick Charles of Hesse—and the suggestion was that he should use this opportunity to begin his suit, as Alix would be there as well. However, they were unable to spend any time together, Alix suffering from an earache, and the exigencies of numerous family members and formal ceremonial leaving no space for more private concerns. The Kaiser presented his Russian cousin with the Order of the Black Eagle, on account of which honor Nicky had to don a "particularly uncomfortable red cloak" in which he nearly "died of heat."

Yet another family wedding took place later that year, in June—of George, Duke of York, to Princess Mary (May) of Teck. Alix did not attend, pleading the need of the Hesse family to be careful with money, but the Russian imperial family had no such concerns and Nicky was sent to represent them, staying at Marlborough House in London. The Prince of Wales, "Uncle Bertie" (whose wife, Princess Alexandra, was Nicky's mother's sister), seems to have taken a rather dim view of his nephew's customary attire, arranging for him to be visited by "a whole bevy of tailors, shoemakers and hatters." "He is very funny in that respect," commented Nicky, "but he has always been extremely attentive and kind to me." Nicky in his turn seems to have been unimpressed by the physical qualities of British women, lamenting the lack of attractive specimens at a state ball at Buckingham Palace. On the next day the party set off for Windsor to visit the Queen—"a round ball on unsteady legs"—as Nicky described her in his diary. Mercifully unaware of such remarks, she presented him with the Order of the Garter. Throughout this stay attention was constantly being drawn to the physical similarity between Nicky and his cousin "Georgie"—"I am getting quite tired of hearing the same thing all the time," Nicky protested. He greatly enjoyed this visit, however, and was sad to leave.

In October Ella, who was visiting her family in Darmstadt, gave Nicky a progress report. Using the "Pelly" nicknames, she told him that there had been no change: Pelly I felt very deeply for Pelly II, but lacked the courage to change her religion from Lutheranism to Orthodoxy, an absolute requirement of the bride of the Russian heir. Nevertheless, Ella continued to hold out hope, for her sister, she reported, was "so utterly miserable that it makes one's heart ache." Alix may indeed have been miserable, but she was also stubborn and in danger of acquiring a talent for misery. Ella's advice to Nicky was in accord with her highly religious nature—she told him that he should get Father John of Kronstadt to come and pray for him.

On November 8, Alix wrote two letters, one to Nicky's sister Xenia, expressing the hope that they could continue to correspond—despite the decision she set out in the other letter, to Nicky himself. In this letter she intimates—without ever quite putting it into words—that she loves Nicky, but is clear that she cannot marry him, and that it would be very wrong of her to change her religion in order to do so. "What happiness can come from a marriage without the real blessing of God?" she asks rhetorically. "For I feel it a sin to change that belief in which I have been brought up and which I love. I should never find my peace of mind again, and like that I should never be your real companion who should help you on in life; for there always should be something between us two, in my not having the real conviction of the belief I had taken, and in the regret for the one I *had* left." She had said all this to Nicky before, but felt that now she had to make it absolutely clear, and in writing. This is the voice of someone who has been brought up not to put personal happiness above everything else; she is used to sorrow—has seen it all around her—and is at home in it. So though her decision makes her unhappy, it also keeps her in what would now be described as her "comfort zone"; the refusal to consider this change in religion—and actually only of one form of Christianity for another—may have been what she felt to be the path of duty, but it was also that of least resistance. Behind Alix's words, one can sense this desire to slip back into the familiar, to have everything be as it was—in short, not to grow up: "I am certain that you will understand this clearly and see as I do, that we are only torturing ourselves, about something impossible and it would not be a kindness to let you go on having vain hopes, which will never be realized."

Nicky received this letter, apparently shattering his hopes, ten days later. His diary entry contains just a hint of resentment at the unilateral nature of the decision: "Yes, it is hard sometimes to submit to the will of God! All day I went about in a daze, it is terribly difficult to appear calm and carefree when the question affecting your whole future life is suddenly decided in this way!" His way of dealing with the disappointment was to indulge in a "four-day binge" with fellow guards officers. Then after recovering from this drinking bout and having allowed a few weeks to elapse, he showed he could be quite as determined as Alix. His carefully crafted letter of December 17 also demonstrates his greater maturity. He begins by letting her know how much she had upset him: "I could not write to you all these days on account of the sad state of mind I was in," but goes on to thank her for "the frank and open way" in which she had written to him. Then, while acknowledging the difficulties Alix would have to face in accepting him, he emphasizes the pain he is enduring through her refusal, not sparing her feelings in forcing her to confront what this means for him: "I knew from the beginning what an obstacle there rose between us and I felt so deeply for you all these years, knowing perfectly the great difficulties you would have had to overcome! But still it is so awfully hard, when you have cherished a dream for many a year and think—now you are near to its being realized—then suddenly the curtain is drawn and—you see only an empty space and feel oh! so lonely and so beaten down!!" Next he turns to the substance of her argument, and points out—tactfully, but firmly—that she has based her opinion on insufficient information: "I cannot deny the reasons you give me, dear Alix; but I have got one which is also true: you hardly know the depth of our religion. If you only could have learnt it with somebody, who knows it, and could have read books, where you might see the likeness and difference of the two—perhaps then! it would not have troubled you in the same way as it does now!" He points out that Alix is reaching her opinion in a vacuum; the suggestion is that that opinion cannot really be trusted. "Your living quite alone without anyone's help in such a matter, is also a sad circumstance in the barrier that apparently stands between us! It is too sad for words to know that that barrier is—religion!" What must have struck Nicky as particularly annoying, and which gave him the impetus to continue the struggle to persuade Alix to change her mind, was that religion was important to him, too; he sincerely believed that to become Orthodox could not in any way be harmful to Alix as a Christian. More than that, he believed that God might yet bring Alix to make this step: "I trust in God's mercy; maybe it is His will that we both, but you especially should suffer long—maybe after helping us through all these miseries and trials—He will yet guide my darling along the path that I daily pray for!" And then he builds to a crescendo, with a heartfelt plea: "Oh! do not say 'no' directly, my dearest Alix, do not ruin my life already! Do you think there can exist any happiness in the whole world without you!" before thanking her for the photograph she had sent (presumably as a token of farewell) and signing off "Ever your loving and devoted Nicky."

Another family event now came to Nicky's aid: Alix's elder brother Ernie, to whom she had been a companion for many years and particularly since the death of their beloved father in 1892, was soon to marry Ducky (Princess Victoria Melita, the daughter of Alfred, Duke of Edinburgh), and Alix confessed in a letter to Queen Victoria that "life indeed will be very different for me, as I shall be feeling myself de trop." In the meantime Nicky, though on one level stricken by Alix's continued refusal and unwilling to give up hope, seemed able to put his anxieties on this score to the back of his mind, his diary entries in the early spring of 1894 hardly giving an impression of misery. He appeared on the contrary to be reveling in his life as a bachelor, regularly getting drunk, being entertained by gypsy singers and dancers, and enjoying the company both of his officer comrades and of a number of attractive women. He describes March 8, for instance, as a "wonderful day"—he had attended a soirée given by his Aunt Michen where the entertainment had been provided by a choir of seventy gypsies and, as usual, he had had more than enough to drink. "I had a lot of fun," he writes, "and I chatted a lot with Countess Pototsky. At 2 o'clock we went downstairs to supper and continued talking as dawn was breaking."

Alix, meanwhile, continued to agonize in Darmstadt, her inclinations at war with her conscience and her masochistic tendencies in full play. A letter she wrote on March 30 to Xenia (who was herself soon to be married to Sandro) demonstrates how she was tormenting herself; she demands Xenia drop the subject of her relationship with Nicky, while being unable to stop herself dwelling on the pain she is inflicting on him. If she really wanted the relationship with Nicky to be over, might it not have been more sensible to stop corresponding so affectionately with his sister? There is something in Alix that likes to pour salt on her wound—or perhaps she is hoping, albeit unconsciously, that her refusal will eventually be overcome. Would she, one wonders, have put up such a fierce resistance if Nicky had shown signs of tiring of the pursuit? How would she have coped if the news had come from Russia that he was about to marry someone else? "Darling," she addresses Xenia, "why did you speak about *that* subject, which we never wanted to mention again? It is cruel as you know it *never* can be—all along I have said so, do you think it is not already hard enough, to know you are hurting first the person whom of all others you would long to please. But it cannot be—he knows it—and so do not I pray you, speak of it again." Alix also knows, however, that her own sister Ella will not allow the subject to be dropped (she will "begin again"), and she anticipates being told that she is "ruining" Nicky's life (both sisters might indeed have considered habitual drunkenness and an addiction to gypsy entertainment to be signs of "ruin"); but she goes on: "can I help it, when to make him happy I should be committing a sin in my conscience. It is hard enough as it is, and beginning about it again is so unkind." And in five days' time, her brother Ernie was to marry Ducky, while she herself was to go and stay with her grandmother, Queen Victoria, as she "would only be in their way here." But first she would have to encounter Nicky again for he, like many more of their mutual relatives, would be attending Ernie's wedding.

And so Nicky and Alix next saw each other at Coburg station, on the afternoon of April 4, 1894, among a crowd of royal relatives. "There was a whole welcoming committee," wrote Nicky, "Uncle Alfred, Aunt Marie, Alix, Ernie, Missy, Ducky, Alfred, and other less exalted persons." They all drove off to the castle, where they were being accommodated. For people as shy and reserved as Nicky and Alix, such a public reunion cannot have been comfortable. The next day the onslaught began, a concerted family effort to persuade Alix to unbend and accept Nicky. Initially, there was no success. "My God! What a day!" Nicky wrote after the first attempt. "After coffee at about 10 o'clock Ernie and Alix came to Aunt Ella's rooms. She has grown noticeably prettier, but looked extremely sad. They left us alone together, and then we began the conversation which I have so longed for and yet so feared. We talked until 12 o'clock, but without success, she is still against changing religion." Later Nicky gave his mother more details of this "long and extremely difficult conversation" during which he had "tried to explain to her that she could not do otherwise than to give her consent! She was crying the whole time, and only answered from time to time in a whisper: 'No! I cannot.'"

During the afternoon Queen Victoria arrived "with great pomp"; all the family presented themselves to her, before returning to their own quarters for tea. Nicky was finding the emotional strain exhausting; "I am weary to my bones today," he wrote. But the next day, fortified by an early morning walk with his

Uncle Vladimir, Nicky returned to the pursuit, with tact: "I touched as little as possible on yesterday's question, it was enough she still agreed to see me and talk to me." Ernie and Ducky's wedding took place on April 7, comprising a civil ceremony followed by a church service. The pastor—who may have been apprised of the situation—"gave a splendid sermon which surprisingly went straight to the heart of [Nicholas's] own problem." Ernie and Ducky set off for Darmstadt after lunch. And finally, on the following day, Alix capitulated. Nicky was able to write: "A wonderful, unforgettable day in my life—the day of my betrothal to my dear beloved Alix."

Central to this change of heart may have been the previous day's service, including the address (for Alix would always take note of what a clergyman had to say), the realization that she was now really on her own, as well as a discussion she had had that morning with Nicky's Aunt Michen, Grand Duchess Maria Pavlovna, the wife of his uncle Vladimir. This consultation had been suggested by Ernie, probably because Maria Pavlovna was also a Protestant (though she, not being married to an immediate heir to the Russian throne, had not been required to adopt Orthodoxy). Nevertheless, with her knowledge of both forms of religious practice, she had managed to allay some of Alix's apprehensions. Alix had also been given a letter from Nicky's mother, which, too, played a crucial role, Nicky relating to Maria Fyodorovna that, after he had handed over the letter, "she could not say anything. This was already a sign for me of the final stage of the conflict which had arisen within her from our first conversation." The couple's mutual cousin Willy was also involved in the persuasion, having a talk with Alix and bringing her to see Nicky on the crucial morning. (Two years later he awarded himself considerable credit for the outcome, referring in a letter to Nicky of the time "when it was my good fortune to be able to help you to secure that charming and accomplished angel who is now your wife.") Again one gets a sense from Nicky's diary that the whole family was determined to bring Alix to this decision, if at all possible—or at least that they were all concerned about it, watching and waiting: "Wilhelm sat in the next room with the uncles and aunts and waited for the outcome of our talk." This family interest and involvement seems to have been almost as much of a trial for Nicky as it must have been for Alix; the issue had become horribly public. Nicky told his mother: "I have to say here that during the whole of those three days I suffered terrible anxiety; all the relatives kept asking me in confidence about her and, expressing their sympathy in the most touching way, wished me all the best. But all this provoked in me even greater fears and doubts that perhaps things would not be resolved."

Once Alix had finally given in, she did so without reserve; it was as though a dam had burst inside her—and inside Nicky: "They left us alone and . . . the first thing she said was . . . that she agreed! Oh God, what happened to me then! I started to cry like a child, and so did she, only her expression immediately changed: her face brightened and took on an aura of peace." Nicky was able to write: "My whole world has been transformed, and everything, nature, people, places, all seem attractive, good and full of joy." Alix, too, was transformed, showing, when happy and relaxed, an entirely new side to herself: "She has completely changed and become gay, amusing, talkative and *tender*." It appears that Nicky had intuited how lovely Alix could be—he had had intimations of this when she was still a child—and that he had fallen in love with her on the strength of this intuition. In her happiness—having finally allowed herself to be happy—she could blossom: "Alix is delightful and has been completely transformed from her state of constant sadness. She is so touchingly sweet with me that I am utterly enchanted."

Dozens of congratulatory telegrams now began to pour in—Nicky had immediately dispatched the joyful news to his parents—and the following morning Queen Victoria's dragoon guards woke him with a serenade beneath his windows. Once he was up, Alix came to collect him and they went to have coffee with the Queen. Nicky's mother's response to the news was effusively affectionate: "Words cannot express with what *delight* and *great* joy I received this happy news! I almost felt *faint* I was so overjoyed! But how sad not to be with you my beloved Nicky at this great moment in your life! Not to be able to kiss you and bless you from the depths of my soul!" Alix was instructed from now on to call her "Motherdear" (a term of endearment favored by both the Danish princesses, Alexandra, Princess of Wales, being called the same by her children). The Emperor Alexander also expressed his joy and gratitude at this eventuality, which he had, in fact, not expected to happen (his letter does rather convey a lack of belief in his son's powers of persuasion, which, if this was his general attitude, goes some way toward explaining Nicky's habitual diffidence). "I have to admit that I did not believe the possibility of such an outcome," he wrote, "and was sure your attempt would fail completely, but the Lord guided you, gave you strength and blessed you, many thanks to Him for His mercy." Alexander now hoped that the struggle would stand his son in good stead to face life's inevitable difficulties.

All the central players in this drama made a habit of invoking God. Up until the last moment, Alix had believed that it was her religion that prevented her from marrying Nicky, while he, despite the celebrations attendant upon Ernie and Ducky's wedding and his own reason for celebration, continued to observe the Orthodox fast of the Great Lent while in Coburg. (Alix and Nicky's engagement took place on the Friday before Passion Week, according to the Orthodox calendar.) Nicky was in many ways a creature of convention and, though happily getting drunk during other seasons of the year, would have considered it a grave sin to have done so during Lent. Religion was also more than convention to him, however, and it was to God that he gave thanks for the gift of Alix.

On April 20, the newly engaged couple had to part, she to travel to Darmstadt and thence to England with her eldest sister Victoria to stay with the Queen, and he to return home to Russia. After Alix had left, Nicky spent the hours before his departure wandering around the places where they had walked together and picking some of her favorite flowers to send to her. He also wrote what was to be the first of many such letters between himself and Alix, at every public parting over the years: "Oh! it was too awful saying goodbye like that, with a lot of people looking on from all sides!" Another action that would become habitual was for one of them to leave a note for the other to find after they had parted; on this occasion, it was Alix who prepared a note to be handed to Nicky. "What a delightful surprise," he wrote to her, "Thank you and thank you for the soothing words that you wrote in it." Nicky and Alix would always find it easier to express their feelings in letters rather than face-to-face, for both were burdened by shyness, even with one another. For Nicky, it seemed that the very depth of emotion he experienced in Alix's presence made him tongue-tied: "I feel very deeply and then I cannot get the words out; it is stupid and tiresome, but so it is." Alix felt the same, telling Nicky: "I also feel shy to express my feelings. I had such a lot I wanted to tell you and ask and speak about and I felt too shy. We shall have to conquer this weakness, don't you think so?" They never did entirely "conquer this weakness," though from his letter it is clear that, on the day when Alix had finally accepted him, Nicky had managed to be eloquent: "I must repeat again the same words I told you my precious little girl, the day of our engagement, that all my life belonged to you and that I could never be enough thankful to you dearest, for all you have done, are doing and are going to do, for me!" Despite their verbal shyness, they were always able to express their affection for one another physically, with few inhibitions (as is evident from the slightly coy references to sex in their correspondence as husband and wife). The couple now expected a fairly long engagement, the separation being "hard" but, at least in Alix's view, it being "better not to hurry." She wanted to learn some Russian and acquaint herself further with the Orthodox religion to which she had agreed to commit herself, before taking the enormous step of going to live in Russia as the wife of the heir apparent.

On her arrival at Windsor, Alix had arranged her room, standing up all her photos of Nicky, "with their beautiful big eyes." She intended to use some of the time for piano practice, which she felt she had been neglecting recently, and over the next few days she played some pieces by Grieg to her grandmother. On the first afternoon, Queen Victoria took her out for a drive, during which she interrogated her on what had taken place in Coburg and what had made her change her mind about accepting Nicky. She asked so many questions that Alix hardly knew how to reply; then, mercifully, the Queen fell asleep. She would have been justifiably horrified to learn that her future grandson-in-law referred to her in his correspondence with his brother Georgy as "belly-woman." He admitted to his fiancée that he had difficulty deciphering the letters "Granny" wrote to him and yet more difficulty in replying, trying to do so in what he thought was a "very grand and old-fashioned like style."

The tone of Nicky's diary entries, and particularly the way he explains various activities and customs, suggest that he is now writing with a definite audience in mind—that Alix will one day read his account of life at his father's palace of Gatchina. He writes on May 14, for instance: "I am on duty today (Lord in waiting) as my Father's a.d.c. and have to appear in church or at the meals in uniform; all my cousins do just the same, we take it in turns with the simple adjutants, having to be on service once a fortnight. Of course, you know, we have nothing hardly to do except sending petitions off to Papa and having to be present at receptions! That's all!" And on his birthday, May 6, he had explained that his brother Misha received presents on that day, too, as Misha's own birthday fell on the same day as his name day and it had been considered unfair that he should receive only one set of presents.

The effect Queen Victoria's strictures regarding her granddaughter's health had on her life have already been considered; there were also consequences arising from the Queen's opinion about how Alix should comport herself in other respects. Not content with the recommendation that the young woman should spend as much time as possible lying down, Victoria also promoted the idea that she should be kept out of public view. "While she is here, alone without you," she wrote to Nicky on April 22, "I think she ought to go about and out as little as possible as she would be stared at and made an object of curiosity which in her present position as *your Bride* would be both unpleasant and improper." This included not going to Ascot that year, a prohibition with which the shy Alix was quite happy to comply. While the intentions of the loving, if domineering, grandmother were entirely directed toward protecting her beloved granddaughter, whom she perceived as fragile, such treatment did not stand Alix in good stead for what awaited her in Russia. A wiser mentor—and one less used to having her own way—might have helped the young woman deal with the inevitable interest of the public by exposing her to it, at least to some extent, while in the safe environment of England. But Victoria did not understand the importance of cultivating public opinion. By this stage in her own life and reign, it may indeed have mattered little (though her stubborn insistence on retreating from public view for years after Prince Albert's death had at one time threatened the stability of the British monarchy), but by implying to her granddaughter that the public's perception of their rulers mattered not at all—that nothing was owed to those who wished to see them, and that no benefit was to be gained by a gracious response—she did Alix no service. It suited someone as shy as Alix to follow her grandmother's counsel and example in this, whereas being forced out of her comfort zone might have done her considerably more good. When she went off to Harrogate for her course of sulphur baths, she was more than happy to abide by Victoria's belief that the public should be ignored. "Of course it is in all the papers that I am here," she told Nicky, "and all the trades people send epistles and beg of one to order things, even a piano and tea were offered. The rude people stand at the corner and stare; I shall stick my tongue out at them another time." It does not seem to have occurred to her that a smile and a wave might have been more appropriate; she was not remotely interested in courting popularity. If only someone could have told her how important it was to cultivate a positive image, how usefully she might have practiced—during this the least stressful period of her life—the art of charming the public. But even if someone had been there to offer such sage advice, she probably would not have listened; one characteristic Alix inherited from her royal grandmother was stubbornness, and she only ever heeded advice that appealed to her. That her shyness could have been overcome, with the right encouragement, is suggested by Nicky's observation to his brother of how her behavior had changed in Coburg, once she had agreed to marry him: "she was completely transformed, she became gay, talkative and not at all shy with the others."

While Alix was living the life of an invalid in Harrogate, Nicky was continuing to indulge in the time-honored habits of a guards officer. He attended a particularly intoxicating dinner at the army camp at Krasnoe Selo on May 24, at which twenty officers insisted on drinking his fiancée's health—that is, a toast, involving tossing back a whole glass of vodka, was drunk to her twenty times. Nicky had to be carried back to his quarters at three o'clock in the morning.

In June he was able to come to England for a few weeks, spending the first few days of his stay with Alix at Walton-on-Thames, where she was staying with her sister Victoria. Here they were able to sit for hours together in the garden, she sewing while he read aloud from the latest works of French fiction, such as Pierre Loti's *Matelot.* Princess Victoria recalled of this happy interlude: "He came quite alone with his old valet and he and Alix were free to spend as much time as they liked together. Then this private intermezzo came to an end and we four [Nicky, Alix, Victoria, and her husband Prince Louis of Battenberg] were fetched by a Royal carriage with an outrider to go to Windsor, much to the surprise of the Waltonians, who never realised who the important people stopping with us had been." It was during Nicky's stay that the future Edward VIII was born, Nicky and Alix being introduced to the baby on June 14, at White Lodge in Richmond, the home at that time of the Duke and Duchess of York. They also attended his christening on July 4, Nicky acting as one of the godfathers. The Queen expected Nicky to behave like all other members of her family while staying in England, even to the extent of his having to acquire "the Windsor tailcoat with red collar and cuffs" to be worn at dinner along with knee breeches and stockings. He did not enjoy wearing this attire, as he told his brother, adding: "It seems funny to me, all this life here and the extent to which I have become part of the English family. I have become almost as indispensable to my future grandmother as her two Indians and her Scotsman." Another visitor to Windsor that year was the Austrian Archduke Franz Ferdinand, in whose honor a dinner was held. On this occasion uniform was worn; it must have been hot, Nicky noting in his diary that he had "sweated a lot." One morning he managed to get himself locked in the lavatory—the key had got stuck—and, after shouting and yelling for forty minutes, was finally rescued by Alix.

Nicky was accompanied on this visit by his confessor, Father John Yanyshev, who was to introduce Alix to the Orthodox faith. For the previous few weeks, Alix had been taking instruction from Dr. Boyd Carpenter, Bishop of Ripon and Chaplain to the Queen. As a future President of the Society for Psychical Research, Dr. Boyd Carpenter may have been influential in preparing the ground for Alix's interest in more esoteric aspects of spirituality, as well as helping her make the transition from Lutheranism to Orthodoxy. While at Windsor, both Nicky and Father Yanyshev attended Anglican services, and the Russian priest was introduced to the Queen. Nicky informed his mother that Yanyshev was "delighted at being in England, and tells everyone with great pride that he has so far never got lost in London. Tomorrow he is going to Oxford, where he has been invited by various divines!"

In July the young couple accompanied the Queen to Osborne on the Isle of Wight. It was during this stay that Alix made her first entry in Nicky's diary, something she was to do on several occasions in the future, when she wanted to write him a special—and lasting—message. This first such message was in response to Nicky's confession of his youthful *amour* with the ballerina Mathilde Kshessinskaya; Alix refers to this as "that little story" and takes a loving but pious and what she imagines to be a very grown-up attitude toward it: "My own Boysy, Boysy dear, never changing, always true. Have confidence and faith in your girly dear who loves more deeply and devotedly than she can ever say. Words are too poor to express my love and admiration and respect—what is past, is past, and will never return and we can look back on it with calm—we are all tempted in this world and when we are young we cannot always fight and hold our own against temptation, but as long as we repent and come back to the good and on to the straight path, God forgives us." She ends her little homily with words from the Book of Common Prayer: " 'If we confess our sins, He is faithful and just to forgive us our sin.' "

And then it was time for Nicky to depart, on his father's yacht the *Polar Star*. The couple planned to meet again toward the beginning of autumn, when Nicky hoped to visit Alix in Darmstadt, but they imagined they would not be marrying before January at the earliest. After such happy weeks spent together, during which their love for, and confidence in, one another had grown ever deeper, the parting was very hard for them both. Nicky wrote from on board the *Polar Star:* "I followed you with my eyes as long as I could from the launch until such a lump came up in my throat that I had to turn away and I sobbed in the boat like I did this afternoon. Luckily it was dark and the men were busy rowing."

Just over three months later Tsar Alexander was dead, Alix had arrived in Russia and been received into the Orthodox Church, and arrangements for an imminent wedding were being discussed. This was no longer a private issue, for the individuals concerned were no longer private people, belonging not only to one another but also to the Russian Empire. Nicky would have preferred the wedding to take place quietly in Livadia, before his father's body was removed, but "all the uncles"—that is, Alexander's powerful and daunting brothers, determined to exert their influence on the young Tsar, their nephew, from the outset—considered it should take place in St. Petersburg, after the funeral. To Nicky this seemed "quite unfitting"; nevertheless, this is the decision that was taken.

Alexander's body, which had quickly begun to decompose, was embalmed. On October 27, the coffin was carried to Yalta, where it was placed, under a canopy and with guards at its four corners, on a yacht called the *Memory of Mercury* on which the family also embarked. Five days later, after having traveled via Moscow where the body lay in state in the Kremlin, the funeral train bearing the coffin arrived in St. Petersburg, to be met by other members of the imperial family.

Once back in the capital, it was straight into work for the new Tsar, even before the old one had been buried. "My dear Alix came to luncheon," Nicky noted in his diary, "it's sad to see her only at intervals!" Seeing Alix, and the rest of his family, "only at intervals" was something the busy Tsar would have to endure for the rest of his reign. In those first days and weeks, Nicky seems to have made a good impression on everyone, and there was much goodwill directed toward him. His ministers were to discover that, despite Nicky's alleged lack of preparation for the enormous task before him, he was actually well informed on most matters of state—apart from those aspects of foreign policy that had been kept highly secret. According to KR, "The young Tsar is the admiration of everyone, wherever His words are heard, either directly or in writing. I hear that the short speech He made in the Kremlin palace to the Moscow nobility was delivered in a loud, clear, assured voice. Yesterday, when receiving the Council of State, He addressed them most beautifully. His modesty suffers from [his] having to be everywhere and always the first." KR also commented on Alix's sweet smile, though he had not yet had the chance to do more than greet her. Nicky's cousin George, Duke of York, in Russia with his parents, wrote to Queen Victoria in similar vein about the new monarch: "Nicky has been kindness itself to me, he is the same dear boy he has always been to me, and talks to me quite openly on every subject. It is really quite touching to see the charming way he treats dear Aunt Minnie [the family name for Maria Fyodorovna]; and he does everything so quietly and nicely and naturally; everyone is struck by it, and he is very popular already."

The funeral of Tsar Alexander III took place in the Peter and Paul Cathedral on November 7. Enormous crowds followed the cortège through the black-draped streets of the capital. Lord Carrington, the British Lord Chamberlain, was in attendance and sent Queen Victoria a report of the service, which lasted for over two hours. "The crush was tremendous . . . ," he wrote, "the Emperor, the Empress [that is, Maria Fyodorovna], and the Princess of Wales in the centre with the Kings of Greece and Denmark and the Prince of Wales: surrounded by the Archdukes, and Duchesses, and other Royal Guests—the future Empress [Alix] looking remarkably handsome. At 12.30 the terrible ceremony of paying the last farewell took place." This must indeed have been a "terrible ceremony," as the corpse had been dead now for nearly three weeks and, despite the embalming, the hands and head were turning black. The central figure in all this was the widow, Maria Fyodorovna: "The Empress with heroic courage walked up steadily, knelt, and then took a last look at the late Emperor and kissed the sacred picture on His Majesty's breast, and then kissed his lips. The Emperor supported and took great care of Her Majesty and all the Royal Personages present kissed the sacred picture." The new Emperor was one of the pallbearers, carrying his father's coffin (now closed) to its final resting place in a vault alongside his imperial forebears. As the coffin was lowered into the vault, salvoes were fired by the artillery of the fortress as well as by the attendant troops, the final military honors being paid to the late Emperor of All the Russias.

The wedding of Nicholas and Alexandra took place in the church in the Winter Palace exactly a week after Alexander's funeral. For Nicky it felt very strange to be preparing for what should have been the most joyful occasion of his life—one for which he had so much longed—in the midst of what was also the greatest sadness he had ever known. He wrote in his diary on the eve of his marriage: "I keep feeling as if it's someone else's wedding—it seems so strange to be thinking about my own wedding in such circumstances!" Poor Nicky was having to grow up so very suddenly.

For the day of the wedding, which was also Maria Fyodorovna's birthday, mourning was discarded. The bridal procession through the Winter Palace to the chapel was witnessed by thousands of officials and dignitaries, among them Lord Carrington, who again wrote an account for the Queen, realizing that her chief interest would of course be her granddaughter: "The Emperor in a very plain uniform walked with the Bride who looked simply magnificent—on her head she wore a circlet of diamonds, with a diamond top which made it into a crown—2 long curls (like the Princess of Wales used to wear) on her shoulders, a splendid necklace and ornaments—and an enormous mantle of cloth of gold, lined with ermine. She looked the perfection of what one would imagine an Empress of Russia on her way to the altar would be and moved along quite simply and with great dignity. She makes very marked bows with her head, when she greets anyone; and this is much noticed and appreciated." Lord Carrington may have been putting a rather positive gloss on Alix's "very marked bows with her head," for these could also look rather stilted and stiff, a sign of her extreme shyness and awkwardness—and possibly of some physical difficulty of bowing other than with her head—rather than of particular courtesy and affability. Cousin George also sent a glowing report to his—and Alix's—grandmother (paying tribute along the way to his mother, Princess Alexandra, for the support she had been giving to her sister since Alexander's death; his father Edward, Prince of Wales—Uncle Bertie to the new Tsar—had also been of enormous help to Nicky in these early, daunting days of his reign): "Poor Aunt Minnie has indeed been brave and has borne her terrible grief in a wonderful way, Mama has been of the greatest possible help and comfort to her, I don't know how she could have got on without her. Dear Alicky looked quite lovely at the Wedding, the Service was very fine and impressive and the singing quite beautiful, she went through it all with so much modesty but was so graceful and dignified at the same time, she certainly made a most excellent impression. I do think Nicky is a very lucky man to have got such a lovely and charming wife; and I must say I never saw two people more in love with each other or happier than they are."

Nicky's best men at the wedding were his brother Misha and three of his cousins: George Prince of Greece and the Grand Dukes Kirill Vladimirovich and Sergei Mikhailovich. Nicky later admitted to his brother Georgy, whose health did not allow him to be present, that it had taken all his strength not to break down during the service, so upset was he at the absence of both father and brother. At the conclusion of the wedding, Alix officially became Empress, and Maria Fyodorovna the Empress Dowager (though the latter would continue to take precedence over her daughter-in-law, in accordance with imperial custom). As the newlyweds rode in a carriage from the Winter Palace to the Kazan Cathedral, and finally on to the Anichkov Palace, where they were initially to live (in a separate apartment but in the same palace as Maria Fyodorovna), the Nevsky Prospekt was thronged with people, the new Tsar having taken the unprecedented step of ordering the route cleared of the usual barrier of soldiers, so that, for the first time in many years, his people could actually see their sovereign. "The cheering was most hearty and reminded me of England," reported the future George V. After appearing several times at one of the palace windows to acknowledge the crowds of well-wishers, the couple spent the evening answering telegrams, had dinner at eight o'clock, and then went early to bed, as the bride had a bad headache.

The description Nicky gives in his diary of his first day of married life contains many of the elements that were to be a stable feature of that life: the presence of close family, praying together (they did so that day at the tomb of "dear unforgettable Papa"), taking physical exercise (on Nicky's part), rigid mealtimes, and enjoyment in sitting quietly together in those intervals when "no one came to disturb" them. Those intervals were, alas, few and far between. "There is very little free time," the new Tsar told his brother Georgy, "there are always reports to be read and endless people to receive." KR noticed the effect this was having on Nicky: "He is so quiet, thoughtful, thin and pale; they are overloading him, he hardly goes into the air, and to stay without moving is bad for him." (It was always believed by his relatives and friends and by Nicky himself that he had to take plenty of exercise, preferably outdoors, for the sake of his health.) Nicky himself expressed the one problem of his early married life: "I am unbelievably happy with Alix, it's only a pity that my work takes up so much of the time that I would like to spend exclusively with her!" This must have been very difficult for Alix, still in her early days of becoming accustomed to such a different life from the one she had known till now; all those hours when Nicky was sequestered with his reports or his officials must inevitably have entailed much loneliness for her. The couple managed four days' respite toward the end of November, when they managed to escape to the Alexander Palace at Tsarskoe Selo. "It's inexpressibly wonderful to live here quietly," Nicky wrote in his diary, "without seeing anyone—all day and night together!" But even here, in between their walks in the surrounding parkland, Nicky had official papers to read. Nevertheless, these few days of relative tranquility and privacy helped make the Alexander Palace forever afterward a special place for the imperial couple, a refuge to which they would always return with relief and joy.

Nicky's diary entry for the last day of 1894 is poignant in its expression of endings and a new beginning: "Read until 7.30 and then went upstairs for the service. It was painful to stand in church and think of the terrible changes, which have happened this year. But putting faith in God I look forward to the next year without fear—because for me the worst has already happened, that which I feared all my life! But together with this irrevocable grief the Lord has rewarded me also with a happiness which I could never have imagined. He has given me Alix."

By late spring Alix and Nicky were making preparations for the arrival of their first child. Their cousin Kaiser Wilhelm would not have been alone in hoping that the result would be "a nice little boy." However, a little girl, Olga (actually not so little, as previously noted), was born on November 3, after an exhausting and protracted labor, and Alix rather startled her grandmother the Queen—who fortunately was too far away to do anything about it—by her insistence on feeding the baby herself (though a wet-nurse was also employed). Several members of the family were allowed to witness this process, which, in its early days, included the babies being swapped over, Alix becoming proficient at feeding the wet-nurse's child while the wet-nurse took care of Olga. Nicky wrote to assure the skeptical Queen Victoria that he believed breast-feeding "the most natural thing a mother can do" and that he thought "the example an excellent one!" Alix reveled in her first month of motherhood, with her baby constantly by her side, and was averse ("in a state" as Nicky described it) to the changes incumbent upon the arrival of an English nanny, who would be bearing the little girl upstairs to the nursery. Nicky, who enjoyed helping to bathe his new daughter, also considered this separation and interference "a pity and rather a bore!" But there seemed no escape; the employment of English nannies was habitual in the imperial family, and Xenia and Sandro were "very happy" with theirs, "an exceptional Englishwoman" who had already been living in Russia for twelve years. The "unbearable" woman who arrived at Tsarskoe Selo on December 17, 1895, was, however, a different prospect. Within twenty-four hours Nicky was telling his brother that she had "something hard and unpleasant in her face" and surmised that things were not going to go smoothly. She upset Alix at once, demanding more rooms for the baby and informing the doting mother that she was visiting the nursery too often. They put up with this disagreeable nurse for just over four months; "what a relief to be rid of her at last!" Nicky wrote on April 29.

Meanwhile, at the very end of 1895, the young family (nurse included) had left Maria Fyodorovna's establishment and moved into their newly decorated and furnished apartments in the Winter Palace, which they liberally strewed with an array of pictures, photographs, ornaments, and icons (what would be perceived by the modern eye as "clutter" was always a feature of Nicky and Alix's private space). They inaugurated their new dining room with a family luncheon on January 1, after having fulfilled the New Year's ceremonial duties together for the second time in their lives. "Thank God," Nicky wrote in his diary, "Alix coped marvellously not only with the church service and the ambassadors' reception, but also with receiving homage from the ladies, the Council of State, the Senate, the court and the suites!" Nicholas was constantly aware of the potential strain—both physical and emotional—on his wife of such ceremonial duties, noting on the occasion of their "first big ball" of 1896: "I suffered for dear Alix, who had to receive a mass of ladies." And at Easter he reported to his mother: "Alix stood up wonderfully to the whole of the midnight service and liturgy; she rested only while I washed my face after the greeting ceremony." This latter ceremony was something of an ordeal as it involved exchanging kisses with about sixteen hundred people—the result being very sore cheeks for the Tsar. Alix was finding it particularly difficult to overcome her shyness; consequently many people never discovered how "sweet and friendly" she could be—unlike KR who described her thus in April after being seated next to her during a lunch. When she felt at ease, she was able to talk quite happily and even intimately; she charmed KR with an account of how she continued to breast-feed Olga once a day, during morning coffee with Nicky. This conversation took place shortly before the imperial couple were due to depart for Moscow for the coronation ceremonies; KR observed that Alix was not at all looking forward to having to wean baby Olga before they left.

The main political event of these months between the accession of Nicholas II and his coronation concerned a speech the young Tsar made to representatives of the nobility and the *zemstvos* (district and provincial assemblies) in January 1895. Through the injudicious use of a couple of words—usually translated as "senseless" or "idiotic" "dreams," and referring to the aspirations of various zemstvo representatives to be more involved in the business of government—Nicky alienated a large proportion of his potential supporters, who might have helped him bring about positive change while avoiding revolution. To the Tsar, his expressed intention of adhering to "the principles of autocracy as firmly and unbendingly as my unforgettable late father" represented a virtue and indeed the fulfillment of a deathbed promise; to his subjects gathered to listen to him in the Winter Palace's Nikolaevsky Hall, it represented disappointment, a dashing of their hopes for a new style of leadership. Nicky, it seemed, had squandered the goodwill and popular enthusiasm that had greeted his accession. His unassuming and charming demeanor, so unlike that of his massive-framed stern-looking father, had appeared to presage a more liberal, forward-thinking approach to running the Russian Empire. But now his hearers realized the change was only cosmetic; Nicholas II might look and sound very different from Alexander III, but in substance he was the same—just as reactionary and just as repressive.

The repercussions of this speech lasted for years; the motives behind it were still being hotly debated in 1905 when W. T. Stead listened to discussions at Prince Dolgoruky's house about "that fatal day when, as if the victim of some baleful spell, Nicholas II flung away the proffered affection of his people, and surrendered himself to the hands of their foes." Nicky himself had been very nervous—"in a terrible state" was how he described it—about delivering this, his first, major speech in public; he had tucked the text of it into his cap so that he had it to hand. When it came to the delivery, however, he appeared confident, addressing the gathering in clear, ringing tones. The debate that went on afterward was over who actually wrote the speech, particularly the "senseless dreams" phrase. Those resistant to the idea of abandoning their idealized, romantic picture of the young Tsar were convinced it was all a plot orchestrated by the Minister of Internal Affairs, Ivan Durnovo—that he had alarmed Nicholas by claiming that an address presented to him by the members of the Tver zemstvo was seditious (so seditious, in fact, that the Tsar himself must not even be allowed to see it) and that the only way to deal with such incipient rebellion was to nip it firmly in the bud. Others, including the German ambassador, General Bernhard F. W. von Werder, held that the offending words were definitely Nicholas's own. For Nicky himself, still bereft—it was, after all, only three months since the death of his "unforgettable" father—and on what we would now call "a very steep learning curve," repeating the kind of formula he could imagine his father using in such circumstances must have felt the obvious thing to do. It is very unlikely he had any idea of the impact his words would have.

Whether or not Durnovo had had a hand in creating the unfortunate incident of the speech to the zemstvo representatives, the suspicion remains that experienced ministers and bureaucrats were prepared and able to manipulate the youthful, inexperienced Tsar. As we have seen, W. T. Stead was convinced that his officials deliberately overloaded him with trivial paperwork in order to prevent him having the time or energy to undertake new initiatives or to question how things had always been done, and, in the weeks leading up to the coronation, Nicky himself comes close to harboring such thoughts. "In general I am terribly fatigued," he told his mother, "there are so many petty meaningless affairs before Moscow, it is as if my gentlemen ministers have decided to wear me out, they are so persistent and tiresome. I'm amazed my head hasn't burst with all the rubbish being stuffed into it."

The Times gave a full account of the coronation of Nicholas and Alexandra on May 14, 1896. The day dawned bright, the sense of expectation very high: "It needed no cannon-firing at 7 o'clock this morning to give notice to the Muscovites and their many visitors that the coronation of the Tsar was to take place to-day in the Cathedral of the Assumption, as most of the inhabitants were off and moving towards the Kremlin at a much earlier hour . . . And a glorious day it was—a cloudless sky with hardly breeze enough to stir a leaf, while the hot sun poured upon the many gilded cupolas of Moscow and the Kremlin till they gleamed like fire." *The Times*'s correspondent seemed almost overcome by the resplendence and variety of the official spectators filling the specially erected tribunes in Cathedral Square and by the gloriously bedecked troops on duty—from the Horse Guards in their eagle-crested helmets, white tunics, and scarlet jackets embossed with golden double-headed eagles, the group of court ladies clad all in white clustered beneath their parasols alongside the Red Staircase, to the members of the diplomatic corps and emissaries of foreign powers, many in national dress. "The most interesting crowd, however, was formed by the selected Russians—Old Believers, delegates of rural institutions, peasant elders, and representatives generally of all the races in Russian Europe and Russian Asia. The dark cloth cap with a peak and long-skirted coat of the Slavonic Russian were predominant, but there were a large number of Eastern types and Oriental dresses in rainbow hues of every possible description." Yet even this starstruck foreign correspondent could not refrain from observing that this crowd was both handpicked and stage-managed; nothing had been left to chance. The "ordinary" Russians present had first been chosen by their respective local authorities and then further scrutinized in Moscow before being deployed, rather like film extras, to cheer vociferously when instructed by "the waving of a handkerchief or the raising of an official's wand."

The first procession—that of the Dowager Empress—began at nine o'clock. This was a very difficult occasion for the forty-eight-year-old widow, for she could not help but be reminded of the coronation of her late husband and herself only thirteen years previously. Every aspect of that ceremony and its attendant celebrations was now being replicated and, though her support of her son was unstinting, her memories must have been painful and acute. So, indeed, were Nicholas's own. In preparation for the appearance of the Dowager Empress, a canopy of gold brocade, supported on four gilt rods and surmounted by black, orange, and white plumes, its hangings embroidered with double-headed eagles, was carried to the foot of the Red [or Beautiful] Staircase. Then the procession started to descend; about two hundred court officials, pages carrying white horsehair plumes, ladies-in-waiting in Russian national costume, and maids-of-honor in white veils and red velvet trains all processed into the Cathedral of the Assumption—and then out again through the north door, this being the usual custom on great occasions as the cathedral was too small to hold all but the most important individuals. Then the Dowager Empress herself came into view at the top of the staircase, wearing a small diamond crown and purple mantle, her train held by several high-ranking dignitaries, to the cheers of the spectators and the playing of "God Save the Tsar." Eight elderly generals held the canopy under which Maria Fyodorovna walked slowly toward the cathedral, surrounded by Grand Dukes and Duchesses. Once she had passed into the cathedral, the crowd had to wait for a further hour before the Tsar himself was due to emerge. A second canopy, resembling the first but much longer, supported by eight rather than four rods, now took its place at the foot of the stairs. At ten o'clock a bugle announced the departure of the imperial procession: First to emerge and descend the stairs was a company of chevalier guards, followed by files of pages and the Masters of Ceremonies. Then came a long double line of representatives of the peasant communes and town municipalities, justices of the peace, government officials, members of the nobility, delegates from Moscow University, from the Holy Synod, and from the Senate. Most of these, as with the earlier procession, passed into the cathedral and out at the other side. They were followed by high-ranking state officials bearing the imperial regalia on brocade cushions—the great seal, orb, and scepter, with two mantles and two crowns—preceded by the sword and banner of State. After a pause, clergy in gold vestments sprinkled the processional route with holy water, ready for the feet of the Tsar.

When Emperor Nicholas II and his Empress Alexandra Fyodorovna finally appeared at the top of the stairs, they were greeted by tremendous cheers. To the playing of "God Save the Tsar" by the massed military bands spread throughout the Kremlin, to the thunder of cannons fired from the ramparts, and to the jubilant clashing of the bells of all the Moscow churches, the Tsar and Tsarina slowly descended. Then, the huge plumed canopy held above them, the bright mid-morning sun glinting on the steel and silver of sword and helmet, shimmering on the golden eagles emblazoned on the hangings, the imperial couple processed toward the Cathedral of the Assumption, where every Tsar had been crowned since Ivan the Terrible in 1547.

The Times's correspondent, fortunate in having secured a place inside the cathedral, described the appearance of Nicky and Alix as they entered: "The Emperor has not the colossal stature which has distinguished so many of the Romanofs, but he is well-built, holds himself erect, and shows in all his movements a great deal of quiet dignity, while his face, which at some moments strikingly resembles that of his cousin the Duke of York, wears habitually a kindly sympathetic expression. He wears the uniform of a colonel of the Preobrazhenski Infantry Regiment, with the red Cordon of Alexander Nevski and the plain Collar of St. Andrew. [It was Paul I, at the end of the eighteenth century, who had begun the custom of wearing military uniform under the imperial mantle, and Nicky was happy to continue it; his colonel's uniform had been made by N. I. Nordenstrem, the best of Russian military tailors, a byword for elegance and taste.] The Empress, always handsome, is to-day looking magnificent in a low dress of silver brocade cut in the ancient fashion, her beautiful brown hair, dressed most simply without jewelry or other ornament, falling in two long thick ringlets on her white shoulders . . . in all her movements she displays an easy grace and dignified composure."

After being clothed in a mantle of gold brocade and ermine, receiving the orb and scepter, placing his own crown upon his head and then crowning his Empress, who knelt before him, Nicholas was anointed with the oil of chrism. The anointing was carried out by the Metropolitan of Moscow, and the Tsar was anointed on forehead, eyes, nostrils, ears, lips, and breast (his uniform jacket having a special flap which opened to expose the breast). Alexandra was also anointed, but on the forehead only. When the imperial couple received Communion, Nicholas entered through the royal doors and received the elements immediately before the altar—where normally only the priests may enter—while Alexandra received outside the sanctuary, like the rest of the laity. Everything was designed to emphasize the divine nature of the Tsar's vocation. This was not lost on the correspondent of *The Times* who, reflecting the next day on the significance of the event, raised the question as to the effect all this must have had on Nicholas himself: "The demeanour of the multitude gathered together from all quarters of the Empire, who assembled to watch the passage of the Sovereigns, shows how the mind of the people is struck by the almost sacred character of the Tsar—a character to which the final seal is set by the rite of yesterday. It is impossible to help wondering how the chief actor in the splendid ceremony is affected by it himself. As he descended from the dais yesterday with the transient sunlight playing auspiciously upon the diamonds of his crown, Nicholas II must have been more or less than man if he were not deeply moved."

CHAPTER SIX

After the Coronation

1896–1904

"Never mind . . ." [the old man] repeated. "Your grief is half a grief. Life is long, there'll be more of good and bad, there'll be everything. Mother Russia is vast!" he said, and he looked to both sides. "I've been all over Russia and seen all there is in her, and believe what I say, my dear. There will be good and there will be bad."

—Anton Chekhov, *In the Ravine*, January 1900

CROWDS WERE ALREADY gathering at the Khodynka Field in the early hours of the morning of May 18, four days after the coronation, though the instructions had stipulated ten o'clock as the time to arrive in order to receive the specially prepared coronation gifts. Wrapped up in colored kerchiefs, the gifts included foodstuffs (sausage, breadrolls, nuts, sweets, and gingerbread) and, most coveted of all—for enamel tableware was rare in most working-class households—a special coronation beaker, featuring the crowned ciphers of Nicholas and Alexandra and the imperial double-headed eagle. Four hundred thousand of these gifts had been prepared and were lying ready on special tables. The field was normally used for military maneuvers, as a training ground for the Moscow garrison. It was hardly an ideal space for a gathering of thousands of excited citizens, for it was pitted with ditches, gullies, and trenches. At about five o'clock in the morning panic suddenly set in; there were already so many people that a rumor had begun to spread that there would not be enough gifts for them all. Some in the crowd started to push, there was no effective crowd control, a barrier broke, and people in their hundreds began to press forward. Those behind were unable to see what was happening ahead, but the impetus shoving them forward made it impossible to stop. People began to fall into the ditches and potholes, others fell on top of them, the panic increased, there was crying and screaming, but no one was able to hold back the press of human beings, surging forward in great waves, more and more falling and being trampled by their fellows who fell in their turn. Over thirteen hundred people were crushed to death that morning, a thousand more injured.

The dead and wounded were carted away, this grisly work continuing even as the more important people began to arrive for the day's festivities. Musical and theatrical performances were scheduled for beween eleven o'clock and midday (by which time it had been envisaged that an orderly distribution of gifts would have been completed) and the imperial family was expected to appear on the balcony of the Emperor's pavilion at two o'clock in the afternoon. These celebrations carried on as planned, the strains of "God Save the Tsar" and "Be Glorified" rising above the field from which the dead were still being removed. "It was awful to have to go to the fete at 2 o'clock, knowing there had been such a misfortune before it had even started," wrote KR. "Although I did not see anything, several people including Mitia [his brother], told me that on the way they had met firemen with large wagons piled with the bodies of the unfortunate victims."

In the evening a ball had been arranged, to be hosted by the French ambassador, Gustave Lannes de Montebello. Nicky and Alix, greatly distressed by the events of the day, felt it would be inappropriate to attend—to dance while their loyal subjects grieved—but the Tsar was overruled. Several of "the uncles" weighed in, to convince him that it would be a discourtesy to the French not to proceed as planned. In retrospect, this was an occasion when the Tsar should certainly have stood up to the interfering Grand Dukes, with their misreading of the situation and complete lack of understanding of the public mood—and of how it mattered. But instead, against their better judgment, the Emperor and Empress agreed to attend, though only for a short while. Once they were there, however, the uncles brought further pressure to bear, telling them it would look "sentimental" if they were to leave before supper, and so they agreed to stay—still leaving before the end, but not until two o'clock in the morning. Meanwhile the "Mikhailovichi"—those cousins of Nicky who were the sons of Grand Duke Mikhail Nikolaevich—who thought that all the festivities should have been canceled, showed their displeasure by leaving ostentatiously after the opening polonaise. The issue showed signs of degenerating into a Romanov family feud, the actual victims in danger of being forgotten.

The number of dead and injured at the Khodynka Field was a matter of speculation and misinformation from the start. The Tsar himself referred to "about 1300 people being trampled." The official death toll was initially 300, though rumor put it closer to 1,500. Xenia gives three possible figures: "They say that by the evening the number of dead had reached 1400, and although Nicky was told 360, in fact it's nearer 1000." On the following morning, KR referred to "more than a thousand people" who had perished. Sergei Oldenburg gives the number of dead as 1,282, while later scholars specify 1,389. So it would seem that Nicky's original information was fairly accurate. On the day after the disaster he and Alix visited some of the wounded in the hospital, and the Tsar donated one thousand roubles each to the families of the victims. Though this may have been of some help to the families, it did little to repair the reputation of the Romanovs.

There were many, including the "Mikhailovichi," who felt that Grand Duke Sergei, as Governor-General of Moscow, should have fallen on his sword and resigned—whether or not he was personally responsible. The elder Grand Dukes, however, Sergei's brothers, considered such a reaction as tantamount to siding with revolutionaries and opponents of the Tsarist regime. Sergei did in fact offer to resign—an offer that was refused—but declined to cooperate with an official inquiry. Nicky had inaugurated one, under the direction of Count Konstantin Pahlen, but when Sergei, supported by at least two other of the bullying uncles, threatened to resign over Pahlen's appointment, he backed down. That Sergei was a difficult person, with whom it was impossible to negotiate and who could not handle criticism, is admitted by KR, who, despite being very fond of him, did not dare tell him what he really thought: "I have been tormented by doubts: should I tell Sergei about what I consider to have been his mistakes? I certainly don't want to talk to him: Sergei does not like anyone to disagree with him, he gets annoyed and loses his capacity to think coolly and logically."

There was no sense in the early days of Nicholas's reign of the family pulling together, of the uncles being prepared to offer their support to the young and inexperienced Tsar. Rather, the reverse was the case, each being determined to keep what power and influence he could for himself. Possibly they feared a repeat of what had happened on Alexander III's accession, when he had dispensed with the services of certain of his own uncles, the brothers of Alexander II. Sandro described the position vividly, if with some exaggeration: "Nicky spent the first ten years of his reign sitting behind a massive desk in the palace and listening with near awe to the well-rehearsed bellowing of his towering uncles. He dreaded to be left alone with them." The Tsar was in an almost impossible position, as would be any new ruler in the midst of a large, close, and intensely vocal family, many of whose members were older and far more experienced than him. He would have needed to be very strong and mature to have disciplined his own brother-in-law and uncle—"Uncle Gega," as he had called Sergei from childhood—to whom he had looked up all his life. Instead, the blame for the Khodynka catastrophe was placed at the door of the chief of the Moscow police, Colonel Vlasovsky, widely seen as a scapegoat.

At the conclusion of the coronation celebrations, Nicky and Alix went to stay for a fortnight with Sergei and Ella at their country residence at Ilinskoye. Nicky seemed to feel that, after the stress of the coronation and attendant festivities, he deserved a holiday. "Awoke with the wonderful realization that everything is over and that it is now possible to live for oneself, quietly and peacefully!" Even a few minutes' consideration should have made him realize that, as long as he remained Tsar, he could never live only for himself; a few more minutes' thought might have led him to the conclusion that, in coming to stay with Sergei and Ella, he was signaling his full support for the Governor-General and exonerating him of any blame for the Khodynka disaster. Perhaps that is what he meant to signal—but it is more likely that he had not given much thought to the public messages his actions were sending, imagining that he really still could operate in a realm of exclusively private actions, at least for a short time, and giving priority to family and personal considerations above the public and political. He seems to have been oblivious to the fact that every action he took from now on would be subject to interpretation, rumor, and conjecture—or else he just did not want to recognize that fact.

The imperial couple, with baby Olga in tow, spent much of the rest of the year paying foreign visits, including to many relatives—Austria, Kiev, Germany, Denmark, England, France, and Darmstadt were all on the itinerary. From August 15–17, they visited Vienna, where they briefly met the Emperor Franz Joseph and his wife the Empress Elisabeth. They returned to Kiev for the consecration of the Cathedral of St. Vladimir, the Tsar also attending the unveiling of a monument to his predecessor and namesake, Nicholas I. The imperial party then traveled on to Breslau and Goerlitz, where the German army was holding maneuvers. *The Times* remarked on the Germans' fondness for Alix as one of their own—an identification that would come to haunt her in later years. In September the same newspaper was keen to point out that the two-week visit of the imperial couple and their daughter to Queen Victoria at Balmoral was of a purely personal and domestic nature, as had been the ten-day visit to Nicky's maternal grandparents in Denmark that had preceded it. Then in France, where a royal guest had not been entertained since 1867, Nicky impressed the populace by his "easy mastery" of his horse and by his "graceful figure, serious countenance, and erect bearing." "It is not surprising," remarked the correspondent, "that he is frantically cheered." We are not told whether Alix was frantically cheered, too, merely that she wore "a green velvet mantle and a boa round her neck." This part of the tour seems to have been a particular success, and the imperial couple were greatly moved at their reception by this republican people. For the latter it presented a perfect excuse for days of partying, and the city's entrepreneurs had also taken every opportunity to capitalize on popular enthusiasm. Russian, or pseudo-Russian, souvenirs abounded: There were cakes of soap labeled "Le Tsar," sweets decorated with the Russian flag and coat of arms, Russian teddy bears, and tableware bearing the portraits of the Tsar, Tsarina, and baby Olga. "The tsar's visage appeared on jumping beans, and the popular toy, 'the peasant and the bear,' became the tsar and Felix Faure. Advertisers exploited the Russian fad. 'Pink pills' were recommended to ensure good health during the tsar's visit; shoemakers and glovers distributed their ads on the backs of free pictures of the tsar. Proprietors of ready-made clothes advertised their sale items as 'presents of the tsar.' One entrepreneur even sold a 'Franco-Russian' Dutch cheese." After the visit to France, Nicky and Alix were able to relax for three weeks with Alix's relatives in Darmstadt.

Where Nicky seemed prepared, and able, to take his uncles on was in small matters—though they did not seem small to him—concerning protocol, or personal relationships, rather than in the arena of politics and statecraft. Thus he wrote sternly to Grand Duke Vladimir in January 1897 over an infringement of protocol at the theater, when Vladimir and his wife Maria Pavlovna had taken the liberty of introducing guests of their own into the imperial box during a masked ball at the Mariinsky Theatre, without even having asked permission (which would probably have been declined). Nicky and Alix were indignant that these older members of their family should have overstepped the bounds in this way, Nicky expostulating to his uncle: "Nothing of the kind ever happened in Papa's day, and you know how strictly I adhere to everything as it was then. It is also unfair to try and take advantage of the fact that I am young, and your nephew." Despite his irritation and feeling of righteous anger (and, one senses, Alix standing over his shoulder, at least figuratively, while he writes), Nicky still found it very difficult to rebuke his elders so. "In future, please spare me the necessity of writing such letters which make me feel abominable," he concluded. Sandro eloquently summed up the problem of the Grand Dukes: "The uncles always wanted something. Nikolai fancied himself a Great Warrior. Alexei ruled the waves. Sergei tried to turn Moscow into his private domain. Vladimir advocated the cause of the Arts. They all had their favorite generals and admirals who were supposed to be promoted ahead of a long waiting list; their ballerinas desirous of organizing a 'Russian Season' in Paris; their wonderful preachers anxious to redeem the Emperor's soul; their miraculous physicians soliciting a court appointment; their clairvoyant peasants with a divine message."

Just as "the uncles" might have helped Nicholas but chose instead to hinder him in seeking to maintain their own spheres of influence, so Maria Fyodorovna might have been of great help to Alix, had the nature of each woman not made the Dowager Empress more of a rival than a mentor to her young daughter-in-law. The laws giving Maria Fyodorovna precedence at all state occasions cannot have helped as far as Alix was concerned, the latter being forced to take third place, after both her husband and his mother. The situation was only made worse for Alix by the fact that the vivacious and popular Maria Fyodorovna was so much more practiced and at her ease on such occasions than she was herself. Comparisons were inevitably made, and they were not usually in Alix's favor. In the autumn of 1896 she had become pregnant for the second time, and was consigned to bed for the first seven weeks of the pregnancy, under the orders of Dr. Dmitry Ott, the imperial obstetrician and director of the Imperial Clinical Institute of Midwives. After she was allowed up, she continued to be treated with great care, "even when changing her position on the divan."

Alix's incapacity during her pregnancy meant that Nicky was accompanied by his mother even more than usual. On January 19, 1897, they went together to an exhibition of English and German watercolorists, organized by Sergei Diaghilev, where they purchased several pictures. This was Diaghilev's first attempt at curating an exhibition; it was modest in size but distinctive in its arrangement. Nicky also regularly attended the theater, opera, and ballet during that winter season, several times in the company of his brother Misha and sister Olga. At the end of January he introduced his other Olga, his fourteen-month-old daughter, to the experience of sledging down an ice hill, holding her on his lap as he tobogganed down. She clung on, both scared and excited. His pregnant wife was not excluded from all entertainment; on the evening of February 7, the balalaika players of the Composite Battalion played in front of the open door of her room. Another excitement at the Winter Palace that year was the showing of some films depicting scenes from the coronation and other imperial occasions. In Nicky's diary entry for February 12, there is a reference to himself and Alix playing piano duets, a joint entertainment they later abandoned. On April 15, Nicky attended a gala performance of two acts of Tchaikovsky's *The Sleeping Beauty* with Emperor Franz Joseph, who was paying a visit of three days, accompanied by his nephew

Archduke Otto. On Alix's name day (April 23) a German choir based in St. Petersburg serenaded her below her windows, alongside the court choir. Her sister Irene had come to stay for a few weeks, and over the next few days performances by cossacks and balalaika players were also laid on for the visitor's benefit. Music played a large part in the lives of the imperial couple at this time, choirs, balalaika players, and chamber ensembles frequently performing in the palaces and with regular excursions to see the latest operas and ballets.

Tatiana Nikolaevna was born on May 29, 1897, at Tsarskoe Selo, this second birth proving both easier and speedier than the first. There is no hint in Nicky's diary of any disappointment over a second daughter; on the contrary, he writes of the "second bright happy day in our family life" on which "the *Lord blessed us with a daughter—Tatiana*." Predictably, other members of the family were less positive in their response, KR remarking "everyone was very disappointed as they had been hoping for a son." Motherhood and breast-feeding again suited Alix, who, so Xenia reported, looked "wonderful." And Tatiana, who of all the daughters would always be closest to Alix, was judged to look "just like her mother! Her mouth is tiny and very beautiful." Just over five months later, on the anniversary of his father's death, Nicky gave a glowing account of his family life in a letter to his mother (who was at the time on a prolonged visit to Denmark): "Our little daughters are growing, and turning into delightful happy little girls. Olga talks the same in Russian and in English and adores her little sister. Tatiana seems to us, understandably, a very beautiful child, her eyes have become dark and large. She is *always* happy and only cries once a day without fail, after her bath when they feed her. The cossacks, soldiers, and negroes are Olga's greatest friends, and she greets them as she goes down the corridor."

Two years after the coronation, and as the mother of two daughters, Alix was still having difficulty fulfilling her role as Empress. This was apparent to KR when he spent half an hour alongside her in a carriage at Gatchina in May 1898. Their conversation was, as always, in English, for though KR did not find this easy, Alix would have found it more difficult to speak to him in Russian. But quite apart from specific language difficulties, Alix had still not mastered the art of making conversation, her shyness proving to be a severe disability. "It's noticeable that she does not have her mother-in-law's charm," commented KR after this awkward half hour, "and still does not, therefore, inspire general adulation." It would appear that, if anything, Alix's difficulties in this respect had increased, for she had earlier seemed at ease with KR, charming him with her talk about her first baby. Part of the trouble was certainly linguistic. Alix had had insufficient time to become proficient in Russian before being cast into the limelight as

Nicholas's bride and, for a shy person, learning in adulthood to speak another language is in itself a challenge—for to speak a new language well requires not only plenty of practice but also a willingness to make mistakes and not to be unduly embarrassed by them; self-consciousness is invariably the enemy of fluency. And to be forced to make one's mistakes in a very public arena, with everyone watching and listening, must be doubly excruciating. In addition, the precipitate nature of Alix's introduction to the Russian court and high society meant that she had failed to grasp all the intricacies of precedence and protocol, so that she had occasionally slipped up and made errors—"irrelevant in themselves but tantamount to formidable crimes in the eyes of St. Petersburg society," as Sandro put it. For someone with Alix's temperament, such faux pas would be almost impossible to laugh off. Consequently her experience "frightened her and created marked reserve in her treatment of visitors." Fearful of making similar mistakes again, she found the simplest—if not the most sensible—remedy was to withdraw. "This in turn gave circulation to the comparisons between the friendliness of the Dowager-Empress and the 'snobbish coolness' of the young Tsarina." Loving both women, sympathetic to both, Nicky was caught in a fix; furthermore, he "resented this malicious matching of his mother against his wife, and very soon the relations between court and society became antagonistic."

In September 1898 Nicky traveled to Copenhagen for the funeral of his maternal grandmother, known to the family as "Amama." By now, when the nickname "Boysy" appears in correspondence between himself and his wife, it is no longer used merely as a term of endearment; rather, it refers to a specific part of his anatomy, the female equivalent of which is "lady." So now he writes to Alix: "Fancy Boysy is so sad that he is alone, that it has made me forget about his very existence. He sends his respects to lady." Boysy was clearly full of vigor once reunited with lady, for by the end of November Alix was again pregnant. She was feeling unwell, as she usually did in the early stages of pregnancy and, during a stay at Livadia, she spent the evenings lying in bed while Nicky read to her. They read *War and Peace* in this way (Nicky reading it for the second time) and then embarked on a recently published biography of Alexander I by Nikolai Schilder, about which Nicky's cousin, historian Nikolai Mikhailovich, had been very enthusiastic. His usual labors pursued the Tsar even in the Crimea, as he told his mother: "Twice a week couriers bring me a mountain of papers, and on those days I am in a bad mood!"

As has been mentioned before, Nicky's tastes in literature were not especially highbrow, and certainly not avant-garde, but neither were they lacking in intellectual content. Likewise, his tastes in music and art were those of the educated middle-of-the-road bourgeois. He did have certain preferences. Musically, he was particularly drawn to the operas of Wagner, an enthusiasm he shared with Alix, their favorite being *Tristan und Isolde*. There was a Wagner season staged in St. Petersburg in the winter of 1898, and Nicky made a point of attending performances of every work and enjoyed them very much. On March 7 that year he and his mother attended the opening ceremony of the new Alexander III Museum (later to be called the Russian Museum) in the Mikhailovsky Palace. He had previously looked around the collection on several occasions and been very impressed. He already knew many of the works exhibited, as they had come from the imperial palaces; later that year he and Alix spent some time at Tsarskoe Selo supervising the hanging of other pictures to replace those removed for display in the museum. Nicky was not oblivious to the new artistic movements taking shape in Russia at the time, however, and was indeed supportive of some of them, particularly those that lay claim to the heritage of the old Russia of icon painting and traditional peasant crafts. This explains his sympathy for the *Mir iskusstva* (World of Art) group and journal of the same name, both of which came into being in 1898 under Diaghilev's leadership; from 1900 until 1904 this journal was even kept afloat by an annual subvention from the Tsar's private funds. In February 1899 he visited the first exhibition staged by the World of Art at the Stieglitz Museum, and in fact rarely missed an exhibition or theatrical performance during these years—even if the opinions he passed on them rarely moved beyond the word "interesting." Anything tending toward the avant-garde, however, was likely to be dismissed by him, whereas he particularly enjoyed the 28th Exhibition of the Society for Travelling Art Exhibitions (connected with the group known as the Wanderers or *Peredvizhniki*), which he attended in February 1900, where he would have seen the kind of works typified by the influential realist critic Vladimir Stasov as "healthy"—as opposed to the "pathological" productions of the so-called Decadent artists. As the World of Art movement also encompassed the Decadents, Nicholas's attitude toward Diaghilev's activities eventually became, at best, ambivalent.

The late summer of 1898 had been marked by Nicholas's springing upon the world a peace initiative, proposing disarmament and the calling of a peace conference, his proposals being made public for the first time in a circular drawn up by the Minister of Foreign Affairs Count Mikhail Muravyov and published in the *Pravitelstvennyi vestnik* (Government Messenger). This was circulated around the world on August 16, though the diplomatic corps had been given a preview of the circular four days earlier, when they had been invited to meet with Muravyov. The central message of the circular was that an end, or at least a limit (the Russian word *peredel* could be interpreted either way), should be put on the progressive development of modern armaments, and the ostensible impetus behind it was the desire to avoid both a huge financial burden for all countries involved in the arms race and a disastrous war. To continue to build up arms would, suggested the circular, "lead inevitably to the very cataclysm that all men seek to avoid and to horrors before which all thinking men must recoil." It concluded with a call to "all governments whose representatives are accredited to the Imperial Court to convene a conference for the purpose of discussing this grave problem."

Part of Nicky's vision in launching this initiative, expounded in interviews he granted to W. T. Stead, who traveled to Livadia to conduct them, appears to have been that the great powers should settle their differences in a similar way to the participants in a duel—using "seconds" who would act as negotiators, in the hope of averting war. One of his inspirations had been a six-volume work, *La Guerre Future,* written by Ivan Bloch, a Polish banker and railway entrepreneur, who had managed to obtain an audience with the Tsar at which he had set out his vision of the horrifying nature of any future major war and of the social collapse and revolution it would carry in its wake.

The initial international response to the Russian proposal was not encouraging. The French could not be expected to be in favor of any disarmament as long as the question of Alsace-Lorraine, ceded to the Prussians after the Franco-Prussian War, remained unresolved. The British government showed no inclination to take the Tsar's proposal seriously, while the German government reacted negatively, fearing they might be requested to relinquish Alsace and asserting the belief that the initiative was designed primarily to lessen Russian military expenditure. During the first few weeks there were positive responses from only Italy and Austria. The Tsar then dispatched Muravyov and the Minister of War, Alexei Kuropatkin, abroad for consultations, urging them to make clear that the suggestion was for a limitation of armaments, not a general disarmament.

A revised circular was issued by the Russian government in December, taking account of the reactions to the first and giving the reassurance that no current treaty obligations or political alignments would be up for discussion at the proposed conference. The revised document set out a number of proposals: All land and naval forces and military budgets should be maintained at current levels; the introduction of new weapons and explosives should be prohibited, along with the hurling of projectiles from balloons; the use of existing explosives should be limited; the use of submarines (the first experimental tests of which were just getting underway) should be prohibited in naval warfare; the Geneva Convention of 1884 should apply to naval warfare, with ships and boats engaged in lifesaving operations being recognized as neutral; and the 1874 declarations on the laws and customs of warfare should be revised. This second set of proposals received an even more negative response than the initial circular, leading Nicky to wonder why he had ever embarked on the process.

Despite all the negativity and hesitations, including by this time Nicky's own (his initial idealism soon being tempered by the realities of international politics), the Hague Conference, involving twenty European and four Asian states, along with the United States of America and Mexico, met from May 6 to July 17, under the presidency of the Russian ambassador to London, Baron Yegor E. Staal. The Hague had been chosen because Holland was one of the more "neutral" countries. Though the final agreement was rather watered down compared with the original circular, prohibitions against explosive bullets, projectiles dropped from balloons, and gas warfare were adopted, and the Geneva Convention was extended to naval warfare with the protection of hospital ships. It was agreed that the articles of war on the treatment of prisoners and wounded would be revised, and a declaration on the peaceful settlement of international disputes through mediation by third parties was adopted. The details of this agreement led to the establishment at The Hague of the Permanent Court of Arbitration (it is still there, housed in the Peace Palace).

For a few years after the Hague Conference (until the Russo-Japanese War showed a very different side of Russian foreign policy), Nicky's standing was high in Europe. When he fell seriously ill in November 1900, a report from Vienna published in *The Times* testified to his popularity on the European stage: "The Tsar's illness has caused genuine and profound regret among all classes in this country. Seldom has a foreign Sovereign excited such universal sympathy. His exemplary private life, no less than his well-known love of peace, has made him one of the most popular members of European Royalty. In conversation, as well as in the Press, he is always spoken of with the utmost respect. Fervent hopes are entertained that he may speedily recover and that his reign may yet be a long one." Unfortunately for the Tsar's reputation in his own country, the Hague Conference received little attention from the Russian public (as would later be the case with the peace negotiations with Japan), the educated members of which were more concerned with domestic politics by the time the conference opened.

Ever since the autumn of 1896 there had been sporadic disturbances in Russia, particularly among university students. In a letter to his uncle Sergei, approving the measures he was taking to quell the disturbances in Moscow, Nicky compared the lives of students in Russia and England, asserting that the British educational system, and particularly its emphasis on "the physical development of the younger generation" was much to be preferred to the Russian, which tended to produce "creatures with effete bodies and souls, torn away from their milieu and not knowing what to do with themselves." Russian students so easily found themselves enticed "along the wrong path," he thought, "incited and led astray by a few dozen scoundrels and rascals!" In the following February there were disorders at the University of St. Petersburg, the rector of which had warned the student body that drunken and disorderly behavior in restaurants, theaters, and other public places would not be tolerated and that the police intended to prevent such disturbances "at all costs." Many students interpreted this warning as an insult, and called for "guarantees." Protests, involving the obstruction of lectures and walkouts, quickly spread to the Institute for Women, the Military Medical Academy, the Institute of Mines, the Institute of Forestry, the Electrotechnical Institute, and the Academy of Arts, before spreading out from St. Petersburg to affect institutions in Moscow, Kiev, and Kharkov. Before long every university in Russia was affected. During the summer vacation of 1899 six ministers met to work out "temporary regulations" on military conscription for students who had been expelled from educational institutions for their part in the disorders. Finance Minister Sergei Witte was in support of this idea, whereas the War Minister, Alexei Kuropatkin, strongly opposed it. Nevertheless the "temporary regulations" created special boards to determine who was to be expelled and for how many years (one, two, or three). Expelled students were assigned to the army for a designated term of service, which could be reduced for good behavior.

In the spring of 1899, on March 18, Nicky, Alix, and their two daughters had moved, as was their custom at the end of the winter season, from St. Petersburg to Tsarskoe Selo, Nicky immediately setting off for a walk in the park on arrival. He was pleased that it took him little time to unpack and arrange his things, as he had arranged to have a complete set of everything he needed in each place. He found that even the more troublesome aspects of his work, such as attending grand receptions, were accomplished more easily at Tsarskoe than back in Petersburg; his enjoyment of his surroundings and particularly the ability to get out into the fresh air for exercise made everything feel less arduous. Alix was suffering from her old troubles with her legs, Nicky reporting to his mother that she felt well in general, but that walking was too painful for her and so she had to use a wheelchair. He made light of this affliction to Queen Victoria when he wrote to her toward the end of May: "Alix is feeling on the whole better and likes being rolled all over the place in her armchair, which is done by her husband!" Maria was born on June 14, and, as with his two previous daughters, there is no suggestion in Nicky's diary of any disappointment over her gender: "A happy day," he wrote, "the Lord sent us a third daughter—*Maria,* who was safely born at 12.10! Alix hardly slept all night, and towards morning the pains got stronger.

Thank God it was all over quite quickly! My darling felt well all day and fed the baby herself." Nevertheless, however supportive and loving her husband was—and in this he could not be faulted—and despite the fact there was nothing she could have done about it, Alix cannot have avoided feeling that yet again she had failed to fulfill the hopes and expectations of family and country. KR was quite explicit about this in his diary: "And so, there's no Heir. The whole of Russia will be disappointed by this news." Neither did Queen Victoria do much to help, with her comment to Nicky: "I am so thankful that dear Alicky has recovered so well, but I regret the 3rd girl for the country." As a consequence, Alix knew she would have to try again.

In addition to the muted and ambivalent happiness of the birth of another daughter, Nicky sustained a great sadness that month with the death from tuberculosis, at the age of twenty-eight, of his beloved brother Georgy, who had been his most trusted confidant for many years. Georgy's final letter to him, written about a fortnight before his death, was ostensibly a letter of congratulation on Maria's birth but sounds a note of farewell, a sense that the writer knew his end was approaching. Georgy writes of his sadness at never having met any of his brother's children, having been confined for the past eight years to his estate at Abbas Tuman in Georgia for the sake of its climate and thermal waters. Despite his avowed submission to the will of God (so like his brother in this), he cannot avoid a slight tone of bitterness when he contemplates the difference between the active life he once enjoyed, particularly his naval service, and what he has now become. Shortness of breath meant he could no longer even walk. He died suddenly, after having been out for a ride on his motorcycle, and was discovered lying by the roadside, having suffered a hemorrhage.

Maria Fyodorovna, who had several times been to visit her son in Georgia, was inconsolable at the news of his death (which Nicky had to break to her). Nicky himself had last seen his brother four years previously, and he, too, wept over his death. At the prospect of having to go and meet Georgy's coffin as it arrived from the Caucasus, he wrote to Alix: "Well! There's nothing to be done, we must as usual take courage and carry our cross patiently, as Jesus Christ bids us. But sometimes it is overwhelmingly hard!" Their younger brother Misha was also deeply affected; in addition to grief at the death of a sibling, he also had now to accept the unwanted burden of becoming the heir presumptive. This unhappy conjunction of events—the birth of the Tsar's third daughter with the death of his former heir—can only have exacerbated Alix's sense of failure at not having secured the succession.

What kept Alix going was the fact that she and Nicky were as much in love as when they had first married. Nicky's tender care for his wife was such that he spent part of the evening before leaving to meet Georgy's coffin writing her a letter to be given to her after he had left, as was often their habit. So that it will come as a surprise to her, he sits writing it in his study while she is close by on her balcony, knowing he is busy writing a letter, but not realizing she is the intended recipient. "I do not want to let a day pass without your hearing from your husband, either from his lips or on paper—how he loves you and the three little ones!" he writes. After expressing sorrow at the thought of setting out to receive his deceased brother, he goes on to talk of his own domestic happiness, of the great joy of having Alix by his side—along with the admission that he still does not find it easy to show his emotions outwardly. He is also determined to let her know how much he loves their children—the "three little cherubs"; never from his lips will Alix hear any criticism or disappointment that she goes on producing daughters. After completing his letter that evening, he joined his wife for a game of bezique. She was overjoyed to receive his missive on the following day, and told him in her reply how much she missed him physically: "The night was a lonely one and each time I woke up and put my hand out, I touched cold pillow instead of a dear warm hand and nobody to shake and poke and bother by waking up."

In the spring of 1900, while staying in Moscow, both Nicky and Alix experienced a deepening of their religious faith and devotion, as practiced in the Orthodox liturgy. Nicky wrote to tell Xenia about what he had been feeling; it is worth noting that the greater importance Nicky began to attach to his faith from now on did not come about as a result of Alix's piety and "religiosity," which has often been assumed, but almost the other way around. "I cannot describe to you the feelings I have experienced here since the beginning of Holy week," he wrote, "but I can assure you it is only now I have realized what it really means to *fast*. Alix shares my feelings completely, which is a great joy to me. We go morning and evening to various churches within the towers; the services in these ancient churches produce a feeling of enchantment." It is significant that this experience occurred in the Kremlin's ancient churches, this being all of a piece with the imperial couple's understanding of the Russian people and the history of Holy Russia—an understanding demonstrated also in their artistic tastes. Such a feeling would not have come so naturally to them in the neoclassical nineteenth-century churches of St. Petersburg; their commitment to old Russia—and its resonance for them with their own religious faith—also explains why they chose old architectural "Russian" (or neo-Russian) models for the new churches they later commissioned (such as the Fyodorovsky Sobor at Tsarskoe Selo). In Moscow they were joined in their devotions by Ella and Grand Duke

Sergei, also a very pious man, who habitually wore round his neck a small golden icon of the Mother of God containing a relic of St. Arseny, a fourteenth-century ascetic and hesychast. Sergei had connections with various monasteries in Russia, and twice traveled to the Holy Land to pray at the Tomb of Christ. This shared religious devotion between the two sisters and their respective husbands makes the later rift between Ella and Alix, as the latter's religious sensibility became ever more entwined with the figure of Grigory Rasputin, all the more striking.

Even in this exalted state, the old playful, slightly childish, Nicky was still in evidence, highly amused at an incident in the Kremlin's Church of the Annunciation. The four of them had taken turns bending down to kiss the church's wonder-working icon, which was surrounded by lamps, and Ella, in so doing, had caught her hat on one of the lamps. She tried to extricate herself by turning her head, but it was no good; she remained attached to the lamp, becoming more and more embarrassed. Meanwhile the priest, not noticing anything, was continuing to tell his august visitors all about the church, while they—apart from the blushing Ella—were trying not to laugh. Finally Dmitry Trepov (at that time head of the Moscow police) managed to detach her, and to hold the lamp steady so that no oil spilled on to her. As they emerged from the church, Ella red and flustered, with her hair in a mess, everyone acted as though nothing had happened, bowing and smiling. Nicky's relish at recounting this story to his sister suggests not only that he retained a sense of mischief, but also that there was something rather priggish about Ella, which led to a certain enjoyment at seeing her embarrassed.

The imperial couple's tastes in art and architecture, their leaning toward the neo-Russian and away from more modernist trends, was one reason why the intelligentsia held them in some derision. Another was their uxoriousness, their embrace of "family life," and even the fact that they often shared a bed. The normal practice among the Russian upper classes was to keep separate bedrooms, with the husband usually sleeping on an ottoman in his study. Members of the intelligentsia also maintained this habit if they could afford it, while sharing a bed was seen as—always that abusive term—"bourgeois." The whole idea of family life and indeed of procreation, of which Nicky and Alix were such prominent exemplars, was held in very low esteem by influential members of the Russian artistic and literary elite, such as Zinaida Hippius and Dmitry Merezhkovsky (who, though married to one another, eschewed anything as mundane as sex) and Alexander Blok (grandson of Nicky's old chemistry tutor).

As for the results of Nicky and Alix's acts of procreation, the two elder girls always gave Maria a rather tough time, tending to exclude her from their games as she grew older and, while she was still a toddler, inclined to knock her over if no adults were watching. She was deeply fond of her father, and hated not being able to see him when, toward the end of October 1900, the usually robust Nicky fell seriously ill while staying at Livadia. Now it was his turn to have dreadful pains in his neck and back, while Alix rose to the occasion and helped to nurse him. A crisis always enabled her to forget her own indispositions, at least temporarily. Initially the imperial doctor in attendance, Dr. Girsh, had been adamant that the Tsar was suffering from influenza and not, as was feared, from typhoid fever. Fortunately Girsh had the good sense—and sense of self-preservation—to call in another, expert opinion. A Dr. Tikhonov arrived, who eventually confirmed that this was indeed typhoid. "It's astounding that influenza should suddenly turn into typhoid!" Xenia remarked disingenuously. At first Baron Fredericks, the Minister of the Imperial Court, found himself in the impossible position of being constantly asked for news and not being allowed to reveal anything. He had to enlist the help of Xenia and Sandro to persuade Alix to allow him to issue a bulletin. She consented, appearing to understand the necessity of keeping the world informed when the Tsar of All the Russias was dangerously ill, agreeing with the others that "there is nothing worse than trying to conceal things!" In later years, in the case of her son, she would take an opposite view. "Thank God Alix is calm," Xenia commented—with the unspoken implication that this was not always the case. Alix had also been persuaded not to share Nicky's bed while he was so ill, and contagious; "at least the doctors have achieved that much," wrote Xenia, this time the implication being that it could be very hard to persuade Alix to do anything she did not want to do. This was a protracted illness, Nicky feeling particularly unwell about ten days after its onset, as his temperature mounted and he became increasingly weak and irritable. The crisis came around the middle of November, the doctors fearing that Nicky might have an intestinal hemorrhage. Then began the slow recovery. He was still convalescent when the news arrived of the death of Alix's beloved grandmother, Queen Victoria, in January 1901. Grand Duke Mikhail set off for England to represent the imperial family at the Queen-Empress's funeral. By now Alix was four months pregnant, and had been unable to spend much of the early part of this pregnancy lying down. This does not seem to have had a bad effect on her—rather the reverse—KR commenting: "[The Empress] is looking very beautiful and despite her pregnancy, feels wonderful, unlike the other occasions; for this reason, everyone is anxiously hoping that this time it will be a son."

On February 14, a former student called Pyotr Karpovich, who had twice been expelled for his participation in student disorders, shot the Minister of Education, Nikolai Bogolepov, who died of his wounds a fortnight later. This was the first act of terrorism in several years, and was designed to attack the imperial government, rather than this particular minister. Bogolepov was still fighting for his life when the first street demonstration erupted in St. Petersburg, in the square opposite the Kazan Cathedral, on February 19, the fortieth anniversary of the emancipation of the serfs. The police herded the two to three hundred demonstrators into the courtyard of the City Duma, where they recorded all their names. More serious disorders took place in Moscow, lasting for five days from February 22–26. But the most violent demonstration took place in St. Petersburg on March 4, again in front of the Kazan Cathedral. In clashes with the forces of law and order, more than thirty demonstrators were injured, as were two officers, twenty policemen, and four cossacks.

Discontent, rioting, and assassinations at home led to massive security operations being launched on the occasions when the Tsar traveled abroad, for there was always the fear that groups of exiled Russian revolutionary elements might take the opportunity of an imperial visit to launch an attack. The security was immense, for instance, when Nicky and Alix paid their second visit to France in September 1901 (by which time they had a fourth daughter, Anastasia). Prior to arriving there, and in accordance with an almost annual custom, Nicky had met his cousin Kaiser Wilhelm at Danzig and watched German naval maneuvers, the two Emperors meeting on board their respective ships, the *Standart* and the *Hohenzollern.* As was usual during the mutual toasts, the Kaiser spoke in German while the Tsar replied in French. Nicky told his mother that all had passed off well during this visit, Willy being "in good spirits, calm and very pleasant." The *Standart* then sailed on to Kiel, where Nicky was joined by Alix before proceeding to Dunkirk. After a windy and stormy night, the *Standart* arrived at Dunkirk on a morning of bright autumn sunlight, entering the harbor "flying the French flag and its own Eagle side by side on the main" and "escorted by two large cruisers with the French colours at the fore." This visit was very different from the one to which the population of France had responded with such enthusiasm in the coronation year, this time the level of security preventing popular participation. The people of Dunkirk had nevertheless been expecting to see something of their imperial visitors and had made preparations to decorate the whole town lavishly—but as it turned out they were informed that the visit would be restricted to a very small area that would be strictly cordoned off. Paris and Versailles were to be avoided altogether as groups of Russian revolutionaries were known to be present there.

After Dunkirk the imperial party proceeded to Saint-Malo, where crowds of people flocked to the harbor to catch what was likely to be their only glimpse of the Tsar. "The *Standart,* which is almost of a size with the French warships, then went slowly ahead, while her escort saluted the French flag with 21 guns. Then, with the Emperor on the bridge, the Imperial yacht steamed slowly down the line. As she forged level with each vessel, the bands on board struck up the Russian Hymn and the Emperor was cheered by the entire ship's company." But even here every precaution had been taken to keep the public as far away as possible, and access was very restricted.

For part of the tour the imperial train was used, its doors and windows veiled by silk curtains displaying double-headed eagles, its eleven carriages resembling, at least to the eyes of the *Times*'s correspondent covering the visit, an armored train, crammed with police agents in "astrakhan hats, long top boots, and long black coats with belts." Every twenty-five meters along the track stood a soldier with a loaded rifle. The *Times*'s correspondent assumed that the extent of the security operation was concealed from the person it was designed to protect, for otherwise the Tsar himself "would be frightened at beholding the terror of those called upon to watch over his security." At Compiègne, where the great château, fallen into disuse since the collapse of Napoleon III's Second Empire, was briefly brought back to life in order to house the imperial guests and their entourage as well as the French President, the Prime Minister, and their staffs, security continued to be very tight. In anticipation of the visit, people hoping to catch a glimpse of the Tsar and join in the festivities at least from afar, having apparently been promised ample facilities and entertainment by the mayor, were pouring into the town, only to be disappointed on arrival. Hotel accommodation and other lodgings quickly ran out, as did supplies of food—and there was nothing to see anyway. The imperial train was too closely guarded for anyone to approach it, and only those on official business could hope to see anything of life at the château. Those few who did see it, however, found the place transformed, ablaze with electric light after having been in darkness for over thirty years, and alive with the sounds and smells of chefs, horses, dogs, soldiers, military bands, and servants bustling to and fro. "Suddenly to see all this and to think of the contrast with what Compiègne had to show to its visitors only a few weeks ago, is to make one fancy that he is living in a world of dreams," enthused the man from *The Times.*

While based at Compiègne, the imperial visitors traveled to Reims to watch maneuvers, where it was noticed that Alix, though looking tired, occupied herself with taking photographs. They also visited the cathedral. Otherwise during their stay, they followed a similar routine to their usual one at home, Nicky getting up early and going out for a long walk with his favorite dog (who had made the trip to France with him), being joined after about an hour and a half by Alix.

Then Nicky would return to his apartments to work until noon on documents that had been sent to him from Russia, and would then give audiences until lunchtime and into the afternoon. Despite enjoying deploying her camera, Alix was unable to relax on this trip, observers noting her unwillingness to forget her imperial rank and treat the wife of the President, Madame Loubet, as of equal standing with herself. It is likely that it was both self-consciousness and the consciousness of being watched by reporters and officials that made Alix so stiff, so jealous of her prerogatives as a sovereign and unable to behave naturally, as well as the fact that she had not been born into such an exalted position. Nicky, who had lived in the rarefied imperial milieu for his whole life, appeared far more at his ease and less threatened than his wife at the prospect of being seen on equal terms with the President of a republic. The Tsar "has been willing with perfect good grace to forget the considerable elevation in which he lives and moves and has his being," commented the *Times*'s correspondent. Nicky was also more aware than Alix of the desirability of maintaining good relations with France and of his own role in helping the wheels of the alliance to turn smoothly. In short, he worked his usual charm, while his wife did her best but could not forget herself sufficiently to charm in anything like equal measure.

In the autumn of 1901, after the visit to France, Alix took a course of mud-baths at Spała, writing to Xenia to tell her about the daily routine—early morning bath, cocoa and rest, reading, getting up for lunch, and resting again before dinner. Alix was very fond of Xenia, beginning her letter "Darling Chicken" and signing off "Your tenderly devoted old Hen." At this stage of her life, she was still riding, at least occasionally, and would have liked to do so more often, had she been able. Her husband, meanwhile, was out hunting stag, accompanied for part of the time by Prince Henry of Prussia, the brother of Kaiser Wilhelm. On his return home, Prince Henry reported to the German chancellor on what he had observed of his cousin's character: "The tsar is benevolent and courteous but not as mild as frequently thought. He knows what he wants, and he won't yield to anyone. He has a humanitarian outlook, but he intends to preserve the autocratic principle. He is open-minded on religious questions but always avoids public controversy with the Orthodox Church. He is a good military man." He also reported that Nicky had "no love for parliaments" and had spoken disparagingly of King Edward VII's lack of real power.

The stay in Spała was spoilt for Alix by the news that her brother Ernie and his wife Ducky were intending to divorce—"*Yes, divorce,*" Nicky wrote in horror to his mother. According to her husband, Alix was trying not to let her grief show, but this grief was very great and not unmingled with a sense of personal disgrace. It is hard for us at the beginning of the twenty-first century to understand, still less to sympathize with, Nicky, Alix, and Maria Fyodorovna—who was equally horrified at this development—when they declare that they would be better able to cope with bereavement than with divorce. "I completely agree with what you say in this instance," Maria Fyodorovna wrote to Nicky, "that the loss of someone near is preferable to the public disgrace of—a divorce." Alix's letter to Xenia on the subject, written on November 7, when she was back at Tsarskoe Selo, is revealing on several counts. She had clearly known for some time that all was not well between Ernie and Ducky, and she imputes the desire for the divorce to the latter (as a fond sister, her brother must be blameless): "It is with a very heavy heart that I write to you today. Yes dear, it is true, Ducky wishes to be divorced and in a few days all will be finally settled. It nearly broke my heart when I got the news, it was so quite unexpected, I always hoped that in time things would come right." As well as being the active party in seeking to divorce, Ducky is blamed for the failure of the marriage: "They have parted friends and each wrote to me saying of the other that they were the truest of friends and would always remain so. Only with her character married life thus was impossible to continue." It would appear from this that Ducky's fault—"with her character"—in the eyes of her sister-in-law, is that to be "friends" was not enough to sustain a marriage; when one bears in mind what Alix does not say—but clearly, even if only subconsciously, knew—that Ernie was homosexual (or at least bisexual), her remarks start to make more sense. What Ducky wanted—or needed—from her marriage was sex, and Ernie had given up having it with her. Alix keeps trying to remind herself that she must be charitable, but she is finding it difficult: "It is not for *us to judge* tho it is an awful step they are taking." There was also the danger—in fact, the likelihood—that Ernie's secret would be talked about, or at least that all sorts of speculation would surround this breakup and that such speculation would redound on his relatives, for Alix pleads: "Only one thing I entreat of you, darling Xenia, whenever you hear nasty gossip, at once put a stop to it, for their sakes and ours. They parted as their characters could impossibly get on together, that is enough for the public." (The Supreme Court of Hesse officially granted the divorce on the grounds of "invincible mutual antipathy." Ernie went on to have two sons by his second wife, Princess Eleonore of Solms-Hohensolms-Lich, whom he married in February 1905.) Try as she will, Alix cannot refrain from criticizing her soon-to-be-ex sister-in-law; in denial about her brother's homosexuality, she can do no other: "She will not be missed in the country, as she never made herself beloved nor showed any liking for the country, alas! Poor girl, she is utterly miserable now without a home, tho' he leaves her the sweet Child. His home is desolate and everything will remind him of her whom he still cares for." Her Panglossian "always all is for the best" sounds in this context like a mantra, something she has learned by heart and is determined to hang on to, despite evidence to the contrary: "But I cannot write any more about it; you can think how we sisters who adore him and are very fond of her, have suffered. But we must believe that always all is for the best." And then comes the nub of it for Alix, the sense of personal embarrassment and shame over what has occurred, making it harder than ever for her to face the autumn and winter season in St. Petersburg with equanimity. Her fondness for Xenia is evident in the openness with which she confides her distress on this count: "It is doubly hard beginning 'society' life again when all know that one's brother and sister in law have gone asunder. All one's pride is crushed out of one."

On April 2, 1902, there was another assassination, this time of Dmitry Sipyagin, who had succeeded Ivan Goremykin as Minister of Internal Affairs in October 1899. Sipyagin was an archconservative, his appointment appearing to signal a policy of retrenchment and further underlining of the autocratic principle. He was also favored by Witte, who may have been behind this appointment—at least insofar as the Tsar had asked for his advice and appeared to have taken it. The man who shot him, a Socialist Revolutionary called Stefan Balmashov, had inveigled himself, dressed in the uniform of an adjutant, into the Mariinsky Palace where the State Council was in session, on the pretext of having a parcel to deliver from Grand Duke Sergei. He then fired one shot at Sipyagin, who died an hour later.

During these years certain characteristics of Nicholas's technique of ruling had begun to define themselves. His sister Xenia complained (not directly to him, of course, but to their mother) that his attitude was too much that of a spectator, that when actions were taken of which he did not approve—such as, for instance, the harsh measures taken to control student protests—the Tsar refused to acknowledge that he could have intervened. Indecisiveness had become the failing most often attributed to him, particularly by those who found themselves affected by it. Neither his relatives nor his officials liked the fact that Nicholas was prepared to listen—unless, of course, he was listening to them. On April 3, 1902, Ella poured out her anxieties to him, passionately if incoherently (punctuation never being her strong point), in a letter written without the knowledge of her husband. This was the day after Sipyagin's assassination, and Ella seems to have feared further shootings if Nicky were not "energetic" (a favorite word of both sisters when they wished to cajole someone into action). She recommended that he appoint Vyacheslav Plehve to take Sipyagin's place, on the grounds of his experience and honesty. Ella sounds confused (she is clearly in much distress) as she criticizes Nicky for what sound like mutually exclusive qualities—that he is too gentle, yet considered unkind: "Don't be so gentle—*all* think you are *wavering and weak,* they *no more* speak of you as *kind* and it makes my heart ache so too too bitterly." It is little wonder if both Nicky and Alix rather dreaded being the recipients of Ella's advice. Perhaps her words make more sense when considered in light of Xenia's earlier comments about Nicky being too much of an observer, and the suggestion is that, by being less gentle with his ministers and advisers, he would be perceived as kinder to his people. Whatever she meant, the desire to instruct, later so dominant in Alix, was likewise central to her sister's character. In both cases, this may have been partly the result of frustration; the two women, daughters of an equally determined and resourceful mother, were full of pent-up energy and undirected intelligence, the not-very-powerful wives of powerful men. They both seem to have felt that, if only they could be in charge themselves, everything would be sorted out; they never, however, managed to work in conjunction with one another, combining their strengths. Instead, particularly as they grew older, they were as frustrated by one another as by everybody else.

Nicky did indeed appoint Vyacheslav Plehve to succeed Sipyagin within two days of the latter's death, though whether he did so in response to Ella's prompting is doubtful. Plehve, apart from "having experience" and being "honest," was known to favor harsh repressive measures (so Ella's advice again sounds contradictory, for how could appointing Plehve make Nicky appear "kind"?). He was also Sergei Witte's bitterest rival, on this occasion Witte having been unable to prevent the appointment, despite having been consulted (a fact that only served to strengthen Nicky's reputation for "indecisiveness," as those asked by the Tsar for their opinions always liked to imagine that his listening to them signified assent). Sipyagin's assassin, it was decided, should be tried before a court-martial rather than in the civil courts—for the reason that only a court-martial could impose the death penalty. Balmashov's subsequent execution by hanging in May was the first political execution of Nicholas's reign.

In August of the following year (1903) Witte was dismissed from his post as Minister of Finance, a dismissal for which he was not at all prepared. Nicky, in the most polite and outwardly considerate way possible, presented him with a fait accompli by announcing during the general course of business that he had already given orders to have Witte appointed Chairman of the Committee of Ministers (replacing Ivan Durnovo, who had died at the beginning of the summer) and that he had selected his successor at the Ministry of Finance. As it turned out, this meant Witte would be well placed in 1905, in the wake of the

October Manifesto, to become Chairman of the *Council* of Ministers, effectively Prime Minister. Neither man foresaw such an eventuality in the summer of 1903, however, Witte merely feeling hard done by and angry with the Tsar, whom he never really forgave. And Witte, a man given to intrigue and plotting for his own ends, was a dangerous enemy to have acquired. In virtually forcing the Tsar to sign the manifesto granting a legislative assembly two years later, he could be seen as getting his own back.

Ernie and Ducky were not the only people connected to Nicky and Alix to be engaging in marital irregularities during these years. In October 1902 Nicky's uncle, Grand Duke Pavel—the youngest of Alexander III's brothers and the one Nicky found easiest to get on with—married a commoner, and a divorcée, called Olga Pistohlkors. The wedding took place in Livorno. As KR commented in his diary, "The affair is made more complicated by the fact that, as I have heard from two different sides, Pavel had given his word, through Vladimir, to the Emperor that he would not marry Olga Pistohlkors." The Tsar heard the news from Plehve, who had himself been informed by the bride's mother. Nicky, hoping his informant was somehow mistaken, sent a coded telegram to his uncle, asking for verification. When it became clear that not only was the news true, but that Pavel had been preparing this act for some time, arranging his finances in readiness for a lengthy stay abroad, Nicky took decisive action, basing his decision on how his "unforgettable Papa" had "dealt with Misha"—that is, with Grand Duke Mikhail Mikhailovich, known as Miche-Miche to the family, who had contracted a morganatic marriage without permission in 1891. Miche-Miche had been exiled from Russia and had lived in England since his marriage. Nicky expostulated to his mother (who was staying in Copenhagen) about the treatment that would now have to be meted out to Pavel—which included his two children by his first wife Alexandra of Greece (who had died in 1891 while giving birth to her son) being handed into the care of Sergei and Ella. "The closer the relative who refuses to submit to our family rules, the more severe his punishment should be. Don't you agree, dear Mama?" wrote Nicky. "The statutes on the imperial family say that morganatic marriages are forbidden," he continued, "and that no marriage contracted WITHOUT PERMISSION is considered real." Nicky felt that he had now to act with exemplary severity, in order to prevent the rest of his uncles and cousins going off the rails in similar fashion. His indignation is almost comic: "What guarantee is there that Kirill won't do the same thing tomorrow, or that Boris or Sergei Mikhailovich won't do it the day after that? A whole colony of the imperial family will be living in Paris with their semi-legal or illegal wives." The other event that had upset Nicky in recent days was the death of one of his beloved dogs—"good old Imam"—which had happened on almost the same day as that of one of his horses, Raven. Both animals were buried on an island close to the Alexander Palace, on which stood the so-called Children's House, a miniature cottage originally designed for the children of Nicholas I.

Maria Fyodorovna's letter on the subject of Pavel and his misdoings crossed with Nicky's, and it shows that her attitude was very similar to his, with some added dislike of Pavel's chosen partner—"that stupid woman"—and a fear of scandal. Pavel himself wrote to his two children—Maria, then aged twelve, and Dmitry, aged eleven—to explain the situation to them; they were understandably shocked and upset—but more by the news that their father was not allowed to return to Russia than that he had a new wife.

All the Romanovs' marital and other disputes were forgotten for one magical night on January 22, 1903, when a costume ball was held in the Winter Palace, which all the guests were instructed to attend in seventeenth-century dress; as Sandro put it in his memoirs, "for at least one night Nicky wanted to be back in the glorious past of our family." A special train had brought roses, lilies, and lilac from the Crimea for the occasion, and champagne and caviar were served by pages in seventeenth-century livery. Greeted by a fanfare of trumpets, Nicky and Alix opened the ball with a polonaise. Nicky was dressed as the second Romanov Tsar, Alexei Mikhailovich, in a braided coat of gold, cream, and raspberry brocade over a pearl-edged kaftan; on his head he wore a cap-crown covered in jewels, with a deep sable border. The costume had been made by Kaffi, the imperial theatrical costumier, and was a copy of Tsar Alexei's formal gala outfit. Some of the accoutrements, such as Alexei's highly decorated staff, had been borrowed for the occasion from the Kremlin treasury. Alix was dressed as Tsar Alexei's first wife, Tsarina Maria Miloslavskaya, in a gold brocade sarafan trimmed with emeralds and silver thread. A traditional domelike headdress studded with emeralds, diamonds, and pearls, from which fell a brocade veil, and extremely heavy earrings, made it impossible for her to bend her head—and indeed, she looks very rigid and somewhat miserable in the official photographs taken of her and Nicky on this occasion. A month later they were able to watch film footage of themselves in these costumes, shown at Tsarskoe Selo by the court photographer Hahn.

CHAPTER SEVEN

Family Matters

1907-1911

Dear little children! Thank you for remembering me, for your sweet words, for your pure heart and your love for the people of god. Love the whole of god's nature, the whole of his creation in particular this earth. The mother of god was always occupied with flowers and needlework.

—Telegram from Rasputin to the imperial children, February 1909

On July 17, 1907, Alix wrote to Nicky from Peterhof, pursuing her practice of writing him a letter that he would find waiting for him once he had set off on a journey (on this occasion he was going to meet the Kaiser in the Baltic off Swinemünde). She told him that their "Friend" Grigory was watching over him, and that consequently all would go well. Any opportunity for the couple to be together on that day of parting had been missed—by the constraining presence of others but also by Alix's own infirmities—this time it was her "stupid neck" that had somehow prevented her from spending time alone with Nicky. In her expressions of love to her husband, her "One and all," there is—despite her infirmities—still a strong physical element in how she feels about him: "Tenderly and fondly with an aching heart—I kiss you—every sweet little spot I love so passionately." Nicky replied from on board the imperial yacht *Standart*. "I feel quite lonely by myself down in the cabins," he wrote. "The doors to yours are open and I look into them often, always thinking I will find my

Wify. I miss you and the children frightfully, so do all the officers!" Nevertheless, he admitted he was relieved Alix was not with him when the ship hit stormy waters and rolled considerably, and many of the younger crew members were sick. Despite the weather, Nicky did what he could to make life on board enjoyable for the officers serving him: "At table, Fredericks sits at your place and Izvolsky on my left. The latter tells me lots of interesting things. I send occasional winks to the boys at the other end and see broad smiles in answer." This was the first meeting between the Tsar and the Kaiser in two years, since Björkö—the secret treaty of which had never come into operation. The toasts exchanged on this occasion were deliberately noncommittal, Nicholas mentioning the "continuation of kindred relations and traditional friendships" and William referring to "the unchangeable friendship between our dynasties and our people."

The summer of 1907 was also a time of yet more family dramas over unsuitable marriage plans, with a continuation of the saga of Misha's relationship with Dina Kossikovskaya (whom KR knew as having played a court lady in his production of *Hamlet* at the Hermitage Theatre). The fear among the family was that Misha would decide to marry this young woman—and that he might do so abroad, where no one would be able to stop him. According to Xenia, her brother had indeed decided to marry Dina, and had even found a priest prepared to conduct the ceremony (for a large sum). But the plan had come to light before it could be put into operation, and Dina had been forbidden to go to her estate, near where the wedding was planned to take place. Misha was upset and furious, and the resultant scenes made his mother distraught. "There was a tempestuous scene with Mama," recorded Xenia. "Misha came to tell her that he was going to town, and she forbade him to go to her ["her" being the lady in question]—he replied that he was going anyway, which he of course did. Mama had to go upstairs after this—she was terribly upset, all day she had palpitations and pains in her arm." Xenia's interpretation of the situation was that it was a plot on the part of Dina and her father to "catch" the Grand Duke "at all costs," and that others were also involved. Misha's aide-de-camp, A. A. Mordvinov, she reported, was "in despair, as indeed we all are, but there is *nothing* to be done, he doesn't want to listen to anyone, and simply doesn't care . . ."

"What harm our family does to itself," lamented KR in his diary, "and how it undermines the Emperor and the ruling house!" Meanwhile, as KR also noted, the Emperor had decided to recognize the marriage of Grand Duke Kirill, thus granting the wishes of his uncle, Kirill's father, Grand Duke Vladimir; Ducky was to be known as Grand Duchess Victoria, and their daughter was to be recognized as an imperial princess. KR (the married active homosexual) found this very difficult to accept; how could Vladimir's request, he wondered, "legitimize that, which is not legal? After all, Kirill married his first cousin, which is not allowed by the church." Implicit in KR's questioning is criticism of his friend and relative, the Tsar: "Where do we have a strong authority, acting with reflection and continuity? One becomes more and more fearful for the future. Everywhere is arbitrary rule, indulgence, weakness." Whatever else may be said about Nicky, his habitual deep-seated reserve is all the more striking when set against the background of his highly emotional family, most of whom (including his mother and younger brother) seem to have been given to turbulent scenes. Perhaps he feared just such a lack of control on his own part, and did not wish to give way to it. Perhaps he, too, could be "turbulent" in private.

The annual summer holiday on board the *Standart* was always a time of particular joy for the imperial family. Each year the children would be eager to see whether any changes had been made since the previous summer, and would greet their old friends among the officers with delight. Once the yacht was anchored at a chosen spot among the Finnish islands, a routine of daily activities was quickly established. The Tsar liked to start his mornings by taking a kayak out to sea. He could not of course expect this to be a solitary expedition, and was followed not only by an officer in a second kayak but also by a light gig manned by seven rowers and with an officer at the helm, ready to give immediate assistance in the event of the Tsar getting into difficulties. It must have been strenuous exercise for all of them, as Nicky handled the kayak with expertise, and it was a challenge to keep up with him. Meanwhile Alix would spend the morning in her cabins, Olga and Tatiana would read or sew, while the three younger children would disembark at about ten o'clock to go and play.

Alexei would be accompanied by his nurse, Maria Vishnyakova; an assistant nurse; and the sailor Derevenko, while Maria and Anastasia were supervised by Mlle Schneider, a woman who fulfilled several roles in the imperial family. In addition, a sailor was designated to watch over each child. The whole group would also be accompanied by the commandant of the yacht, Chagin, and a chief officer. On the coast, the group would divide into two, Alexei and his party going off to play separately from his sisters. While this move was designed partly to afford the hemophiliac child extra protection in his games, it was presented to him by his parents as a privilege—to prevent the little girls spoiling his important manly pursuits—and so he went off quite happily, his vanity duly flattered. Maria and Anastasia were also content with the arrangement, particularly as Mlle Schneider was hardly a stern supervisor: "Slender, fragile, self-effacing, this young lady was active everywhere, and ready for any sacrifice. . . . She adored the Empress and the children. Her capacity for work was astonishing. She taught Alexandra Fyodorovna Russian, and was at the same time her private secretary; she did all the shopping for Her Majesty; she accompanied the children whenever they went out. She was infinitely sweet-tempered and good-hearted. One sole shortcoming she had: The children paid not the slightest attention to anything she said."

In the summer of 1907, the three-year-old Alexei's favorite game was leapfrog, which he loved to play with the burly Derevenko. He would accomplish his "leap" by climbing up onto the tall and sturdy sailor and then sliding down over his back with his legs apart. Once he had done enough "leaping" himself, he would get down on all fours and call out: "Your turn, Derevenko!" The burly sailor would set off at a run and jump over the little boy, just brushing him with his hand, to the child's immense delight. Anyone who owned a camera—and photography was an immensely popular hobby for most of the participants on these trips—loved to take pictures of the chubby little Tsarevich, dressed in his white sailor suit, a tiny velvet bag containing his handkerchief worn over his shoulder. But he usually had to be caught unaware, as whenever he saw a camera pointed at him, he would pull a face. Spiridovich was very pleased to have managed to catch him in his leapfrog position, just as he was calling: "Your turn, Derevenko!"

Everyone would return to the yacht midmorning, in plenty of time for luncheon at half-past twelve, prior to which the whole family would walk along the row of officers and salute them. Luncheon was attended not only by the yacht's officers and members of the retinue but also by officers of the other ships in the squadron, according to a roster. The men would begin with *zakuski* and vodka (the Emperor drinking two shots at most), and then they would take their seats at the table, where the Empress and the two elder girls would be waiting, along with the maids-of-honor and Ania Vyrubova. The only wine Nicky drank during the meal was port, sent to him by the King of England. He drank one glass of it, out of a special golden cup. Count von Benckendorff, Grand Marshal of the Imperial Court, sat at the opposite end of the table from the Emperor, keeping a watchful eye on everything that went on during the meal. These were relaxed occasions, during which Nicky would chat happily and without constraint. After 1908, the last year during which Alix's health was tolerable, at least sporadically, the Empress no longer came to the table. Instead she would lie in an armchair on the bridge, in order to be able to see the Emperor through the window. She would then summon the officer on watch to come and talk with her. Spiridovich comments: "She always spoke to the officers in Russian, of which she had perfect command, although she spoke it rather slowly. She also spoke Russian to her children in front of strangers. But when addressing the Emperor, she always spoke in English, and it was also English which she spoke to the children when they were alone."

After dessert, the Emperor would say, "Gentlemen, you may smoke," and would take out his gold cigarette case, a gift from the Empress, containing Turkish cigarettes sent to him every year by the sultan. Coffee would follow, after which everyone would rise and make the sign of the cross, the guests would make a deep bow to the Emperor and Empress, and all would go out onto the bridge. Here Nicky would engage one or two people in conversation, and then the guests would depart. The afternoons would be devoted to walks, Alix still being able to join in as late as 1908, she and her daughters all wearing white dresses and straw hats and carrying walking sticks.

The summer of 1908 marked a high point in the life of the imperial family. Elections to the Third State Duma had taken place in September and October 1907, the resultant membership consisting in large part of people prepared to work with, rather than against, the government. The Duma's first session had opened without ceremony on November 1. The session of November 13 included a stormy debate over the wording of a proposed message of salutation to the Tsar; the argument was over whether the greeting should include the word "autocracy" and whether it should mention "the constitution." In other words, it concerned the contradiction at the heart of the attempt to introduce a form of democracy, however limited, into the Tsarist system. The rightist members wanted the salutation to read "To His Majesty the Sovereign Emperor, Autocrat of All the Russias," while the Kadet (Constitutional Democratic) and Progressive factions insisted that they would only vote for the greeting if it contained no reference to "autocracy." The vote went in favor of the latter elements, and so the right-wingers refused to subscribe to the message and instead sent the Tsar a separate greeting of their own. Nicholas was outraged that his title should be rejected in this way by the Duma, and he never forgot this episode. Nevertheless, he was prepared to believe that this Duma would get on with its work satisfactorily, if the members demonstrated a willingness to do so. He left the running of it to his Prime Minister, Stolypin. The only serious clash that occurred during the first session of the Duma concerned naval reconstruction, the Duma proving unwilling to approve the funds necessary for getting on with this at once. So by and large in 1908 the worst of the political upheavals seemed to be behind the imperial family, and the children were happy and appeared healthy, as did the Empress. There is a clear sense in Spiridovich's account of that year's holiday of the power of Alix's personality. When she was happy, so was everyone else; the obverse would be equally true: "There had been a particularly agreeable atmosphere that year in the fjords. The Empress's constant good mood, her appearance of good health, everyone's desire to please her, had created an exceedingly pleasant ambience, happy with the happiness of youth."

On some afternoons there would be games instead of a walk, everyone, including Nicky and Alix, playing "cat and mouse" with enthusiasm. Even the rather overweight Ania joined in, lumbering around and making everybody laugh. Nicky played very energetically, particularly when chasing a very agile engineer-mechanic called Savchenko, who did his best to evade capture. The Tsar was genuinely delighted when he finally managed to catch him. Tea would be served back on the yacht at five o'clock (Nicky drank one glass of tea with milk, followed by another without), after which the Tsar would put in nearly three hours' work in his cabin-study. At eight o'clock a drumroll would call everyone to prayer. The crew would line up on the poop, the chaplain would arrive, prayers would be chanted, and then the men would retire. A private dinner was served at half-past eight, to the accompaniment of balalaikas, after which the women of the imperial family would entertain themselves while Nicky played dominoes with some of the officers. At eleven o'clock the girls would go to bed (Alexei having been dispatched several hours previously), while the adults gathered in the dining room for evening tea. Nicky and Alix would talk for a while, before retiring to their cabins at about midnight. Nicky would then write up his diary. Toward half-past twelve, the sailor in charge of the cabins would inform the watch officer that "His Majesty has deigned to go to bed." Through the night, the floodlights of the accompanying destroyers illumined the adjacent shore, where the men of Spiridovich's detachment were silently keeping watch.

The cruise was interrupted by a voyage to Reval, where Nicky and Alix went to meet the President of France, Armand Fallières. During such official events, the ambiguous position of Ania Vyrubova was especially noticeable. Not being a maid-of-honor or holding any other position, she had, in accordance with court etiquette, to keep out of public view. The French President had brought gifts for the imperial children. The girls all received dolls, for which they thanked him politely, but meanwhile Alexei, coming last, was bursting with impatience. Unable to contain himself any longer, he approached the final box, standing on tiptoe in order to try to see inside. At last the mysterious box was opened to reveal a magnificent railway train. The delighted child started to play with it immediately, his faithful companion Derevenko being appointed as conductor.

During the cruises on the *Standart,* Alix seems to have relaxed the firm control she usually exercised over her children—particularly over her daughters. For the rest of the year she was stricter, frequently using letters as a medium of exhortation. In December 1908 her eldest daughter, Olga, lamented the fact that she never seemed able to spend time alone with her mother, and that all their communication had to be via "little notes." Nevertheless she tried valiantly to compose her own apologetic "little note," despite her difficulties with having to write it in English: "With all my heart I thank you sweetest Mama dear for your dear little note and kiss you tenderly for it and will never through it away from me. I will trie to do what you wrote to me in the little note. So sorry that never see you alone Mama dear, can not talk so should trie to write to you what could of course better say, but what is to be done if there is no time, and neighter can I hear the dear words which sweet Mama could tell me." Alix marked the beginning of 1909 with a particularly exhortatory letter, the thirteen-year-old Olga being enjoined to "be an example of what a good little obedient girlie ought to be." As the eldest, it was up to Olga to "show the others how to behave." She was to "Learn to make others happy, think of yourself last of all." The maternal commandments continued: "Be gentle and kind, never rough nor rude. In manners as well as in speech be a real lady. Be patient and polite, try to help sisters in every possible way." In the fulfilling of these recommendations, the child was also to be a little ray of sunshine: "When you see somebody sad, try to cheer them up and show them a bright sunny smile. You know so well to be sweet and gentle with me, be so towards sisters too." The suggestion here is that relations among the sisters were not always particularly "sweet and gentle," and also that Alix used her own invalid state to extort sweetness and gentleness from her daughters. The admonishments end with a veiled threat, an appeal to that ultimate source of authority, using belief in an all-seeing God as a form of control: "Above all, learn to love God with all the force of your soul and He will ever be near to you. Pray to Him with all your heart. Remember He sees and hears everything. He loves his children dearly, but they must learn to do His will." It is clear from a further mother-to-daughter letter, written only a few days later, that Olga has not been observing this recipe for the perfect little girl. She has, however, requested a letter; is there here a suggestion that one reason for her less than perfect behavior is that she is missing her mother and seeking by this means to gain her undivided attention? "Girlie mine," writes Alix, "you must remember that one of the first things is to be polite and not rude, neither in manners nor in words. Rude words in the mouth of little children is more than not nice." A heavy burden is placed on Olga in her position as eldest child; spontaneity is firmly discouraged:

"They [that is, the three younger daughters] are small and don't understand things so well, and will always imitate the big ones. Therefore you must think of every word you say and what you do." The final paragraph is more gentle than the rest of the letter and implies for the first time, with the sentence, "Now try your best, and I shall be happy," that Olga is not really expected to be a complete paragon, provided she makes the effort to be one.

The liturgy to mark the new year of 1909 was held in the church of the Catherine Palace at Tsarskoe Selo, the Dowager Empress Maria Fyodorovna arriving from Gatchina, and Olga and Tatiana being allowed to stand with the adults in the church, while Maria and Anastasia remained out of sight in the gallery. Alexei was ill with a hemophiliac attack, but even a relative as close as KR did not know the details of what was wrong with him: "he has a bad leg," KR recorded in his diary, "they say it's an inflammation of the knee joint, but I don't know for sure." Alix, though present at the liturgy, was feeling weak; she "avoids getting tired," wrote KR, "and is being careful." Consequently, she did not join Nicky at the customary reception of the diplomatic corps. By this time Alix's illness had acquired a psychological dimension, as is clear from Nicky's uncharacteristically candid reply to KR when the latter asked him whether he might stage his play *The Bride of Messina* in the Chinese theater at Tsarskoe Selo. Nicky had told him that "the Empress is very unwilling to receive, and is fearful of people, especially in crowds." One of her main symptoms was tiredness, which prevented her getting up and seeing her daughters, but did not (as previously noted) prevent her seeing her friend Ania.

During the previous few months the influence of Grigory Rasputin in the imperial household had begun to grow noticeably and to become a matter of increasing concern to the wider family. The impressions of Nicky's younger sister, Olga, may come closer than most to providing an accurate depiction of Rasputin, as she had a more measured reaction to him than was usual, being prepared to admit his sincerity and the good effect he appeared to have on the imperial children, while never being able to bring herself to like him personally. Her recollections begin with a happy domestic scene, little Alexei in particular being very relaxed with Grigory: "When I saw him I felt that gentleness and warmth radiated from him. All the children seemed to like him. They were completely at their ease with him. I still remember their laughter as little Alexis, deciding he was a rabbit, jumped up and down the room." Grigory then decided it was time to pray; again, the picture Olga paints is of the small child's complete trust in his friend: "quite suddenly, Rasputin caught the child's hand and led him to his bedroom, and we three followed." From Olga's description, Rasputin had a calming effect on this excitable and boisterous child, who could usually be controlled only by his father: "There was something like a hush as though we had found ourselves in church. In Alexei's bedroom no lamps were lit; the only light came from the candles burning in front of some beautiful icons. The child stood very still by the side of that giant, whose head was bowed. I knew he was praying. It was all most impressive. I also knew that my little nephew had joined him in prayer." It was this experience that convinced Olga of Grigory's "utter sincerity." What she disliked about him, however, was his curiosity—"unbridled and embarrassing." She had no intention of allowing him entry into her own personal life: "In Alicky's boudoir, having talked to her and Nicky for a few minutes, Rasputin waited for the servants to get the table for the evening tea and then began plying me with most impertinent questions. Was I happy? Did I love my husband? Why didn't I have any children? He had no right to ask such questions, nor did I answer them. I am afraid Nicky and Alicky looked rather uncomfortable. I do remember I was relieved at leaving the palace that evening and saying, 'Thank God he hasn't followed me to the station,' as I boarded my private coach in the train for St. Petersburg." Olga's discomfiture arose partly from Grigory's questions being very pertinent. He was either extremely perceptive or very well-informed, as Olga's marriage was indeed unhappy.

Rasputin's growing influence had come about partly as a result of Ania Vyrubova's attachment to and championing of him, which in turn increased at the end of 1908 with the death of Father John of Kronstadt, who had previously been the focus of her veneration. The rumors that were already common currency in St. Petersburg society over the "unnaturally" close relationship between Ania and the Empress were given additional fuel by the introduction of this even more mysterious third party. There were also plenty of people prepared to use either Ania or Grigory in order to gain access, or so they imagined, to the seat of power. This, in turn, led both Ania and Grigory to see themselves as powerful, the latter becoming increasingly convinced that he was "predestined to do something great and beautiful for the Tsar and for Russia."

Nicky and Alix's trust in Rasputin appeared to be justified in the early years of their acquaintance by the company he kept. In the early evening of February 4, 1909, the imperial family received a visit at Tsarskoe Selo from Grigory, accompanied by Archimandrite Feofan, Inspector of the St. Petersburg Theological Academy and the Empress's confessor. As Spiridovich pointed out, "How could they not trust their spiritual director, not give credence to the words of a man whose solid religious convictions, whose vast theological knowledge and unshakeable devotion to true orthodoxy were universally acknowledged, at least among the clergy?" Feofan had even, at Alix's request, been to visit Rasputin's native village of Pokrovskoe to make some investigations into his background and had brought back a very favorable report of him. Archimandrite Feofan's support for Rasputin counterbalanced, in Nicky and Alix's eyes, the negative reports connected both to his personal life and to his association with a controversial cleric, the fanatical, extremely right-wing, and anti-Semitic monk, Iliodor, who had been preaching demagogic sermons against the local authorities in his monastery in Tsaritsyn. Steps had been taken to have Iliodor removed to Minsk, and it was in order to contest this sanction that the monk himself turned up in St. Petersburg in the spring of 1909 to canvas support—even, he hoped, imperial support, through the agency of Rasputin, whom at that time he counted as a friend. On this occasion Iliodor was successful, and was even received by Alix at an informal meeting at Ania's house. He was authorized to return to Tsaritsyn, as Nicky, acting against ministerial advice, had expressed the desire to give him one last chance, out of sympathy for his followers.

In addition to semiofficial visits, such as when he was accompanied by Feofan, and to planned meetings often held at Ania's house, Grigory would on occasion arrive unexpectedly at the Alexander Palace. For such unplanned visits, he would bypass official palace procedures for visiting the imperial family by ostensibly arriving to see their nurse, Maria Vishnyakova; this semisecrecy was maintained by the family choosing the nursery in which to sit and talk with him. Nicky and Alix never betrayed the slightest anxiety about his spending time alone with their children, Alix remarking in a note to Olga on April 3, 1908: "I'm glad you had him so long to yourselves."

Most of the people around the imperial family, however, held very different views. Vladimir Dediulin, the Palace Commandant, asked by the Tsar for his opinion of Rasputin, replied with commendable frankness: "He is a wily peasant, false, intelligent, and possessing a certain power of suggestion which he knows how to use." None of the members of the imperial retinue had any time for him, some actively disliking him while others merely shrugged their shoulders. Only the aide-de-camp Nikolai Sablin maintained relations with him; being a special friend of the imperial family, he had little choice but to do so. The Emperor's personal protection force was ordered, at least for the time being, to pay no particular attention to him, his relationship with the imperial family being regarded as private and posing no security threat. Police interest was nevertheless taken in him, the following events taking place, as far as Spiridovich could remember, either at the very end of 1908 or the beginning of 1909:

We nevertheless greatly desired to rid ourselves of the suspect "*starets*." And my boss, General Dediulin, personally pleaded with Gerasimov [head of the St. Petersburg Department of Security] to have Rasputin watched and to check out the bizarre rumours which were circulating about him. Stolypin, for his part, ordered the gathering of information about him in the Tobolsk region. The facts furnished by the exterior surveillance, as much as the information collected in Tobolsk, turned out to be unfavorable to Rasputin: the man really had deplorable morals. Gerasimov imparted the information received to Stolypin. Stolypin recommended that he should say nothing to anyone, but that he should write a memo of which he, Stolypin, would make use in compiling a report for the Emperor.

Gerasimov, who often came to see my boss in those days, used to say to him: "Get rid of this adventurer! What is he doing here?" He would be answered with a smile that it was up to the minister to get rid of the adventurer. Why did he not banish the "*starets*," if he believed there were serious reasons for doing so? Dediulin discussed the matter again with Stolypin who begged Gerasimov to write, in secret, a decree ordering Rasputin's deportation to his village, as an administrative measure, with a ban on returning to the capital within five years.

Stolypin signed the decree and charged Gerasimov with its execution. One day when the "*starets*" had travelled to Tsarskoe Selo, the Okhrana, who had been having him watched for some time, had taken all the measures to arrest him on his return to Petersburg, during the journey from the station to his apartment. But then something odd happened. Had Rasputin been warned by someone, or did he suspect something? This isn't known; in any case as soon as he arrived in Petersburg, he ran across the station, jumped into a waiting car and, gaining speed on the agents who had rushed in pursuit, he arrived at the palace of Grand Duke Pyotr Nikolaevich and his wife Militsa.

Despite day and night surveillance, the security agents did not manage to see him leave the palace a single time in the space of three weeks. And then, at the end of three weeks, a telegram arrived from the Governor of Tobolsk, announcing that Rasputin had returned to his native village of Pokrovskoe.

General Gerasimov asked Stolypin what should be done and whether the ban on Rasputin returning to Petersburg within five years should be upheld. The minister gave a gesture which meant "forget it" and gave the order that the decree should be destroyed.

In November 1909 Rasputin went to visit Iliodor in Tsaritsyn, where he received a rapturous welcome, Iliodor having told his flock that Rasputin was a genuine "*starets*," a defender of the poor and humble before the Tsar. Rasputin took care always to appear in Tsaritysn in the company of the Bishop of Saratov, Hermogen, which only served to raise his authority further in the eyes of the people. The news of Rasputin's great success with the devoutly Orthodox population of Tsaritsyn, where he was hailed as a new John of Kronstadt, inevitably reached the ears of the Emperor and Empress and made a profound impression on them, strengthening their belief that their Friend was indeed a man of God.

In July 1909 the imperial family had visited Cherbourg, in return for the visit that President Fallières had paid them the previous year. During a review of the French fleet, the Empress and all her daughters enjoyed taking photographs of the submarines (having first obtained permission to do so). There was also a further presentation of gifts to the imperial children: "To the Tsarevich the President gave twelve miniature rifles of different models, as well as models of military drums and trumpets and a military tent with complete furniture. The Grand Duchess Olga received a garniture for a writing table in silver and blue enamel, the Grand Duchess Tatiana a traveling clock in blue enamel, the Grand Duchess Maria a completely furnished doll's house of two stories with a lift and electric light, and the Grand Duchess Anastasia a magnificent doll's *trousseau.*"

During the late summer the family visited Cowes on the Isle of Wight, as the guests of King Edward VII. Nicky was made an honorary member of the Royal Yacht Club, which gave him great pleasure. He also received onboard the *Standart* the Lord Mayor and Aldermen of London, who presented him with an Address of Welcome in a gold box. Afterward he and Alix boarded the royal yacht *Britannia* and left to attend the races. In the evening they paid a half-hour visit to Empress Eugénie, widow of Emperor Napoleon III, who was staying on a private yacht. In the meantime the imperial children had been driven to Osborne and spent the morning playing on the beach.

After lunch, Olga and Tatiana, aged thirteen and twelve respectively, had what was for them a great adventure, setting off into the town without their parents, in the company of several members of the retinue. They loved the simple experience, so rare for them, of being able to walk along the streets, almost like ordinary girls, without being recognized. While this happy situation lasted, they went shopping for postcards and souvenirs, traveling by ferry from one part of the town to another and taking great delight in being able to buy their own tickets. Unfortunately, but inevitably, members of the public soon guessed the identities of these pretty and lively girls, in their grey dresses. Before long they had attracted large crowds of curious onlookers, who gathered outside the shops to try to catch a glimpse of them as they emerged. The police had to start clearing a path for them, and the members of the retinue became increasingly anxious. So back they all went to the landing stage. But there the young Grand Duchesses looked at the time and decided it was still too early to return to the squadron. And so they hailed two taxicabs that took them into the town, having decided they wanted to visit the local church—where a delighted vicar gave them an impromptu tour, which included showing them the chair in which their great-grandmother Queen Victoria used to sit when she attended services. Highly pleased with themselves and their outing, the girls returned to the *Standart* in time for tea.

By late summer, when the family returned to Peterhof, Alix was very unwell. Dr. Botkin attended her daily and the rumor began to spread in court circles that she was suffering from some mysterious illness. Earlier in the year a Doctor Fischer, a specialist in nervous diseases attached to the palace hospital at Tsarskoe Selo, had been summoned to see her. He had concluded that the Empress needed absolute rest and advised that she should be separated from everything likely to irritate her or to affect her nerves in any way. Unfortunately, he had included Ania Vyrubova in his list of likely irritants, as he thought her constant presence was having a harmful effect on Alix. He was thanked for his advice and never asked to return. And so, as Spiridovich put it, "The treatment of the Empress was then entrusted to E. S. Botkin who obeyed his patient in all things. He conducted her treatment, not as it should be done, but as the Empress desired."

Alix's faith in God helped give her strength on the rare occasions (at this period) when Nicky went traveling farther afield than from one imperial palace to another. One such occasion was in late June 1909, Alix following her custom of writing a letter to accompany her husband on his journey to Sweden to visit the King. "You will read these lines when the train will already be carrying you far away from Wify and children," she writes. "It is very hard letting you go all alone—the first journey in the country since all the troubles—but I know you are safe in God's hands." On the following day, Alix and the children were to receive Holy Communion and, in preparation for this, they would be making their confessions that evening at the house of Ania's parents, the Taneevs. In expressing her love for her husband, and thanking him for loving her, for being "so pure and unselfish, trusting and kind," Alix alludes to the aspect of Nicky's character that often made him so hard to fathom: He is, she writes, "always serene, no matter what battle may be going on inside." And her comment that there is from him "never a word of rebuke if I am naughty" suggests that he dealt with his wife's illness and invalidism in the same way that he faced the problems of being the Tsar—he kept the battle to himself, "inside."

On October 6, 1909, Alix had to write another farewell letter to Nicky, this time from Livadia. He was about to embark on what she referred to as a "long and lonely journey"—to Italy. Initially the plan had been for the whole family to travel there by sea, on the *Standart*. But this project had been abandoned on account of the Empress's illness and other considerations, and the Emperor's journey was now going to be by rail, avoiding Austria, with whom relations were strained on account of the annexation of Bosnia and Herzegovina, which had taken place the previous September. Serbia and Montenegro had protested over the Austrian annexation, the Montenegrin King being supported in his calls for war and the intervention of Russia by his son-in-law, Grand Duke Nikolai Nikolaevich. That no intervention took place has been attributed, at least in part, to the influence of Rasputin, and may have contributed to the falling out between Rasputin and the Montenegrin princesses and their friends. In addition, Rasputin had spoken in denigrating terms about Grand Duke Nikolai's marriage to Stana, which both drove a wedge between him and the Montenegrins and made Nicky and Alix realize that they had been manipulated into supporting this marriage.

As Nicky set off for Italy, the sorrow of parting and the weight of illness were both bearing down considerably on Alix. She was no longer gaining any enjoyment from her invalid status, her lack of strength having become a burden, particularly the awareness that she was not always able to control herself in public: "I dread the moment of goodbye and yet I want to come with you to the last, I hope God will give me strength to behave well, formerly I could always master myself, now I have less strength to and it's my despair." She promises to try hard to get better by the time her husband returns, "so as to be able to accompany you at least by motor sometimes." Her one consolation as the moment of parting looms is that, at least to begin with, Nicky will be traveling on the *Standart;* she hopes he will seek out the company of the officers and play dominoes with them. Not only God, but also Grigory, is enlisted to keep her husband safe on his journey. In conclusion, she reverts to baby language: "It is so hard to let you go—me not like it."

Alix's methods of bringing up her daughters, her cajoling letters combined with her frequent inability, or refusal, to communicate with them except by letter, had a particularly deleterious effect on her third daughter, Maria, who had always struggled to find her place within the family. As a ten-year-old, in March 1910, she was finding it hard to believe anyone loved her—hardly surprising when her mother enjoined her "always to be good and obedient little girly, then all will love you." If Alix loved her daughters unconditionally, she certainly did not let them know it. Maria seems to have been displaying some jealousy of her younger sister's relationship with their mother, for Alix adds: "I have no secrets with Anastasia, I do not like secrets." A further letter from Alix to her daughter shows the effect this constant iteration of conditional love was having on the little girl, though it seems to have come as a surprise to her mother, who does not realize that she herself has planted this idea on Maria: "Your letter made me quite sad," wrote Alix. "Sweet child you must promise me never again to think that nobody loves you. *How* did such an extraordinary idea get into your little head? Get it quickly out again." She goes on to try to counteract the impression she has given in some of her other notes (though without realizing quite what that impression had been): "We all love you *very tenderly,* only when too wild and naughty and won't listen, then must be scolded; but to scold, does not mean that one does not love, on the contrary, one does it so as that you may cure your faults and improve." It would appear that Maria had been getting herself into a vicious circle, staying away from her older sisters, imagining that they did not want her, and playing instead with her cousin Irina (Xenia's daughter). Consequently Olga and Tatiana imagined she did not want to be with them, whereas, according to their mother, "now you are getting a big girl it is good that you should be more with them." Alix concludes her letter reassuringly: "Now do not think any more about it, and remember that you are *just* as precious and dear as the other 4 and that we love you with all our heart. God bless you Darling Child. I kiss you ever so tenderly."

On March 8, it is Tatiana's turn to apologize to her mother for some unspecified misdemeanor. The juxtaposition of her rather anguished plea for forgiveness with an inquiry as to her mother's health ("How is your head?") suggests that Alix used her invalidism, even if unconsciously, as a controlling mechanism—her daughters knew they had to behave in a way that would not displease her, as otherwise she might be made ill, or more ill, through them: "Please forgive me that I have not did what I would last day. I am so sad that I did that, what I knew you would not like. Please forgive me I did not want to do it really Mama dear. I never, never wont do something I know you don't like and I won't do it without asking you my sweet Mama. How is your head?" There is also here not so much a sense that Tatiana has done something genuinely wrong, or something she considers wrong herself, but something her mother does not like. Tatiana's letter then alludes to the trouble brewing around the girls' governess, Sofia Ivanovna Tyutcheva ("S.I." in Tatiana's letter) and Rasputin; Tatiana is very afraid that S.I. is going to speak "about our friend some thing bad" to "Maria"—the latter most probably being the nurse, Maria Vishnyakova, for Tatiana adds: "I hope our nurse will be nice to our friend now." In fact Vishnyakova claimed that spring to have been raped by Rasputin during a visit to his hometown of Pokrovskoe, a visit she had been encouraged to make by Alix. This had allegedly taken place during the last month, so it was understandable if Maria was not being "nice" to Rasputin and was instead highly receptive to Sofia Ivanovna's criticism of him. Tatiana herself would not have understood what was going on; she would just have been aware of the undercurrents of dislike, gossip, and the necessity not to talk about their "friend" to those who wished him ill. Again, the placing of these sentiments within her contrite note to her mother suggests that this—her concern for Grigory and that their domestic staff should be "nice" to him—will please Alix; it is impossible to know what Tatiana herself really thinks (if indeed she knows herself). All her effort is bound up in keeping her mother happy and in that way helping her to be well (or at least less sick). Tatiana's note concludes with an apology to her father as well, amid further anxiety over her mother's health: "Please tell Papa that I also ask him my pardon. I am so sad I made that what you and Papa don't like. Sleep well my own sweet Mama darling and I hope that tomorrow your poor head wont each [sic] any more."

In fact Sofia Ivanovna had already been talking more widely than just to the children's nurse. On March 15, Xenia recorded in her diary that she had been sitting with Alix's lady-in-waiting, S. D. Samarina, who was in a state of shock over what the governess had been telling her about the goings-on at Tsarskoe Selo and "the attitude of Alix and the children to that sinister Grigory." Despite the lack of any concrete evidence, it was the opinion of all these women that Rasputin was a "*khlyst,*" a member of a flagellant sect, while the misguided Alix and her offspring saw him as a saint. Just a few weeks earlier this precise charge against Rasputin—that he was a flagellant sectarian and "a sex maniac" had been leveled against him by the writer, churchman, and friend of Alix's sister Ella, Mikhail Novoselov, in the *Moscow Gazette* in an article entitled "A Spiritual Quack."

Though explicit words are not used by Xenia, the implication in what she has been told is clear—that Rasputin has been sexually abusing the imperial daughters: "He's always there, goes into the nursery, visits Olga and Tatiana while they are getting ready for bed, sits there talking to them and *caressing* them. They are careful to hide him from Sofia Ivanovna, and the children don't dare to talk to her about him. It's quite unbelievable and beyond understanding." Xenia declares that she was "simply crushed by this conversation." She and her sister Olga had dinner that evening with their mother at the Anichkov Palace, and the allegations concerning Rasputin were the only topic of conversation. They had all heard "the most terrible rumors" about him, but felt powerless to intervene. Ella was involved in these discussions, too—Sofia Ivanovna Tyutcheva was another of her friends—and Nicky noted in his diary on March 17 that he had had a conversation with Ella after tea about Grigory. His sister-in-law had warned him that it was possible to be mistaken and that "not all who seem holy are." When Sofia Ivanovna took these allegations to Alix and Nicky, they refused to believe them. According to the deposition she made to the Provisional Government's Extraordinary Commission of Enquiry in 1917, she had been told by the Tsar that he had only survived all these difficult years through Rasputin's prayers and that, as for the slanders about him, "the pure always attract everything dirty." All that can be known for sure is that, where their children were concerned, both Nicky and Alix trusted Grigory completely, and that the children themselves never brought any allegations against him. As a result of her suspicions—and the fact that she had talked openly about them, and about the other rumors concerning Rasputin—Sofia Ivanovna Tyutcheva was dismissed.

This was not the only family trouble with which Nicky had to deal in March 1910. His brother Misha had recovered from the love affair he had been so desperate about three years previously only to fall in love with yet another unsuitable woman. This one was the wife of a captain in the Cuirassier Regiment of which Misha was the commanding officer. Her name was Natalia Wulfert and she was now already five months pregnant with Misha's child. He was determined she should be divorced without delay, as he could not countenance her husband having any rights over his child. He had confessed all this to Nicky when they had last met, and now, on March 29, he wrote to press his request that the Tsar should speed up Natalia's divorce. He reiterated that his sole concern was over his paternity: "I have no intention of marrying her, of that I give you my word" but, at the same time, he was very insistent: "Once more, my dear Nicky, I very, very much ask you to help in this matter."

That year Ella had become Abbess of the Order of nuns (the Convent of Sts. Martha and Mary) that she had created in 1908, three years after the assassination of her husband, Grand Duke Sergei; she now dressed "all in white, her head and forehead covered by a wimple, over which was a white veil, with a pectoral cross and a rosary." Felix Yusupov, the future husband of Xenia's daughter Irina, stressed the elegance and style Ella brought even to her nun's habits: "With a last touch of worldliness, for she had been a woman of extreme elegance and great taste, she had the dress of her Order designed by Mikhail Nesterov, a Muscovite painter and also a devout Orthodox Christian, a long pearl-grey robe of fine wool, a lawn wimple which framed the face, and a white woollen veil that fell into long classical folds."

News of the death of King Edward VII arrived in Russia on April 27, 1910. Maria Fyodorovna and Misha went to London for the funeral (Maria Fyodorovna's reason for attendance also being to console her sister, Queen Alexandra, who had been so helpful to her in her own bereavement), while Nicky attended a requiem at the British Embassy in St. Petersburg. On George V's accession there was an exchange of letters between the cousins, Georgie assuring Nicky: "Yes, dearest Nicky, I hope we shall always continue our old friendship to one another, you know I never change and I have always been very fond of you." He had some concern for the future, but believed the problems were not insurmountable: "there may be difficulties with Germany, but I think they can be overcome. If only England, Russia and France stick together the peace in Europe is assured."

During the trip to the fjords that summer, Nicky undertook many strenuous walks in the islands. On one occasion the nine-year-old Anastasia, who prided herself on being a tomboy, begged to be included in the party, and her father agreed. But he made absolutely no concession to her age. They walked for about eleven miles; the Tsar was always a fast walker and soon everyone, apart from him, was flagging. Poor little Anastasia got so tired that she started to cry, and the members of the entourage (but not Nicky himself) took it in turns to give her a piggyback. This walk was talked about for a long time afterward, some of the men who had been on it weighing themselves before and after and claiming to have lost about two pounds. Anastasia would think twice before begging to be included in the Emperor's serious walking expeditions again. Alix, for the most part, stayed on the yacht during this trip, Ania, Olga, or Tatiana always sitting with her. She only left the *Standart* seated in an armchair carried by two sturdy sailors. Dr. Botkin was of the view that she ought to keep as still as possible, for the sake of her heart, and Alix was happy to comply.

On October 22, Alix wrote Nicky a sad little note from Tsarskoe Selo, after he had left to meet with Kaiser Wilhelm at Potsdam. Her state of health was making it very difficult for her to withstand unhappiness, to keep her emotions under control. "It is so sad and empty in the little house without you," she wrote, "I miss you quite too terribly. After you left I remained in your room a little trying to be brave, though not succeeding. After my bath I prayed long and read the whole Akathist [a sequence of prayers] to the Kazan Mother of God and then got calmer. It took ages before I got to sleep. Baby Sweet [Alexei] came in his dressing gown to wake me and drew up the curtains." Alix's chief symptoms at this time consisted principally of aches and pains—her head ached frequently, as did her whole body. Massage sometimes helped to ease the pain, which she also found to be affected by the weather, rain and cold making it worse. From that point of view, St. Petersburg and its environs, with its short hours of daylight during the winter and its damp and gloomy atmosphere, must have been one of the worst places to live.

A letter from Alix to Maria (whom she addresses as "My little childy") on December 6, 1910, shows that this third daughter was still unhappy as the year drew to a close. Her mother had noticed this but had decided not to ask her about it—"because one does not like it when others ask." This is indicative of Alix's own tormented need for privacy, her fear of self-revelation, her dislike of anyone interfering with her private thoughts and feelings; it is not necessarily how her little girl felt. Maria's sadness seems connected at least in part with having an invalid mother; Alix recognizes the difficulty this presents her family, without showing any real desire to do anything about it (in this case submission to the will of God can also be read as permission to do nothing, to make no effort to change). She is still also quite prepared to use her poor health as part of her armory to instill good behavior in her children. "Then loving your old Mama who is always ill does not make life bright for you poor children," she tells Maria. "It is my great sorrow not to be able to be more with you all, and to read and shout and play together—but we must bear all. He has sent His cross which must be borne. I know it's dull having an invalid mother, but it teaches you all to be loving and gentle. Only try to be more obedient, then you make it easier for me, and you show the little ones a good example." Maria's other problem is that she has become too fond of some boy or young man, possibly a member of the Corps de Pages, or a young officer on the *Standart*—certainly someone with whom she comes into regular contact but who can never be an acceptable suitor for "a little Grand Duchess." "I know well your feelings for . . . poor little one," writes her mother. Grigory knows about it, too, and he has advised Maria not to think too much about the object of her affections, advice with which her mother concurs. Above all, she must hide her feelings: "Try not to let your thoughts dwell too much on him, that's what our Friend said. You see, others might see your looks when you are with him and speak unkindly. Now that you are a big girl [she was eleven], you must always be more careful and not show those feelings. One must not let others see what one feels inside, when one knows it's considered not proper." Whoever it is that Maria has fallen for—and she is a young girl crying out to love and be loved—likes her "as a little sister" and, asserts her mother, "would like to help you not to care too much, because he knows you, a little Grand Duchess, must not care for him so." But now Alix must bring her letter, on however important a subject, to a close: "Deary, I can't write all, it takes too long and I am not alone." This is a kind and understanding letter, and reveals something of why her children were so fond of Alix, despite her tendency to withdraw; yet she could have been of so much more help to her daughters, if only her own state of invalidity could have been overcome. "Be brave and cheer up and don't let your thoughts dwell so much upon him," she concludes. "It's not good and makes you yet more sad. Had I been well I should have tried to amuse and cheer you up, so all would have been easier—but it's not so and nothing can be done. God will help you. Cheer up, little one—try to be good and don't think yourself horrid."

As was usual during the winter season, Nicky made several trips into St. Petersburg in early 1911 to theatrical, musical, and operatic performances, and generally did so with relish. On February 9, he took his two elder daughters with him to see a performance of Tchaikovsky's *Evgeny Onegin*. They all enjoyed it very much, and were back home by midnight despite a violent snowstorm. On the 13th he went with his mother to the jubilee performance of his erstwhile flame, Mathilde Kshessinskaya. And on the 17th he took all his daughters to see the ballet *The Sleeping Beauty*. Whenever he could escape for an hour or two from his work during the daylight hours (brief in the northern midwinter), he would enjoy playing in the snow with the children, tobogganing or building snow towers. He also visited various exhibitions, including, on March 9, those of the Wanderers (the 29th Exhibition of the Society of Travelling Art Exhibitions, held at the Society for the Encouragement of the Arts) and of the Moscow Artists. He also attended meetings of the Imperial Historical Society.

From time to time the imperial couple would spend part of the evening with Rasputin, Nicky making mention of one such occasion—the meeting taking place at Ania's house at Tsarskoe Selo—on February 12, 1911. A few days later Grigory was set to leave, however, on a trip to the Holy Land, something that brought sadness to all the family (unless the sensitive Maria, in expressing her sadness on this subject to her mother, is expressing her awareness of her mother's feelings, rather than her own—that is, Maria is sad precisely because she knows Alix is, too): "Loving thanks, Maria Darling, for your sweet letter. Yes, I too am very sad that our beloved friend is now leaving—but while he is gone we must try and live as he would have wished. Then we will feel he is near us in prayers and thoughts." What seems so extraordinary to anyone outside this magic circle is that Rasputin, with his reputation for licentiousness and drunkenness, should have been seen by the irreproachable Alix as an arbiter of behavior, that she and her family should defer to him and make his instructions their rule of life. This is all the more startling, and demonstrates Alix's absolute trust in Rasputin in the face of compelling evidence against the wisdom of such trust, when one considers that the reason for his sudden decision to go on a pilgrimage to the Holy Land was that he was in disgrace, and had actually been forbidden to reappear at Tsarskoe Selo. This had come about as a result of inquiries having been made into the monk Iliodor's behavior in Tsaritsyn, where he had once again been infuriating the authorities. Nicky had dispatched one of his trusted aides-de-camp, a Captain Mandryka, to Tsaritsyn to find out what had been going on, and in the course of his investigations Mandryka had also uncovered many disreputable stories about Rasputin's own doings in Tsaritsyn, including allegations that he had had numerous affairs with women and had been preaching against marital fidelity. Alix had been present when Mandryka presented a verbal report on his findings, Mandryka himself being so upset by what he was having to tell the Emperor and Empress that he burst into tears and had to be calmed down. Nicky, presumably with Alix's agreement, took the decision to ban Grigory from making further visits to them; their subsequent behavior, however (and indeed Alix's letter to Maria quoted above), would suggest that they did not really believe what they had been told and that the ban was more a matter of expediency than of genuine outrage. Grigory's departure for the Holy Land, presented as a penitential pilgrimage, also seems in the nature of a cooling-off period, a way of making himself scarce until all the trouble had died down. The ploy worked, and Grigory was received back at Tsarskoe Selo with open arms, Nicky noting the joy of seeing him again, after his return from Jerusalem and Athens on June 4. Rasputin's erstwhile supporters in the Church, however, had by now had second thoughts about him, and he increasingly came to be seen as a man of God only within his own small circle of faithful followers.

On May 10, 1911, Ella came from Moscow to stay with Alix and Nicky for some weeks. In the same month KR had a conversation with the Dowager Empress (whom he refers to by the family name of "Minnie"), in which she gave vent to some of her concerns about her daughter-in-law (including the complaint, also attested to by others, that Alix kept her rooms too cold, having something of an obsession with fresh air) and her grandchildren. "She spoke openly," KR confided to his diary, and continued:

> It is sad to see that if her relations with the Empress are not exactly bad, they are not quite right either.
>
> She criticised the cold and constant draught in her daughter-in-law's rooms, blaming this for the latter's continual ill health. [Minnie] catches cold at Tsarskoe because of it.
>
> She is distressed that they continue to receive in secret some God's fool, Grisha, who orders the Empress A. and the children to keep it secret and not to say that they have seen him. It can hardly be beneficial to accustom the children to such dissimulation.

KR may have been right about this; on the other hand, with his secret life, he was hardly in a position to criticize anyone else for "dissimulation."

In his diary for January 1911, KR had recorded a famous theatrical incident, which took place when Nicky attended a performance of *Boris Godunov* at the Mariinsky Theatre with his mother and eldest daughter (the other three girls being convalescent after a bout of chicken pox). Fyodor Chaliapin was playing the title role. Unexpectedly, at the end of the first act, the curtain opened to reveal the entire cast, with Chaliapin in the center. They began to sing "God Save the Tsar," at which point the audience stood and the actors all dropped to their knees, facing the imperial box. The occupants of the box—Xenia and Irina, KR and his wife, as well as the Dowager Empress and Olga—leapt to their feet when they realized what was happening, the Emperor standing, too. The orchestra took up the anthem, and everyone in the hall was applauding as the anthem was sung three times, the whole auditorium joining in with enthusiasm. Maria Fyodorovna pushed her son forward (he had been standing in the corner, hidden from the public by the curtain), and he bowed to the actors and the audience, amid wild cheering. It appeared to be a spontaneous and emotional outburst of patriotism, a triumphant acknowledgment of the Tsar's popularity with his (opera-going) subjects, and KR declared: "I had not experienced a moment of such intensity for a long time, and was unable to hold back my tears." The secret police soon discovered that this demonstration of loyalty to the Tsar had been arranged by the opera singers in support of a petition they hoped to present to him, connected with a dispute they were having with the director of the imperial theaters. Pure patriotism had therefore not been the motive, though this was not known at the time by the audience who had joined in so enthusiastically—demonstrating, if nothing else, the power of music and spectacle to stir the emotions.

During that year's holiday a new entertainment was devised, the impetus coming from the commandant of the destroyers accompanying the *Standart,* a

Captain Trubetskoy. He decided it would be a good idea to organize a picnic for the Grand Duchesses and, after having got Ania Vyrubova to check whether the Empress was likely to agree to the plan (she was), he presented an official request, doing so after lunch one Sunday. Alix replied that she would give her daughters permission to attend, but would not be able to be present herself, because of her state of health. Nicky, who was listening, turned to Trubetskoy and said, "And what about me, Prince, am I not invited?" He duly was.

An imperial picnic was no casual affair, and the sailors spent days preparing for it. A suitable piece of grass was selected, a little way inland; it was covered with a carpet and provisions began to be amassed. (One can begin to understand from all these preparations for one afternoon's entertainment just how unusual—and hence how enjoyable—Olga and Tatiana's impromptu excursion around Cowes had been two years before.) On the designated afternoon, Nicky, the girls, Ania, members of the retinue, and the yacht's officers all disembarked and made their way on foot to the picnic area, recognizable from afar by the nautical flags that had been hoisted. There they found not only the carpeted lawn, surrounded by fir trees, but also a specially constructed lodge and a tent containing all sorts of delicacies, including the pastry chef Ivanov's famous strawberry tarts. The young people—and the Emperor—played games, including blind man's buff (always an imperial favorite, Catherine the Great having loved playing it with her grandchildren), races, and a game called "Cossack brigands," while the older men sat comfortably on rugs spread in front of the lodge, talking and relaxing. One gets the impression that the afternoon was particularly relaxing as the Empress had been left behind on the yacht. Everyone enjoyed themselves until six o'clock, when the Emperor gave the signal to depart. Even then the entertainment was not quite over, for they traveled back to the landing stage in Finnish two-wheeled carts, which was a new experience for them. The carts rolled along making a dreadful noise, shaking the travelers and throwing them against one another, to the accompaniment of shrieks and gales of laughter.

This was the first of several such outings, each one more ambitious than the last. The next one—more a party than a picnic—was organized for the Dowager Empress's and little Maria's name day, July 22, and involved a meadow being completely transformed into something resembling an amusement park, with tents, "Russian mountains" (that is, constructions designed for sliding down, like miniature dry ski slopes), trapezes, and swings. As before there was plenty to eat and drink, and on this occasion both Alexei and Alix were also in attendance. The little boy loved the Russian mountains, climbing up and rolling down the rubber slope repeatedly. His mother was at first understandably anxious that he would hurt himself, but was reassured by the way the officers in charge of the entertainment took care of him. Her presence had at first been rather constraining for the young people, but as she was in a good mood she actually contributed to everyone's enjoyment, and the party was deemed a great success. It had been organized this time by the officers of the *Standart,* and now the Emperor wished to return the favor and appointed some of his own staff to devise an outdoor entertainment. This turned out to be the most inventive of all, involving the production of huge pyramids of "snowballs," made out of white calico and damp straw, with which the imperial family, the retinue, and officers were invited to pelt one another. The idea had arisen when the Emperor had remarked during the previous picnic, "I really feel like playing snowballs." Battle commenced, and continued until everyone was exhausted and one or two people were bruised. Fortunately, Alexei had not been included in this entertainment; neither was the Empress well enough to attend.

The question of how to bring up a boisterous little boy, who had to be protected as much as possible from giving himself the knocks and bruises that are a normal part of childhood, while not allowing him to become too spoiled and helping him learn how to control himself instead of always being controlled by others, presented an endless headache to his parents. In some respects he did appear rather spoiled, various observers commenting on his bad table manners, for instance; but, despite the attendant risks, his parents—his father in particular—did not believe in keeping him entirely wrapped in cotton wool, and he was allowed to learn some lessons the hard way. At six years old, he went through an aggressive phase and took to beating up one of his small playmates (the child of a member of the retinue). When Nicky heard about it, he told his son he would soon have no friends if he carried on like this and he advised the other little boy, who had been rather hesitant about hitting the Tsarevich back, to stand up for himself and return blow for blow. He duly did so—which completely amazed and affronted Alexei, who burst into tears and went running off to Derevenko. After a further talk with his father, he realized the error of his ways and the two feisty little boys became the best of friends. And fortunately the childish fighting produced no lasting ill effects. Nicky was, however, the only person (apart from, arguably, Rasputin) who could effectively control his son. As Spiridovich commented, "It was sufficient for the Emperor to say to him severely: 'Alexei!' for the child to stop his mischief immediately, such as splashing about in the water when he wasn't supposed to. He would obey at once, while all the reprimands his mother might utter to him were without effect."

Soon after the summer holiday Olga again attended the theater with her father, this time with Tatiana, too; this occasion was marked by a less happy event than the "spontaneous" acclamation featuring Chaliapin. The date was September 1, and the venue was the municipal theater in Kiev, where the imperial family was attending the festivities to celebrate the unveiling of a monument to Tsar Alexander II; the opera was Glinka's *A Life for the Tsar*. Security was tight, as the Kiev police had received information that terrorists were planning an assassination, but the Tsar had insisted that the crowds of people attending the festivities should not be prevented from seeing him. Admission to the theater was by special pass, and there were security men stationed at every entrance. During the second interval the tall, stately figure of Prime Minister Stolypin, who had been sitting in the first row of the stalls, could be seen alongside Court Minister Baron Fredericks, leaning on the balustrade of the orchestra pit, both men deep in conversation. Most of the audience had gone out into the foyer. Kokovtsov, then acting as Stolypin's deputy, came up to him and Baron Fredericks, to ask if there were any messages for him to take back to St. Petersburg, as he would be leaving for the capital straight after the performance. "No," answered Stolypin, "there are no messages; but I wish you could take me with you." Kokovtsov said good-bye, and moved off to speak to some other people. As he did so, he heard "two muffled detonations like those made by firecrackers." Stolypin had been shot.

The Tsar described what had happened in a letter to his mother on September 10: "I was getting quite tired, but everything had gone so well and smoothly and our spirits were high, when on the evening of the 1st the filthy assassination of Stolypin took place. Olga and Tatiana were with me, and we had just left our box during the second interval, as it was very hot in the theatre. At that moment we heard two noises, like the sound of an object falling, and, thinking that a pair of binoculars must have fallen on someone's head from above, I ran back into the box." Stolypin remained standing for a few seconds, then he slowly turned toward the imperial box and made the sign of the cross, before crumpling into a chair. He was wearing a white jacket, through which a bright red stain now began to seep. There was pandemonium in the theater, shouts of "help!" as Fredericks and a Professor Rein helped Stolypin to unbutton his jacket, while in the corridor a group of men tackled the assassin, who had calmly walked in wearing a black tailcoat. General Dediulin stood with a drawn sword near the imperial box. As the Tsar appeared in the box, looking, according to Kokovtsov, "pale and agitated," the national anthem was played and the Tsar bowed to the people who were returning to the auditorium and cheering him. Olga and Tatiana had followed their father back into the box, and had seen what had happened. They were all three now quickly hustled away by the police. Tatiana in particular was badly upset and crying, and neither girl could sleep that night. Not only was it the first time they had seen someone they knew mortally wounded, but they had also realized the danger threatening their beloved father whenever he appeared in public. According to one account, Tatiana had tried to prevent him from going back into the box, fearing he would be shot.

The Prime Minister was taken to the clinic of a Dr. Makovsky, and Kokovtsov went there, as did the Governor-General of Kiev, F. F. Trepov, once he had seen the Tsar and his daughters safely back to the Nikolaevsky Palace. A bullet had lodged in Stolypin's back; he was conscious and in great pain. His attacker had been arrested and was being questioned. Kokovtsov's immediate concern was to prevent a pogrom, as the people had learned that Stolypin's attacker, Dmitry Bogrov, was a Jew. The Jewish inhabitants of the city were in a panic, many of them already packing their belongings and getting ready to leave, while other members of the population were, it was asserted, preparing to massacre them. Order was restored by the recall of three regiments of Cossacks who had been on the point of leaving to take part in the following day's maneuvers. They reentered Kiev early the next morning and provided a visible, reassuring presence in those areas inhabited by Jews. No pogrom ensued.

Despite some initial hope that Stolypin's iron constitution might pull him through, it became apparent after thirty-six hours that recovery was very unlikely. His wife and brothers-in-law arrived in Kiev on September 4, by which time he had begun to lose consciousness. He died at about five o'clock in the afternoon of the 5th. Meanwhile, on September 2, the Tsar (after visiting the clinic but being discouraged from seeing the patient, for fear the resultant emotion would have a negative effect) had fulfilled his original program of troop inspections, and on the 4th had left for Chernigov to venerate the relics of St. Feodosia Uglitsky, who had been canonized during his reign in 1896. He returned to Kiev on the morning of September 6, and was due to leave for the Crimea, via Sebastopol, that evening. On his arrival back in Kiev, Nicholas went straight to Dr. Makovsky's clinic to pay his respects to the deceased and to offer condolences to his widow. "I returned to Kiev at 9 in the morning," he told his mother. "Here I learnt at the landing stage from Kokovtsev that Stolypin had died. I went straight there, and there was a special requiem in my presence. The poor widow stood there, unable even to cry; her brothers are with her." On September 7, the Emperor and his family left Kiev for the Crimea.

It had become clear almost immediately that General Kurlov, commander of the Special Corps of Gendarmes, and his staff had made significant errors, particularly in allowing the assassin to gain access to the theater—where, not only had he shot the Prime Minister but he had been within firing range of the Tsar. It turned out that the twenty-four-year-old Bogrov was known to the police as an informer and, through misplaced trust on the part of the Kiev secret police chief, he had been granted an entry pass. His motive was not merely to assassinate a prominent member of the government, but to do so in such a way as to promote mutual suspicion and discord among the security forces, as well as to derail Stolypin's economic and agrarian reforms, which threatened the very raison d'être of the revolutionary movement. He also wanted to expiate himself in the eyes of that movement, for having earlier been a traitor to the cause. The head of the Tsar's personal protection force, General Spiridovich, was necessarily implicated in this lapse of security, and for some weeks the Tsar refused to speak to or acknowledge him and his men (whom he and Alix habitually referred to as "the yellow men" on account of the color of their uniforms or "nature-lovers" because they always seemed to be staring intently up at the sky or into the bushes). An official inquiry was also launched. The military trial of Bogrov took place on September 9, he was sentenced on the 10th and executed on the 11th; all this was unusually and extraordinarily fast, which in itself gave rise to rumors that this had been a government plot to do away with an inconvenient minister. (Stolypin had been on the point of resigning as Prime Minister, having failed to secure the support he needed for his proposal to spread the zemstvo system into the southwestern provinces of Russia. His disproportionate reaction to this personal setback had also resulted in the loss, to some extent, of Nicky's trust in him.)

On arrival in the Crimea, the imperial family had been hoping to move into the new palace at Livadia, which they had commissioned from Yalta's most fashionable architect, Nikolai Krasnov, but it was not yet completely ready and so they had to spend a fortnight on the *Standart,* docked at Sebastopol. During this time Nicky traveled on a destroyer to attend a mine-placing exercise, inspected the docks, reviewed some troops, and visited the Brotherhood War Cemetery. Here he was received by the Archbishop of Tauride, who delivered an unacceptably political speech, in support of increased freedom for the Russian people. The Tsar's displeasure was apparent to those who knew him well: Throughout the speech he was constantly adjusting his belt and fiddling with his moustache. On September 16, the *Standart* arrived at Yalta, dropping anchor near the pier; the family stayed on board for a few more days, while the finishing touches to the new palace were being feverishly accomplished. Spiridovich was greatly relieved when, during one of Nicky's walks along the jetty, he made a point of greeting each of his "yellow men." Two days later, the Tsar shook hands with Spiridovich himself, signaling his intention of putting the matter of Stolypin's assassination behind them. "I felt solid ground beneath my feet again," commented Spiridovich.

On October 1, Kokovtsov made his first trip to Livadia as Prime Minister. Nicholas received him on the 4th, and showed him around the new palace, where the family had finally taken up residence. Built in "le style moderne" (which in later decades came to be known as Art Deco), it resembled an Italian villa rather than a royal palace, and the imperial family became very fond of it. The ground floor comprised a very large gala dining room, a drawing room, reception room, the Emperor's official study, galleries, and a small interior "Moorish" courtyard. The corner room on the first floor, its windows looking out over Yalta and the sea, served as the Empress's study while a similar corner room on the other side of the palace, facing the resort of Alupka and more sea, became Nicky's private study. The children's rooms were on the same floor, as was the family's private dining room and another drawing room. The furniture, also "style moderne," had been designed by Russian artists, and the upholstery and curtains were of cretonne. Everything had been done in the way Nicky and Alix liked it, as a comfortable family home—albeit on a rather grand scale. Being so closely involved with the palace's conception and design had its pitfalls, as Spiridovich enumerated: "The Empress had put so much care into organizing, installing and decorating the Palace that she would not tolerate the slightest criticism of it. But the entourage took a malign pleasure in numbering its defects and in denigrating Krasnov."

On October 2, Alix engaged Kokovtsov in conversation for an hour; for this, he was summoned to her side as she sat in an armchair after lunch, for, as Kokovtsov remarked, she found it painful to stand for any length of time. He soon realized that his predecessor had been no favorite of the Empress's; she had felt that Stolypin had "overshadowed his sovereign," and she begged Kokovtsov not to make the same mistake.

In the afternoons Nicky would go off for excursions, leaving the town by car (his favorite make of car was Delaunay-Belleville) and then taking a long walk, followed and accompanied by officers (as well as by the inevitable security police). Nicky, as is evident from the time he had exhausted Anastasia, took his walking very seriously. He refused to allow any business talk during these excursions, but liked to be entertained with amusing anecdotes. The walks usually took place along the coast for about a dozen kilometers, the cars having been sent on ahead to an agreed meeting point. There was also some hill walking, when the Tsar's companions would frequently have difficulty keeping up with him. It was not only Anastasia who was occasionally reduced to tears. Nicky would have planned out the itinerary in advance and would not stop until halfway, when he would suggest that everyone sit down and have a cigarette, offer barley sugars to the nonsmokers, and set off again after a five-minute rest. The men would return from these climbs soaked through, and would have to have a complete change of clothing. Such long expeditions were rare, however, as they took too much time out of the Emperor's working day. The usual walk, along the coast, lasted from two to five o'clock, when they would all return for tea. The public would often be massed on the quay to await the arrival of the cars.

In addition to his walks, Nicky loved playing tennis—which again he did with great seriousness, having as partners and opponents a number of the *Standart*'s officers. A routine developed whereby Tatiana would telephone the *Standart* at two o'clock, to announce whether there would be an excursion or a game of tennis. In the latter case, the tennis-playing officers would get in a car sent from the imperial garage and be driven to Livadia. They would play until teatime, the imperial daughters joining in—apart from one of them, who would sit with Alix, watching the game and doing some needlework. Tea was usually taken in the pavilion alongside the courts.

The other activity undertaken by the family at Livadia was at Alix's inspiration, and this was a charity bazaar in aid of the poor of Yalta and its surroundings. The imperial daughters, maids-of-honor, and selected officers all joined in with the preparations, making various objects for sale. Many of the local ladies were also involved; there was much competition to have a stall in the same room as the Empress, or to be part of her committee. The bazaar of 1911 opened on September 25, in the boys' school. In the main hall behind a large semicircular table stood Alix, all her daughters, and one of their cousins, assisted by the maids-of-honor, members of the retinue, and a number of officers. A host of magnificent objects were on display, many of which—cushions, sachets, lampshades, boxes, and frames—had been made by the Empress herself. Several of the artifacts bore portraits of the imperial family, particularly of Alexei, who also made his appearance from time to time behind the table. Other members of the nobility, including Grand Duchess Militsa Nikolaevna, had their own stalls nearby. The bazaar proved immensely popular with the local populace, all eager to see the imperial family and buy something from their hands. Despite feeling unwell, Alix made every effort to be charming, while her daughters enjoyed signing postcards and selling them. Even Nicky came in to greet the enthusiastic crowds. Alix felt in control here and in her element; this was the sort of event her mother, Princess Alice, might have organized in Darmstadt. If this sort of charitable activity could have constituted the regular occupation of a Russian Empress—rather than the exhausting and grandiose imperial receptions in St. Petersburg—Alix would have been much happier. For the security detachment, this whole three-day event was a nightmare.

The other excitement of this autumn in Livadia was a ball to mark Olga's sixteenth birthday on November 3. It was preceded by a dinner served at small tables, with Nicky, Alix, and several of their imperial relatives (including the Montenegrin princesses and their husbands, suggesting that the reports of their mutual antipathy by this time have been somewhat exaggerated) seated at a round table in the center. Olga, wearing a pink dress and with her hair up for the first time, presided over a separate table with the aide-de-camp Nikolai Sablin acting as her partner for the evening. Tatiana was alongside her, with another officer from the *Standart* for her partner.

They also had for company the Emir of Bukhara and two Generals. Maria and Anastasia were present, too, as were a number of other imperial children, the maids-of-honor, members of the retinue, local society ladies, and a variety of military officers, including a delegation of the 9th Regiment of Hussars from Elizavetgrad, of which Olga was the chief.

At the conclusion of dinner, various guests were presented to Nicky and Alix while the tables were cleared away and the room prepared for dancing. Formalities were slightly relaxed, in that it was announced that the gentlemen might invite the Grand Duchesses to dance without having to ask for a special authorization each time they did so. The music was provided by the band of the Crimean regiment, the dances being directed by its commander.

Alix watched the dancing from an armchair, the seven-year-old Alexei standing next to her in his customary white sailor suit. He was tired and beginning to yawn, but resolutely determined not to leave. The Empress told him to go to bed, but he didn't move—despite the fact that he could hardly keep upright. And so Nicky had to tell him it was time to go, and off he went at once with his tutors, pouting. Nicky meanwhile spent the ball playing bridge, frequently getting up from the table to look at the young people enjoying themselves. The final mazurka ended at two o'clock, Nicky and Alix having stayed to the end. The guests made their formal good-byes, and the imperial family retired to their private apartments.

Various works of fiction suggest themselves as comparisons when considering the lives of the last Romanovs. The Emperor and Empress liked to cast themselves as the hero and heroine of sentimental Victorian novels, such as *Through the Postern Gate,* by Florence L. Barclay, while to an observer the works of Chekhov, with their atmosphere of indecisive, passive melancholy, might seem more appropriate. *War and Peace* is another possibility, the character of Nicholas II having already been compared with that of Tolstoy's peasant philosopher, Platon Karatayev. In one respect, however, their lives contained all the fearful secrecy, the hidden family burden, of a *Jane Eyre* with its unmentionable curse hidden away in the attic. This is the kind of unspoken menace—so menacing precisely because unspoken, unadmitted, and hence giving rise to rumor upon rumor—hinted at in this telling paragraph from Pierre Gilliard's memoirs: "During the years following I had increasing opportunities of seeing Alexei Nikolaevich, who made a practice of escaping from his sailor nurse and running into his sisters' schoolroom, from which he was soon fetched. And yet at times his visits would suddenly cease, and for quite a considerable period he was seen no more. Every time he disappeared everyone in the palace was smitten with the greatest depression. My pupils betrayed it in a mood of melancholy they tried in vain to conceal. When I asked them the cause, they answered evasively that Alexei Nikolaevich was not well. I knew from other sources that he was prey to a disease which was only mentioned inferentially and the nature of which no one ever told me." The same sense of hidden, unmentionable threat is present in Spiridovich's account: "The terrible disease, which the parents carefully tried to hide from the entourage, but which, like the sword of Damocles, hung, menacing, over the imperial family, began to show itself by signs which allowed no equivocation. And, despite all the efforts made to keep the disease a secret, the news of this misfortune was not slow to traverse the walls of the palace and the surroundings of Livadia."

CHAPTER EIGHT

Grigory the Wonder-Worker

1912

Simple-lifers, utopian socialists, spiritualists, occultists, theosophists, quietists, pacifists, futurists, cubists, zealots of all sorts in their approach to life and art, later to be relentlessly classified into their respective religious, political, aesthetic or psychological categories, were then thought of by the unenlightened as scarcely distinguishable one from another: a collection of visionaries who hoped to build a New Heaven and a New Earth through the agency of their particular crackpot activities, sinister or comic, according to the way you looked at such things.

—Anthony Powell, *The Kindly Ones*—on the "unsorted ideas" prevalent throughout Europe in the decade leading up to the First World War

On January 6, 1912, the Emperor authorized his uncle Grand Duke Pavel, who had been living abroad since his marriage to Olga Pistohlkors, to return to Russia. Pavel received back his grade of general aide-de-camp and his title of regimental chief, while his wife was authorized to take the name and style of Countess of Hohenfelsen. This was also the day on which Pavel's son, Grand Duke Dmitry Pavlovich, who attained his majority that year, swore his oath of fealty to the Tsar and the Fatherland.

On January 14, Nicky and Alix visited the Academy of Arts in St. Petersburg to see an exhibition of ancient Russian icons and traditional craftwork, such as embroideries. This was part of the second All-Russian Congress of Artists, opened under the aegis of Grand Duchess Maria Pavlovna (the elder, widow of Grand Duke Vladimir), the president of the Academy of Arts. It covered art education, aesthetics, museology, folk art, conservation, and some aspects of the avant-garde, and included academicians as well as members of the World of Art movement. Its aim was to give a full survey of the attainments of Russian art at this vibrant period, which later came to be known as the "Silver Age."

Around the turn of the year Bishop Hermogen of Saratov and the monk Iliodor had both definitively fallen out with Rasputin. They did not like the fact that their creature, like Frankenstein's monster, had gone beyond their control, was moving in more powerful circles than theirs, and in fact no longer needed them or was prepared to operate in their interest. Hermogen, who had recently been appointed to the Synod in an attempt to "tame" him (he was another of extreme right-wing views), had demanded to see Rasputin and had berated him, in Iliodor's presence, for his dissolute lifestyle and interference in the imperial household and had attempted to insist he return to his native village of Pokrovskoe and stay there. It is even possible that the two clerics had set upon Rasputin and physically attacked him. He managed to escape, but from now on he and the other two dubious characters were sworn enemies. Hermogen requested to see the Emperor, wanting to put his side of the story and denounce Grigory, but he was too late, Grigory having got there first. Hermogen was dismissed from the Synod, and exiled to a remote monastery in the province of Minsk. These events now became virtually the sole topic of conversation among the wider imperial family, as is clear from Xenia's diary entry of January 25:

> I went to see Alix, whom I found in bed, in her large room. We talked about Hermogene, Iliodor and most importantly, Gr. Rasputin. The papers are forbidden to write about him—but a few days ago his name was again mentioned in several of them, and those issues confiscated.
>
> Everybody already knows and talks about him, it's terrible the things they say about him, about Alix, and everything that goes on at Tsarskoe. The Yusupovs came to tea—always the same conversation—and at the Anichkov in the evening and over dinner I recounted all I had heard. How will it all end? It's terrible.

It is somehow typical of this whole episode and of the court that while, on the one hand, Xenia laments all this gossip and wonders where it will all end, she happily joins in promulgating it, recounting "all that [she] had heard." She notes further on January 26: "A motion was tabled in the Duma, and adopted unanimously, on the question of the confiscation of certain newspapers because of Rasputin; the unfortunate ministers now have to answer! It's all simply terrible."

Having fallen out with Rasputin, Iliodor had lost his support with the imperial family and hence there were to be no further interventions on his behalf. He was at last exiled to the Florishchevsky Monastery in Vladimir province.

Nicky then took the decision to have the case against Rasputin—that he belonged to the sect known as the *khlysty*—reexamined. He was himself convinced that the "*starets*" did not, and that the evidence previously collected by Bishop Anthony of Tver was conclusive in this regard. He therefore imagined that a reexamination would end this particular piece of speculation once and for all and help to dampen down press interest. But in his commissioning of Mikhail Rodzianko, the President of the Duma, to report on the earlier report, the wires seem to have become crossed as Rodzianko interpreted the commission as a request to conduct a completely new examination, by collecting afresh all relevant documents and interviewing witnesses. Moreover, he seems to have believed that the conclusion he was supposed to reach would indict Rasputin and free the court and government from his influence. Nicholas, on the contrary, was expecting Rodzianko to find the rumors of Rasputin's sect membership to be false and to put a stop to them (and, presumably, to all other derogatory rumors). Kokovtsov perceived that some misunderstanding was afoot and, by his own account, tried to limit it: "I reminded [Rodzianko] that he had been asked only to study the matter and not to hold a second inquiry, and warned him that by making too much of his task he might only revive and prolong the scandal and further compromise his Emperor. Apparently my advice had some effect, but not enough to alter Rodzianko's conviction that he had been entrusted with the mission of saving the Tsar and the country from Rasputin."

On February 11, Grigory met with the imperial family, including all the children, in Nicky's study at Tsarskoe Selo. Nicky noted that it was "a great comfort to see him and listen to him talk." Four days later, Maria Fyodorovna came to tea and engaged Nicky and Alix in conversation about him. The Dowager Empress then reported on this conversation to her daughter Xenia; it seems to have at least afforded her some relief and not worsened her relationship with her son and daughter-in-law, though Alix was intransigent and Nicky seemed unable, or unwilling, to act. "In general everything [Alix] said was besides the point," declared Xenia, "and there is obviously a lot she doesn't understand—she castigated society (dirty-minded gossips), Tyutcheva for talking too much and lying, and the ministers 'all cowards.'" The theme of Alix "not understanding" was to become a common one among the wider Romanov family; the feeling was entirely mutual.

Rasputin now began to be talked about regularly in the Duma—during, for instance, the sessions of the budget committee in February. Soon after the falling-out between him and his two erstwhile cronies, letters that purported to have been written by Alix and her children to the "*starets*" began to circulate in the capital, the person responsible for their dissemination being Alexander Guchkov, Rodzianko's predecessor as Chairman of the Duma. The letters dated from 1908 to 1909 and, though innocent in themselves, were capable of other interpretations, particularly by those hostile to the Empress. The originals (of which hectograph copies had been made) appeared to have been stolen from Rasputin, and the culprit was most probably Iliodor.

The Minister of Internal Affairs, Alexander Makarov, tried to stop the press writing about Rasputin, but to no avail. Kokovtsov's efforts to influence the press fared no better. He took the view that Rasputin—or the idea of Rasputin—was being used as a weapon to beat the monarchy and the tsarist system, rather than being of genuine significance in himself: "I made use of a visit to M. Suvorin and Mazaev to try to make them see that the constant mentioning of Rasputin in the papers only gave him so much publicity and, what was infinitely worse, played into the hands of all the revolutionary organizations that were trying to undermine the prestige of the Monarch. Both men agreed with me but insisted that they could do nothing." The Tsar's initial response to all the publicity had been to seek for ways to strengthen the censorship of the press, but this met with no encouragement from his ministers; he had first made his displeasure felt on the subject of the newspaper campaign against Rasputin in January, when he sent an irritated note to Makarov, "demanding that he 'take firm measures to bring the press to order' and prohibit them from printing anything about Rasputin."

Meanwhile Rodzianko, with the help of two of his colleagues, spent about a month compiling his report on Rasputin and then presented it to the Tsar. Nicholas expressed amazement at its size, thanked Rodzianko, and said he would summon him again once he had absorbed the report. Nothing happened immediately, and Rodzianko began to suspect that the Tsar was refusing to see him, as his request for an audience to discuss Duma matters was ignored. This suspicion led Rodzianko to threaten resignation, on the grounds that he could not permit such an "affront" to the President of the Duma. Kokovtsov was in the process of trying to calm Rodzianko, telling him he was sure the Tsar's silence was unintentional, when evidence to the contrary arrived. "Great was my astonishment," recorded Kokovtsov, "when in the midst of our conversation a courier delivered a large envelope from the Tsar, and on opening I found, among other things, Rodzianko's request for an audience, sharply scored in the Tsar's handwriting." Kokovtsov did not let on to Rodzianko what had just arrived, and the latter left feeling reassured. When Rodzianko had gone, Kokovtsov read the Tsar's comments, which he records as follows: "I do not wish to receive Rodzianko, especially since I saw him but a few days ago. Let him know this. The conduct of the Duma is deeply revolting. . . . I shall be very glad if my displeasure is made known to these gentlemen; I am tired of always bowing and smiling to them." This latter sentiment seems to have been increasingly felt by Nicky.

When Kokovtsov saw the Tsar the following morning, he attempted to convince him of the folly of giving offense to Rodzianko, which would only precipitate conflict with the Duma and thereby antagonize public opinion—the importance of which the Tsar still only grasped sporadically. Kokovtsov sensibly sought for a way out: "to make it easier for the Tsar to reverse his former decision I asked him to write Rodzianko a personal note saying that he had not a minute to spare before his departure, requesting that all reports be forwarded to Livadia, and promising to receive the President of the Duma as soon as he returned." Nicholas agreed to Kokovtsov's proposal to smooth things over for now and, thanks to the latter's diplomacy and tact, the incident ended happily: "At about five that same afternoon Rodzianko telephoned me and announced in the most cheerful tone that he had received a very gracious note from His Majesty, that he considered the incident liquidated, and that he hoped I had not spent too much effort in presenting the affair to the Tsar." Perhaps overoptimistically, "All is well that ends well," said Kokovtsov to himself.

The imperial family left St. Petersburg for Livadia in mid-March, and Kokovtsov's account of their departure gives a clear impression of the mood of the imperial couple: "The Tsar was in his usual good humor, and on bidding me farewell said jokingly: 'You are probably envious of me, but I am not envious of you; I am only sorry for you who have to remain in this bog.' The Empress passed us all without saying goodbye to anyone, and boarded the train with the Dowager Empress." They were accompanied by the tutors, Petrov and Gilliard, who were lodged in a separate house on the estate, where they initially took their meals with some of the court officials and officers. The family was joined at luncheon only by the retinue and various visitors; in the evening they dined entirely *en famille*. After a few days, the Empress invited the tutors to join the imperial luncheon parties. Alix herself, however, rarely made an appearance at these meals—which her daughters also found rather long and tedious—as she usually ate in her own rooms, along with Alexei.

The level of privacy maintained by Alix and Nicky about their family affairs becomes clear when one realizes that it was not until Alexei was almost eight years old, in March of this year, that Alix had finally admitted to her sister-in-law Olga that he suffered from "that terrible illness." She linked her own state of health to that of her son, adding that "she herself has become ill because of this and will never fully recover." She had also been seeking to explain something of her trust in Rasputin: "As far as Grigory is concerned, she said how can she not believe in him, when she can see that the boy feels better the moment he is near him, or prays for him." Xenia, on hearing about the situation from Olga, could not help feeling immense sympathy for Nicky and Alix, while at the same time continuing to be appalled by all the rumors and wishing that her sister-in-law could understand more clearly the results of some of her actions. Those of the family who were not fully apprised of the situation merely observed that Alexei was rather spoiled and badly behaved, as did KR's wife during that same month: "Recently," wrote KR, "my wife had lunch with their Majesties, and was embarrassed by the behaviour of the Heir. . . . He wouldn't sit up, ate badly, licked his plate and teased the others. The Emperor often turned away, perhaps to avoid having to say anything, while the Empress rebuked her elder daughter Olga, who was next to her brother, for not restraining him. But Olga cannot deal with him."

Kokovtsov arrived in Yalta to report to the Emperor on the evening of April 21. He was well aware throughout that spring and summer that the Empress was displeased with him, and that this vitiated his relationship with the Emperor. He had been trying to convince the Tsar to receive the members of the Duma on his return from Livadia, but it had been proving difficult to evoke a positive response: "Finally, towards the end of the first week in June, all that remained was to take a final vote on the parish-school credits and to celebrate a mass. Still the Tsar did not give me an answer. I was obliged to write him a letter, asking him to fulfil his promise to the Duma members. That evening I received a brief answer, 'I have no time to receive the Duma.'" Immediately on the family's return to Tsarskoe Selo in June, Kokovtsov met with the Tsar to dissuade him from offending the Duma. Kokovtsov's record of this conversation and its aftermath gives a rare glimpse of Nicky when annoyed:

> I was forced to undertake the difficult and thankless task of persuading the Tsar not to take this dangerous step but to overcome his personal irritation for the sake of the common good. I requested a special interview, and the next morning (June 10) at nine o'clock I set about

> persuading the Tsar to receive the Duma members. To all my arguments, to all representations of the harm that would result from such an unfortunate ending of the five years of Duma work, I received no reply. I had to have recourse to an argument which I disliked to advance: I reminded the Tsar that he, through me, had definitely promised the Duma members that he would receive them should they adopt the naval program.
>
> The Tsar looked at me with frank irritation: "This would mean that I will deceive the Duma members if I refuse to see them?"
>
> "Yes, Your Majesty," I answered, "you have given your word, which heretofore you have always kept. Or, perhaps I overstepped my authority and permitted myself to make a promise without having received your permission to do so. In this case I must bear the responsibility for having overstepped my authority."
>
> "No, indeed," said the Tsar. "You are right; I have no right to break my promise and I thank you once again for having persuaded me not to take a wrong step. I shall receive the Duma members the day after tomorrow. I do not know what I shall tell them; their speeches have been very disagreeable and even revolting to me, and it will be difficult for me to refrain from telling them so."

Kokovtsov then drafted a conciliatory speech for the Tsar to deliver to the members, thanking them for their service and looking forward to seeing again those of them who would be reelected for the next term of office. Kokovtsov described the occasion:

> The reception of the Duma members took place on Friday, June 12, at 11:-00 a.m., at the Alexandrovsky Palace. Only myself, Baron Fredericks, and the aide-de-camp on duty were in attendance. The Tsar entered the room along the three walls of which the members stood according to the alphabetical order of their constituencies. He greeted me and the President of the Duma, and walked along in front of the members, speaking at some length with some of them. To Guchkov he limited himself to a remark, "I believe you are from the gubernia of Moscow?" then walked into the center of the room, took a sheet of paper from his hat, and made his address, glancing at the text from time to time. It followed my draft quite closely, but contained a very sharp sentence which mine did not contain. "I was much distressed

> with your opposition to the matter of parish schools, which is particularly dear to me as having been bequeathed to me by my unforgettable father."

Through this expression of displeasure, the Tsar seemed to have scored an own goal:

> This addition made a great impression upon the majority of the Duma members. They exchanged glances in silence, and when the Tsar had gone and everybody was invited into an adjoining room where tea and sandwiches were served there were expressions of disappointment and discontent on all sides. On that same day, the Duma by an overwhelming vote declined several remaining credits for these parish schools which had remained undecided from former sessions. Thus ended the work of the Third Duma.

The Duma was dissolved on June 20, and the imperial family immediately set off to meet Kaiser Wilhelm in Port Baltic in Estonia. Nicky's diary entry for June 21 reads: "Got up early to a wonderful, clear morning. At 9.30 we saw the German ships. At exactly 10 o'clock the *Hohenzollern* dropped anchor between us and the *Polar,* and its cruiser *Moltke* in among our ships. I went over to Wilhelm and at 11 o'clock returned to the yacht. Then he and his son Adalbert came over to us and stayed for lunch." On the following day Nicky went aboard the cruiser *Moltke,* which he inspected together with Wilhelm. In the evening the whole of the imperial family, except for Alix, visited the German imperial yacht, the *Hohenzollern*. There, the Kaiser gave them presents, and they dined, listened to music, and watched a film, before returning to the *Standart*.

During this meeting, the Kaiser engaged Kokovtsov in a spirited discussion about the future of the European oil-producing nations, and was disinclined to break it off when Nicholas became impatient (another indication that the mask could sometimes slip; however courteous Nicky might be as a general rule, he was not used to being kept waiting or to being excluded): "The sun was scorching. The Tsar did not want to interrupt our conversation, but behind Emperor Wilhelm's back he made signs of impatience to me. The Kaiser, however, continued to answer my arguments with increasing fervor. Finally the Tsar seemed to lose all patience, approached us, and began to listen to our conversation, whereupon Emperor Wilhelm turned to him with the following words (in French): 'Your Chairman of the Council does not sympathize with my ideas, and I do not want to permit him to remain unconvinced. I want you to allow me to prove my point with data collected at Berlin, and when I am ready I should like to have your permission to resume this conversation with him.'" After this meeting, the Tsar was nevertheless, according to Kokovtsov, feeling cheerful: "The Tsar was in fine spirits, mentioned several times that Emperor William had assured him positively that he would not permit the Balkan complications to become a world conflagration. 'Nevertheless,' said the Tsar, 'we must get ready. It is a good thing that we succeeded in adopting the naval program; besides, we have to prepare our land defense.'" Nothing of a practical nature emerged from this meeting; "the official communiqué made it clear that no realignment of the European powers was to be expected."

A happy event of 1912 was the building of the Fyodorovsky Sobor, or the church of St. Theodore, at Tsarskoe Selo, an initiative of the Empress, and funded by her. Nicky and Alix had been to watch the crosses being lifted onto the cupolas on February 26, before inspecting the church's interior. It was consecrated on August 20. This church was designed "in pure Russian style" and furnished with objects selected by Alix. The lower church included a small room for herself, alongside the sanctuary, from where she could both see the altar (dedicated to St. Serafim of Sarov) and make her private devotions. Here Alix was able to indulge her taste for mysticism: "She visited this room alone, mostly during mass but sometimes at other hours, and it was there that she gave herself up to her religious moods. It was there that her faith in the miraculous grew within her, and it was to the solace of that room that she turned whenever she felt assailed by the doubts, worries, and cares of life. Those close to her often said that she emerged from her solitude in the Fyodorovsky Church as someone completely changed and transfigured. On several occasions they had heard her say that in her solitude she felt all her doubts dissolved in a way she could not explain; her most poignant sorrows left her, and in their place came calm and peace of heart." Countess Anastasia Hendrikova, who became a lady-in-waiting to the Empress around this time and soon became one of her closest friends, explained to Kokovtsov something of the nature of Alix's religious beliefs: "The Empress believed that one's whole life should be based upon complete faith in the Almighty and obedience to His will. Nothing was impossible for God, she believed. He would hearken to every prayer of the pure in heart; faith in Him would overcome all obstacles. Even though miracles might not be understood, He worked them none the less, and they were to be accepted with meekness and humility." It is possible to read Alix's future acts and words through the prism of these beliefs; it is, nevertheless, also possible to perceive how she underestimated her determination to impose her own solutions on events, her own interpretation of what was the will of God and what should be done to bring it about.

At the beginning of September the family spent a fortnight in the forest of Białowieza, from where Nicky wrote to KR (whom he addressed as "Kostia") explaining his reservations, which he shared with the Holy Synod, about the wisdom of a public staging of KR's play *King of Judea*. He had been deeply moved, he wrote, when he read aloud this play to Alix, and this is precisely why he feels a public performance could be dangerous, although he would be happy for it to be staged as a private court performance. The nub of the problem centered on the fear of stirring up the latent, but ever-present, anti-Semitism of the Russian people. "I told your wife in conversation," wrote Nicky, "that, as well as the lofty sentiments which it inspired in me, I was also fired by a hatred of the Jews, who crucified Christ. I think the common Russian man would feel the same thing, if he saw it on stage, and from there it would not be far to the possibility of a pogrom." Nicky went on to tell KR about the recent celebrations at Borodino and Moscow, commemorating the hundredth anniversary of the battle of Borodino: "The tour of the Borodino field made an indelible impression on me, especially the thought that every clod of earth under our feet had been washed in the blood of one of 58,000 of our heroes, both dead and wounded, during those two days! And then to meet and talk with a *survivor of the battle*—a 122-year-old former sergeant major! I felt as I would in the presence of the greatest relics! In Moscow everything went well and successfully, but for me at least, Borodino was far greater and more intense!"

At Białowieza disaster struck, when Alexei, despite the best efforts of his sailor-protector Derevenko, bruised himself badly. The accident had happened at bath time, when the child had been feeling particularly lively. It was a large bath made out of majolica, and had to be climbed into via several steps. Alexei had climbed up on to the edge and had then decided to show Derevenko how the sailors on the *Standart* leaped into the sea when they wanted to get washed. He jumped—and hit himself against the side of the bath, where it jutted out. It hurt, but not too much at first, so he said nothing—but several minutes later he fainted. A serious internal hemorrhage had begun.

The child's condition was spoken about as little as possible, Alix and Dr. Botkin directing the treatment—which essentially consisted of nothing except bed rest. When he began to be a little better—that is, he was in less pain but still could not walk—he was given some fresh air by being carried outside in the arms of a Cossack. In mid-September, when Alexei was still suffering and unable to walk, the family left Białowieza for Spała. Here, when the weather was mild enough, he was taken out for rides in a small carriage, but one day, when he was riding along with Alix in a barouche, the jolts of the carriage set off his hemorrhage again. The swelling in his groin, the result of his first accident and starting to lessen, now increased again and he had to return to bed, in terrible pain. His groaning and crying could often be heard all through the palace. Dr. Botkin was with him constantly, but was unable to ease his pain, which was so great that the little boy could not bear to let anyone touch the tumor. He lay on one side with his leg drawn up, unable to eat or sleep.

Professors Fyodorov (the court surgeon) and Rauchfuss (a pediatrician) were summoned from St. Petersburg, arriving on October 4, the eve of Alexei's name day. Nicky wrote in his diary on the 5th: "We did not spend a happy name day today, as for the last few days Alexei has been suffering from a second internal haemorrhage. The first time happened in Bieloveji. Professor Fyodorov arrived yesterday. Thank God he found a certain improvement today. There was a service and a lunch with the house suite. Played a little tennis. The weather was warm and grey." Despite the reported "certain improvement," the child grew steadily worse, his temperature rising. On October 6, the doctors declared the situation was desperate. In another case, Fyodorov might have tried cutting open the tumor, but the danger of provoking a fatal hemorrhage was too great, particularly when the patient was the heir to the throne. There was a very slight chance—only about one in a hundred—that the tumor might be reabsorbed spontaneously, but the situation looked hopeless. Yet with all this going on in the little boy's bedroom, the perceived need for secrecy meant that elsewhere in the palace life proceeded as normal; "one shooting-party succeeded another, and the guests were more numerous than ever."

Gilliard paints a vivid picture of the strain endured by the family, particularly by the anguished parents, a strain exacerbated by their refusal to allow anyone outside a very tight, closed circle to know the nature of Alexei's condition, the extent of his suffering, and the danger he was in:

> One evening after dinner the Grand-Duchesses Marie and Anastasie Nikolaevna gave two short scenes from the *Bourgeois Gentilhomme* in the dining-room before Their Majesties, the suite, and several guests. I was the prompter, concealed behind a screen which did duty for the wings. By craning my neck a little I could see the Czarina in the front row of the audience smiling and talking gaily to her neighbours.
>
> When the play was over I went out by the service door and found myself in the corridor opposite Alexei Nikolaevich's room, from which a moaning sound came distinctly to my ears. I suddenly noticed the Czarina running up, holding her long and awkward train in her two hands. I shrank back against the wall, and she passed me without observing my presence. There was a distracted and terror-stricken look

> on her face. I returned to the dining-room. The scene was of the most animated description. Footmen in livery were handing round refreshments on salvers. Everyone was laughing and exchanging jokes. The evening was at its height.
>
> A few minutes later the Czarina came back. She had resumed the mask and forced herself to smile pleasantly at the guests who crowded round her. But I had noticed that the Czar, even while engaged in conversation, had taken up a position from which he could watch the door, and I caught the despairing glance which the Czarina threw him as she came in. An hour later I returned to my room, still thoroughly upset at the scene which had suddenly brought home to me the tragedy of this double life.

As Alexei became more and more ill, his mother spent more time closeted with him, while his father continued to exercise his iron self-control, appearing outwardly calm and behaving as usual, joining in the shooting parties and entertaining his guests in the evening. There is in this crisis, however, an indication that Nicky's self-control was not solely the result of a code of behavior he believed to be right, but also indicative of an inability, or refusal, to engage emotionally—a fear, if he allowed himself to see and feel too much, of complete collapse. Self-control was, for him, at least in part a form of self-protection. Later, to his mother, he was able to express some of the anguish he had experienced, as well as describing the awful pain the little boy had had to endure: "The days from 6th–10th October were the worst. The poor little mite suffered terribly, the pains gripped him in spasms, which reoccurred practically every quarter of an hour. He was delirious day and night from the fever, and used to sit up in bed, a movement which immediately brought on the pain again." All the child could do was moan and keep repeating "Lord have mercy" (the oft-repeated phrase from the Orthodox liturgy—*Gospodi pomilui, Gospodi pomilui, Gospodi pomilui*). "I could hardly bear to stay in the room," Nicky confessed, "but I had to relieve Alix, as she was understandably exhausted from spending days at a time at his bedside."

As the little boy's temperature continued to mount and his pulse to weaken, Baron Fredericks finally managed to persuade the Tsar that information needed to be given out to the public; KR mentioned having seen a bulletin in the *Evening Times* about the Tsarevich's illness on October 9. There was clearly a genuine fear that he would die. Now that the seriousness of Alexei's illness had finally been admitted publicly—even if the precise nature of it was not made clear—prayers could also be said in public for his recovery, and this began to happen in

Spała twice a day, the services being attended by many of the local peasantry. In fact, at about the same time that Alexei's condition was at last made public, he started very slowly to show signs of recovery; this must have been the crisis. Nicky wrote on October 9: "I stayed in Alexei's room until 2 o'clock, when he began to quieten down and fall asleep. He had quite a good day in general, and slept frequently, his temperature was back to 39.5." On the next day his temperature had dropped further; he received Communion and was then "quite quiet and cheerful for the rest of the day." Everyone began to cheer up, and Nicky managed to get out for a longer walk with all his daughters. Nicky told his mother about this day: "On 10th October we decided to give him communion, and he *immediately* felt better, his temperature dropped from 39.5 to 38.2, the pains almost ceased and he fell into a peaceful sleep for the first time."

What Nicky does not mention to his mother was that, as the crisis approached, Alix had telegraphed to Grigory to beg for his prayers. All hope seemed to be lost, Alexei believed himself to be dying, and then a telegram arrived in reply. "The illness does not appear dangerous," it read. "Don't let the doctors tire him." To anyone as steeped in the Gospels as were Nicky and Alix, this message would immediately remind them of some of the miracles of healing performed by Jesus, particularly the healing of children—when he did not even have to be present, but would send a few words to say all would be well. In another telegram, Grigory announced that he was praying, that God listened to his prayers and would grant them. The tension immediately lifted from Alix, and Alexei began to recover, the one-in-a-hundred chance of spontaneous reabsorption having begun to take place. The child's fever continued to abate, and on October 12 it was possible for him to be lifted out of bed and carried over onto a sofa, where he had a nap. Little wonder if, in the words of Spiridovich, "The mother, in all her joy, could see only one thing: it was from the 'friend' that salvation had come, it was his prayers that had saved the child's life."

During this time of crisis, as in several others, Alix had managed to overcome her own invalidity. She paid the price afterward, however. "She withstood it all better than I did while Alexei was so bad," Nicky told his mother, "but now that the danger has, thank God, passed, she is feeling the consequences of what she went through. It has taken its toll on her poor heart. However she is taking greater care of herself and spends the days lying on the couch in Alexei's room." Nicky's way of coping, once the crisis was over, was to go hunting; he had also continued to observe his normal work pattern as far as he could throughout the period of Alexei's illness.

In order that the young patient, as he began slowly to recover, should be able to benefit from continual specialist care, Professor Fyodorov summoned one of his assistants, Dr. Vladimir Derevenko, from St. Petersburg. Dr. Derevenko now became a constant and welcome presence in the life of the imperial family. The doctors had warned the child's parents that Alexei's recovery would be slow, and that he would still feel pain in his left knee, which he could not yet bend. It was important that he be kept quiet and still, in order for the tumor to continue to subside, and he would need to be carefully nourished as he had become very thin.

The attempt made by Alix and Nicky to keep their son's diagnosis a secret resulted, as was so often the case with their PR strategy, in having the opposite effect to the one they intended. Instead of keeping speculation about Alexei's condition to a minimum, it increased it enormously. In the absence of clear and accurate information, the wildest stories abounded. It also meant that the sympathy they might have garnered as loving, anxious parents was lacking; in particular, this entirely valid and understandable reason for Alix's frequent absences from court events, for her look of strain and unhappiness, was never presented to the world. Yet again they misunderstood the nature of public opinion, and missed an opportunity to engage public sympathy. The small amount of news released officially, and the obvious delay in Alexei's illness being reported at all, inevitably gave rise to all sorts of rumors, as can be judged even from the reports in those newspapers that denied them: "There is not a single word of truth in the rumors about a plot," stated *The Times*.

Another consequence of Alexei's brush with death came from nearer home. On October 16, despite his earlier promise of having no intention of marrying his mistress, Natalia Brasova (Nicky had granted this surname to Natalia Wulfert in 1911, after she had had children by Misha), Misha had done precisely that. At the end of the month, he wrote from Cannes to confess the same to his mother and brother. It seems that what had propelled him to take the step at this time was Alexei's illness and the fear that he himself would once again become Nicky's heir—and then it would be impossible for him to marry Natalia. He explained this to his mother, at the same time reiterating that his relationship with Natalia had been deeply important to him for several years. Misha also claimed to be in torment over knowing how much this would hurt his mother and brother, but felt unable to act otherwise. To his brother he gave a similar explanation. "Our wedding took place at the Serbian church of St. Savva in Vienna on 16/29 October," he told him. "I know that punishment awaits me for this act, and am ready to bear it."

Maria Fyodorovna's reaction was quite as horrified as Misha had anticipated, as she wrote to Nicky of this "*terrible cruel new blow.*" Her letter is full of anguished underlinings and hyperbole, as she contemplates the consequences of yet more marital scandal in the imperial family, and seeks for some form of damage limitation:

> I simply can't believe it, and can hardly understand what I am writing, it's so unspeakably awful in every way, and has *completely killed me!*
>
> I only ask that it should remain a secret, so there shouldn't be *another scandal,* there have been other marriages in *secret,* which everyone *pretended not to know about.* I think it's really the only thing that can be done now, otherwise I won't be able to show myself any more, it's such a *shame and a disgrace!*

Nicholas himself was both appalled and hurt by his younger brother's action, as he explained in his reply to their mother:

> Yes, dear Mama, I say as you do—may the Lord forgive him! Unfortunately everything is over between him and me now, because he has broken his word.
>
> How many times did he tell me, without my asking, *he himself gave* his word that he would not marry her. And I believed him implicitly! What upsets me particularly—is that he refers to Alexei's illness as having forced him to rush into this ill-considered step! He doesn't seem concerned with either your distress, or our distress, or the scandal this event will cause in Russia. And at such a time, when everyone is talking of war, and just a few months before the Jubilee of the Romanov dynasty!!! It's shameful and awful!

The Tsar can see no way of avoiding this scandal being made public: "My first thought was also to keep the news quiet, but on reading his letter two or three times I realized that it's impossible for him to return to Russia now. Sooner or later everyone here will find out, and will be surprised if nothing has happened to him, as the others were dealt with very severely." Both Nicky and his mother, backed up by Misha's former aide-de-camp Mordvinov, rationalized their feelings over this marriage by casting the lion's share of the blame onto the woman in question, Nicky writing in exceptionally strong language for him: "Poor Misha is evidently not responsible for his own actions at the moment; he thinks and reasons as she tells him, and it's utterly useless to argue with him. Mordvinov has very much asked us NOT TO WRITE to him AT ALL, as she not only reads any telegrams, letters and notes, but takes copies which she shows to her people and then keeps in

Alix and Nicky, shortly after their engagement in 1894.

RIA Novosti

A family photograph in 1903, including Nicky (back, far left), Alix (back, second from left), Ernie (back, far right), Ella (front, second from left), Ducky (front, second from right), and Sergei (front, far right).

RIA Novosti

The young Nicky on a hunting expedition.

Private collection of Alexandre Tissot-Demidov

The Coronation procession on May 14, 1896. *RIA Novosti*

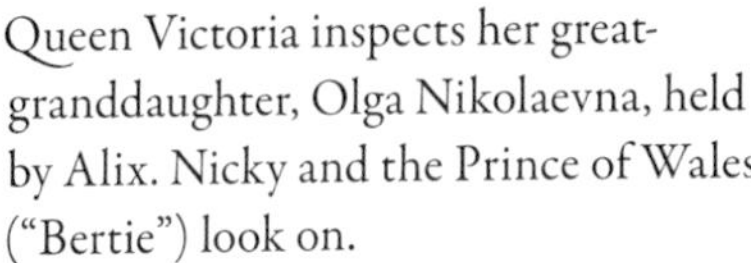

Queen Victoria inspects her great-granddaughter, Olga Nikolaevna, held by Alix. Nicky and the Prince of Wales ("Bertie") look on.

Private Collection / The Bridgeman Art Library

Nicky holding his baby son, Alexei. By now (June 1905) Nicky and Alix already knew that Alexei was a hemophiliac.

RIA Novosti

Maria and Alexei. "Alexei Nikolaevich was the center of this united family, the focus of all its hopes and affections. His sisters worshipped him and he was his parents' pride and joy." *Beinecke Rare Book and Manuscript Library, Yale University*

Alexei with his personal bodyguard, the sailor Derevenko.

Private Collection / Peter Newark Military Pictures / The Bridgeman Art Library

Alix with her three younger children – Anastasia, Alexei, and Maria.

Beinecke Rare Book and Manuscript Library, Yale University

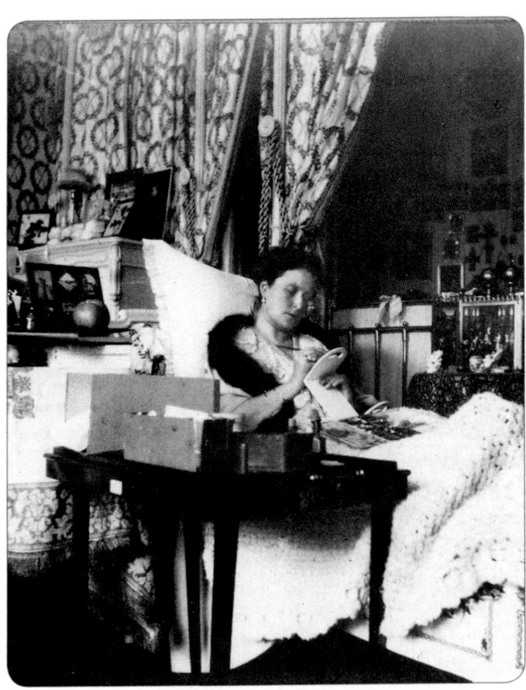

Alix keeping herself busy while resting on her daybed. Note the profusion of icons and other objects of devotion on her wall.

Beinecke Rare Book and Manuscript Library, Yale University

The two invalids – Alexei and his mother.

Beinecke Rare Book and Manuscript Library, Yale University

Alix in earnest conversation with one of her little "girlies," on board the imperial yacht.

Beinecke Rare Book and Manuscript Library, Yale University

The opening of the State Duma in April 1906, representatives of the imperial court and members of the newly elected Duma facing each other across the Great Throne Room as the Tsar addresses them.

RIA Novosti

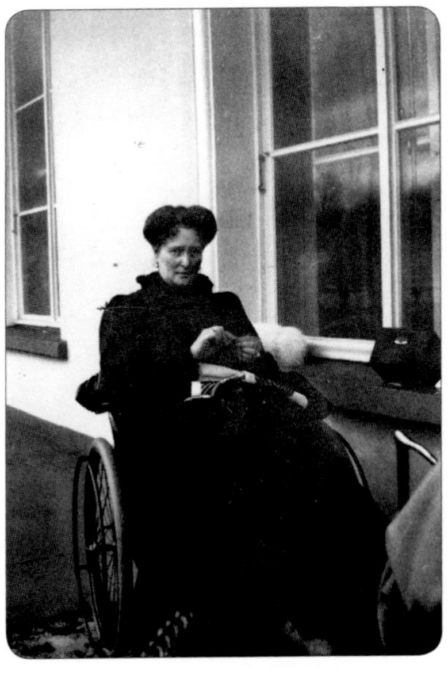

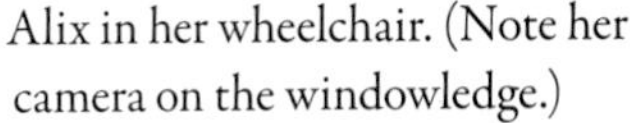

Alix in her wheelchair. (Note her camera on the windowledge.)

Beinecke Rare Book and Manuscript Library, Yale University

Nicky with his mother, the Dowager Empress, on the imperial yacht. Maria Fyodorovna rests a proprietorial hand on her son's leg.

Beinecke Rare Book and Manuscript Library, Yale University

On the imperial yacht: Alix and Tatiana are employed in sewing, while Maria, looking bored, holds her camera, and Anastasia, looking cross, holds her dog.

Beinecke Rare Book and Manuscript Library, Yale University

Alexei plays with kittens on board the imperial yacht.

Beinecke Rare Book and Manuscript Library, Yale University

Something Anastasia has said seems to have amused the Tsar (the habitual cigarette in his hand).

Beinecke Rare Book and Manuscript Library, Yale University

One of the most well-known Romanov family groupings (clockwise, from bottom: Alexei, Alix, Maria, Tatiana, Olga, Anastasia, Nicky).

RIA Novosti

An afternoon expedition in the Crimea.

Beinecke Rare Book and Manuscript Library, Yale University

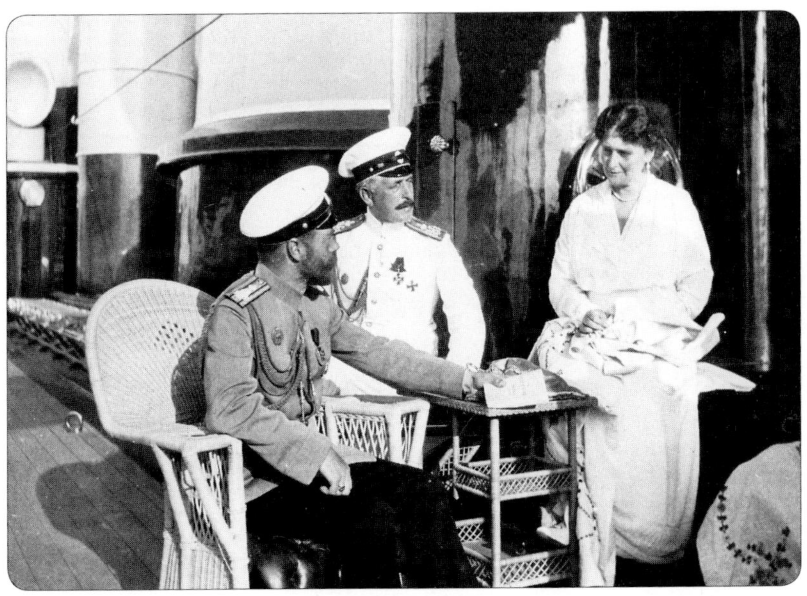

Nicky and Alix with their friend "NP," on board the imperial yacht.

Beinecke Rare Book and Manuscript Library, Yale University

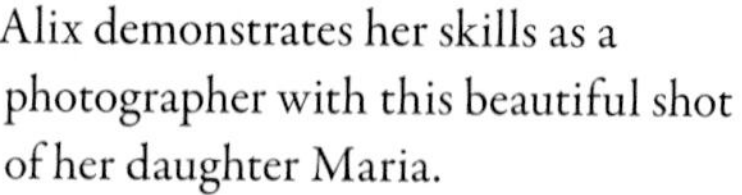

Alix demonstrates her skills as a photographer with this beautiful shot of her daughter Maria.

RIA Novosti

Alix captures something of Anastasia's restless spirit in this photograph, taken, as was that of Maria, on the balcony of the Alexander Palace.

RIA Novosti

"Our Friend," Grigory Rasputin, raising his hand in blessing.

Private Collection / The Bridgeman Art Library

Ania Vyrubova seated at the feet of the Empress, in a consciously intimate pose.

Beinecke Rare Book and Manuscript Library, Yale University

Tea during a tennis match. The three-way relationship of Nicky, Alix, and Ania Vyrubova is especially striking here: Ania stares at the camera, while Alix watches Nicky, who is looking at Ania.

Beinecke Rare Book and Manuscript Library, Yale University

Alexei entertaining his tutor, Pierre Gilliard, on the imperial yacht.
Beinecke Rare Book and Manuscript Library, Yale University

A walk through the Kremlin during the Romanov Tercentenary celebrations: the stout Alix is doing her best to look friendly, while Alexei, unable to walk after a severe bout of illness, is carried by a Cossack.

RIA Novosti

The Tsar appears on the balcony of the Winter Palace, after the declaration of war with Germany in July 1914.

Beinecke Rare Book and Manuscript Library, Yale University

Ania, Tatiana, Alix (sitting), and Olga, in their uniforms as Red Cross nurses during World War I.

Beinecke Rare Book and Manuscript Library, Yale University

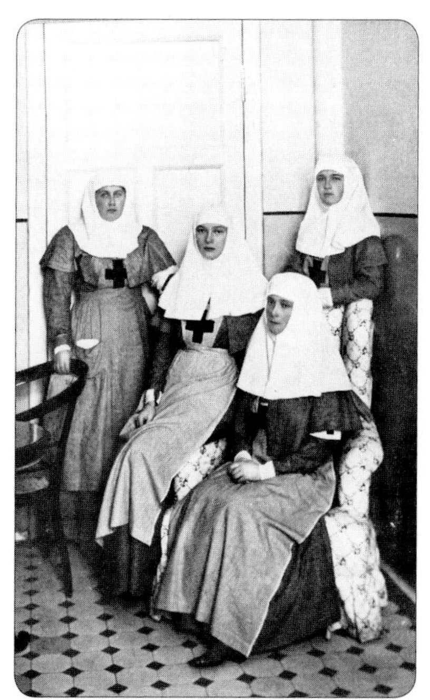

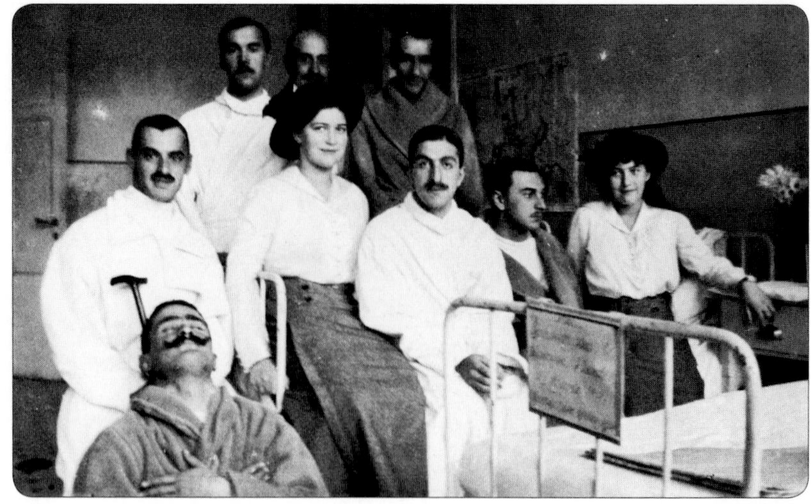

Maria and Anastasia, too young to train as nurses, nevertheless spent time with some of the wounded officers. Judging from this photograph, the experience was one of mutual enjoyment.

Beinecke Rare Book and Manuscript Library, Yale University

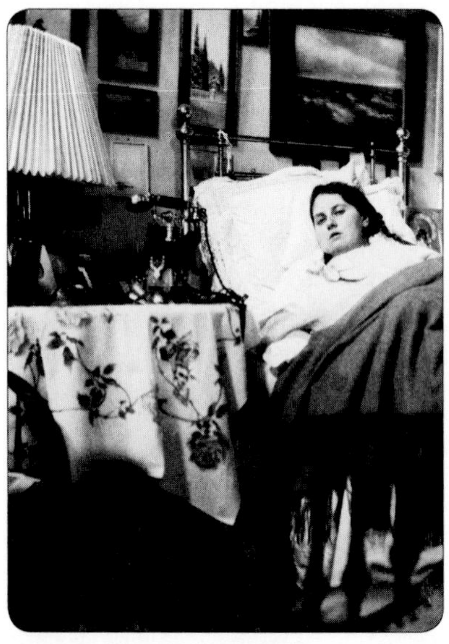

Ania in bed after her accident in January 1915. (Note the telephone within easy reach.)

Beinecke Rare Book and Manuscript Library, Yale University

Nicky and Alexei during World War I.

RIA Novosti

The Tsar exchanging the triple kiss with soldiers, and distributing eggs, to celebrate Easter in April 1916.

RIA Novosti

The Tsar with the heads of the allied military missions in September 1916. From left to right: Baron Rickel (Belgium), General Sir John Hanbury-Williams (Great Britain), Tsar Nicholas II, Marquis de Guiche (France), Colonel Londkievic (Serbia).

RIA Novosti

Nicky (soon after having assumed command of the Russian Army) discussing a plan of military operations with Generals Alexeev (right) and Pustovoitenko.

RIA Novosti

The ex-Emperor under guard at Tsarskoe Selo.

RIA Novosti

The ex-Tsar and his children getting some fresh air on the roof at Tobolsk.

Private Collection / Peter Newark Military Pictures / The Bridgeman Art Library

the bank together with the money. She's such a cunning, wicked beast that it's disgusting to even talk about her." There appears never to have been an imperial change of mind about Natalia, Nicky's sister Olga noting in her memoirs: "Neither the Emperor nor either of the two Empresses ever received Misha's wife."

In early November, with infinite precautions being taken over Alexei, the family set off for Tsarskoe Selo. General Hesketh, the director of the Vistulan railways, was instructed to ensure that the journey was carried out without jolts, the slightest tremor being potentially dangerous for the Tsarevich. Hesketh recommended the train driver not to use the brakes, and this is how the journey was accomplished, Alexei, constantly watched over by Dr. Derevenko, experiencing no discomfort all the way. In St. Petersburg Nicky and his daughters transferred to a sledge for the rest of the journey, Alix and Alexei following in a car.

Gilliard sums up Alexei's condition after this crisis: "Alexei Nikolaevich's condition required assiduous and special medical attention. His illness at Spała had left behind it a temporary atrophy of the nerves of the left leg, which remained drawn up and could not be straightened out by the boy himself. Massage and orthopaedic appliances were necessary, but in time these measures brought the limb back to its normal position." But he was no longer the small cuddly-looking child he had been. Back at Tsarskoe, Alexei was cheerful and well enough to be able to play in bed, and sometimes to sit in an armchair. He also, like his mother, had a wheelchair, in which he persuaded his sailor-nurse, Derevenko (his having the same name as Alexei's new doctor did give rise to some confusion), to push him up and down the corridor for hours.

The other unfortunate event of this autumn was the suicide of Admiral Chagin, the commandant of the *Standart,* well-liked by all the family. He had in recent months become involved with a young girl from Yalta, an initial flirtation having developed into something more serious and threatening to become a scandal. She had followed him back to St. Petersburg, and her parents had begun, not unreasonably, to make demands. Chagin had decided the only honorable course of action was to marry her, but for this he needed the Emperor's permission. He had set off for Spała, determined to make a clean breast of it, but on learning of the critical condition of the Tsarevich, he had decided he could not now bother the Tsar with his own troubles and had returned home—where, after the girl had visited him again, he had gone into his study, arranged his papers, and shot himself in the mouth. Nicky was deeply upset, telling Nikolai Sablin: "I find it very painful to think that Ivan Ivanovich left us, without reflecting how much his death would grieve us."

CHAPTER NINE

Upsets at Home, and the Beginning of War

1914–1915

I spoke to Nicky and he replied that Willy was a bore and an exhibitionist, but he would never start a war.

—Memoirs of Nicky's sister Olga

VLADIMIR KOKOVTSOV WAS dismissed as Chairman of the Council of Ministers on January 29, 1914. Nicky's letter informing him of this fact was characteristic:

Vladimir Nikolaevich:

It is not a feeling of displeasure but a long-standing and deep realization of a state need that now forces me to tell you that we have to part.

I am doing this in writing, for it is easier to select the right words when putting them on paper than during an unsettling conversation. . . .

I appreciate highly your devotion to me and the great service you have performed in achieving remarkable improvements in Russia's state credit; I am grateful to you for this from the bottom of my heart. Believe me, I am sorry to part with you who have been my assistant for ten years. Believe also, that I shall not forget to take suitable care of you and your family. I expect you with your last report on Friday, at 11:00 a.m. as always, and ever as a friend.

With sincere regards,
Nicholas

Kokovtsov was sure that the Tsar's decision had been forced on him: "Then as now I could see clearly that the Tsar had written the letter under the influence of that pressure which had been brought to bear upon him for the purpose of removing me. Evidently the Tsar did not trust himself during a conversation with me, fearing that I might advance arguments which would force him to change his mind; on the other hand, the persons enjoying his confidence persisted in their purpose, and therefore he had decided to take a step which made his decision with respect to me irrevocable." Their final, friendly interview was painful for both men: "Both of us had to struggle against the emotions that surged within us. For some moments neither of us could speak; the Tsar could not hold back the tears." As the meeting drew to a close, " 'Tell me again,' [the Tsar] said, 'that you bear me no enmity and that we part as friends.' I assured him of my undying love for him and my unending gratitude for all his past kindness. Then he embraced me, and I withdrew."

Kokovtsov's leave-taking interview with Alix, though requested by him, never took place. "I did not press the matter," he recorded, "for I knew Her Majesty was not well disposed toward me. Thus I did not see the Empress again."

In February the Tsar was concerned, as so many Russian rulers have been since, with curbing the level of alcohol abuse in the country, and he proposed to do this by ending the state monopoly on the sale of alcohol. *The Times* reported Nicholas's initiative with approval, particularly as it appeared to be in line with the views expressed in the Duma, especially by the peasant representatives: "The Imperial Rescript which the Tsar has addressed to M. Bark, the new Russian Minister of Finance, will be read with even deeper interest than was the news of M. Kokovtsoff's retirement. It was a twofold importance—social and political. It declares that the most crying of all the moral evils that afflict Russia—the evil of national drunkenness—must be dealt with by the State. It declares further that the Emperor's conviction of the imperative need of this reform, based upon personal observation during his recent tour, is confirmed by the views expressed by the Legislative Chambers in their late debates upon the spirit monopoly of the State. Western opinion always looks with pleasure upon the cooperation of the Tsar and of the constitutional organs of the nation."

In late April 1914 there was a crisis involving Ania Vyrubova, Nicky, and

Alix. Precisely what form the crisis took is difficult to ascertain, though it is clear from remarks Alix made later that it included "stories and love-scenes and rows." It took place in Livadia, where the imperial family had arrived at the beginning of April. Alix wrote to Nicky from Livadia on the 28th of that month, when he had set off on a two-day expedition to the nature reserve at Askania-Nova, telling him that though she would miss him "*horribly*," she was glad for his sake that for the space of those two days he would "get new impressions and hear nothing of Ania's stories." Whatever Ania had been carrying on about, she had been upsetting not only her friend the Empress but also the Empress's husband, for Alix is quite clear that "she gives you worries and disagreeable conversations, no rest for you either." Alix is very bitter about whatever has happened; she feels her trust and love have been betrayed, the family's generosity in opening their hearts and home—"our private life even"—taken advantage of and in some way thrown back in their faces. What is more, this is not the first such betrayal to have occurred; something horrible had also happened over their former friendship with Princesses Militsa and Stana and their husbands—now referred to by Alix as "the black family." "My heart is heavy and sore," she tells her husband, "must one's kindness and love always be repaid thus?"

In Ania Vyrubova's own brief account of what had happened, she is inevitably concerned to portray herself in the best light. She declares that Alix became jealous of her relationship with Nicky, and imputes the main blame for this jealousy onto Alix herself, commenting: "In letters written during this period, especially from the Crimea during the spring of 1914, the Empress said some very unkind and cruel things of me, or at least I should consider them cruel if they had not been rooted in illness, and in physical and mental misery." Ania's interpretation of events is that, with the invalid Alix unable to give Nicky what he needed in terms of companionship, he had come to depend on Ania and had in fact fallen for her. "I have, I think, spoken frankly of the preference of the Emperor for my society at times," she wrote, sounding decidedly pleased with herself, "in long walks, in tennis, in conversation. In the early part of 1914 the Empress was ill, very low-spirited, and full of morbid reflections. She was much alone, as the Emperor was occupied many hours every day, and the children were busy with their lessons. In the Emperor's leisure moments he developed a more than ordinary desire for my companionship, perhaps only because I was an entirely healthy, normal woman, heart and soul devoted to the family, and one from whom it was never necessary to keep anything secret. We were much together in those days, and before either of us realized it the Empress became mortally jealous and suspicious of every movement of her husband and of myself."

Spiridovich provides another take on what had occurred between the imperial couple and Ania:

> That season, everything was not going as might be wished in the imperial family. The Empress was extraordinarily nervous. Her long prayers often ended in tears, sobs, veritable crises of hysteria.
>
> A serious falling-out took place at that time between the Empress and her friend A. A. Vyrubova. By her excessive attentions towards the Emperor, to whom she demonstrated on every occasion limitless admiration and solicitude, the latter provoked jokes from some, including from the Emperor himself, and jealousy from the Empress.
>
> This situation was aggravated by the fact that, according to various rumours which spread beyond the Palace, Mme Vyrubova had spoken in derogatory terms of both the Emperor and the Empress. As a consequence of all these incidents, the attitude of Their Majesties towards Mme Vyrubova changed profoundly. And as she had become to some extent a member of the imperial family, the change of attitude towards her could not help but trouble its own tranquility and confidence.

Against this background of trauma, with even the imperial daughters beginning to show obvious signs of annoyance with Ania, there were discussions going on about a possible marriage—between the eighteen-year-old Olga and Prince Carol of Romania. Pierre Gilliard believed that the parents on both sides were in favor of the match, though Nicky had promised Olga she would not be made to marry the Prince if she did not wish it. In general she professed herself very disinclined to leave Russia. At the official banquet in Romania, where these discussions were pursued, Olga was seated next to Prince Carol and was her usual charming self, while her sisters, all rather bored, kept watching her, then catching Gilliard's eye and winking. On the following day it was clear that the projected marriage was either off altogether or postponed indefinitely. The prince's apparent lack of cultivation and "mop of badly combed hair" had probably done nothing to promote his cause.

At the beginning of June the family arrived back in Odessa and visited Kishinev (then in Bessarabia) to attend the unveiling of a monument to the memory of Alexander I, before traveling on to Tsarskoe Selo. There the Tsar received a brief visit from the King of Saxony. Soon afterward the family transferred to Peterhof before setting off at the beginning of July for a brief cruise in the Finnish fjords. On embarking on the *Standart* at Kronstadt, Alexei banged his ankle in misjudging a jump, and by the evening he was in increasing pain.

This was to be a disturbed cruise in another way, too. During it, news arrived that Rasputin had been stabbed in the stomach by a young woman in his home village, and his life was in danger. There were very mixed feelings on board the *Standart,* as Gilliard makes clear: "There was great excitement on board, whisperings and mysterious confabulations which suddenly stopped whenever anyone suspected of being an adherent of Rasputin came near." There was no knowing what the Tsar thought about this; he was, according to Spiridovich, "as impenetrable and cheerful as ever." Alix was out of sight, tending to her son. Ania, still included in the holiday despite the falling-out, was vocally indignant. Meanwhile an eminent surgeon, Professor Wreden (who had also advised on an orthopedic contraption for Alexei) had been dispatched to Pokrovskoe to operate on Rasputin. It was considered that he saved his life. Other news that had arrived just before the cruise, of rather more significance—though few people on board (apart from the Tsar) may have realized it, preoccupied as they were with the drama surrounding Rasputin—concerned the assassination of Archduke Franz Ferdinand in Sarajevo.

Partway through this holiday, the imperial family returned to Peterhof for the four-day visit of the President of France, M. Poincaré. Though Alexei was by now recovering, he was still unable to walk and had to be carried off the yacht. Nicky noted in his diary on July 7: "At exactly two o'clock the French squadron put into port. At 7.30 there was an official dinner with speeches. After the talks, we bid goodbye to the kind president and returned home at 10 o'clock." Maurice Paléologue, the French ambassador to Russia, also wrote of this dinner in his memoirs:

> I kept an eye on the Tsarina Alexandra opposite whom I was sitting. Although long ceremonies are a very great trial to her she was anxious to be present this evening to do honour to the President of the allied Republic.
>
> She was a beautiful sight with her low brocade gown and diamond tiara on her head. Her forty-two years have left her face and figure still pleasant to look upon. After the first course she entered into conversation with Poincaré who was on her right.
>
> Before long however her smile became set and the veins stood out in her cheeks. She bit her lips every minute. Her laboured breathing made the network of diamonds sparkle on her bosom. Until the end of

dinner, which was very long, the poor woman was obviously struggling with hysteria. Her features suddenly relaxed when the Tsar rose to propose his toast.

The departure of M. Poincaré coincided with war becoming a virtual inevitability, Austria having reacted to the assassination of Franz Ferdinand by presenting Serbia with a clearly unacceptable ultimatum and all the great imperialistic powers of Europe being drawn in to defend their own interests and those of their allies. Gilliard (his informant having been Anastasia) describes the scene at Peterhof, in the Lower Palace at Alexandria, on the evening of the day Germany declared war on Russia (July 19). Nicky had gone to his study to read the dispatches that had arrived for him while they had all been at church, and had immediately telephoned his Minister of Foreign Affairs, Sergei Sazonov, and asked him to come to the palace as soon he could: "Meanwhile the Czarina and the Grand-Duchesses were waiting for him in the dining-room. Her Majesty, becoming uneasy at the long delay, had just asked Tatiana Nikolaevna to fetch her father, when the Czar appeared, looking very pale, and told them that war was declared, in a voice which betrayed his agitation, notwithstanding all his efforts. On learning the news the Czarina began to weep, and the Grand-Duchesses likewise dissolved into tears on seeing their mother's distress." Sazonov arrived at nine o'clock and went off into the study with the Tsar; during the course of the evening the British ambassador, Sir George Buchanan, also arrived.

Nicky's own report of this momentous day was characteristically laconic: "Went for a walk with the children. At 6.30 we went to church. On our return we learnt that *Germany* has declared war on us. . . . During the evening, the English Ambassador Buchanan arrived with a telegram from Georgie. Spent a long time with him composing a reply. Then I saw Nikolasha and Fredericks. Had tea at 12.15." King George V, Nicky's "very devoted cousin and friend," also wrote to him at further length. "Both you and I did all in our power to prevent war," Georgie declared, "but alas we were frustrated and this terrible war which we have all dreaded for so many years has come upon us. Anyhow Russia, England, and France have clean consciences and are fighting for justice and right. I feel sure D.V. that we shall be victorious in the end, for the right spirit exists in all our troops and Navies. I deeply sympathize with you in these anxious days and I trust that your troops will soon be able to move, ours will shortly be in France cooperating with the French. I trust for all our sakes that this horrible war will soon be over and peace once more exist in Europe." Earlier in the day the Tsar had informed Grand Duke Nikolai Nikolaevich of "his appointment as

Commander-in-Chief until such time as I joined the army," showing both that he was expecting Russia to be soon at war even before the declaration from Germany had been received and that he all along intended Nikolasha's appointment to be only temporary and that he himself would take over the command when the time seemed right.

On the following day, the imperial family (minus, to all their chagrin, Alexei, who had suffered another minor accident that delayed his recovery and had to be left behind in bed) set off for St. Petersburg, where the Tsar was to make the official declaration to his people that Russia was at war. Gilliard recalled that "He looked even worse than on the previous evening, and his eyes sparkled as if he had the fever." Nicky himself wrote of that day that it was "good . . . particularly from the point of view of morale." In the morning he had gone to church with Maria and Anastasia, and in the afternoon, accompanied by his wife and daughters, he embarked on the *Alexandria* to sail to St. Petersburg, completing the journey to the Winter Palace by carriage. Again Nicky provides a straightforward factual account of what then took place:

> I signed the manifesto of the declaration of war. From the Malachite room we went to the Nikolaevsky hall, where the manifesto was read out and a Te Deum celebrated. The whole hall sang "Save us, Lord" and "Many years."
>
> I said a few words. On our return the ladies rushed to kiss our hands and jostled Alix and myself slightly. Then we went onto the balcony over Alexander Square and bowed to a huge mass of people. At about 6 o'clock we went out onto the embankment and made our way back to the cutter through a large crowd of officers and public. We returned to Peterhof. Spent the evening quietly.

On July 27, Nicky and all his family were present to greet Maria Fyodorovna on her return to Peterhof after her visit to England and a difficult journey home (she had been refused permission to travel through Germany). Nicky and the children frequently visited her for supper during the following days. For Alexei's tenth birthday on July 30, his grandmother gave him a little donkey, which he liked very much. On Sunday, August 3, with the departure for Moscow planned for that evening, Nicky went mushroom picking in the company of his mother and daughters. Florence Farmborough, a young Englishwoman working as a governess and subsequently as a Red Cross nurse in Russia, was in Moscow to see the arrival of the Tsar. "The city was astir at an early hour," she wrote of the day when he was due to attend a solemn liturgy in the Kremlin's Cathedral of the Assumption, "and the streets were packed with excited crowds. The Emperor's reception by the people would be very sincere and warm, for he ranged side by side with God in the affection and estimation of the peasant masses. What *Batyushka* Tsar could not do for them, *Batyushka* God would bring about, and what *Batyushka* God would not do, *Batyushka* Tsar could bring to pass." Florence describes the moment when the imperial family came into view: "The waiting seemed endless and the atmosphere had become tense with expectancy when, in the distance, a group appeared. As they drew nearer, figures and faces became recognizable. The Tsar and Tsarina walked in front: he, a slim, refined figure in full uniform with many decorations; she, tall and elegant, moved slowly in step with him at his side. The four young Grand Duchesses followed, walking slowly two by two: Olga and Tatiana, Anastasia with Maria. They were lovely girls and exquisitely dressed in long frilled frocks and large picture hats. They walked easily, but with dignity." And behind them came Alexei, carried by "a tall, massive, broad-shouldered Cossack, in full Cossack uniform." All that Florence, in common with most of the people watching, knew of Alexei's condition was that he "was of delicate frame and sickly constitution; not allowed to walk far, lest he should overtire himself." Gilliard recalled of that day: "When Alexei Nikolaevich found he could not walk this morning he was in a terrible state. Their Majesties have decided that he shall be present at the ceremony all the same. He will be carried by one of the Czar's cossacks. But it is a dreadful disappointment to the parents, who do not wish the idea to gain ground among the people that the Heir to the Throne is an invalid." Florence watched as "The Imperial party bowed and smiled, acknowledging the vociferous acclamations of the crowds, moving towards the ancient cathedral, where the highest ecclesiastics were gathered." After the liturgy the imperial family knelt to pray at the tombs of their ancestors.

While in Moscow Gilliard used to go out for a drive with Alexei every morning, and on one occasion the car containing himself and the Tsarevich (followed by another car containing the sailor Derevenko) got held up in a crowd. Not only were the people (characterized by Gilliard as "humble folk and peasants from the district who had come into the city to shop or in the hope of seeing the Tsar") excited at seeing the heir—they were also desperate to touch him, in the same way that they might, in church, have expressed their devotion and intercession to an icon by the touch of hands or lips:

> The crowd surged towards us, surrounded us, and came up so close that our way was blocked, and we, so to speak, found ourselves prisoners of

> these moujiks, workmen and shopkeepers who struggled and fought, shouted, gesticulated, and behaved like lunatics in order to get a better view of the Tsarevich. By degrees some of the women and children grew bolder, mounted the steps of the car, thrust their arms over the doors, and when they succeeded in touching the boy they yelled out triumphantly: I've touched him! . . . I've touched the Heir!
>
> Alexei Nikolaevich, frightened at these exuberant demonstrations, was sitting far back in the car. He was very pale, startled by this sudden popular manifestation, which was taking extravagant forms which were quite novel to him. He recovered himself, however, when he saw the kindly smiles of the crowd, but he remained embarrassed at the attention bestowed upon him, not knowing what to say or do.

Eventually they were rescued by two policemen, who dispersed the crowd.

On September 14, the young Dmitry Pavlovich lunched with the imperial family at Tsarskoe Selo, having just been with Grand Duke Nikolai at the army General Headquarters (known as "Stavka" and based at Baranovichi, between Warsaw and Vilna). "It was so pleasant to see him," commented Nicky, "especially with the St. George cross on his chest. Sat with him for an hour and a half, and talked about many things." In the evening Grigory—eventually—arrived (Nicky noting that they had had to wait for him for a long time, Grigory being the only person apart from Ania Vyrubova with the temerity to keep the Emperor and Empress waiting). Once he had turned up, they sat with him "for a long time."

Alix wrote to Nicky on the eve of his first departure for Stavka, expressing her sorrow at several things: his departure, the fact that war had begun, and sorrow both for her adopted and her native countries, especially for her brother and sister now officially on the side of the enemy. Far from being sympathetic toward the German cause, as many came unjustly to suspect of her, Alix is embarrassed by the possible association of herself with what she feels Germany has become: "And then the shame, the humiliation to think that Germans would behave as they do! One longs to sink to the ground." From the start, no matter how difficult it was for her personally, Alix supported Nicky's determination to spend time with the armed forces. "I must rejoice with you that you are going and I do," she told him, "but yet egoistically I suffer horribly to be separated—we are not accustomed to it and I do so endlessly love my very own precious Boysy dear."

Alix's letter to Nicky of the following day (September 20) tells us several things. Nicky has now set off for Stavka, and, after saying farewell to him, Alix has come home and broken down in tears. She has pulled herself together by praying, having a lie down, and smoking cigarettes—so, whatever her heart condition, smoking was not considered to affect it badly, but rather the reverse. Nicky was himself a chain-smoker and had been for years; so was his mother (who would try to hide her cigarette behind her back at official functions, oblivious to the column of smoke rising above her) and, judging from photographs, at least two of his own daughters took up the habit. When her eyes were less swollen from crying, Alix went to Alexei's room and lay there on the sofa, near him, in the dark, and felt better for having had this rest. She also sends "much love" to Nicky from Ania (referred to simply as "she"), and so from this we can gather that relations had been restored, if not completely, with Ania (this is five months after the crisis); that Ania is permitted to express affection, indeed love, for Nicky; and that Ania is significant enough to be referred to, and understood, merely as "she." Ania is currently staying in "the big palace" at Tsarskoe Selo, rather than in her small house, and she is somewhat unwell. She has a bad leg, which ailment includes "obliteration of veins" (thought to be a result of phlebitis) and the cure being to "keep quiet a few days." Earlier that day (this may all have occurred the day before if Alix is writing in the morning), Ania had driven (or, rather, been driven) into St. Petersburg to see Rasputin ("our Friend"), whom Nicky had also seen prior to his departure. Rasputin is, Alix asserts, anxious about Grand Duke Nikolai Nikolaevich, believing that his supporters want him to be put in charge of Petrograd (the wartime name for St. Petersburg) or Galicia, but Alix purports not to share this anxiety as she believes Nicky would never risk giving Nikolasha too great a place of power. He was already, of course, Commander-in-Chief of the army. According to Alix, it is Grigory who cannot bear the idea of "N" playing a significant part, because he (Grigory) loves the Tsar jealously; Grigory was adept at knowing what Alix herself thought and felt and feeding it back to her as reinforcement, so it is not unreasonable to assume that these are also Alix's own feelings about Nikolasha. Alix then tells Nicky that she is premenstrual ("Apparently the engineer-mechanic is near"), and that she has pain in her teeth and jaw, in consequence of which her "face is tied up." Her eyes are still sore and swollen from crying.

Alix's period (this time referred to as "Bekker") duly arrived the next day, on which she had lunch on her sofa (always spelt "sopha") with her daughters ("the girlies"). Alexei was still confined to bed, and his mother spent an hour or two lying near him, but she was also active at this time—at least at intervals—and went off to meet a trainload of wounded soldiers in the second part of the afternoon. In the evening she went to see Ania again, finding her daughters there already—so relations between Ania and the girls have not been permanently disrupted by whatever passed between her and their parents—along with the family's friend Nikolai Sablin. Princess Vera Gedroitz (the first woman-surgeon in Russia and in charge at the hospital set up by Alix at Tsarskoe Selo) called in to inspect Ania's leg, and Alix bandaged it for her.

In Nicky's reply (dated September 22) he inadvertently gives away one of the reasons he enjoys being at Stavka; it is not just that he has always liked to think of himself as a military man, at home in the company of officers, but also because he has less to do when he is there. Not being as inundated as usual with paperwork and reports to receive, he is now "so free" that he has time "to think of my Wify and family." "Strange but true!" as he remarks himself. In addition to sending blessings and kisses to his wife and all his children (referring to Alexei as "agoo wee one"; even more excruciatingly, when the couple indulge in their habit of babytalk, Nicky himself is sometimes referred to by Alix as "Agoobig-weeone"), he signs off by sending love to Ania. Evidently a decision has been made that this is what he will do; the implication is that this will keep her quiet.

The children's letters to Nicky are full of love, as well as giving him factual accounts of what they have been doing—rather in the style of his own letters and diary. One also gets the sense from the early letters that they were expecting the war to be short and victorious. On September 21, Maria congratulated him on the "victory" (one of the early Russian victories in Galicia), and went on to describe how her mother and her two elder sisters had been "bandaging" in the hospital set up in the Catherine Palace, while she and her brother had been "through all the wards and talked to almost every soldier." She also reports on her little brother's health ("Alexei, thank God, is all right") and ends with enormous affection: "You have to take me with you next time, or else I will jump onto the train myself, because I miss you. Sleep well." The ten-year-old Alexei's letter to his "Darling Papa" is very brief, but also loving and cheerful: "I am delighted by the victory. I'm better. I am still in bed. Anastasia was trying to strangle M. Gilliard. We are all waiting for you." Anastasia's own letter of September 23 is a mixture of affection, information, and her own irrepressibility: "My brilliant Papa!" she begins, "I am writing again, while Shura brushes my hair for the night. Olga is having a meeting, Tatiana is also there. Ania had dinner with us, now she is on the couch, Maria is writing to you, and Mama went to see Alexei. Today we studied, then all four of us went to the store, we worked a lot plus it was rather jolly." "I don't want to go to bed," she continues. "I want to be there with you, wherever you are, as I don't know where it is." She, too, reports that "Alexei is better, he's in bed and in very good spirits."

A constant source of irritation to Nicky—but particularly to Alix—during his visits to Stavka concerned the restrictions placed on his movements. The imperial couple shared a romantic notion that the Tsar should be visiting a lot of fighting troops—to boost morale and remind them what (and who) they were fighting for—but Grand Duke Nikolai Nikolaevich and other officers in the field obviously had reservations about letting the Tsar go off anywhere he pleased, potentially endangering both himself and others, and he would not actually disobey the Commander-in-Chief (even if Alix, and Rasputin, thought he should).

The drops that Alix took for her heart trouble (referred to by her as Adonis drops, Adonis vernalis still sometimes being given as a homeopathic remedy to regulate the pulse) and for her frequent headaches could not, she believed, be taken during her period, and so she sometimes felt particularly ill at those times of the month. Normally she took drops three or four times a day, believing that otherwise she would not be able to keep going. Nevertheless, despite her period, neuralgia, headache, and enlarged heart, she showed remarkable stamina at this time, being trained as a Red Cross nurse along with her two elder daughters (and, to a lesser extent, Ania) and assisting at operations for several hours a day.

Her complaints about Ania generally concern the latter's alleged selfishness, her expectation that her friend the Empress will spend several hours every day with her, despite her health problems and the work she is undertaking—and the fact that Ania herself is not exactly neglected. Thus Alix complains to Nicky on September 23, "Ania was offended I did not go to her, but she had lots of guests, and our Friend for three hours." Ania does have something the matter with her at the moment, centering on her leg; one almost gets the sense that she is competing with Alix in the illness stakes. It is certainly a curious relationship, in which this woman of no particular standing at court can demand so much time and attention from the Empress—as though she herself were the Empress, and Alix a rather unsatisfactory lady-in-waiting. Ania's ailments also seem to have been timed to suit herself, as Alix is aware, but cannot counteract. It is almost as though Ania is playing Alix at her own game—and winning. She has become a sort of caricature, a slightly vulgar version of the Empress—a not-quite-malign doppelgänger, like a character out of Gogol or the "petty demon" of Fyodor Sologub, the "*nedotykomka,*" the embodiment of "*poshlost,*" a concept that has elements of both evil and banality, the frightful mirror into which Alix is forced to look—lying on a couch while other people run around her—and this at a time when Alix herself is running around and being far more active than usual. And so Alix comments to Nicky on September 24: "Ania's leg is much better to-day, and I see she intends to be up for your return—I wish she had been well now and the leg next week bad, then we should have had some nice quiet evenings cosily to ourselves." It is extraordinary that the Emperor and Empress could not demand "some nice quiet evenings cosily" to themselves, if that was what they both wanted. Ania now seems to be back in her own little house—Alix had to rush over there for half an hour in the afternoon, as Grigory was there and wanted to see her, and she returned in the evening with her daughters and Sablin. Ania has really got Alix under her thumb, the latter now indulging in a litany of complaints about her "friend" (not "the Friend") to Nicky; the picture she paints is almost comic: "She is not over amiable these days & only thinks of herself & her comfort & makes others crawl under the table to arrange her leg on lots of cushions, & does not trouble her head whether others sit comfortably—spoilt & badly brought up." Alix is sure that Ania will make the most of Nicky's absence, by letting him know when he returns how "wretched" she has been "the whole time," despite having people come to see her all day long. Ania is also determined to rub in, and let everyone see, how devoted she is to Nicky, and to suggest, by having an array of photographs of him, taken by herself, around her ("She is surrounded by several big photos of you enlarged ones of hers—in every corner & heaps of small ones") a shared, even reciprocal, intimacy. Ania seems to be succeeding in making herself, and not Alix, the center of the life of the imperial family.

Maurice Paléologue was not alone—though he was particularly eloquent concerning it—in finding Ania's position vis-à-vis the imperial family very puzzling. "What a curious person Madame Vyrubova is," he wrote in his memoirs. "Physically she is coarse and heavily-built, with a round head, fleshy lips, limpid eyes devoid of expression, a full figure and a high colour. She is thirty-two years of age [actually she was thirty at this time]. She dresses with a thoroughly provincial plainness and is very devout, but unintelligent." With this last remark, Paléologue underestimated Ania. "No one else ever enters the family circle," he went on. "They play draughts and patience, do puzzles; occasionally a little music. Highly proper novels, English novels for preference, are read aloud. When the children have gone to bed Madame Vyrubova stays with the sovereigns until midnight and thus takes part in all their conversation."

Nicky spent much time coming and going in the early months of the war, and on October 20, he is just about to depart again from Tsarskoe Selo, at a time when at least anxiety for Alexei ("Baby sweet" and "agoowee one") seems to be over for the time being. Alix suffers very much at Nicky's departures, and is sensitive to his own loneliness, but at this stage she was able to use work and activity, rather than invalidity, as a partial cure for unhappiness. "I felt so sad seeing your lonely figure standing at the door," she wrote to him on October 21, "it seems so unnatural your going off alone—everything is queer without you, our centre, our sunshine. I gulped down my tears & hurried off to the hospital & worked hard for two hours." Neither was her hospital work just a way of passing the time and taking her mind off her troubles; rather it was genuinely useful, and the abilities she was able to deploy gave her a great sense of satisfaction. Part of Alix's problem all along may have been frustration at not having a role in life that fulfilled her and made proper, constructive use of her considerable intelligence and talents. And in nursing the wounded she was following in the footsteps of her own mother, whom she had loved and lost so young. She is in fact returning to her earliest childhood, when as a tiny girl she accompanied her siblings and Princess Alice every Saturday in taking flowers to the sick in the hospital the latter had founded. "Very bad wounds," she told Nicky that day; "for the first time I shaved one of the soldiers legs near and round the wound—I worked all alone to-day, without a sister or Dr.—only the Princess came to see each man and to [see] what was the matter with him & I asked her if it was right what I intended doing." This was far more the kind of activity Alix believed the wife of a sovereign should be doing, rather than attending endless court receptions, dinners, and other ceremonies.

The two elder daughters, Olga and Tatiana, were not only training as nurses themselves but also taking an active role in various committees concerning relief for the wounded, and their mother was very keen to encourage them in these activities. "Now O. & T. are at Olga's Committee," she tells Nicky on October 21, "before that Tatiana received Neidhardt alone for half an hour with his doklad [report]—its so good for the girls & they learn to become independent & will develop them much more having to think & speak for themselves, without my constant aid." In the same letter Alix expresses her belief that women should not only be engaged in nursing physical wounds but should also be trying to "bring people more to God." She has even been telling the priest at the hospital that, in her opinion, the clergy should be doing more of this, too, that they should speak to the wounded "quite simply & straight out, not sermonlike." These are the ordinary soldiers she is speaking about, as she makes clear, whose souls are, in her opinion, "like children & only at times need a little guiding." Then she disingenuously remarks: "With the officers its far more difficult as a rule." This was no doubt true, officers, being better educated and more sure of themselves, proving less willing to be patronized and told what to believe, even by their Empress.

Alix's letter to Nicky of October 25 contains the first indication of her intention, prompted by Grigory and with Ania also active in the background, to involve herself in politics and affairs of state in the temporary absence of her husband, and to start making decisions that properly belong to him. The issue concerned the Crimea; Grigory—on the evidence of a woman who had been to see him—believed that N. N. Lavrinovsky, the Governor of the Crimea, was "ruining everything" by the approach he was taking to the Tatars and should be replaced by General Knyazhevich. Grigory wanted Alix to speak at once to Interior Minister Maklakov—"as he says one must not waste time until your return"—so that is what she had decided to do. She did have her doubts as to whether Nicky would welcome this intervention—"pardon my mixing in what does not concern me"—but is determined to do it anyway, as "its for the good of the Crimea." Her idea was that Maklakov should write a report, to which Nicky would merely need to append his signature on his return. Alix's tone in this first attempt to act in advance of Nicky's agreement, and following Grigory's instructions, is a combination of anxiety about her husband's response and a desire to hurry him up to make a decision. "Please don't be angry with me," she writes (and the fact that she recognizes this as a possibility shows that she knows Nicky can be—and maybe has been in the past—angry with her), "& give me some sort of an answer by wire—that you 'approve,' or 'regret' my mixing in—& whether you think Kn. a good candidate, it will quieten me."

On October 27, Alix was again "grumbling" to Nicky about Ania, who had been "not amiable" and "queer" with her. She had also been flirting with "the young Ukrainian" and generally enjoying herself on an outing to Petrograd with a group of wounded soldiers, despite claiming to be missing and longing for Nicky. Alix tells him: "You will see when we return how she will tell you how terribly she suffered without you, tho' she thoroughly enjoys being alone with her friend." And then she makes a very peculiar request of her husband: "Be nice & firm when you return & don't allow her foot-game etc. Otherwise she gets worse after—she always needs cooling down." From this it would appear that Nicky has not been completely discouraging of Ania's advances toward him, that he is not always "nice & firm" with her, but has previously allowed her to play this intriguing "foot-game etc." Was this just playing footsie under the table? Is the "etc." some kind of tickling game perhaps? Whatever it was, after which Ania would need "cooling down," it was certainly odd behavior for the Empress's best friend to be indulging in with the Emperor, and very strange of that Emperor to allow it. And why had Ania, after presumably forgetting herself in this way in the spring at Livadia, not simply been sent away? Was it because, despite all the anger and complaints she provoked, she was still needed by Alix, and therefore by Nicky, in whose interest it certainly was to keep his wife calm and reasonably contented? Or was it also because Ania provided a vital link between the imperial couple and Rasputin? I would contend it was for both these reasons and more: that Ania was a necessary component in the relationship between Alix and Nicky, that without her Alix's neuroses would have been ungovernable and that therefore Nicky felt he had to keep her sweet; that Alix also knew that without Ania, Nicky would not be able to cope with her, Alix; and that Ania knew all of this, recognized her indispensability and knew she could therefore act as she pleased. She also had Grigory's support in this, as her constant presence made it so much easier for him to have access to the imperial family. The imperial children, particularly the four girls, also seem to have recognized the necessity of Ania. All this would certainly suggest that the relationship between Nicky and Alix was not, after all, a cloudless romantic idyll as it has so often been portrayed.

On October 28, Anastasia tells Nicky how she has been helping "our soldier" to read, which she has enjoyed very much. The girls are also becoming accustomed to the presence of death: "Two more poor things died, we sat with them only yesterday." But Anastasia, rather like her father, cannot sustain a serious register for long: "Olga is hitting Maria, and Maria is shouting like an idiot." The imperial daughters were not always the demure, white-clad maidens of popular representation, as this youngest of them is happy to admit. At times, feelings ran high in the imperial household about Germany; from an apologetic letter Tatiana wrote to her mother on October 29, it is also clear that the consciousness of having a German mother did not make things easy for the girls. "Please forgive me, my Mama Sweet," Tatiana wrote, "if I ever hurt you involuntarily by saying something about your former home, but really if I do say something, it is always without thinking that I can hurt you, or something like that, because really, when I think of you I only think that you are our angel, Mama dear—a Russian, and always forget that it was not always so, and that you had another home before you came to Papa here." "I am *quite* Russian, as you say," responded her mother, "but I can't forget my old home."

At the end of October Alix traveled to join Nicky for a short time; this was the first time she had been separated from Alexei for more than a few hours, and she found this very difficult. "My very own boy!" she wrote to him, "*I am terribly sad* because you are not with me, but I know that Papa is anxiously awaiting us. My prayers and all my thoughts will be with you all the time. Study well, eat quickly and a lot—do not run too much." A particular part of each day that Alix normally shared with her son was his evening prayer time, so now she tells him: "You may pray with your sisters in the evening—and at that time I shall think about you."

In her letter of November 17, Alix is again preoccupied with Ania, though claims to be less so than before the trouble in the Crimea—so the implication here is that her friend's "rudenesses and moods" have been going on for a long time, since well before whatever she did to provoke Alix and Nicky earlier in the year. "I take all much cooler now," Alix declares to her husband, "& don't worry over her rudenesses & moods like formerly—a break came through her behaviour & works in the Crimea—we are friends & I am very fond of her & always shall be, but something has gone, a link broken by her behaviour towards us both—she can never be as near to me as she was." It is evident that Ania, while still declaring herself to love Alix, believes herself to be in love with Nicky—or at least that is what she says—and that both the object of her infatuation and his wife have decided to accept this and live with it: "One tries to hide one's sorrow & not pride with it—after all its harder for me than her, tho' she does not agree as you are *all* to her & I have the children—but she has me whom she says she loves." There is also a suggestion in what Alix writes that Nicky keeps himself at a distance from all this, letting the two women work out their relationship, while he is content to be the passive object of their veneration: "Its not worth while speaking about this," writes his wife, "& it is not interesting to you at all." And, indeed, in the letters Nicky writes from Stavka he does rather give the impression of not being interested in the emotional goings-on of his women. He does, after all, have other things to preoccupy him. Neverthless, he also found the partings from Alix and his family very difficult, writing on November 18, while on the train: "This time I managed to keep myself in hand the moment of parting, but it was a hard struggle." For him, as ever, his way of overcoming emotional distress was—apart from smoking—through physical exercise: "My hanging bar proved to be very practical and useful! I hung on it and climbed lots before eating. It is really good for one in the train and shakes the blood and the whole system up!" Both he and Grigory were pleased to see Alix being active and busy, and encouraged her in this: "It is such joy and comfort to see you well and doing so much work for the wounded. As our Friend said, it is God's mercy, that at such a time you should be able to do and to stand such a lot." Nicky also seems to want to encourage her to be less dependent on himself: "Believe me, my sweet love, do not fear, but be more *sure* of yourself, when you are alone, and everything will go off smoothly and successfully."

His letter of November 19 shows his awareness of one of the major problems for the Russian forces: "The one serious difficulty for our armies is this—we are again running short of our artillery ammunition." Alix is soon to travel to meet Nicky, without the rest of her family or Ania and, after more than twenty years of living in Russia as the Empress, she still sounds daunted at the prospect: "I shall be so shy on the journey—I have never been alone to any big town—I hope I shall do all properly & your wife wont make a mess of herself." Is she perhaps being at least partly disingenuous, presenting herself to Nicky as the poor, helpless wife, while at the same time determined to take an increasing part in "helping" the Tsar?

In November *The Times* printed an article by an American journalist based in Warsaw, Stephen Graham. Headed "The Great White Tsar," it was subtitled "An Outstanding Figure of the War" and would suggest that at this point Nicholas was at the height of his popularity—both at home but, more particularly, abroad, among the allies. "It will be years before we can regard the Kaiser with clear eyes," declared Graham, and continued:

> But meanwhile there is one other figure in this war that stands out in the popular vision very remarkably, and that is the Tsar Nicholas II, once called the Great White Tsar.
>
> When the Tsar came to the throne he showed himself to be an idealist, an even Utopian idealist, by his passionate efforts for the establishment of universal peace. The cause of peace was chiefly associated with the name of the Tsar. It was strange that this great absolute monarch should associate himself with the cause dearest of all to democrats and liberals, strange that he should be the colleague of men like W. T. Stead and Andrew Carnegie. Many said that the Tsar was not sincere. The sarcastic and cynical found Nicholas delivered wholly to their untender mercy when at last Russia wilfully broke peace by declaring war on Japan. But a worse denial of ideals was to follow when the great revolutionary outburst was put down ruthlessly by military force. The Tsar became "the man of blood." People associated the ghastly carnage of the war with the dreadful loss of life at the Coronation crush in Moscow, and with the firing on the workmen at Father Gapon's procession, and with many another incident in which the Tsar's name was connected with the injury and death of his subjects. Perhaps no one has been more hated in his time than the Tsar. No one has been more cursed.
>
> And yet despite all that seemed against him many people quietly kept their faith in him. The most touching example is perhaps that of W. T. Stead. Stead and many others saw in the Tsar the granter of the Duma, a new Peter the Great, a God-chosen monarch

> leading his nation through the most difficult and hazardous ways of national evolution. They held that it was comparatively easy for Alexander II to give liberty to the serfs, but that it needed a stupendous genius to cope with the difficulties that that liberation would lead to. . . . It must always have been said of him, even if he had been stricken in the revolution, that he was confronted by problems that only genius or sacred simplicity could solve. . . .
>
> The Tsar's life and personal character are a mystery. . . . The Tsar to-day has outlived the accusation of insincerity, has outlived all his unpopularity, and has given the lie to all that has been said against him. . . .
>
> Before the Tsar passed the uniform for the common soldier in the war he asked that a complete suit be sent to him and with it boots and rifle and full kit. And he himself put off his royal clothes and put on the soldier's uniform and shouldered the kit and the gun and walked in them on his estate in Livadia some two hours. He was photographed so, and has allowed the photograph to be reproduced for common sale and for distribution among the soldiers.
>
> He is a simple man. He inherits the awful power of his ancestors, but he would like to spend a day as a common soldier in the trenches. Such an action would resound throughout history—win the hearts of the whole non-German world. But necessarily the Tsar is to the peasants someone unearthly, a giant, a demi-god. They would not really be well influenced by such an action, probably would not understand it. Still, who knows? Noble deeds take care of themselves.
>
> As the war goes on the sincerity and the nobility of the Tsar will be a great factor in the giving of victory. The sacred simplicity, kindness, and earnestness of the Tsar emerge as a guarantee of the ultimate issue of this struggle, but also of the marvellous and healthful future of the vast Russian Empire and of the wonderful Russian people. It is good to see in the idealist, the Peace Tsar, the same personality of to-day, but made wiser, stronger, simpler by suffering and responsibility—the Great White Tsar.

The comfort Alix was able to bring to some of the wounded men in her charge is evident from her letter to Nicky of November 19, in which she mentions a "poor boy" whom she was with the day before "during his dressing awful to see, & he clung to me & kept quiet, poor child." All the hours she had spent next to the bedside of her own son, as well as being so frequently ill herself, had added to her understanding of how to impart sympathy and strength to the suffering. And in turn the sense that she was being useful seems to have given her strength to carry on despite her own continuing ill health. "Yes, God has helped me with my health," she tells Nicky, "& I keep up—tho' at times am simply deadtired—the heart aches & is enlarged—but my will is firm—anything only not to think." The desire "not to think" encompassed all of Alix's feelings about this terrible war, the impact of which on young lives she was seeing firsthand, and in which she was at the center of a divided Europe and a divided family; intensely loyal to Russia (whatever the gossipmongers may have said to the contrary), she could not help but be aware that the "enemy" included various of her own close relatives, including her beloved brother. No wonder she didn't want to think.

On November 20, Alix gives Nicky some gruesome details of what her nursing work entails. That day she and Olga were present at their "first big amputation (the whole arm was cut off)," with herself giving the instruments and Olga threading the needles. And then she found herself (without her daughters this time, for she would not have wished them to see these injuries) working with some men who had been wounded in their most private parts: "I had wretched fellows with awful wounds[—]scarcely a 'man' any more, so shot to pieces, perhaps it must be cut off as so black, but hope to save it—terrible to look at. I washed & cleaned, & painted with iodine & smeared with Vaseline & tied them up & bandaged all up—it went quite well & I felt happier to do the things gently myself under the guidance of a Dr.—I did three such—one had a little tube in it. Ones heart bleeds for them—I wont describe any more details, as its so sad, but being a wife & mother I feel for them quite particularly—a young nurse (girl) I sent out of the room."

According to Alix, Ania displays none of the sympathy she herself brings to her charges: "Ania looked on so coolly, quite hardened already, as she says—she astonishes me with her ways constantly—nothing of the loving gentle woman like our girlies—she ties them up roughly when they bore her, goes away when she has had enough—& when little to do, grumbles." It seems that Alix is determined that, whatever Ania's feelings for the Tsar may be, she is going to make sure they are not reciprocated—despite the frequent assertions that she loves Ania and her overt encouragement to Nicky to send her loving messages, too. (The next day: "I send you papers & a letter from Ania.—Perhaps you will mention in your telegram, that you thank [her] for papers & letter & send messages. I hope her letters are not the old oily style again.") It is all very odd. If Ania is really as horrible as she is presented here, why do Alix and her whole family appear to love her? What elaborate game is being played out? Can Alix only love people whom she feels to be inferior to herself? She goes on to describe the very different reactions to becoming a Red Cross nurse displayed by Ania and the imperial women: "Its not a play—she wanted & fidgeted for the cross, now she has it, her interest has greatly slakened [sic]—whereas we feel now double the responsibility & seriousness of it all & want to give out all we can to all the poor wounded, with slight or serious wounds, equally lovingly." On November 21, Alix tells Nicky of an encouraging telegram she has just received from Grigory: "When you comfort the wounded, God makes his name famous through your gentleness and glorious work." "So touching," comments Alix, "and must give me strength to get over my shyness."

On November 25, Alix tells how she, her two elder daughters, and Ania had witnessed their first death on the operating table: "Hemorrhage. All behaved well, none lost their head—& the girlies were brave—they & Ania had never seen a death. But he died in a minute—it made us all so sad as you can imagine—how near death always is! We continued another operation." On the same day Nicky, writing while on board the imperial train, tells Alix that he has just received a "most comforting" telegram from Grigory, delivered to him at a small station where he got out for a run.

On November 28, Alix recounts having visited her mother-in-law at the Anichkov Palace for tea. "Motherdear" is looking well, apparently, but Alix believes her to be "astonished" at the journeys she herself has been undertaking alone as part of her work for the wounded. If Maria Fyodorovna was indeed "astonished" (and her own diary entries confirm that she was), it may have been more because such active behavior was so unlike anything her usually ailing daughter-in-law had managed to do before than because she had any disagreement with Alix's assertion that "we women must all, big & small, do everything we can for our touchingly brave wounded." Grigory is also, it seems, encouraging her to undertake such journeys (as usual, even if he sincerely believes the Empress is doing the right thing, he is also giving her the advice she wants to hear).

In mid-December Alexei hurt his foot, but not seriously. We also learn from Alix's letter to Nicky of December 14 something of how these early-twentieth-century women handled their monthly periods (that is, by retreating for at least part of the time to bed). Tatiana has hers ("Mme Becker") and so she does not get up until lunchtime. Alix is also in bed on this day, on Dr. Botkin's instructions, as her heart is "still very much enlarged & aches & I cannot take medicines"—from which we know she was having her period, too. She also feels "horribly tired & achy all over." She was expecting Grigory to arrive back in

St. Petersburg tomorrow—Ania would be going to meet him, and he had sent a message in advance of himself to say that "better news from the war" would be coming soon. Alix seems to be about to act in a way that may have helped give some credence to the false idea that she was pro-German; this concerned the issue of Christmas trees, which were being frowned upon in some quarters as representing a custom originating in Germany. While Alix may be right that this was a ridiculous killjoy thing to do, the way she went about defending the "tannenbaum" may not have been very sensible or tactful—better, perhaps, to have let someone else speak for her, rather than "make a row" herself: "One says the Synod gave an order there should be no Xmas tree—I am going to find out the truth about it & then make a row, its no concern of theirs nor the Churches, why take away a pleasure fr. the wounded & children, because it originally came from Germany—the narrow-mindedness is too colossal."

On December 15, Alix was still unable to work, or to receive guests, as her heart was "still enlarged and aches," she had a headache, and felt giddy. Her daughter Maria was also unwell—apparently with "angina," though this seems unlikely for one so young. Alix tried to do what she could while lying down, her mind not being at all inactive, as she made clear in her letter of the following day: "I feel still not famous [one of her favorite expressions for being under the weather], such a nuisance not to work, but I go on with my brain doing business."

On January 2, 1915, Ania was involved in a train accident on the line from Tsarskoe Selo to St. Petersburg and was severely injured. She was taken to the hospital in the Catherine Palace, where Nicky (back home for Christmas and the New Year) visited her at eleven o'clock that evening. Her parents were there already, and later Grigory arrived. Nicky went back to see her the following afternoon with his daughters and sat with her. His diary for January 4 reads: "We visited Ania in the infirmary; thank God she is better, although she is in pain all over her body. Walked in the darkness before tea. At 6 o'clock received Trepov. Read the whole evening."

Pierre Gilliard's account of Rasputin's prediction over Ania's recovery does suggest the "*starets*" had a talent for making pronouncements that would be "true" whatever happened:

> She was nearly dead when she was dragged from under the fragments of a shattered carriage, and had been brought to Tsarskoe Selo in a condition which seemed desperate. In her terror the Czarina had rushed to the bedside of the woman who was almost her only friend. Rasputin, who had been hastily sent for, was there also. In this accident the

> Czarina saw a new proof of the evil fate which seemed to pursue so relentlessly all those whom she loved. As she asked Rasputin in a tone of anguish whether Madame Vyrubova would live, he replied:
>
> "God will give her back to you if she is needed by you and the country. If her influence is harmful, on the other hand, He will take her away. I cannot claim to know His impenetrable designs."
>
> It must be admitted that this was a very clever way of evading an awkward question.

Alix wrote to her old friend Bishop William Boyd Carpenter (canon and subdean of Westminster by now, having resigned his see on grounds of ill health in 1911) on January 20, 1915, replying to his New Year wishes. It was a letter such as one would expect from someone at the center of this particular conflict, written to someone who had known Queen Victoria and, consequently, most of her grandchildren. "You, who know all the members of our family so well," she writes, "can understand what we go through—relations on all sides, one against the other." While appalled at what she perceives is happening to Germany ("a country morally sinking into such depths"), Alix is rather buoyed up by the idea that a previously anticlerical France is actively recruiting army chaplains. She tells the Bishop of the importance of "prayer and work" in surviving such sorrowful times, and regrets that she herself has had to give up her hospital work for the time being, having "overtired" her heart again.

On the following day, Nicky being on his way back to Stavka, Alix informs him that she will always give him news about Alexei, and about Ania, to whom she will refer as "A" or the "invalid." Why she imagines such semisecrecy should be necessary is hard to fathom, as no intelligence officer or spy worth his or her salt would be unable to work out who this character was. She also reminds Nicky—as if he might need reminding—to ask after Ania's health from time to time in a telegram, as she will "sorely" miss the visits he has been making to her while she has been so ill after the accident. Alexei has had another hemophiliac attack, Alix reporting on January 22 that "Baby spent the day alright & has no fever, now he begins to complain a little of his leg & dreads the night." Alix herself, perhaps buoyed up by other people's illnesses, is back at work, at least in the mornings; she spends the afternoons sitting with Ania. She also passes on a message from Grigory, which has been transmitted via Ania. It is another anti–Grand Duke Nikolai Nikolaevich message; the Tsar "must be sure," says Grigory, "not once to mention the name of the commander in Chief, in your manifest—it must solely come fr you to the people."

By January 26, Ania was hoping that she would soon be able to leave the hospital and return to her own house—a prospect Alix regards with some dread, realizing how much more tiring it will be for her and her daughters to have to visit Ania there rather than in the hospital where they are working anyway. And she also has a warning for Nicky, for when he returns home: "lovy, fr the very first you must then tell her that you cannot come so often, it takes too much time—because if now not firm, we shall be having stories and love-scenes & rows like in the Crimea now, on account of being helpless she hopes to gain more caresses & old time back again—you keep fr the first all in its limits as you did now—so as that this accident should be profitable & with peaceful results." So we do now have confirmation that what happened in the Crimea in April 1914 involved "stories and love-scenes and rows"; there is in addition a clear indication that "caresses" of some sort have been exchanged beween Ania and Nicky, and that there was a time, which Ania preferred to the current situation, which could be referred to as the "old time." Nicky seems to have been guilty in the past of, at least, not discouraging Ania's advances—of not keeping "all in its limits"—and possibly, even, of reciprocating them. In her letter of the following day Alix continues to remind Nicky that he must be careful not to let the situation get out of hand again, and she also—partly unconsciously—seeks to emphasize Ania's unattractiveness, as a further discouragement, should it be needed, for her husband to be led astray: "Ania gets on alright tho' her right leg aches, but the temp is nearly normal in the evening. Only speaks again of getting into her house. I foresee my life then! Yesterday evening I went as an exception to her, & so as to sit with the officers a tiny bit afterwards, as I find her stomach & legs colossal (& most unapetising [sic])—her face is rosy, but the cheeks less fat & shades under her eyes. She has lots of guests; but dear me—how far away she has sliped [sic] from me since her hideous behaviour, especially autumn winter, spring of 1914—things never can be the same to me again—she broke that intimate link gently during the last four years—cannot be at my ease with her as before—tho' she says she loves me so, I know its much less than before & all is consecrated [concentrated?] in her own self—& you. Let us be careful when you return."

Alix's letter of January 29 makes it clear that what she fears in regard to Grand Duke Nikolai Nikolaevich is that he is trying to usurp Nicky's rights by attempting to exercise control in more than merely military matters. She brings in Court Minister Fredericks to lend support to her point of view. "I am so glad you had good talks with N," she begins disingenuously. "Freder. is rather in despair (rightly) about many orders he gives unwisely & wh only aggravate, & things one had better not discuss now—others influence him & he tries to play your part wh is far from right—except in military matters—& ought to be put a stop to—one has no right before God & man to usurp your rights as he does—he can make the mess & later you will have great difficulty in mending matters. Me it hurts very much. One has no right to profit of one's unusually great rights as he does."

On February 27, when Nicky was once again about to set out from Tsarskoe Selo—and this time with the firm intention of seeing actual frontline troops—Alix expresses enthusiasm about his endeavors, an enterprise also backed by Grigory, who has blessed the Tsar before he set out. (A lot of blessing goes on among the Orthodox; Alix will have blessed him, too, so this may not be as significant as it sounds to the non-Orthodox.) "God bless you quite particularly on this journey," she writes, "& give you the possibility of seeing our brave troops nearer! Your presence will give them new force & courage & be such a recompense to them & consolation to you. The Stavka is not the thing—you are for the troops, when & where possible—& our Friend's blessing & prayers will help. Such a comfort for me that you saw Him & were blessed by Him this evening! Sad I cant follow you out there—but I have the little ones to look after. I shall be good & go once to town before M-me B comes & visit some hospital, as they are impatiently awaiting us there." Nicky himself has left in an unusually calm state of mind—"which even astonishes me," he told his wife. He is unsure as to what to attribute the "calm peace" in his soul: "Does it come from having talked with our Friend last night, or is it the paper that Buchanan gave me, Witte's death [Count Sergei had just died], or perhaps a feeling of something good going to happen at this war—I cannot say, but a real Easter comfort is rooted in my heart." "Calm peace" can, unfortunately, be illusory and misleading; neither may it provide the best guidance for wartime decision-making.

Nicky's letter also has some revealing things to say about the two days he has just spent at Tsarskoe Selo. He laments—in a way that is reminiscent of the letters this couple used to send one another when they were first engaged—his inability to express himself fully face-to-face: "I was so happy to have spent two days at home—perhaps you noticed it, but I am stupid, & never say what I feel." And then, despite how much they long for one another when they are apart, they do not actually spend that much time together when they are in the same place. There is work to do in the mornings—"Such a nuisance to be always so occupied & never to sit quietly together & talk!"—and in the afternoons there is Nicky's compulsion to take vigorous exercise outside—"In the afternoon I can never remain at home, such a yearning of getting into the fresh air." And so as a consequence, "all the free hours pass & the old couple is very rarely together." At least when Ania was well and turned up at the palace all the time, they spent some time sitting together. Alix's response to this letter is also interesting. First, she seems surprised to have received it—"What an unexpected joy yr precious letter was, thank you for it from all my loving old heart"—which underlines the fact that even this limited amount of self-revelation from Nicky was unusual. And then, in regretting that they have not made the most in the last couple of days of "A" not being in the house, she seems to look back to a time before Ania—"It reminds one of bygone evenings—so peaceful & calm, & no one's moods to bother & make one nervous." Again this begs the question as to why, if Ania's presence was so bothersome, the imperial couple also found it necessary. It is as though, if they are to spend time together, Ania must be there as well.

In the afternoons of that winter, Pierre Gilliard used to take Alexei out for drives in about a twenty-mile radius of Tsarskoe Selo, feeling he needed less of a sheltered life and to see more of what was going on around him. Alexei greatly enjoyed these drives, during which they would stop to talk to unsuspecting peasants, and he also became very interested in the local railway lines and stations. Inevitably, such activities provoked security concerns: "The palace police grew alarmed at these excursions, which took us beyond the guarded zone, especially as our route was not known beforehand. I was asked to observe the rules in force, but I disregarded them, and our drives continued as before. The police then changed their procedure, and whenever we left the park we were certain to see a car appear and follow in our tracks. It was one of Alexei Nikolaevich's greatest delights to try and throw it off the scent, and now and then we were successful." Alexei also acquired a new friend and playmate, in the person of Dr. Derevenko's son, who was more or less the same age as himself.

On March 2, Alix reports to Nicky that she has intervened in the case of one of her wounded officers who has received orders to return to active service at a time that she seems to feel is too early—or else she does not like the harsh army regulations existing in time of war and considers the Russian army particularly harsh in its treatment of the wounded. Her instincts about trying to prevent bitterness among the fighting troops were undoubtedly sensible. The "fat Orloff" to whom Alix refers is Prince Vladimir Orlov, stationed at Stavka as the director of the Tsar's infantry chancellery (and not to be confused with Nicky's late friend General Alexander Orlov). She later comments that he is Grand Duke Nikolai Nikolaevich's "colossal friend," which would explain her undertone of animosity: "I have told Vil'chkovsky to send fat Orloff a printed paper one of the wounded received from his chief—far too hard orders & absolutely unjust & cruel—if an officer does not return at the time mentioned he must be disciplinied [sic]

[and] punished etc. I cant write it, the paper will tell you all. One comes to the conclusion that those who are wounded are doubly badly treated—better keep behind or hide away to remain untouched & I find it most unfair—& I dont believe its everywhere the same, but in some armies.—Forgive my bothering you my Love, but you can help out there, & one does not want bitterness setting in their poor hearts."

On the evening of that same day (March 2) Alix wrote again to Nicky, to unburden herself of something that had upset her very much, and which would affect her for weeks, if not months, to come. In fact, it was a grief that incapacitated her for some considerable time, and ended a period of her nursing activity. This was the death of a young officer called Grobov, of whom Alix had become very fond over the weeks he had been in her hospital—fonder of him, perhaps, than either she or anyone else had realized. He seemed to have filled a vacuum in her life during Nicky's absence, a vacuum that no one else had been able to fill. And now she pours out her heart to her husband, who must have not known quite what to make of this letter. "Wify feels hideously sad," she tells him, because her "poor wounded friend has gone!" She had been in the habit of spending time with him every day, often more than once a day, and always brought flowers for him; on the day of his death: "I was as usual with him in the morning & more than an hour in the afternoon." The way she describes him—"his big shiny eyes," "his lovely smile"—suggests that he reminded her in some ways of Nicky in his younger days, strengthening the sense that there was a sentimental, if not romantic, element to this relationship for Alix. After seeing Grobov that afternoon, she had had a premonition that all might not be well: "I rested before dinner & was haunted with the feeling that he might suddenly get very bad in the night & one would not call me & so on—so that when the eldest nurse called one of the girls to the telephone—I told them that I knew what had happened & flew myself to hear the sad news." The three younger daughters then went off to visit Ania, while Alix and Olga went to see Grobov's body. "He lay there so peacefully," Alix tells her husband, "covered under my flowers I daily brought him, with his lovely smile—the forehead yet quite warm. I cant get quiet—so sent Olga to them & came home with my tears." This is an extreme reaction for someone daily involved with the wounded and dying. This particular officer, though, seems to have been a favorite with all the nurses: "The elder sister [nurse] cannot either realise it—he was quite calm, cheery, said felt a wee bit not comfy, & when the sister, 10 m. after she had gone away, came in, found him with staring eyes, quite blue, breathed twice—& all was over—peaceful to the end. Never did he complain, never asked for anything, sweetness itself as she says—all loved him—& that shining smile." Grigory, it seems, with his talent for knowing what Alix wanted to hear (but also being vague enough for various interpretations to be attached to his words), had told her "he will not soon leave you," which had made her sure Grobov would recover, albeit slowly. She is aware that to write so heartbrokenly to her husband of another man's death is rather unusual and might provoke jealousy, but feels sure that Nicky will understand: "Forgive my writing so much about him, but going there, & all that, had been a help, with you away & I felt God let me bring him a little sunshine in his loneliness." "It must not make you sad what I wrote," she adds, "only I could not bear it any longer—I had to speak myself out." Alix is using her letter to Nicky as a way of trying to calm herself; one wonders whether, when he was present, she did the same thing out loud, using his constant—and hard-won—calmness as a counterbalance to her own turbulence. For the time being, she has to make do with his "dear cushion": "I am writing to you now in bed, I am lying since an hour already, but cant get to sleep, nor calm myself, so it does me good talking to you. I have blessed & kissed your dear cushion as always."

On this day when Alix was so preoccupied with Grobov and his death, Nicky wrote a fairly optimistic letter from on board the new imperial train at Stavka: "At the front all is pretty well. N is in good spirits and as usual wants rifles and ammunition. The question of our coal supplies for the railroads & fabrics is of a precarious nature, so I have asked Rukhlov to take it all in his hands. Think only if our war material fabrication stopped & that on account of lack of coal or rather from not getting enough of it out of our coal mines in the south! I feel confident that energetic measures will pull us out of these difficulties." From his usual tone when writing, one can imagine that Alix must at times have felt frustrated at the difficulty of eliciting a response from him at the same emotional level on which she generally lived.

On the same day, Sir John Hanbury-Williams, head of the British military mission at Stavka, commented in his diary on Nicky's walking habits. "I met the Emperor on one of his long walks at Headquarters," he records, "and as usual got off the road so as to be out of his way, for which he called me over the coals at lunch. . . . He is a tremendous walker, fairly walks his staff off their legs, and said I must walk where I liked, and not mind meeting him and his retinue, which is a pretty large one, as there are mounted police scouring about all the time."

It was quite clear to Sir John that Nicky had no intention of deserting the allies and every intention of fighting on until the war was won; he also had no inclination to defend the actions of his cousin Willy. He also found the Tsar full of characteristic concern for his interlocutor: "He inquired after my family, and later on sent me all the English papers, illustrated and others, which he kindly continued to do all the time I was at Headquarters. He is looking very well, and as attractive and good-tempered as ever."

Nicky's brother Misha was now redeeming himself in the Tsar's eyes, after his unfortunate marriage, by performing well in the war: "Yesterday N brought me a report of Ivanov from Brusilov . . . about Misha's division's excellent conduct in the battles in February, when they were attacked by two Austrian divisions in the Carpathians. The Caucasians not only repulsed the enemy but attacked them & were the first to enter into Stanislavov, Misha being himself the whole [time] in the firing lines. They all beg me to give him the St. George's Cross, wh I am going to do. . . . I am happy for him because I think this military reward really is deserved by him this time & it will show that he is, in the end, treated like the others, & that for doing his duty he gets also recompensed!" Alix's response to this is to be pleased, but to wish that the offending wife could somehow be removed: "I am sure this war will make more of a man of him—could one but get her out of his reach! Her dictating influence is so bad for him." (A case here, one might think, of people in glasshouses throwing stones . . .)

The ever-understanding Dr. Botkin now dictated that Alix should retire to bed. Her heart was "a good deal enlarged," she had a cough, her period had arrived, and she was feeling "rotten, in every respect." Ania has continued to be a source of exhaustion, demanding at least two visits per day and apparently never satisfied. Dr. Botkin, it appears, has been trying to intimate to Ania that the Empress needs to conserve her energy, but Ania has not taken the hint. Neither can she understand Alix being so upset over Grobov's death. Alix herself explains the reason for the strength of her feelings thus: "I cannot do a thing by halves & I saw his joy when I came twice daily—& he all alone . . . he had no family here."

The letter Nicky sent in reply to his wife's outpouring of grief is very typical of him. He is sympathetic—"I so well understand your grief about the poor fellow's sad death"—but chooses to focus on the least complicated aspect of Alix's sadness—that it is because Grobov was alone, far away from his family—"with nobody of his own near him!"—and to avoid discussing the sentimental attachment that she had so clearly formed for him. Then he goes on to make a more general, and banal, comment about death in war—"Truly, it is really better to be killed at once . . . because death in action comes in presence of whole unit or regiment and gets written down in history!"—before changing the subject to the weather! "Today the weather is fine, but frosty & lots of snow. The sun shines so prettily through the trees in front of my window." By the end of the brief paragraph, he is positively jocular: "We have just returned from our afternoon walk. The roads in the fields are abominably slippery and my gentlemen fall down occasionally."

On March 5 (the day on which Nicky wrote the above letter) Alix was still in a state of incapacity and distress, to Ania's continued chagrin: "She is very put out, that I do not go to her again, but B keeps me in bed till dinner, like yesterday. The heart is not enlarged this morning, but I feel still rotten & weak & sad—when the health breaks down its more difficult to hold oneself in hands. Now he is being buried." She encloses with her letter to Nicky one from Ania, with the curious comment that the latter had said "I was to burn hers if I thought you would be angry—how can I know. I answered her that I would send it, so I hope she does not bother you with it—she can not grasp that her letters are of little interest to you, as they mean so much to her." It is clear from this that Alix respects Ania's privacy and does not open her letter to Nicky before sending it on to him—and also that Nicky's own feelings in the matter are a closed book to both women. Alix is probably right and what Ania has to say means little to him, which in turn suggests that his main fault has been that of leading her on, of not putting a stop to her infatuation when it first became apparent. This was, after all, a man whose usual way of showing anger was to look out of the window or adjust his belt; his way of dealing with an unwanted infatuation was most probably to ignore it with a kindly smile, and hope it would depart of its own accord. Unfortunately such behavior is open to all sorts of misreadings. And Nicky continues to "encourage" Ania, with Alix's full support; he sends the following message via his wife on March 7: "Give A my love and tell her I liked the verses she copied out for me." "I at once sent Ania your message, it will have given her pleasure," Alix responded. "She probably thinks that she alone is lonely without you." So again there is an ambivalent attitude, a desire both to criticize and to console her friend.

Alix also expresses her annoyance that the Tsar is still being prevented from going wherever he wants in the theater of war; it is her opinion that he should just set off without telling the Commander-in-Chief where he is going: "Dont you tell N & go off where it suits you & where nobody can expect you—of course he will try to keep you back, because one won't let him move—but if you go, I know that God will hold you in safe keeping & you & the troops will feel comforted." If Alix's ideas about warfare were unrealistic, her faith in a protecting God was certainly very strong and enabled her to attain a degree of selflessness, if not of good sense, in her advice to her husband. In his reply Nicky tries to explain that all is not quite as Alix sees it: "You seem to think that N keeps me back for the pleasure of not allowing me to move & see the troops—but really it is not quite so. A fortnight ago, when he wrote to me to come—he told me that I might have easily visited *three* army corps, because they were massed together in the rear. Since then much has changed & they have all been sent to the front lines, which is true, I get the proof every morning during the reports." Alix's response to this is to write: "I see now why you did not go more forward, but surely you could go still to some place before returning, it would do you good & cheer the others up—anywhere."

"I wish I were near you," Alix had added in her letter of March 5, "as I am sure you go through many difficult moments, not knowing who speaks the exact truth, who is partial & so on." The clear implication here is that, if she herself were present, she would be able to tell Nicky whom to believe, whom to distrust. This belief in her own power of instant judgment, inculcated in her initially by Monsieur Philippe and encouraged by Grigory, was very dangerous—but it was a danger to which the Empress herself was blind. (She mentions Philippe's remark in a letter to Nicky on June 16: "our first Friend gave me that Image with the bell to warn me against those, that are not right & it will keep them fr approaching, I shall feel it & thus guard you from them.")

On March 6, Alix was still unwell, her heart feeling as though it had "slipped to the right." Dr. Botkin was now going to intervene to try to make Ania understand the Empress's need for rest: "A fidgets for me to come to her but Botkin is going there, so as to tell her, that I cannot yet, & need quiet still some days." She has had to abandon nursing for the time being: "Thank God, the wounded officers in both hospitals are pretty well, so that I am not absolutely necessary this moment & the girls were at soldiers' operations again yesterday." She is generous in not appearing annoyed with Nicky's rather lame—or evasive—response to her grief, and comments: "Your walks are surely refreshing, & the different falls must cheer up the monotony (when not too painful)." But then she returns to her preoccupation: "Yesterday they buried the poor fellow & sister Liubusha said he had still his happy smile—only a little changed in colour, but the expression we knew so well, had not faded. Always a smile, & he told her he was so happy & wanted nothing more—shining eyes which struck all & after a life of ups & downs, a romance of changes, thank God he was happy with us." Meanwhile Ania continues to "fidget" and make her demands: "I am to telephone & come in the evening, when we daily explain I can't yet; so tiresome of her, & heaps of letters every day!—its not my fault, & I must get quite right & only by quiet lying (as can't yet take medicine) can help me.—She only thinks of herself & is angry I am so much with the wounded—they do me good & their gratitude gives me strength—whereas with her, who complains about her leg always, it's more tiring—one gives out so much of oneself, moral & physical all day, that in the evening little is left." Grigory is of the opinion that Alix should get out more into the sun—"says it will do me good (morally) more than lying." But for once she seems reluctant to take his advice: "But its very cold, I have a cough, the cold I keep down, then feverish again & so weak & tired."

The invalid Alix seems to have met her match in the invalid Ania, the latter being the only person ever really to berate her for staying in bed. As this is a case of the pot calling the kettle black (though at this point Ania can at least boast actual physical injuries), the attack misses its target and only makes Alix more cross. Ania has also touched a raw nerve—grumbling about Alix's visits to Grobov is something only she would dare to do. "You see I am looking after my tired old self," writes Alix to Nicky on March 7, "& to-day again only get up for 8. Ania won't understand it, the Dr, children & I explain it to her, & yet every day 5 letters & begging me to come—she knows I lie in bed, & yet pretends to be astonished at it—so selfish. She knows I never miss going to her when I only can, & dead tired too she still grumbles why I went twice daily to an unknown officer & does not heed Botkin's remark, that he needed me & that she always has guests all day long almost." For once, Alix is riled enough to feel her friend needs putting in her place: "If she would kindly once remember who I happen to be, then she might learn to understand that I have other duties except her." It is unlikely, however, that she has said precisely this to Ania, though the Empress has said it about the Emperor—to no avail, of course: "100 times I told her about you too, who you are, and that an E never goes daily to a sick person—what would one think otherwise, & that you have your country first of all to think of, & then get tired from work, & need air & its good you should be with Baby out, etc. It is like speaking to a stone—she won't understand, because she goes before everybody." When pleading is ineffectual, Ania turns to other tactics, or so Alix asserts: "She offers to invite officers in the evening for the children, thinking to get me like that, but they answered that they wished to remain with me, as its the only time we are quietly together." "We have too much spoiled her," Alix concludes, and it is hard to disagree. What is more bewildering is to understand why, though perhaps the clue, or part of the clue, is contained in Alix's description of Ania as "a daughter of our friends," by which she probably does not mean, or does not only mean, the Taneevs' daughter, but a disciple belonging to the mystic circles around Dr. Philippe and Grigory. As such a "daughter," Ania ought, thinks Alix, "to grasp things better & the illness ought to have changed her." She then brings the subject to a close with "Now enough about her, it's dull—it has stopped worrying me as it used to"—in which case, one can hardly begin to imagine how it must have worried her previously. No wonder Nicky tries so hard to avoid getting involved in his wife's emotional entanglements. The Romanov girls, in the meantime, have been enjoying using their father's large sunken bath, a treat Alexei had enjoyed a few days previously. "I went first," Anastasia reported happily to Nicky, "there was lots of water. I was able to swim all round it and then jumped in from the side, it was lovely. Fantastic! Then I splashed around some more with Maria, then it was unfortunately time for me to get out. Ortipo was there barking the whole time. Then Olga and Tatiana had their bath and really enjoyed themselves!!! It was awfully good."

CHAPTER TEN

The Great Fight

1915

Its not my brain wh is clever, but I listen to my soul & I wish you would too my own sweetest One.

—Alix to Nicky, June 15, 1915

ON MARCH 9, 1915, Alix was looking forward to Nicky's imminent return: "What happiness to know that the day after to-morrow I shall be holding you tight in my arms again, listening to your dear voice & looking into your beloved eyes. Only for you I regret, that you won't have seen anything. If I could only be decent by the time you return." Nicky was at home for four weeks (Easter was on March 22), and it was not an easy time, Alix writing to him on April 4, the day of his departure: "Once more you are leaving us, & I think with gladness, because the life you had here, all excepting the work in the garden—is more than trying & tiring." Part of the reason for this is that Nicky found his work simpler when not surrounded by all the politicking of Petrograd. Another reason is that Alix has been ill throughout the whole period of his stay, and so they have actually had very little time together: "We have seen next to nothing of each other through my having been lain up. Full many a thing have I not had time to ask, & when together only late in the evening, half the thoughts have flown away again." What Alix has been unable to say in person, she now takes up her pen to say in writing, for it is from this point that she becomes increasingly forceful in her letters to Nicky. It seems to have been during this interlude at Tsarskoe Selo—despite her not having seen much of her husband—that she has become more than ever convinced that he is too soft with his subordinates, too malleable—particularly in relation to "Nikolasha." "Forgive me, precious One," she now writes, "but you know you are too kind & gentle—sometimes a good loud voice can do wonders, & a severe look—do my love, be more decided & sure of yourself—you know perfectly well what is right, & when you do not agree & are right, bring your opinion to the front & let it weigh against the rest. They must remember more who you are & that first they must turn to you." Charm is all very well, Alix seems to be saying, but something more is needed: "Your being charms every single one, but I want you to hold them by your brain & experience." It is Grand Duke Nikolai who has really irritated her—"Though N is so highly placed, yet you are above him"—and Rasputin is also behind this attack. Clearly, though she has not been able to have many conversations with her husband during this past month, she and Grigory have been in communication: "The same thing shocked our Friend, as me too, that N words his telegrams, answers to governors, etc in your style—his ought to be more simple & humble & other things." Is there a suggestion in what Alix writes next that one of the reasons for her lack of spoken communication with her husband is that he does not wish to hear these comments from her and avoids such conversations? For her letters, he is more of a captive audience: "You think me a meddlesome bore, but a woman feels & sees things sometimes clearer than my too humble sweetheart." Alix wants to change Nicky, an enterprise inevitably doomed to failure: "Humility is God's greatest gift—but a Sovereign needs to show his will more often. Be more sure of yourself and go ahead—never fear, you won't say too much." Yet despite the clearly unsatisfactory nature of the last few weeks, Alix was very upset at Nicky's departure and only the presence of Alexei with her forced her to hold back tears. "It is so hard every time," she tells Nicky, "it wrenches at one's heart & leaves such an ache & endless longing." Even the dog, Ortipo (a French bulldog, belonging to Tatiana), feels sad, she says, and jumps up at every sound, hoping it is Nicky returning. The latter has evidently extracted a promise from his wife that she will take care of herself, for she concludes: "I shall be careful Deary, I promise you—because I really feel still rather rotten & weak." Nicky, too, was upset at leaving—despite Alix's professed belief that he was glad to go; he wrote to her from Stavka: "I felt very sad & low, leaving you not quite well yet & was in that mood until I went to bed."

From a comment in Alix's next letter, it is evident that their daughter Tatiana was well able to stand up to Grigory and Ania, that she had no fear of expressing her opinion (and then reporting back to her mother on the conversation): "Tatiana & Anastasia were [at Ania's] in the day & found our Friend with her. He said the old story that she cries & sorrows as gets so few caresses. So Tatiana was much surprised & He answered that she receives many, only to her they seem few." By this answer, Grigory demonstrated both his diplomatic and psychological skills. Alix is anxious that her peace is about to be disturbed, because Ania has now progressed to being pushed in a wheelchair and "is preparing to invade upon us often when you return & she will beg to be wheeled in the garden, as the park is shut (so as to meet you) & I wont be there to disturb." So Alix is plotting to have her let into "the big park" instead. She has already encountered this apparition—"what a sight! Covered by a shuba [fur coat] & shawl on her head—I said better a tennis cap & her hair plaited tidily will strike less!" Alix is frequently—and unintentionally—very funny when writing about Ania. "I foresee lots of bother with her," she declares now; "all hysteria! Pretends to faint when one pushes the bed, but can be banged about in the streets in a chair." Again, it is like looking at herself in a distorting mirror, though she seemed to be unaware of this. And in the midst of these very domestic concerns, Alix has been rereading Rasputin's book (the publication of which she had paid for herself) of reflections after his pilgrimage to Jerusalem in 1911; her thoughts lead her to remark: "This war can mean so colossaly much in the moral regeneration of our Country & Church—only to find the men to fulfil all your orders & to help you, in all your immense tasks!" She is also concerned that the Russians should be careful not to mistreat Muslims or any Islamic holy places during their conquests, despite her great hope that one day Mass should again be celebrated at St. Sophia in Constantinople: "Only give orders that nothing should be destroyed or spoiled belonging to the Mahomedans, they can use all again for their religion, as we are Christians and not barbarians, thank God!"

Ania was finally allowed to visit Alix on April 6, a lovely sunny day, on which Maria and Anastasia went for a drive between their lessons. Alix was feeling a little better, though had by no means yet recovered: "The Dr. lets me get up more, only to lie when the temp rises, heart nearly normal, but feel horribly weak yet." The visit seems to have gone off tolerably, if not with great enjoyment on either side: "Well, Ania came, & she has invited herself to luncheon one of these days. Looks very well, but did not seem so overjoyed to see me, nor that had not seen me for a week, no complaint, thank goodness—but those hard eyes again wh she so often has now." Afterward Alix had to get back into bed after three hours on the sofa.

Rasputin's comments as to what the Tsar should or should not do, though inappropriate for him to make given their relative standing, were by no means always lacking in sense, and the one Alix mentions now is a case in point: "Au fond, our Friend wld have found it better you had gone after the war to the conquered country, I only just mention this like that." At this stage, Alix is clearly wary of proffering Grigory's advice—with which she agrees (or is it the other way round?)—too strongly. It is also clear from Alix's letter of the next day how the Tsar's travel plans were communicated to Grigory "in secret"—the route being Nicky to Alix, Alix to Ania, Ania to Grigory—all because Alix wanted "His special prayers" for the Tsar. This lapse of security—and there were others to follow—shows Alix's complete trust in Grigory, or her appalling naïveté and lack of caution. The campaign being waged against Grand Duke Nikolai by his former "friend" and by the Empress is now in full swing: "Does not like N going with you, finds everywhere better alone—& to this end I fully agree." Nicky is quite clear that they are wrong on this point, and he refers only to Alix's, not Grigory's, opinion in his response: "Darling mine, I am not of your opinion that N ought to remain here while I go to Galicia. On the contrary, just because it is a conquered province that the Commander-in-Chief must accompany me. I think that all my people find this right. He accompanies me not I in his suite." At this stage Alix knows when to accept a fait accompli: "Well now all is settled, I hope it will be a success, & especially that you will see all the troops you hope to, it will be a joy to you, & recompense to them."

The imperial couple exchanged loving words on the anniversary of their engagement, April 8. "Have I not also thought of you and of this day 21 years ago?" Nicky wrote to Alix. "I wish you health and everything a deeply loving heart can wish and thank you on my knees for all your love, affection, friendship and patience you have shown these long years of our married life!" "How the years go by!" wrote his wife. "21 years already! You know I have kept the grey princess dress I wore that morning? And shall wear your dear brooch. Dear me, how much we have lived through in these years—heavy trials everywhere, but at home in our nest, bright sunshine!" "I am finishing my letter to you on the sofa," she continued. "The big girls are in town, the little ones walked, then went to their hospital and now have lessons. Baby is in the garden. I lay for ¾ of an hour on the balcony—quite strange to be out, as it happens so rarely I get into the fresh air."

Grigory is now starting to give advice on internal political matters. There is no indication Nicky has asked for such advice, or will consider taking it—but, rather as has been the case with Ania, he does not convey any clear instruction telling Grigory to desist. On the contrary, he sends friendly messages to him via telegram. Grigory's advice is of the "common sense" variety; he envisions an old patriarchal, almost fairy-tale society, where people can be summoned by the Tsar or his representatives to have their heads banged together. This very much suits Alix's way of looking at things, too. "Gr is rather disturbed about the 'meat' stories," Alix tells Nicky on April 10, "the merchants wont lessen the price tho' the government wished it, & there has been a sort of meatstrike one says. One of the ministers he thought, ought to send for a few of the chief merchants & explain it to them, that it is wrong at such a grave moment, during war to highten [sic] the prizes [prices], & make them feel ashamed of themselves."

Alix also reported to Nicky on April 10 that their daughter Maria was going to the cemetery to lay flowers on Grobov's grave. "40 days to-day!" Alix exclaimed—and she had been ill for the whole of that time, and was not yet better. She does not herself appear to have made that connection.

Having reconciled herself to Nicky's too-early trip to the recently conquered province of Galicia, Alix now expresses her full support for it and for him, writing to him on April 11: "Now I have read in the *Novoe Vremia* all about you, & feel so touched & proud for my Sweetheart. And your few words on the balkony [this is how Alix always spells "balcony"]—*just the thing!* God bless & unite in the fully deep, historical & religious sense of the word, these Slavonic Countries to their old Mother Russia! All comes in its right time & now we are strong enough to uphold them, before we should not have been able to. Nevertheless we must in the 'interior' become yet stronger & more united in every way, so as to govern stronger & with more authority.—Wont E[mperor] N[icholas] I be glad! He sees his greatgrandson reconquering those provinces of the long bygone—& the revenge for Austria's treachery towards him." She is also, for the time being at least, reconciled to the way Nicholas governs, backing off from her demands that he be more overtly tough: "And you have personally conquered thousands of hearts. I feel, by your sweet, gentle, humble being & shining, pure eyes—each conquers with what God endows him—each in his way."

In Nicky's subsequent description of his excursion he seems particularly pleased to have slept "in old Franz Joseph's bed" in Lvov. On the next day he saw enough troops even to keep Alix happy: "There, on a large field, was drawn up the mass of troops of the 3rd Caucasian Corps.... I walked along the three long lines on a ploughed field & nearly fell several times, it was very uneven.... As there was little time left, I passed the [remaining] troops in a motor to thank them for their fine service. We were awfully tossed about N and I. I got back to the train completely hoarse, but so pleased & happy to have seen them." From the fortifications near Przemysl he sent Alix a flower that he had "dug up with [A. N.] Grabbe's dagger."

On April 12, spring appeared to have arrived at Tsarskoe Selo and Alix actually lay outside on the balcony for two hours, as she did on the following day, too. Her heart was not enlarged and she was feeling better and stronger. But on the 14th it was snowing again. Nevertheless Alix was still feeling better and had decided she would put on her stays for the first time since her collapse on the day of Grobov's death (whom she still mentions from time to time though not, curiously, without getting his name wrong—she refers to him as Grabovoy). Her improved condition also seems to be making her better disposed toward Ania, whose own recovery is faltering somewhat: "Poor Ania has got again flebitis [sic] in her right leg & strong pain, so one has to stop massage, & she must not walk—but may be wheeled out, as the air is good for her—poor girl, she now really is good & takes all patiently & just as one was hoping to take off the plaster of Paris (gypsum). Yesterday morning for the first time she walked alone on her crutches to the dining room without being held. Awful bad luck!" Ania seems yet again to mirror Alix's own mood; as one becomes more cheerful, so does the other, and vice versa.

On April 15, despite its being a very cold day—with the ice from Lake Ladoga that had broken up with the thaw flowing down the Neva—Alix had arranged to meet Grigory, at his request, at Ania's. Grigory was not there for long but he was, reported Alix, "very dear." He also "asked lots" about Nicky.

On April 17, Alix reported having had a "long, dear letter" from her brother Ernie, which contained a first, tentative suggestion of the possibility of Germany concluding a separate peace with Russia—"He had this idea, as in Germany there is no real hatred against Russia." Ernie wants to open secret talks with Nicky and, to this end, he had sent "a man of confidence" to Stockholm, in the hope that Nicky might send such a man from his side—"privately" (that is, secretly)—to start negotiations. Alix has sent an answer to "the gentlemen" to tell him the Tsar is still away so he had better return home (as Ernie had said he could only spare him for a week, and his letter seems to have taken a long time to reach Alix, so that the "gentleman" had already been there for two days when she received it), and also to say that though "one longs for peace, the time has not yet come." She has dealt with the whole matter herself immediately, she writes, because she knew it would be "unpleasant" for Nicky.

On April 20, Alix managed at last to visit the hospital for three quarters of an hour, though her heart had again been "enlarged" over the previous couple of days. Ania was starting slowly to recover, and Alix's description of the improvements she was making show the extent of the injuries she had suffered in the train accident: "Yesterday evening Hagentorn took off Ania's gypsum from round her stomach, so that she is enchanted, can sit straight, & back no longer aches. Then she managed to lift her left foot, for the first time since 3 months, wh shows that the bone is growing together."

Nineteen-fifteen was the first year since they were married that Alix and Nicky were unable to spend his birthday together as, after having briefly been back at Tsarskoe Selo at the end of April, by May 6 he had left again. "Hard not to be able to give you a birthday tender kiss & blessing," Alix wrote to her "own sweetest of Sweets." She gave him a present of candlesticks and a magnifying glass, which she hopes will be "useful for the train." Ania sent him a card, and Grigory a telegram.

The war was now going badly for the Russians (Przemysl would be recaptured by the enemy on May 21, and Lvov on June 9), and the news is taking its toll on Alix's health—"Slept not famously—heart heavy of anxiety, hate not being with you when trying times." Nevertheless, she is back at work in the hospital in the mornings. In the afternoons she is gaining support from Grigory, meeting him at Ania's, where they talk and pray together and Grigory assures her that "still God will help." Alix and her daughters also made a trip by train and car to Vitebsk at this time, which she feels has gone very well, despite her aching back, which she ascribes to kidney stones ("crystals"), one of her recurrent ailments. Tatiana's dog Ortipo has also been taken along on this journey: "Ortipo climb onto my lap, have sent her off several times without success—so yet more difficult writing on the top of her back in a shaking train." Back at Tsarskoe, Alix is relieved, for his sake, that Nicky is not there, too, as when the war news is bad it is received in the capital "in a different tone"; only the wounded, she asserts, "understand all much more normally."

Something Nicky appreciated in Sir John Hanbury-Williams was his straightforwardness, his lack of obsequiousness vis-à-vis the Emperor, his readiness to say what he meant. "With the Emperor on both these days," Sir John recorded on May 7 and 8. "He suddenly turned round to me at lunch and said: 'I do like people who look you straight in the face, and no one would accuse you of doing otherwise.'" In his letter to Alix of May 11, Nicky complains that for the last week he has been as busy with the receiving of reports, conversations, and going to church as he would have been at home. As a result he has been suffering from headaches, but at last "that is past & now everything's become better & normal, as it used to be." He then goes on to explain to Alix what he has learned since arriving at Stavka, and the reasons Grand Duke Nikolai has given him for the retreat: "When I arrived the prevailing feeling was a depressed & low on[e]. In a halfhour's talk, N explained the whole situation very clearly. Ivanov's Chief of the Staff, poor Gen. Dragomirov, went off his head & began telling right & left that it was necessary to retreat to Kiev. Such talks coming from the top, of course acted strongly on the minds of the commanding generals, and coupled with the tremendous German attacks & our terrible losses, brought them to the conclusion that nothing remained for them but to retreat. . . . Dragomirov was replaced by Gen. Savvich, an excellent man who came with his Siberian corps from Vladivostok. Ivanov gave orders to evacuate even Przemysl! I felt that all along, before N told me about it. But now, after the nomination of Savvich, thank God, thanks also to his [Savvich's] strong & calm will & clear head, the generals' mood has changed." As far as the state of the army in general is concerned, Nicky maintains that "The moral state of our troops is splendid, as usual; but the only thing which causes anxiety, as in the past, is the lack of ammunition." Nevertheless, even this does not cause the Tsar as much anxiety as it might, as rumors have been reaching the Russians that the Germans are in the same plight. Nicky further reports that Grand Duke Nikolai is very pleased with General Alexeev (who had become a commander on the Russian western front and whom Nicky refers to as "my squinting friend"), finding that he is "the right man in the right place." The Grand Duke himself had been very distressed over the situation, as Nicky is at pains to tell Alix; he seems to want to counteract the negative views he knows his wife holds as to his cousin's attitude: "Poor N cried in my cabin when he had explained all this & even asked me whether I was not thinking of replacing him by any other more capable man. He was not in the least excited: I felt he meant what he had said. He thanked me over & over for remaining here longer, because my presence calmed him personally."

In May KR became ill, writing in his diary on the 12th: "I have been feeling unwell. During the day I have had several attacks of spasmodic pain in the chest, which makes me feel very depressed." Three weeks later he was dead, his twelve-year-old son Georgy coming to tell the Tsar in person on June 2. That evening Nicky and Alix went to Pavlovsk (the home of KR and his family) for the first requiem service. By his relatively early death at fifty-six from natural causes, KR was spared much. The funeral took place at the Peter and Paul Cathedral on June 8; the Tsar was accompanied by his sister-in-law Ella and his three elder daughters. Alix did not attend. KR, despite his double life (about which his family never knew, he having left instructions that his diaries were not to be read for ninety-nine years), had been much loved. "It was sad to look at Aunt Olga [his sister], Mavra [his wife] and particularly poor Tatiana [his daughter] when they lowered Kostia's body into the grave!" commented Nicky.

Alix found her separation from Nicky particularly hard to endure when he left again on June 10, and from now on her desire to be of assistance to him emerges more and more clearly. Whatever the results of her "help" may turn out to be now and in the future, her motivation cannot be in doubt. "It is with a heavy heart I let you leave this time," she tells her husband, "everything is so serious & just now particularly painful & I long to be with you, to share your worries & anxieties. You bear all so bravely & by yourself!—let me help you my Treasure. Surely there is some way in wh a woman can be of help & use." She is particularly annoyed by political discord—"the ministers all squabbling amongst each other at a time, when all ought to work together & forget their personal offenses—have as aim the welfare of their Sovereign & Country—it makes me rage." This seems nothing short of treachery to her, as the opposition and revolutionary forces will feed off it—"because people know it, they feel the government in discord & then the left profit by it." This leads her to return to her earlier strictures—that Nicky needs to change his style: "If you could only be severe, my Love, it is so necessary, they must hear your voice & see displeasure in yr eyes; they are too much accustomed to your gentle, forgiving kindness." And she brings in their "Friends," Monsieur Philippe & Grigory, to bolster her argument. Nevertheless, as yet, the tone of her instructions is still comparatively soft: "Sometimes a word gently spoken carries far—but at a time, such as we are now living through, one needs to hear your voice uplifted in protest & reprimand when they continue not obeying yr orders, when they dawdle in carrying them out. They must learn to tremble before you—you remember Mr. Ph & Gr say the same thing too."

Alix's letter of the next day demonstrates how desperately seriously she took Grigory's opinions, to the extent of believing that everything could go wrong with the war and the country if his advice was not followed—particularly as he has been shown to be right in his opinion that it had been too soon for the Tsar to make a victory trip to Galicia. Grand Duke Nikolai had recently issued an order that men categorized as "second class" were now to be conscripted into the army, and Grigory is convinced this is wrong and has expressed the desire that the Commander-in-Chief's order be rescinded. Alix has already written to Nicky about this (the previous day) and is now sounding obsessed by it: "I hope my letter did not displease you but I am haunted by our Friend's wish & know it will be fatal for us & the country if not fulfilled. He means what He says, when speaks so seriously—He was much against your going to L & P—it was too soon, we see it now. . . . Please, my Angel, make N see with your eyes—don't give in to any of the 2-nd class being taken—put it off as long as only possible—they have to work in the fields, fabrics, on steamers etc.; rather take the recroutes [sic] for next year now—please listen to His advise when spoken so gravely & wh gave Him sleepless nights!—one fault & we shall all have to pay for it." It almost sounds as though Grigory is blackmailing her to make sure his advice is followed. Her language at times sounds almost biblical; Grigory to her is far more than a man, he is like an Old Testament prophet. And, to a Christian, her use of the initial capitals—our Friend, He, Him—is always troubling, for it implies that Grigory is being put by Alix on the same level, or very nearly the same level, as Christ: "No, harken unto our Friend, believe Him, He has your interest and Russians at heart—it is not for nothing God sent Him to us—only we must pay more attention to what He says—His words are not lightly spoken—and the gravity of having not only His prayers, but His advice—is great. The Ministers did not think of telling you, that this measure is a fatal one, but He did."

Alix's (first) letter of June 12 gets to the nub of the problem as far as she is concerned over why Grand Duke Nikolai Nikolaevich is the wrong man to be in control of the war. It is because he has "turned against a man of Gods"—that is, Grigory—and this will inevitably bring "bad luck" to his work. And in addition "those women"—Stana and Militsa—will prevent him from changing his attitude. Alix's second point—that Nikolai Nikolaevich has been feted at too early a stage in the war ("he received decorations without end & thanks for all—but too early—its pain to think he got so much & nearly all has been retaken") is a reasonable one, but this is not the main point for her, except insofar as it is all connected, and these latest reversals are only to be expected when a man who has "turned against a man of Gods" is in command.

On a personal level, Ania continues to irritate: "yesterday it was very hot & Ania's temper beastly, wh did not make me feel better—grumbling against everybody & everything & strong hidden pricks at you & me."

On the conscription question, all had not yet been decided and Nicky was able to report that he and the Grand Duke had discussed the issue: "He told me he understood the gravity & that he had a letter from Goremykin on the subject. Everything in one's power shall be done to put it off." Alix is pleased to hear this news—"Thank God N understood about the second class"—but her anxieties are now starting to mount, as is her compulsion to express them and interfere in anything she (and Grigory) dislike. In particular, anything advocated by Grand Duke Nikolai is likely to come in for criticism as being inevitably misguided. As is so often to be the case, she starts and ends with a semi-apology for expressing her criticism, but does not hold back: "Forgive me, but I don't like the choice of [Polivanov as] Minister of war—you remember how you were against him, & surely rightly & N too I fancy. He works with Xenia too—but is he a man in whom one can have any confidence, can he be trusted? How I wish I were with you & could hear all yr reasons for choosing him! I dread N's nominations, N is far from clever, obstinate & led by others—God grant I am mistaken & this choice may be blest—but I like a crow, croak over it rather."

Nicky was now also experiencing some kind of heart trouble; this came upon him during times of particular anxiety and may have been more psychological than physical. "Yes, my sweet one," he told his wife on June 12, "I begin to feel my old heart. The first time it was in August last, after Samsonov disaster [an early disaster in the War when Samsonov's army was encircled by the Germans and most of the troops were killed or captured], and now again—so heavy on the left side when I breathe!" Alix is sympathetic, and seems to understand that part of the trouble may be Nicky's tendency to keep all his anxieties and emotions bottled up inside. "I am sad your dear heart does not feel right," she tells him, "please let Botkin see you upon yr return as he can give you drops to take from time to time when you have pains. I feel so awfully for those who have anything with the heart, suffering from it myself for so many years. Hiding ones sorrow, swallowing all, makes it so bad & it gets besides phisically tired—your eyes seemed like it at times. Only always tell it me, as I have after all enough experience with heart complaints & I can perhaps help you. Speak about all to me, talk it out, cry even, it makes it phisically too, easier sometimes." She also urges, however, that Nicky should "walk less," as she believes that she "ruined" her own heart "walking at the shooting & in Finland before speaking to the Drs. & suffering mad pain, want of air, heartbeating." That Nicky might have consented to such a restriction is unthinkable.

Grigory's latest request is that the Tsar should personally order a church procession to pray for victory, and that it should happen soon, during the two-week fast leading up to Petertide (the feast of St. Peter and Paul on June 29). Alix's insistence as she conveys this message to Nicky is beginning to acquire the edge of hysteria that will be so dominant later on, so fearful is she of the consequences if Grigory's instructions are not followed to the letter: "He begs you most incessantly to order quickly that on one day all over the country there should be a church procession to ask for victory, God will sooner hear if all turn to Him—please give the order, any day you choose now that it should be done—send yr order (I think) by wire (open that all can read it) to Sabler that this is yr wish . . . please Darling, & just that its to be an order from you, not from the Synod. I could not see Him to-day—hope to-morrow." Nicky's response to this proposal is positive, though he has not followed Grigory's instructions to the letter, as he has discussed—rather than ordered—the proposed procession with the head Chaplain of the Army, Georgy Shavelsky, and the idea now is that it should take place on July 8, the feast day of the Mother of God of Kazan.

On June 14, Alix reported to Nicky on a visit she had had from his uncle Grand Duke Pavel, from which it is clear that rumors about Russia being willing to conclude a separate peace with Germany were rife. Alix's account is clear and sensible, and contains no suggestion at all that she herself was anything less than fully committed to the Allies' war aims. She is also astute enough to know perfectly well what the rumormongers will be saying about her: "I warned him he wld next hear, that I am wishing peace to be concluded." In the same letter Alix warns Nicky that she has heard (also from Grand Duke Pavel) of the possibility that one of the generals at Stavka—Yuri Danilov, previously head of the Intelligence Section of the Russian Main Staff—is a spy, and recommends he be watched (without telling Nikolai Nikolaevich). (Nicky's response to this is: "What concerns Danilov—I think the idea of him being a spy not worth a straw.") The superstitious element in Alix's faith in Grigory—and for her the borderline between religion and superstition was very blurred—is obvious in the attachment she formed for certain objects, such as she now describes: "I send you a stick (fish holding a bird), wh was sent to Him from New Athos to give to you—he used it first & now sends it to you as a blessing—if you can sometimes use it, wld be nice & to have it in yr compartment near the one Mr. Ph touched, is nice too." Later, in August, she instructs Nicky to "Remember to comb your hair before all difficult talks & decisions, the little comb will bring its help." Again, the comb has come from Grigory, with his blessing.

During a recent evening gathering at Ania's Grigory had regaled the company on his understanding of the nature of the Russian autocracy—which, happily and hardly coincidentally, matched and bolstered Alix's own. "Tho' other Sovereigns are anointed & crowned," he had declared, "only the Russian one is a real Anointed since 300 years." And the way such an autocrat ought to behave is, according to Grigory, simple: He should just issue orders and have them obeyed. It should therefore, in his view, be perfectly easy to solve the ammunition problem, for instance; the only people making it difficult are the bureaucrats who waste time talking: "Finds, you ought to order fabricks to make Ammunition," Alix reports, "simply you to give the order even choose wh fabrick, if they show you the list of them, instead of giving the order over through commissions wh talk for weeks & never can make up their minds. Be more autocratic my very own Sweetheart, show your mind."

There were now moves afoot to replace Vladimir Sabler (not to be confused with the imperial family's friend, Nikolai Sablin) as Chief Procurator of the

Holy Synod. In his letter of June 15, Nicky demonstrates a rather nervous awareness that his wife will not approve of the proposal for Sabler's successor; nevertheless he is attempting to stick to his guns: "During our talks [Shavelsky] mentioned Sabler's name & said how necessary it is to change him. It is curious how all understand it & want a pure, religious & well intentioned man in his place. Old Gorem[ykin] and Krivoshein and Shcherbatov all told me here the same thing & they find Samarin the best. I remember now that Stolypin wanted to have him some six [years ago] & with my permission spoke to him, but he refused. I allowed Gorem to send for him & propose him that place. I am sure that will not please you, because he comes from Moscow, but the changes must happen now & one must choose a man whose name is known in the whole country & who is unanimously estimated. With such people in the government one can work & they will all stick together—that is quite sure." While Nicky was writing this letter, Alix was also composing one to him, from which it is clear that Nicky was absolutely right in knowing that she would not like the appointment of Samarin; she had also been hearing other rumors about which she—but particularly Grigory—was most anxious: "Town is so full of gossip, as tho' all the ministers were being changed—Krivoshein first minister, Manukhin instead of Shcheglovitov, Guchkov as aide to Polivanov & so on & our Friend, to whom A went to bid goodbye, was most anxious to know what was true. (As though also Samarin instead of Sabler, whom it is better not to change before one has a very good one to replace him, certainly Samarin wld go against our Friend & stick up for the Bishops we dislike—he is so terribly Moscovite & narrowminded.) Well, A answered that I knew nothing."

Alix now passes on a message from Grigory, who has by now assumed enormous importance in his own eyes: "you are to pay less attention to what people will say to you, not let yourself be influenced by them but use yr own instinct & go by that, to be more sure of yourself & not listen too much nor give in to others, who know less than you. The times are so serious & grave, that all your own personal wisdom is needed & yr soul must guide you. He regrets you do not speak to Him more about all you think & were intending to do & speak about with yr ministers & the changes you were thinking of making. He prays so hard for you and Russia & can help more when you speak to Him frankly." Though Nicky seems never to have responded to Rasputin's request to treat him as a kind of unofficial prime minister and discuss everything with him prior to doing so with his ministers (the Tsar would not have treated his ministers in such a way), there is one element of Rasputin's advice that did chime with his own way of thinking and may unfortunately have strengthened that particular tendency—and that was Nicky's belief that, as Tsar, he could be in direct communication with God and had only to listen to his own soul to know what to do. This belief led him at times to ignore the advice of others, to imagine that a feeling of inner peace was sufficient confirmation that his decisions were right, and made him susceptible—at least when in Grigory's presence—to some of what the *"starets"* told him.

Another revealing thing about this very interesting letter is the light it casts on Alix's motivation for what has so often been seen merely as interference in matters that should not have properly concerned her. Part of the reason why she feels so strongly that she must join in and be involved in everything Nicky is doing is because she is lonely. She is so used to their being together nearly all the time—even if that "togetherness" actually meant that he was in his study for long stretches of time while she concerned herself with the children or with being an invalid—that she hates feeling so separated from what he is doing, and is determined to overcome the separation, mentally and spiritually if she cannot do so physically. "I suffer hideously being away from you," she writes. "20 years we shared all together, & now grave things are passing, I do not know your thoughts nor decisions, & its such pain." And partly in order to assuage that pain, she involves herself more and more in the ruling of her husband's Empire.

And then, even before she has sent off this letter, arrives the one from Nicky containing the dreaded news about Alexander Samarin. Alix responds immediately, in a state of near panic; Samarin is so clearly on the wrong side: "Yes, Lovy, about Samarin I am much more than sad, simply in despair, just one of Ella's not good, very bigoted [sic] clique, bosom friend of Sophie Iv. Tiutchev and that bishop Trifon [the Bishop of Dmitrov, decorated in 1915 for his work at the front]. I have strong reason to dislike him, as he always spoke & now speaks in the army against our Friend—now we shall have stories against our Friend beginning & all will go badly. I hope heart & soul he wont accept—that means Ella's influence & worries fr morn to night, & he against us, once against Gr & so awfully narrowminded a real Moscou type—head without soul. My heart feels like lead, 1000 times better Sabler a few months still than Samarin!" And then she reverts to the procession question—why is Nicky not getting on with it in the way she told him to? "How the church procession now, don't go putting it off, Lovy, listen to me, its serious, have it quicker done, now is lent, therefore more appropriate, cho[o]se Peter & Paul day, but now soon." She is so convinced she is right, and that if only she were with Nicky, she would be able to convince him, too: "Oh, why are we not together to speak over all together & to help prevent things wh I know ought not to be." Her last piece of advice is the one he will eventually take, and which will prove fatal: "Its not my brain wh is clever, but I listen to my soul & I wish you would too my own sweetest One."

In the evening (of June 16) Alix puts pen to paper again, continuing to express (at length—"Just a few words before the night," she begins) the fear that only bad things can come from not listening to "our Friend" and doing what he says. The hectoring of her husband—for that is what this is—can only really be understood in light of her fear. Grigory has succeeded in making her very afraid—of the consequences of not listening to him, of the influences that may be brought to bear on Nicky when he is away from herself and from him, of the evil inherent in anything Grand Duke Nikolai says or does: "The heart is, oh, so heavy & sad!—I always remember what our Friend says & how often we do not enough heed His words! He was so much against yr going to the Headquarters, because people get you round there & make you do things, wh would have been better not done—here the atmosphere in your own house is a healthier one & you would see things more rightly—if only you would come back quicker. I am not speaking because of a selfish feeling, but that here I feel quieter about you & there am in a constant dread what one is concocting—you see, I have absolutely no faith in N—know him to [be] far fr clever & having gone against a Man of God's, his work cant be blessed, nor his advice be good." Grigory himself is clearly distraught over Samarin's nomination: "When Gr heard in town yesterday before He left, that Samarin was named, already then people knew it—He was in utter despair, as He, the last evening here, a week ago to-day, begged you not to change him Sabler just now, but that soon one might perhaps find the right man—& now the Moscou net will be like a spiders net around us, our Friend's enemies are ours, & Shch [Prince Nikolai Shcherbatov, Minister of Internal Affairs from July to September 1915] will make one with them, I feel sure. I beg your pardon for writing all this, but I am so wretched ever since I heard it & cant get calm." Alix is firmly of the belief that her strength is needed to keep Nicky strong and to guide him into the right decisions: "People are afraid of my influence, Gr said it (not to me) & Voiekov, because they know I have a strong will & sooner see through them & help you being firm. I should have left nothing untried to dissuade you, had you been here, & I think God would have helped me & you would have remembered our Friend's words." But behind all her bullying lies the fear: "When He says not to do a thing & one doesnt listen, one sees ones fault always afterwards."

To Nikolasha Alix imputes deliberate malice toward Rasputin, asserting that it is "N's campaign" to turn people against their Friend and that this is what he will do with Samarin, if the latter accepts his appointment as Chief

Procurator. To combat this, Nicky must "speak very firmly" to Samarin as soon as he sees him: "Tell him severely, with a strong & decided voice, that you forbid any intrigues against our Friend or talks about Him, or the slightest persecution, otherwise you will not keep him." A particular fear for Alix is that Samarin is a friend of the children's former governess, who had accused Rasputin of abuse; therefore, Nicky must "tell it him all, his bosom friend S. I. Tiutchev spreads lies about the children, repeat this & that her poisenous [sic] untruths did much harm & you will not allow a repetition of it." Her next words—"Do not laugh at me"—are interesting, as they suggest that laughter may be one of the reactions Nicky has previously had when his wife is beset by anxieties and launches an attack on him (for in this lengthy stream-of-consciousness epistle one can hear Alix's voice when she is speaking out loud). Nicky must not laugh now, Alix insists, for this is a matter of life and death: "You know what this war is to me in every sense—& that the man of God's who prays incessantly for you, might be in danger of persecution—that God would not forgive us our weakness & sin in not protecting him." And she is clear that these particular battle lines are drawn: "You know N's hatred for Grig is intense." (This seems to me to have to do with Nikolasha's marriage and Grigory's condemnation of it—rather like Herod vis-à-vis John the Baptist—at least in Alix's mind. She could surely imagine Stana and Militsa wanting to serve up Grigory's head on a platter.) Someone about whom Alix had no doubts, on the other hand, is Vladimir Voeikov, Commandant of the Imperial Palace and Count Fredericks's son-in-law (Fredericks had been made a Count in 1913), for she tells Nicky: "Speak once to Voeikov, Deary, he understands such things because he is honestly devoted to you." Then, yet again, Alix returns to the question of the projected procession: "Lovy, remember, quicker the church procession, now during lent is just the most propicious [sic] moment, & absolutely from you, not by the new Chief Procurator of the Synod." From her next remark it is clear that she shared her tendency to preach, and to be long-winded over it, with her sister—and that she and Nicky have commented on this proclivity of Ella's: "Reading this letter you will say—one sees she is Ella's sister." (One might also be tempted to say: "one sees they are both Queen Victoria's granddaughters.")

To be added to "Nikolasha's" crimes, in the eyes of Grigory and Alix, is the fact that he supported the idea of inaugurating the Duma in 1905. Indeed, the very fact that Nikolasha was in support of this makes Alix doubly sure that the whole idea of a move toward constitutional government for Russia was completely wrong. Now she and Grigory are weighing in against the Duma being convened: "Now the Duma is to come together in August, & our Friend begged you several times to do it as late as possible & not now, as they ought all to be working in their places—& here they will try to mix in & speak about things that do not concern them. Never forget that you are & must remain authocratic [sic] Emperor!—we are not ready for a constitutional government, N's fault & Wittes it was that the Duma exists, & it has caused you more worry than joy. Oh I do not like N having anything to do with these big sittings wh concern interior questions!—He understands our country so little & imposes upon the ministers by his loud voice & gesticulations." Alix's fear of not doing as Grigory bids is particularly clear in this letter: "You are remaining still long away, Gr begged not—once all goes against His wishes my heart bleeds in anguish & fright." She is also aware that such letters may not be welcomed by Nicky, but feels she has no option but to write them: "Do my long, grumbling letters not aggravate you, poor wee One? But I only mean all for yr good & write fr the depths of a very suffering, tormented heart."

Nicky's reply to all this outpouring of anxiety is evasive and, largely, dismissive; this, one can surmise, is how he was accustomed to dealing with his wife's outbursts. He thanks her for her "dear letters," and for all the "devotion & love" she shows him. "It gives me strength," he writes. Then he goes on: "Bless you my beloved One. It is too hot to write about such serious questions." He clearly perceives her as being overwrought and unnecessarily panic-stricken; he tells her he is glad she has seen "the old man"—by which he means Ivan Goremykin (reappointed Chairman of the Council of Ministers from 1914 to 1916), whom Alix herself has referred to as "dear old Goremykin"—and asks whether he has "calmed" her. He then goes on to assure her that his own health is fine after all, the unpleasant feeling in what he had taken to be his heart having gone away (and having turned out to be lumbago anyway).

In her letter of June 22, Alix has added another "enemy" to her list—Vladimir Dzhunkovsky, Assistant Minister of Internal Affairs and Commander of the Corps of Gendarmes, guilty of disseminating nasty stories about Rasputin. "Ah dear," she tells Nicky, "he is not an honest man, he has shown that vile, filthy paper (against our Friend) to Dmitri who repeated all to Paul & he to Alia . . . ah, its so vile—always liars, enemies—I long knew Dzh hates Gr & that the 'Preobrazhensky' clique therefore dislikes me, as through me & Ania he comes to the house." This leads her on to remonstrate once more with Nicky—her tone seems "more in sorrow than in anger"—that he should lay the law down and stop people behaving in this way: "Ah my Love, when at last will you thump with your hand upon the table & scream at Dzh & others when they act wrongly?—one does not fear you—& one must—they must be frightened of you, otherwise all sit upon us,

& its enough Deary—don't let me speak in vain. . . . Oh my Boy, make one tremble before you—to love you is not enough, one must be afraid of hurting, displeasing you! . . . If your Ministers feared you, all would be better. The old man, Gorem also finds you ought to be more sure of yourself & energetically speak, & show more strongly when you are displeased." In a further letter later that day, Alix again acknowledges that she is in danger of displeasing Nicky herself: "I fear I aggravate you by all I write, but its only honestly & well meant, Sweetheart—others will never say anything, so old Wify writes her opinion frankly, when she feels its right to do so." She is again feeling ill: "I remain quiet today, as heart again enlarged, pulse rather weak & head aches. Am lying on the balkony—all are out & away & Ania gone to Peterhof." She continues to ask about the projected church procession: "Wonder what you have settled for the day of the cross, hope you have said its to be done by your order."

In his letter of June 23, in which Nicky again ignores most of Alix's questions but fills her in on the military situation—the Germans have almost broken through the Russian lines but have been repulsed by a vigorous counterattack—he asks her specifically to keep what he tells her to herself: "Of course, this is only for you to know, please don't speak about it, my darling."

Tsarskoe Selo on an early midsummer morning is wonderfully evoked by Alix: "Slept little this night & at 3 looked out of the window of my mauve room. A glorious morning, one felt the sun behind the trees, a soft haze over all, such calm—the swans swimming on the pond, steam rising from the grass—oh so beautiful, I longed to be well & go for a long, long walk as in bygone days."

She continues to be dubious about War Minister Alexei Polivanov, writing of him on June 24: "Saw Polivanov yesterday—don't honestly ever care for the man—something aggravating about him, cant explain what—preferred Sukhomlinov, tho' this one is cleverer, but doubt whether as devoted." She goes on to urge Nicky once again to visit troops, unrealistically insisting he should go anywhere he pleases, with her usual simplistic understanding of what it means—or, in her view, ought to mean—to be the Emperor and with her continued distrust of Nikolasha: "say you are going off again for a trip;—had I been there, I should have helped you going off—Sweetheart needs pushing always & to be reminded that he is the Emperor & can do whatsoever pleases him—you never profit of this—you must show you have a way & will of yr own, & are not lead by N & his staff, who direct yr movements & whose permission you have to ask before going anywhere. No, go alone, without N., by yr very own self, bring the blessing of yr presence to them." From what she writes next—"don't say you bring bad luck"—one can surmise that this is precisely what a depressed Nicky did say, after his visits to Lvov and Przemysl and their subsequent recapture. But, no, Alix assures him, this only happened "because our Friend knew & told you it was too early, but you listened instead to the Headquarters." And, just as Alix and Nicky have always previously made a distinction beween the "people" and St. Petersburg—the former representing "real" Russia, supportive of the autocracy, with the latter standing for all the falseness, artificiality, and deceit of high society; the bureaucracy; and, of course, the revolutionaries—she now makes a similar distinction between the "Active Army" and "Headquarters." And that is one of the reasons why the Tsar should go off and meet some real troops. Such an action on his part will, she is sure, be valued by those loyal troops she has in mind: "bless the troops by your precious Being, in their name I beseech you to go—give them the spiritual rise, show them for whom they are fighting & dying—not for Nikolasha, but for you! 1000[s] have never seen you & yearn for a look of yr beautiful, pure eyes." Alix has the most lurid and strange ideas of what goes on at Stavka. Nicky should not tell Nikolasha where he is going, she insists, because that way spies will find out and inform the Germans, who will then set out to drop bombs on the Tsar. Whereas if he just goes off in a convoy of three cars, no one will notice at all and he will be quite safe—provided of course that he has sent a coded message to Alix so that she can pass it on to Grigory, who will pray for him. All this would be comic were it not so sad.

On June 25, Alix is again arguing against the Duma being allowed to convene: "Deary, I heard that the horrid Rodzianko & others went to Goremykin to beg the Duma to be at once called together—oh please dont, its not their business, they want to discuss things not concerning them & bring more discontent—they must be kept away—I assure you only harm will arise—they speak too much. Russia, thank God, is not a constitutional country, tho' those creatures try to play a part & meddle in affairs they dare not." She also continues to inveigh against Grand Duke Nikolai, whom she is convinced wants to usurp the Tsar's power for his own malevolent ends: "All are shocked that the ministers go with report[s] to [Nikolasha], as tho' he were now the Sovereign. Ah my Nicky, things are not as they ought to be, & therefore N keeps you near, to have a hold over you with his ideas & bad councels [sic]. Wont you yet believe me, my Boy? Can't you realise that a man who turned simple traitor to a man of Gods, cannot be blest, nor his actions be good—well, if he must remain at the head of the army there is nothing to be done, & all bad success will fall upon his head—but interior mistakes will be told home upon you, as who inside the country can think that he reigns besides you. Its so utterly false & wrong." Yet again Alix betrays her awareness that Nicky may be annoyed by these hectoring, distraught letters of hers, but she cannot stop herself from writing and sending them: "I fear I anger & trouble you by my letters—but I am alone in my misery & anxiety & I cant swallow what I think my honest duty to tell you." A feeling of helplessness, of being too far from the field of action and decision-taking, while being convinced that she (and Grigory) know what ought to be done, what decided, exacerbates her misery: "Remember our Friend betted you not to remain long—He sees & knows N through & through & your too soft & kind heart.—I here, incapable of helping, have rarely gone through such a time of wretchedness—feeling & realising things are not done as they should be,—& helpless to be of use—its bitterly hard; & they, N knows my will, & fears my influence (guided by Gregory) upon you; its all so clear." And, finally, she still wants to know about the planned processions: "Please answer me, are the cross Processions going to be on the 29th, as such a great holiday & the end of lent? Excuse bothering you again, but so eager to know, as hear nothing." She was again not at all well, telling Nicky on the following day: "Fear can't meet you at station, as Church will already be a great exertion & do feel so rotten still! . . . Miss my hospital & feel sad not to be able to work & look after our dear wounded."

Nicky was then back home throughout the whole of July and for more than half of August. During this time a struggle went on at Tsarskoe Selo, the ultimate victors of which were Alix and Rasputin. But in her letter to Nicky of August 22, as he set off back for Stavka (now transferred to Mogilev, on account of the "retreat before the advancing enemy")—this time to take over as Commander-in-Chief—she is concerned to express her belief that the real victory is his. "You have fought this great fight for your country & throne," she tells him, "alone & with bravery & decision. Never have they seen such firmness in you before & it cannot remain without good fruit." And in Nicky's absence—for now he will not be able to return to Tsarskoe so frequently—Alix has every intention of "helping" him to rule. "Lovy, I am here," she assures him, "dont laugh at silly old wify, but she has 'trousers' on unseen, & I can get the old man [as she calls Goremykin] to come & keep him up to be energetic—whenever I can be of the smallest use, tell me what to do—use me—at such a time God will give me the strength to help you—because our souls are fighting for the right against the evil." This is the crux of what is motivating Alix—the belief that she, Nicky, Rasputin, and the few others on the side of their "Friend" are waging spiritual warfare against the powers of evil (personified, for Alix, in the figure of Grand Duke Nikolai as well as various members of the Duma, of the Synod, and indeed anyone opposed to her "Friend" and herself). So much more is at stake, she believes, than mere questions of territory and secular power. In waging the external war against Germany and Austria, and the internal war against the forces of revolution (which include, in Alix's eyes, supporters of a democratic constitution for Russia), Nicky is upholding his right to rule as the divinely anointed autocrat, he is fulfilling his spiritual destiny—and working to bring about that of his son, the heir. "It is all much deeper than appears to the eye," Alix tells Nicky, "we, who have been taught to look at all from another side, see what the struggle here really is & means—you showing your mastery, proving yourself the Autocrat without wh Russia cannot exist." Such a belief makes Alix completely impervious to the remonstrances of others, however well-meaning, for they—including many of the wider Romanov family over the coming months, including her own sister Ella—do not look from the same "side," do not perceive what the struggle really means, and so they cannot be expected to understand and there is no point in listening to them. "God anointed you at your coronation," she reminds her husband, "he placed you where you stand & you have done your duty, be sure, quite sure of this & He forsaketh not His anointed. Our Friend's prayers arise night & day for you to Heaven & God will hear them."

Alix is so convinced that this decision is the right one and that God will make everything come right because of it that she is even willing to let her beloved and vulnerable little boy accompany his father to army headquarters; in fact, she is encouraging this plan: "your Sunbeam will appear to help you, your very own Child—won't that touch those hearts & make them realise what you are doing, & what they dared to wish to do, to shake your throne, to frighten you with internal black forebodings—only a bit of success out there & they will change."

This letter of Alix's also gives some indication of the pressure to which she (with the help of Grigory) has subjected Nicky during this time at Tsarskoe Selo (the climax seems to have come during the last two days) until he both capitulated and managed to hold fast against the opposition from various of his ministers to his—insofar as it was his—decision: "forgive me, I beseech you, my Angel, for having left you no peace & worried you so much—but I too well know yr marvellously gentle character—& you had to shake it off this time, had to win your fight alone against all. It will be a glorious page in yr reign & Russian history the story of these weeks & days—& God, who is just & near you—will save your country & throne through your firmness." There is no indication, at least by the time the battle was over, that Nicky felt he had been bullied or outmaneuvered by his wife; "Remember last night, how tenderly we clung together," she writes. The daughters—at least the elder two—also had some awareness of the struggle going on between their parents, Tatiana writing to her mother on

August 15: "I pray for you both dearies, the whole time, that God will help you now in this terrible time. I simply can't tell you how awfully sorry I am for you, my beloved ones. I am so sorry I can in no way help you or be useful."

Alix is in fact still worried that her husband will not be able to keep up his firmness once he is back at Stavka and has to act on his decision, without her there to keep him going. "Be firm to the end," she adjures him, "let me be sure of that otherwise shall get quite ill from anxiety. Bitter pain not to be with you—know what you feel, & the meeting with N wont be agreeable—you did trust him & now you know, what months ago our Friend said, that he was acting wrongly towards you & your country & your wife—its not the people who would do harm to your people, but Nikolasha & set Guchkov, Rodzianko, Samarin etc." Alix will not be able to stop worrying, she declares, until "all is done at the Headquarters & Nikolasha gone." And her great fear is that, once Nicky is away from her, others will be able to influence him and all his promises to be firm will evaporate; hence her need to keep on and on, repeating her strictures until even her poor impressionable husband will be unable to forget them: "near you all is well—when out of sight others at once profit—you see they are affraid [sic] of me & so come to you when alone—they know I have a will of my own when I feel I am in the right—& you are now—we know it, so you make them tremble before your courage & will. God is with you & our Friend for you—all is well—& later all will thank you for having saved your country." Alix appears convinced that "the left" had been planning to "use" Nikolasha for some plot of their own—presumably to bring down the autocracy, possibly by losing the war. (Pierre Gilliard suggests, and this is corroborated by later letters, that Alix had got wind, via Ania, of a plot emanating from Stavka to seize her during the Emperor's absence and have her confined in a convent. There is no evidence that Nikolasha was involved in any such plot, however.) Now, she believes, "the left are furious because all slips through their hands & their cards are clear to us."

Alexei Khvostov has now been suggested—by Alix and Rasputin—to take over as Minister of Internal Affairs. "I do hope Gorem will agree to your choice of Khvostov—you need an energetic minister of the interior—should he be the wrong man, he can later be changed—no harm in that, at such times—but if energetic he may help splendidly & then the old man does not matter. If you take him, then only wire to me 'tail alright' & I shall understand." ("Khvost" is the Russian for "tail," hence Alix's instructions about the telegram—it is hardly likely, however, that this would provide much secrecy as the pun is so obvious.) Her views on the Duma and on all the political wranglings and disturbance are that they are all a load of "empty noise," quite without substance and of no real concern, as she has made clear to Goremykin and repeated to Nicky: "I begged him not to worry about it, that I am convinced its not so serious & more talking than anything else & that they wanted to frighten you & now that you have shown a strong will of your own, they will shut up. . . . I tried to cheer him up, & a wee bit I think I did, as I showed him how little serious, au fond, all this empty noise is." Nicky's response to this turns out to be another fatal mistake; he encourages Alix in her ambitions to "help" him while he is away and betrays no trace of annoyance at all her hectoring—rather the reverse. "I am delighted you spoke & soothed dear old Gor," he writes on August 25. "Fancy, my Wify, helping Huzy when he is away! What a pity you did not perform that duty long ago, or at least now during the war! Nothing gives me more pleasure than to feel proud of you, as I have all these last months when you worried me thoughly [sic] to be firm & stick to my opinion." He concludes by sending his "fond love" to Ania. One could be forgiven for wondering if Nicky has gone mad. Alix's delighted response is inevitable: "Oh Sweetheart, I am so touched you want my help, I am always ready to do anything for you, only never liked mixing up without being asked—only here I felt too much was at stake."

From Alix's remark on how Nicky had looked when he set off, and after he had been subjected to whatever took place when Grigory had been there, it almost sounds as though he had been hypnotized: "Such calm filled my soul (tho' terribly sad) when I saw you leave in peace and serene. Your face had such a lovely expression, like when our Friend left." Whatever did take place, Nicky ended by choosing the path of least resistance—having been bullied into submission by Alix and Grigory, and it had always been so much easier for him to agree than to put up a fight with anyone—and he mistakes the sense of calm that now enters him (which is really the calm of retreating to his comfort zone, of abrogating his responsibility to think and decide, to use his mind as well as his soul) as confirmation that he is right, that he is obeying the promptings of God. He describes this sense of calm to Alix on August 25: "Thank God it is all over and here I am with this new heavy responsibility on my shoulders! But God's will be fulfilled—I feel so calm, A sort of feeling after the Holy Communion!" His eventual abdication is merely the outward form of the mental renunciation that has already taken place.

Despite this calmness, Nicky sounds quite excited—for him—in his diary entry on the day of his arrival at Mogilev, August 23: "At 3.30 arrived at *my headquarters,* one *verst* from the town of Mogilev. Nikolasha was waiting for me. After talking with him, received General Alexeev with his first report. It all went well! After having tea, went to look at the surrounding area. The train is standing in a small, thick wood. We dined at 7.30. Afterwards went for another walk. The evening was splendid."

Grand Duke Nikolai Nikolaevich seems to have taken the change of command—and his "promotion" to be viceroy of the Caucasus and to command the Russian armies facing the Turks—in his stride, even with relief. Only his aides-de-camp were furious. "N came in with a good cheery smile," Nicky reported to Alix of his first meeting with the Grand Duke on his return to Stavka, "simply asked for my order when he was to leave. I answered, in the same manner, that he could remain for two days; then we spoke about questions concerning the military operations, about some generals and that was all. The following days at luncheon & dinner he was very talkative & in a good humour that we all have rarely seen him in for many a month. Pet[ia] also, but his a.d.c.s were black in their expressions—it was even funny." Part of the reason behind the Grand Duke's calm was the knowledge that it would not actually be the Emperor making military decisions, but General Alexeev as Chief of Staff: "N repeated to me that he leaves this place with a quiet feeling knowing I have such a help as Alexeev under me." He also claimed to be pleased to be going to the Caucasus—"he likes it & interests himself in the people & fine nature, but he begs to remain long after the end of the war"—and he would be joined on the journey by his wife and sister-in-law—"the whole collection of black women," as Nicky termed them. The latter concluded: "Now begins a new clean page, and what will be written on it only God Almighty knows? I signed my first prikaz [order] & added a few words with a rather trembling hand!"

CHAPTER ELEVEN

From Command to Abdication

1916-1917

Be firm, I, your wall, am behind you & won't give way.

—Alix to Nicky, December 13, 1916

ALIX'S FIRST LETTER to Nicky of 1916 is a rather needy, peculiarly revealing epistle. She has slept badly, has a headache, and her heart is enlarged, so she has been consigned to bed for the day. She is suddenly cheered by the unexpected arrival of a particularly loving letter from her husband, and now she pours out to him how much she misses him, longing to be in his arms, and to receive the kisses that he, being shy, only gives her in the dark. She declares that she "lives" by these kisses, caresses, sweet looks, and any tender word; the impression conveyed is that tender words from Nicky are not quite as frequent as Alix might like—for one thing, he is always busy. But, unlike Ania, Alix hates "begging" for these signs of affection. From this we gather that Ania continues to be smitten with Nicky and to make demands on him. Ania also continues to insist that she is lonely, which greatly annoys Alix, who protests (to Nicky, rather than directly to Ania) that she sees plenty of the children and herself, coming to see them twice a day and spending every evening with them as well, whereas Nicky himself is genuinely alone. There is also more than a hint of jealousy in Alix's words (this in her letter of January 2) that there is someone else—that is, Ania—who "dares call you 'my own'—you nevertheless are mine, my own treasure, my life, my Sun, my Heart!" Alix seems to have had little, if any, genuine reason for jealousy. From a letter of a few days later, there can be no doubt that Nicky still finds his wife sexually attractive; he writes: "I press you passionately to my heart—& lower (forgive me)"—to which Alix responded wholeheartedly with "lady thanks for the caress wh she returns with great love!" (A constant refrain throughout these wartime letters concerns the fear that Alix will be having her period when Nicky returns home on short breaks, an eventuality that neither of them desires.) Nevertheless, there is still some kind of relationship between Nicky and Ania, even if it is one-sided, and no effort is made to stop Ania writing love letters to him. Alix asks on January 6: "Lovy, you burn her letters so as that they should never fall into anybody's hands?" and Nicky replies: "I always tear A's letters into small pieces after reading them, so you need not worry. None of her letters will be saved for posterity." How deeply frustrating for the biographer!

After her intense beginning to the year's correspondence, Alix changes register to tell Nicky that the eleven-year-old Alexei has now begun to keep a diary of his own; Maria helped him to make a start on it on New Year's Day—and his spelling is rather "queer." Two days later Alexei is still taking his diary writing very seriously, but amusing his mother by writing about what he had for dinner before he has actually had it, as he claims not to have enough time to write it all up in the evening. The diary was clearly going to be in the same factual style as his father's. Nicky was predictably approving of this enterprise, giving as the reason for maintaining the habit that it taught one how to express thoughts "clearly and concisely." This message encouraged Alexei to keep going, as after a week he was already getting rather bored.

In addition to the "Adonis" drops that Alix took to quell her heart palpitations, she was also taking opium to relieve the stomach pains that she thought might be a side effect of the drops. In mid-January she was feeling very ill, the symptoms of her heart condition troubling her throughout the month. At the beginning of February toothache, with an accompanying swollen face, was added to her ailments. Alexei was ill also, having hurt himself while sledging; both his arms were bandaged, aching, and hard to bend, but Grigory had assured them the problem would pass in two days. Earlier in the year Anastasia had been suffering from bronchitis and communicating with her mother by telephone, which is how the daughters now customarily kept in touch with Alix whenever any of them was too indisposed to come down one floor to see her (and vice versa). Nicky made occasional brief visits home from Stavka, to attend to official business. One such visit occurred in late January, and during this visit his "Aunt Michen" (Grand Duchess Maria Pavlovna) mooted the possibility of Olga marrying her son Boris. Alix disliked the idea very much, and Nicky pleaded with her not to brood over it. They also both knew that the young woman herself would not be at all susceptible to the suggestion; Olga's interests lay elsewhere, though her mother does not give any details.

Throughout the winter "the cow" continued to send Nicky "fat letters of love," Alix signing off crossly on February 4: "Goodbye Lovebird, my own & not hers, as she dares to call you." What remains inexplicable is that they never put a stop to this, despite Alix's annoyance and Nicky's apparent lack of interest. He was still always concerned to ensure that Ania should not feel neglected by him. There is a suggestion in what Alix writes on March 3 that there was some truth in Ania's assertion that Nicky valued talking to her. "A is sad she never had an occasion to see you alone," Alix wrote, "personally I think she gets calmer & more normal, less aggressive when she has less chance,—because the more one has, the more one wants,—if you need talks, then of course its another thing. But she gets over those things much better now,—you have trained her & in consequence her temper is calmer & we have no stories." Even that phrase "you have trained her" suggests a relationship between Nicky and Ania that did not directly involve Alix herself. Nicky seems to have gone back to Stavka feeling particularly cheerful, at least from Hanbury-Williams's perspective: "The Emperor after an absence of some time returned to Headquarters yesterday. He is always so bright and cheerful that one cannot but be cheerful with him. It is a wonderful temperament for a man who must have such cares and anxieties on his mind and I am sure is a good inspiration for others."

Alix was still not well by early spring, having now added a cough to her woes. She was continuing to experience a lot of pain and was feeling "cretinised" because of it. Much of the pain was in her face, which Dr. Derevenko kept "electrifying" for her. She was also having trouble with her eyes, which she believed to be partly caused both by crying and by holding back unshed tears. Her optician connected it to her neuralgia, opining that both complaints were symptoms of gout. Whatever the root cause, the symptoms sound horribly painful: "My eye has been hurting me madly all day (& head too)—its from the *triplex nerve* in the face. One branch to the eye, the one took the upper row of teeth, the other the lower, & the knot before the ear. . . . Its fr a chill in the facial nerves, the cheek & teeth are much better, the left jaw goes popping in & out this evening, but the eyes ache very much." In early April, just before Easter, Alexei suffered another very painful hemophiliac attack, after having overexerted himself using a spade. Again it was one of his arms that was affected; it swelled up so that he could not bend it and he was in great pain for several days.

The many changes of ministers that occurred during the last fifteen months of the reign of Nicholas II were symptomatic of a growing instability. From January to November 1916 the Chairman of the Council of Ministers (or Prime Minister) was Boris Stürmer; he was replaced for only two months by Alexander Trepov, Nikolai Golitsyn taking over until the Revolution. At the Ministry of Internal Affairs Alexei Khvostov (referred to by the imperial couple as "Fat Khvostov") was in charge from September 1915 until March 1916, Boris Stürmer holding the office concurrently with that of Prime Minister from March to July, Alexander Khvostov (Fat Khvostov's uncle) taking over from July to September, with Alexander Protopopov succeeding him until the Revolution. The Minister of Finance, Peter Lvovich Bark, fared much better, staying in office throughout the period, as did the Minister of Marine, Ivan Grigorovich. Sergei Sazonov served as Minister of Foreign Affairs until July 1916 (having been appointed in September 1910), Boris Stürmer was given this third responsibility from July to November, and was succeeded by Nikolai Pokrovsky for the final few months of the dynasty. The Minister of War was Alexei Polivanov from June 1915 until March 1916, when he was replaced by Dmitry Shuvaev, who was replaced in turn, in January 1917, by Mikhail Belyaev. Alexander Khvostov was Minister of Justice from July 1915 to July 1916 (when he became Minister of Internal Affairs for three months), being succeeded at the Ministry of Justice by Alexander Makarov from July to December, the final incumbent being Nikolai Dobrovolsky. From October 1915 to August 1916, Alexander Volzhin served as Chief Procurator of the Holy Synod, being replaced by N. P. Raev. V. N. Sakovsky was Minister of Commerce and Industry from February 1915 until the end. Alexander Naumov was Director of Agriculture from November 1915 to July 1916, at which point Alexei Bobrinsky took over, being himself replaced in November by Alexander Rittikh. At the Ministry of Public Education Pavel Ignatiev lasted from January 1915 until December 1917, when he was replaced by Nikolai Kulchitsky. Alexander Trepov was Minister of Ways of Communication from November 1915 until November 1916 (when he briefly served as Prime Minister), and was succeeded by Eduard Krieger-Voinovsky. The State Comptroller was Pyotr Kharitonov from September 1907 to January 1916, when he was replaced by Nikolai Pokrovsky, who served until November, before being replaced himself by Sergei Fyodosev.

The frequent changes of minister, suggestive of a spiral of confusion and backstabbing, have usually been attributed to the machinations of Alix and Rasputin, working in concert to influence Nicky, insisting on the appointment only of people whom they believed to be supportive of themselves. This is the charge most frequently leveled at Alix—that she assisted in the collapse of the Empire by overseeing this frenetic, ill-conceived, and calamitous whirligig of ministers. Nicky is perceived as having consistently given in to the importunate demands of his wife and her mentor. How accurate can we judge these perceptions to be, if we take as our evidence the many letters that passed between the imperial couple during this period? Alix's own view of the situation is encapsulated in a remark she made on March 4, 1916: "One gets so bitterly disappointed in Russian people,—they are so far behind still we know such masses & yet when one has to choose a minister,—none is capable to hold such a post." So, as far as she is concerned, it is good material that is lacking—it is always the fault of the chosen, never of the chooser. For Nicky, it was a constant nightmare. On August 16, 1916, he told Alix: "Sometimes my head feels like wanting to crack when I turn over those questions about naming this or that name & trying to guess how it will go." That was a revealing comment, with its suggestion that ultimately the choice of ministers relied on guesswork.

Nicholas had been casting around for a replacement for "old man" Goremykin as Chairman of the Council of Ministers at the beginning of the year, and had asked Minister of the Interior "Fat Khvostov" for his opinion on Boris Stürmer (who had accompanied the imperial party on the trip along the Volga during the tercentenary celebrations) as a candidate for the post. Khvostov's reply was that Stürmer was "too old and his head is not as clear as once." Alix disagreed, believing Stürmer's head to be "plenty fresh enough" and correctly perceiving that Khvostov would rather like the job himself, so that his opinion on the matter was not entirely trustworthy. Her advice is that Stürmer would do "for a bit" (from which it is clear she sees no problem with chopping and changing ministers); she adds that Stürmer should be discouraged from changing his German-sounding name—this at a time when there was widespread Germanophobia and a tendency to see spies everywhere—and she quotes Rasputin as her source for this advice. The clincher for her is that Stürmer "very much values Gr[igory] wh[ich] is a great thing." The fact that this right-wing nonentity was not a popular choice was of no concern to Alix; people would always "scream" at any nomination, but Stürmer was "loyal" and would keep everyone else in hand. When the Tsar returned to Tsarskoe Selo for a few days later that month, he duly appointed Stürmer, in whom he decided he had "unlimited confidence." Over the next few months Stürmer, realizing how to stay in favor, made a point of letting Rasputin have access to him; Rasputin, in turn, advised Stürmer to consult with Alix every week. For certain other posts, those within Stürmer's control, Alix was, by the autumn of 1916, making the decisions herself, without reference to anyone else. On September 20, she wrote to Nicky: "Sht[ürmer] has not yet found a Chief of police for town—those he proposed wld never do—have told him to hurry up & think again."

Stürmer's appointment—particularly his triple appointment as Minister of Internal Affairs and of Foreign Affairs *as well as* Prime Minister—was a disaster, and in November, by which time his days in all his posts were numbered, he was unburdening himself to Alix over his distress at the upset being caused to the Tsar on his account. Alix's opinion was that he ought to go on sick leave for three weeks, in order to avoid stirring up further fury in the Duma ("that madhouse"), for whom he was "the red flag." He could return, she thought, once the Duma had been prorogued in December. She suggested that Nicky wire her his agreement, and she would then tell Stürmer this decision herself, to spare Nicky the unpleasantness of writing what might appear to be a critical letter to his Prime Minister. She realized that in the meantime Alexander Trepov, as Stürmer's deputy, would have to take over as Chairman of the Council of Ministers; she did not like Trepov, but was prepared to put up with him as a temporary measure. Nicky's letter of November 8 confirms that the widespread opposition to Stürmer's continued tenure is proving burdensome: "All these days I have been thinking about old Sht who is, as you rightly say, the red flag but not only to the Duma, nearly that of the whole country—alas! I hear of that from all sides; people don't believe him & become angry one sticks to him. Much worse than last year with old Goremyk." Nicky himself is displeased with Stürmer for being too "prudent," and for being apparently incapable of taking responsibility on himself and making the other ministers, and the Duma, get on with their work. This sounds rather like an autocrat wanting to have his cake and eat it. Stürmer was expected at Stavka on the following day, and Nicky would then himself tell him to go on leave for a time. As to whom to appoint to this most important position in the future, the Tsar wanted to talk that over with his wife when he next saw her. And so Trepov took over temporarily. According to Rasputin, however (as reported by Alix), there was no real need for Stürmer to stop being Prime Minister immediately; the trouble stemmed from his being also the Minister of Foreign Affairs—a situation that Grigory had, he asserted, realized in the summer, telling Stürmer that this would be his downfall. Furthermore, Alix believed that Stürmer had gone wrong only because for several months he had ceased to listen to Grigory's advice. But Nicholas was clear that Stürmer would have to leave "completely," as no one had any confidence in him. General Hanbury-Williams was at Stavka when Stürmer came to see the Tsar, and the atmosphere over lunch, among the suite and the heads of the allied military missions, seems to have been rather uncomfortable: "Stürmer being the Minister for Foreign Affairs, and his appointment not having given much pleasure in Russia, conversation was rather limited, as he sat on the other side of the Emperor. Trepov, whom I knew and like, seems pleased about railway matters, and I only hope he is not too optimistic. He is very keen, and everyone I know has a good opinion of him, but his task is a very difficult one. Stürmer is near the end of his tether."

When Stürmer saw Alix after having seen the Tsar, he shocked her by reporting that he had been relieved of all his responsibilities—that he was no longer even a member of the Council of Ministers. So it would seem that on this occasion, Nicky did not entirely follow Rasputin's advice, as mediated by Alix, but took more account of what he had heard of general opinion in the country. "I remember even Buchanan told me last time I received him," he wrote, "he got reports from english consuls in Russia, saying that there would be serious troubles in the country if he remained. And longer every day I hear more and more upon the same subject. One has to reckon with this." Alix, though not contesting the decision to retire Stürmer, nevertheless regretted it, as he liked (or gave the impression of liking) "our Friend" and was "so right in that way." Both Goremykin and Stürmer were of the "good old sort," she felt, unlike Trepov, whom she not only does not like but fears does not trust either herself or Grigory—in which case, she asserts, "things will be difficult." She has instructed Stürmer to pass on instructions to his successor over how to behave with regard to Rasputin and to make sure that he is always safeguarded. Despite the mutual antipathy that she senses between Trepov and herself, she still hopes to be able to exercise some influence over him, asking Nicky to tell him to come and see her sometimes, in order that she may get to know and "understand" him. It is striking how, in these times of crisis, when Alix feels that she has a vital role to perform, her earlier, much-vaunted "shyness" seems to have vanished. "I am no longer the slightest bit shy or affraid [sic] of the ministers & speak like a waterfall in Russia[n]!!!" she announced on September 22. This suggests that it always was, at least in part, a mechanism to help her avoid doing anything she did not want to do.

A month later, it is clear from the correspondence that Alexander Trepov's appointment as Chairman of the Council of Ministers is not working out. Alix's methods of determining a man's probity and suitability for office are simplistic in the extreme. "Lovy," she writes on December 9, 1916, "look at their faces—Trepov & Protopopov [now Minister of Internal Affairs]—can't one clearly see the latter's is cleaner, honester and more true." (This seems rather akin to her faith, expressed in a letter of December 4, that good weather is a propitious sign.) Her husband, true to form, is not proving fierce enough. "You *know* you are right," Alix declares, "keep up yr head, order Trepov to work with [Protopopov]—he dare not be against your order—bang on the table." Just in case her written exhortations are insufficient, Alix is even prepared to visit Stavka for a day, if her husband needs her to bolster his "courage and firmness." "Be the *Master*," she insists, cheerfully oblivious to the fact that she is herself bullying him, treating him as anything but "the Master."

Alix's tendency to adopt a near-hysterical tone in her letters should not, however, blind one to the fact that her perceptions were sometimes accurate. She did have her ear to the ground and on occasion understood more about the political situation than did her husband. Now she tells Nicky that "Trepov flirts with Rodzianko [the Chairman of the Duma]—all know it, & to you he slyly fibs its out of politics." Nicky himself seems to have been trying to act a little slyly at this juncture, wanting Trepov (whom he also disliked and distrusted) to take on the difficult and thankless task of "shutting up" the Duma, after which he could be "kicked out," leaving his successor to inherit a less onerous responsibility. That successor was Nikolai Golitsyn.

At the Ministry of Internal Affairs, meanwhile, the appointment of Alexei "Fat" Khvostov, so much canvassed by Alix, Ania, and Rasputin in August 1915, had turned out to be an unmitigated disaster, Khvostov actually becoming implicated in a plot to murder both Rasputin and Ania. Alix was understandably mortified by this, telling Nicky on March 2, 1916: "Am so wretched that we, through Gregory recommended Khvostov to you—it leaves me no peace—you were against it & I let myself be imposed upon by them." Nevertheless, she managed to rationalize what had happened, by explaining that "the devil" must have "got hold of" Khvostov. It was on account of this debacle that Stürmer had been made Minister of Internal Affairs, concurrently with being Prime Minister, that month. Nicky himself alludes to his typical way of dealing with his ministers and other officials, when he describes a conversation he had with Rodzianko in late June, during which the latter made various ministerial suggestions: "I smiled and thanked him for his advice," Nicky told his wife. Stürmer's appointment to the Ministry of Internal Affairs was in the nature of a stopgap; he was succeeded briefly by Fat Khvostov's uncle Alexander (who worked very capably for the two months he was allowed to do so), but then, in September, Grigory took up the cudgels on behalf of Alexander Protopopov, a right-wing member of the Duma who would therefore know, thought Alix, how to deal with that troublesome body. Grigory easily convinced Alix that Protopopov was the right man for the job. Stürmer had intended to recommend Prince Obolensky, but he was contaminated in Alix's eyes by having served at Stavka under Grand Duke Nikolai; instead she tells Nicky in a letter of September 7, that Grigory begged him "*earnestly*" to appoint Protopopov. Two days later she reiterates her plea: "Please, take Protopopov as minister of the Interior, as he is one of the Duma, it will make a great effect amongst them & shut their mouths." About this she and Rasputin did perhaps have a point; the selection of one of their own number for such an important post might indeed be expected to surprise, maybe even silence (at least temporarily), the Duma members. Nicky was far from sure about this suggestion; he had already heard of Protopopov, as Rodzianko had suggested him several months earlier for the post of Minister of Commerce and Industry—it may have been the connection with Rodzianko that gave Nicky pause for thought. "I must think that question over as it takes me quite unexpectedly," he told Alix. "Our Friend's ideas about men are sometimes queer, as you know—so one must be careful especially in nominations of high people." But Alix does not appear to have learned from the disaster over Alexei Khvostov; she continues to have infinite trust in Rasputin's judgment—and plenty in her own. Nicky also had serious doubts about the wisdom of such frequent changes of minister, and of changing more than one at a time. "All these changes exhaust the head," he wrote. "I find they happen much too often. It is certainly not at all good for the interior of the country because every new man brings changes also into the administration." But Alix continued to press for Grigory's choice, insisting that Prince Obolensky would be no good as he was "of the opposite clan & not a 'friend,'" and within a few days Nicky had put aside his better judgment and agreed. "God bless yr new choice of Protopopov," Alix wrote to him on September 14, "our Friend says you have done a very wise act in naming him."

Alix wanted to get to work with Protopopov at once, including implementing her idea of sending out their own spies ("nice, honest people") and propaganda agents into the army, to counteract those of the left, who she was well aware were filling the ears of the soldiers with "bad ideas." Some of these "bad" propagandists, she asserted, were to be found in the ranks of (Jewish) doctors and nurses. (How history repeats itself: that other anti-Semitic Russian leader, Joseph Stalin, believed, or professed to believe, he was being plotted against by a cabal of Jewish doctors in 1952.) Alix does not intend to put up with this, and, again, to a certain extent one can sympathize with her; she did have a point when she wrote, "I dont see why the bad shld always fight for their cause, & the good complain, but sit calmly with folded hands & wait for events."

Alix's trust in Rasputin extended well beyond his judgment of individuals and into the sphere of practical logistics. On September 22, she told Nicky that there was no need to worry too much about the food supply question—Grigory had said so; according to him, things would "arrange themselves," Protopopov already being busy at work on the issue. In fact, Nicky was desperately worried about the food supply question, as well he might be; more disturbingly, though, he was perplexed by it, completely out of his depth. "I don't see another way out of it," he told Alix on September 20, "than by giving it over to the military authorities, but that also has its inconveniences! The most d-d question I ever came across. I have never been a merchant & simply do not understand those questions about provisions & stores!" Arguably, it was ludicrous that the Tsar should need to understand such questions (did George V understand them? or Kaiser Wilhelm? or even Emperor Franz Joseph, approaching the end of his sixty-eight-year reign?), but unfortunately the autocratic system meant that everything, ultimately, devolved on to Nicholas, and he had to shoulder the responsibility for all of it. Even so, Hanbury-Williams believed that the Tsar was never told the full truth about the situation, having noted at the beginning of June: "I am afraid from all I gather that the reports about food, transportation, fuel, etc., which reach the Emperor are too rosy coloured. It is not so much a question of the stuff itself, but of the transportation."

Alix advised Nicky on how he should receive Protopopov on the first occasion of his visiting Stavka as Minister of Internal Affairs. Nicholas should show his "power of will and decisiveness," she told him, so that the new minister would be suitably energized. She also encouraged a meeting between Protopopov and General Alexeev, in order that the latter should see that "he has to do with a clever man who wastes no time."

Despite all Alix's optimism regarding the new minister, by November the Tsar had had enough of him, his own initial doubts about the appointment (he had clearly heard some of the rumors that Protopopov was in the final stages of syphilis) having been realized. And so he had taken the decision to remove him, without telling Alix beforehand, writing to her on November 10: "When you get this one you will have heard fr Sht about the changes wh are absolutely necessary now. I am sorry about Prot, a good honest man, but he jumped fr one idea to another & could not stick to his opinion. I remembered that fr the very beginning. People said he was not normal some years ago fr a certain illness (when he went to Badmaev). It is risky leaving the min of Int in such hands at such times!" Nicholas intended that the Duma should be closed for a week while the ministerial changes (which included the forced retirement of Stürmer, mentioned above) were being made, in order to avoid the impression that they were coming about as a result of Duma pressure. And Nicky is very clear at this point that he does not want Grigory to be involved at all in his decision-making: "Only please don't mix in our Friend!" he tells his wife. "It is I who carry the responsibility I want to be free to choose accordingly."

Alix, predictably, was horrified at this show of independence on the part of her husband the Tsar; his intentions have, she declares, "put me awfully out." She entreats Nicholas not to change Protopopov now, convinced that he will be able to sort out the question of food supply as soon as he gets a chance. Her unstinting support for Protopopov is based both on Grigory's recommendation and on her conviction that he is on the side of herself and Nicky—that he is "honestly *for us*," as she puts it. She is aware that those who are not "for" them, a segment of whom she characterizes as the "rotten upper sets," have been intriguing against Protopopov; this, in itself, is enough to justify her own support for him. She admits that she acts and speaks from instinct rather than from reason, but is convinced this very fact makes her right: "I may not be clever enough—but I have a strong feeling & that helps more than the brain often." She begs Nicky not to change any of the ministers until she has had a chance to talk it all over quietly with him. She realizes that, in writing like this, she once again risks annoying her husband, but cannot stop herself. "*Quieten* me, promise, forgive, but its for you & Baby I fight."

The next day she continues her assault: "Lovy, my Angel—now about the chief thing—don't change Protopopov." She has no doubt that the rumors about his sanity are entirely false, and that all the opposition to him is the result of intrigue. And that intrigue, she believes, is similar to the one about which she had successfully warned Nicholas the previous year, when he had taken over as Commander-in-Chief. "It's the same story as last year," she tells him now—"again against wify." The Tsar, she believes, does not realize how serious the intriguing is: "They [that is, the various statesmen opposed to her influence] feel I am your wall & it aggravates them—ah, lovy, dont let them do this, its more serious than you think. It took you long to realise that last year—& now its the bad party, who have got behind Trep[ov]." Again, the rising note of hysteria undermines the argument; one is tempted not to take the writer seriously at this point, to see everything Alix writes as delusional. But just because no plot against her came to fruition does not mean that none existed. "Lovy, it's no joke," she insists, "more serious, as its a hunt against wify. Categorically answer you have quietly thought it over & do not for the present intend changing any of your ministers." She is also in distress, upset that someone she has found herself able to trust—Protopopov—may be taken away from her; one senses in this the immense loneliness she was experiencing at Tsarskoe Selo at this time, despite her best efforts to put on a brave face: "Its difficult writing & asking for oneself, I assure you, but its for yr & Baby's sake, believe me. I don't care what bad one says of me, only when one tries to tear devoted, honest people, who care for me—away—its *horribly unfair*. I am but a woman fighting for her Master & Child, her two dearest ones on earth—& God will help me being your guardian angel, only dont pull the sticks away upon wh I have found it possible to rest." Alix is writing prophetically in her letter of November 12, 1916. Again the heightened tone, the sense of near-madness, can blind the reader to the accuracy of some of her predictions; perhaps she was indeed being driven mad, but that was partly because she could perceive the danger the dynasty was in—even if her ideas about how to avert that danger were misguided and counterproductive: "Darling, remember that it does not lie in the man Protop or x.y.z., but it's the question of *monarchy & yr* prestige now, which must not be shattered in the time of the Duma. Dont think they will stop at him, but they will make all others leave *who are devoted* to you one by one—& then ourselves." Her arguments appear to have convinced the Tsar, and Protopopov remained in post as Minister of Internal Affairs until the Revolution. Alix's insistence (backed by Rasputin) that Alexander Makarov, Minister of Justice from July 1916, was also "an enemy (of me absolutely, therefore of you too)" likewise bore fruit, the "*bad* man" Makarov being replaced in December by the "sure man" Nikolai Dobrovolsky.

The post of Minister of War was another upon which Rasputin had an opinion to offer. In January 1916 Alix reported that he was anxious for "Ivanov" (most probably General N. I. Ivanov) to be named as Alexei Polivanov's successor. Nicholas seems to have taken no notice of this suggestion, however, declaring that he intended to appoint Dmitry Shuvaev, whom he felt he could trust "absolutely." He certainly concurred with the desire to remove Polivanov, despite the excellent progress he had made in improving the organization of the Russian war effort. Alix was convinced that he was "simply a revolutionist under the wing of Guchkov"; he had particularly incurred her displeasure during the previous year's crisis, when he had tried to persuade the Tsar not to dismiss Grand Duke Nikolai as Commander-in-Chief and had leaked the news that the Tsar was going to do so to the Council of Ministers, thereby ensuring yet more opposition to the scheme). General Alfred Knox, British liaison officer to the Russian Army, reported that General Polivanov was dismissed as War Minister on March 20, 1916, the Emperor having said that he felt "in serious times like the present he must have as Minister of War a man whom he could trust to work in less close co-operation with non-official organisations that were openly hostile to the Government." Knox went on to state that Polivanov was undoubtedly the ablest military organizer in Russia and his dismissal was a disaster. Alix would have preferred Mikhail Belyaev (who did not take over until January 1917) to have been appointed straightaway, for she believed him to be honest, devoted, and more "of a gentleman" than Shuvaev. The latter, to whom she admitted she had spoken only once, she had found "most obstinate." Rasputin still supported General Ivanov, on account of his popularity with the army, but Nicky still showed no inclination to accept this advice; for once Alix did not press the point and Shuvaev was duly appointed. Nicky's view of Belyaev, expressed later in the year, was that he was "a very weak man—he always gives way & is a slow worker." But for Alix, the fact that Belyaev seemed "exceedingly willing" and did "try his best" outweighed other considerations.

Not only was Grigory anxious to express his opinion about who should be appointed as Minister of War; he also had plenty to say about how the war itself should be conducted. On a "common sense" level, on which Alix also operated, much of what he said sounds valid enough. He tended to be against anything that he thought likely to result in great loss of life; "he is always praying & thinking when the good moment will come to advance, so as not to uselessly loose [sic] men," Alix reported on January 6, 1916. Nicky was anxious—justifiably so—that Alix might tell Grigory more than he, or anyone, ought to know. On March 9, the Tsar wrote to his wife that the next offensive would begin in a few days, before the spring thaw flooded the trenches and made forward movement impossible. "I beg you not to tell *anyone* of this," he added. But, given how well Nicky knew Alix and her unbounded trust in Rasputin, either he was being unutterably stupid in telling her so much—or he intended her to tell Grigory. On balance, stupidity seems the more likely explanation. Rasputin's "advice" to Nicky in June was again concerned with minimizing Russian losses: "He begs we should not yet strongly advance in the *north* because he says, if our successes continue being good in the south, they will themselves retreat from the north, or advance & then their losses will be very great—if we begin there, our losses will be very heavy." This time Rasputin's opinion seems in line with the decision that was in fact taken, Nicky telling Alix on June 5: "A few days ago Alexeev & I decided not to attack fr the north, but to concentrate all our efforts lower down.—But *please don't mention this to any body,* not even our Friend. Nobody must know this." Nicky inadvertently gives a very clear impression of his Chief of Staff's attitude toward this leakage of information, when he reported two days later: "I told Alexeev how interested you were in military questions & about those details you asked me in your last letter No. 511. He smiled and listened silently." Perhaps he had learned such a response from the Tsar. (Alexeev did try to talk to the Tsar about the state of Russia, about the need for a responsible

Ministry, and about Rasputin, but he was none the wiser for doing so. General Anton Denikin wrote of these efforts that "he invariably met with the impenetrable glance, so well-known to many, and the dry retort: 'I know.'") On this occasion, Alix appears to have respected Nicky's request that she keep such sensitive information to herself; he was still extraordinarily unwise to have sent it to her. He could not have been much more specific, writing: "You must not be astonished if there is a lull in the operations for a few days. Our troops down there won't move until reinforcements come up & until another diversion is made near Pinsk. Please, this is only for *you,* not another soul must hear about it!" Later in the year, Alix asks for details of planned attacks, in order that Grigory may pray for their success, and it is clear from what she writes that she did pass on to him the orders Nicky gave to General Brusilov in September: "Our Friend says about the new orders you gave to Brusilov etc: 'Very satisfied with father's orders, all will be well.' He won't mention it to a soul, but I had to ask His blessing for yr decision." Those orders were in connection with the halting of the advance, and Brusilov, it would appear from Alix's letter of September 24, did not immediately obey them, a dereliction about which Grigory was "much put out"—again on account of his primary desire to avoid "useless losses." Nicky justified what had happened in his next letter, but tried—probably uselessly—to deter Alix from giving further details to Grigory: "Just got your wire where you say our Friend is put out that my plan is not followed out. When I gave this order I did not know that Gurko decided to draw nearly all his available forces & prepare an attack together with the guards & neighbour troops. That combination makes our troops doubly stronger at this point & gives one faith in the possibility of success. That is why when Al read the explanation telegrams from Brus & Gurko begging to continue the operation, wh was in full development—the next morning I gave my consent.... These details are only for you—please Lovy! Tell Him only: 'Papa prikazal prinyat' razumnie meri!' [Papa has ordered sensible measures taken!]." Alix remained unconvinced, fearing that this continued offensive would prove to be "a second Verdun," entailing the pointless loss of thousands of lives. Nicholas explained further about the new combined attack with which all the generals were in accord, and Alix appeared to accept this. Nevertheless, she and Rasputin remained unhappy about following the advice of the generals, Alix writing on September 28: "In any case our Friend says to go by your ideas, your first are always the most correct."

Alix and Grigory also involved themselves in the appointment of Chief Procurator of the Holy Synod, Alix suggesting that N. P. Raev might replace Alexander Volzhin (whom she found "an obstinate nuisance") and, once Raev had been duly appointed, Grigory giving his imprimatur of approval. "He spoke with Raev over an hour," Alix reported, "says he is a real God's send, & spoke so well about all Church questions & in such a *spiritual* way."

The overwhelming impression of many of Alix's wartime letters to Nicky—an impression that has sometimes contributed to their prophetic element being overlooked—is that of an extreme bossiness. She frequently treats her husband abominably in these letters, figuratively beating him over the head, and the cumulative effect of reading them one after the other can be for that bossiness and verbal violence to obscure everything else. Her letter of March 12, 1916, in which she is urging the immediate removal of Polivanov as Minister of War, is a particularly vivid example: "Lovy mine, don't dawdle, make up yr mind . . . be quicker about it . . . *hurry up* Sweetheart, you need Wify to be behind pushing you! . . . Please, do the change at once. . . ." In September she provides her husband with a whole list of what to remember to say to Protopopov, the list having been initially compiled by Rasputin; she is anxious that Nicky, being so busy, may forget some of these items, so she will undertake to be his "living notebook"; "Keep this paper before you," she tells him, once she has written out her precise list. Nicky appears not to mind being treated like a schoolboy who might forget his lessons, responding: "Tender thanks for your sweet letter & tidy instructions for my talk with Protop." Occasionally, however, the worm turned—though even then Nicky's response was humorous rather than angry. But most of the time he encouraged Alix in her efforts, furthering her self-belief and conviction that she was thinking, speaking, and acting correctly. One senses that for him her current busyness and sense of satisfaction was a welcome relief after years of invalidism and neurosis. "Oh, you precious Sunny," he wrote to her on September 23, "I am so happy you have at last found the right work for yourself. Now I will certainly feel quiet & no more worried, at least for the interior." And yet he should never have felt more worried.

One of the saddest aspects of the story of Nicholas and Alexandra is the mismatch between desire and outcome. Alix so clearly wanted to do whatever was best for Nicky and his position as monarch. "I pray so hard for God to give me wisdom & understanding so as to be a real help for you in every way; & to advise you always rightly," she wrote to him on September 4. But wisdom and understanding seem to have been precisely the qualities that were lacking in many of her responses to the political situation; either her prayers were not granted, or her entrenched attitudes—her unwavering, unshakeable belief in autocracy in the form advocated by Alexander III as well as her conviction that God was speaking through Rasputin—precluded her from recognizing wisdom when it was offered. Her sister Ella made one last attempt to convey what she believed to be wise words, but her effort was spurned: "In December 1916," Ella testified in her deposition to the Provisional Government's Extraordinary Commission of Enquiry, "I had a final, decisive conversation with the Tsar and Tsarina on the subject of Rasputin. I pointed out that Rasputin rankled society, was compromising the imperial family and leading the dynasty to ruin. They replied that Rasputin was a great man of prayer, that all the rumours about him were slanders, and asked me not to touch on the question any further."

This must be a central question when considering these last fateful months of the regime: Why did the imperial couple evince such confidence in Grigory Rasputin? Why was it that this man, so vilified by almost everyone else who came into contact with him, with his reputation for loose living, his known consorting with prostitutes (even though there was disagreement as to what he actually did with them—one woman testified to the police that he bought her two bottles of beer, asked her to undress, looked at her body, paid her two roubles, and then left; this might possibly be interpreted as some kind of spiritual exercise), the suspicion by some that he might be a German spy, the controversy that raged around him in court circles—why was it that this man was their beloved "Friend," the one Alix in particular trusted above all others? Why could they believe no ill of him, despite evidence that had been presented to them many times over the years?

For an answer, one might do worse than turn to the Gospels, so well known to Nicky and Alix, and to such passages as: "And it came to pass, as Jesus sat at meat in the house, behold, many publicans and sinners came and sat down with him and his disciples. And when the Pharisees saw it, they said unto his disciples, Why eateth your Master with publicans and sinners?" [Matthew 9: 10–11]. And "Then was brought unto him one possessed with a devil, blind, and dumb: and he healed him, insomuch that the blind and dumb both spake and saw. And all the people were amazed, and said, Is not this the son of David? But when the Pharisees heard it, they said, This fellow doth not cast out devils, but by Beelzebub the prince of the devils" [Matthew 12: 22–24]. Or "And when the sabbath day was come, he began to teach in the synagogue: and many hearing him were astonished, saying, From whence hath this man these things? and what wisdom is this which is given unto him, that even such mighty works are wrought by his hands? Is not this the carpenter, the son of Mary, the brother of James, and Joses, and of Juda, and Simon? and are not his sisters here with us? And they were offended at him. But Jesus said unto them, A prophet is not without honour, but in his own country, and among his own kin, and in his own house" [Mark 6: 2–4].

Alix saw parallels all the time between the way Jesus was vilified by the Jewish establishment of his time and the way Grigory was attacked by the equivalent Russian authorities. "During the evening Bible I thought so much of our Friend," she wrote on April 5, "how the *bookworms* [a rather delightful rendering of the more usual "scribes"] & Pharisees persecute Christ, pretending to be such perfections, (& how far they are from it now!). Yes, indeed, a prophet is never acknowledged in his own country." Once having made this identification, having recognized in Grigory Rasputin a Christlike figure—and, as mentioned previously, the use of the uppercase in "He," "our Friend," and so on would suggest that the identification had been made early in the imperial acquaintance with him—then everything that happened, every unpleasant rumor attaching to him, every attack made upon him, even the very fact that hardly anyone else could recognize Him for who He was, only made that identification clearer to those who believed in Him. His wonder-working powers, particularly the fact that he was able to calm Alexei and that his prayers were efficacious (the "many wonderful escapes to those he prays for at the war who know Him—not to speak of Baby & Ania"), served to strengthen that identification, but they were not necessarily the first or most important proof of it, and by 1916 Alix's faith in him was so strong that even a failure on his part to effect a miracle would not have threatened it. Alix's letter of April 8, 1916, the twenty-second anniversary of her engagement to Nicky, contains an explicit reference to what Grigory, and Monsieur Philippe, have meant to the imperial couple. She is absolutely clear about this, writing first of her reciprocated love for her husband, and continuing: "And the love for Christ too—& it has always been so closely linked with our lives these 22 years! First the question of taking the orthodox faith & then our two Friends sent to us by God."

Nicky's attitude toward Grigory is more ambiguous and his belief at times seems to waver. Though he allowed himself to be heavily influenced by him in the days before he took over as Commander-in-Chief, he showed less inclination afterward to follow his advice, and certainly did not regard every word Grigory spoke as God-given. He was far more prepared than his wife to make a distinction between spiritual and practical advice, and did not assume that Grigory's spiritual gifts—in which he undoubtedly believed—necessarily translated into every other sphere. His hesitations in this regard are clear from Alix's letter of November 11, 1916 (one of her longest and most forceful epistles): "Ah, Lovy, I pray so hard to God to make you feel & realise," she writes, "that He is our caring, were He not here, I dont know what might not have happened! He saves us by His prayers & wise counsils [sic] & is our rock of faith & help." She returns to the theme on December 5: "To follow our Friend's councils, lovy—I assure is right—He prays so hard day & night for you—& He has kept you where you are—only be as convinced as I am & as I proved it to Ella & shall for ever—then all will go well." Rasputin's occasional apparent lapses in judgment—such as his initial strong support for the treacherous Alexei Khvostov—she excuses and rationalizes away: "if they [i.e. the people Rasputin has supported] later on change that is already not His fault—but He will be less mistaken in people than we are." As was the case with many of the biblical prophets, Grigory's dreams constitute divine messages for Alix. She also feels that she has plenty of evidence that following his advice leads to good results, while the opposite is also true: "Even the Children notice how things don't come out well if we do not listen to Him & the contrary—good when listen." The recollections of Rasputin's daughter Maria offer further evidence that Nicky was not nearly as inclined to follow Grigory's advice as his wife, or Grigory himself, would have liked: "Sometimes, swayed by the various influences that pressed about him and pushed him to make some fatal concession or to believe in the efficiency or the good intentions of this or that Minister," wrote Maria Rasputina, "he obstinately refused to take some decision that my father or some other enlightened and devoted counselor represented as being urgent. 'Our Little Father is very good, but he is stubborn, as difficult to budge as a post!' my father would sometimes say to Varvara and me, doubtless after some fruitless discussion." Nicky's technique, as ever, would be to make no comment, in order not to provoke an argument; he would merely ignore any advice he did not wish to follow.

If Nicky's belief and trust in Grigory were not always as wholehearted as Alix could have wished, he entirely shared with her a rather sentimental taste in fiction. In 1916 they were particularly enjoying the novels of Florence L. Barclay, and the one they loved most of all—because it reminded them of their own story—was *Through the Postern Gate,* the young hero of which, Guy Chelsea, was affectionately known by the heroine, Christobel Charteris, as "little Boy Blue," a term that Alix took up and applied to Nicky. One can understand much about the way Nicky and Alix viewed themselves, and their love, through their attachment to this "healthy" and delightful little novel. It is a love story in which duty appears to conflict with the fulfilment of desire—Guy loves Christobel, who reciprocates his love but believes herself bound to marry a much older man—until almost the final pages, when it becomes clear that Christobel is mistaken in this belief, and that her duty in fact resides in marrying the man she loves. The novel reminded Nicky and Alix of the struggle she had undergone in allowing herself to succumb to her love for him, and the idea that by so doing she was fulfilling a sacred duty—rather than reneging on an existing one—resonated with them. "The stone was very great," declares the heroine at the moment of her capitulation; "but lo, as we reached it, the Angel of the Lord had rolled it away." "I don't know why, but it reminded me of Coburg & Walton!" wrote Nicky (probably realizing perfectly well why it did). But their mutual delight in this book also demonstrates one of Alix's blind spots. Another of the characters is a self-centered and very bossy "invalid" called Miss Ann, who "fancies herself in a bath-chair" and spends most of her time "upon a comfortable sofa in her tiny drawing-room; or reclining on a wicker lounge beneath the one tree in her small garden; or being carefully wheeled out in a bath-chair." Miss Ann also "had a way of keeping everybody about her . . . on the move; while she herself presented a delicate picture of frail inactivity." The similarities with Alix are obvious, but the Empress was as oblivious to the traits she shared with this fictional character as to those she shared with Ania Vyrubova. And if Nicky noticed the similarity, he was far too tactful—and peace loving—to say so.

The fact that Nicky was spending most of his time at Stavka (where Alexei joined him for several months) shielded him from the reality of the political situation as it slipped inexorably toward revolution. To him, the rumors from Petrograd were only that—rumors—the same old gossip and troublemaking from the usual suspects and not to be taken seriously. When Alix wanted him to return to the capital for a couple of days in September, he did not take her concerns seriously, replying that it was impossible for him to get away. "I am afraid it is the atmosphere of Petrograd which is worrying you," he wrote, "& wh you do not feel here." Alix was aware that not everyone at Stavka was as oblivious to the political ferment as Nicky appeared to be, telling him on September 18: "Now a correspondence between Alexeev & that brute Guchkov is going on & he fills him with vile things—warn him, he is such a clever brute & Al will certainly, alas, listen to things against our Friend too—& that wont bring him luck." Rasputin himself was advising her not to worry too much; God would "help out at the war," he declared. Alix's health had once again broken down, her heart felt "more enlarged again," and she was having difficulty breathing. She nevertheless struggled on with her self-imposed responsibilities, receiving ministerial reports and trying to take Nicky's place in his absence. At Stavka the presence of Alexei did much to lighten the mood. "Babykins, you keep him in hand," Alix instructed his father on September 25, "see he does not play at table or put his arms & elbows on the table, please—& dont let him shy breadballs." He particularly enjoyed playing jokes on General Hanbury-Williams, who enjoyed his company enormously. One day toward the end of May Alexei entertained himself by pushing everything on the lunch table—"cups, bread, toast, menus, etc."—toward Hanbury-Williams's place and then drawing his father's attention to how greedy the General was being. As this was shortly after the news had been received of Lord Kitchener's death at sea—while on his way to visit Russia at the behest of the Tsar, Hanbury-Williams inevitably feeling some responsibility for having encouraged, or at least not discouraged, the fatal voyage—Alexei's attempts at cheering him up were welcome, and indicate the boy's sensitivity toward his friends. Alexei's empathy was again in evidence several months later, when Hanbury-Williams suffered a personal tragedy. "I heard the news of the death of my eldest son, which was not unexpected," the General recalled. "I was in the ante-room next the Emperor's before dinner, when, being alone, the little Tsarevitch came out of his father's room, ran up to me and sat next me, saying: 'Papa told me to come to sit with you as he thought you would feel lonely to-night.'" Alexei's innate ability to know what to do and say in such situations was inherited from his father, Hanbury-Williams also noting: "The Emperor himself most kind and sympathetic, saying, as was his nature, just the right thing."

In lighter moments Nicky also enjoyed joining in his son's pranks; after a short leave of absence earlier in the year Hanbury-Williams had returned to Stavka toward the end of June to find Alexei in high spirits: "He dragged some of us off after lunch in the tent to a round fountain in the garden which has porpoise heads all round it, with two holes in each to represent the eyes. The game was to plug up these holes with one's fingers, then turn on the fountain full split and suddenly let go. The result was that I nearly drowned the Emperor and his son, and they returned the compliment, and we all had to go back and change, laughing till we nearly cried." (This was not what Alix had in mind when she urged Nicky to behave more like Peter the Great, renowned for the trick fountains he had installed at Peterhof in the early eighteenth century.) Though Alexei occasionally hurt himself and had to take to his bed for a few days, the condition was never serious enough to warrant his returning home at this period. He had had to return home from a shorter visit to Stavka at the end of the previous year, when he had suffered a severe nosebleed, but on the whole his attacks of hemophilia seemed by now to have settled into a fairly predictable pattern, with swelling being followed by gradual reabsorption. He always had to cope with pain, to a greater or lesser degree, but he seemed to be learning how to manage his condition, knowing what to expect at each stage of the process.

During 1916 and early 1917, several family members made attempts to communicate their concerns either to Nicky or Alix, but with no more success than Ella. One of the most bizarre incidents involved Grand Duke Nikolai

Mikhailovich—Sandro's brother, the historian. Toward the end of April 1916 he asked to meet Alix alone—"cannot simply imagine why," Alix told Nicky—and they duly met for an hour on May 1. Alix reported that he was "very interesting about the letters he wrote you etc & he wants me to talk all over with you." And though she did not like him, she considered that "he meant & spoke well." Then in the autumn Nikolai Mikhailovich visited Nicky at Stavka, where they had a long talk on the evening of November 2. Nikolai left some letters with Nicky, which the latter claimed not to have read and instead sent them on—unread—to Alix. Unfortunately the letters were extremely uncomplimentary about Alix, and she was both absolutely furious and deeply hurt. Nikolai asserted that Alix was being "led astray by the evil circle" surrounding her, that as a result everything she said was "the result of clever fabrication and not the truth" and that Nicky had to find a way of ending "this system"—that is, the "system" of ministers being selected on Rasputin's say-so, via the mouthpiece of Alix. If the Tsar did not make this change, and also introduce a Ministry responsible both to himself and to "constitutional legislative institutions," then Nikolai Mikhailovich predicted "a new era of disturbances" and assassination attempts. It is striking that one of the things Nikolai tells the Tsar is almost word-for-word what Alix and Grigory have already told him—namely: "Your first impulses and decisions are always remarkably right and to the point, but as soon as other influences come in, you begin to hesitate and end up by doing something other than what you originally intended." Where they disagree is in the definition of "other influences," each "side" viewing the other as malign and guilty of manipulating the Tsar.

What is extraordinary is that Nicky—whether he had read these letters or not himself—sent them on to Alix, for, even without having read them, he must have had some idea of the contents, given that Nikolai—who was known both in the family and without for his plain speaking, not to say rudeness—had been telling him of his concerns. Unsurprisingly, on receipt of the letters, Alix exploded, telling Nicky that she was "utterly disgusted." Nicky ought, in her opinion, to have stopped Nikolai Mikhailovich while he was talking and threatened deportation to Siberia if he dared once more to speak so disrespectfully of his Empress—"as it becomes next to high treason." "He has always hated & spoken badly of me since 22 years," she went on, "but during war & at such a time to crawl behind yr Mama & Sisters & not stick up bravely (agreeing or not) for his Emperor's Wife—is loathsome & treachery." She worked herself up to a real pitch of fury, declaring: "He is the incarnation of all that's evil, *all* devoted people loathe him, even those who do not much like us are disgusted with him & his talks." Nor can she entirely disguise her anger that her husband does not stand up for her more strongly, as she tells him: "He & Nikolasha are my greatest enemies in the family, not counting the black women—& Sergei.... I don't care personal nastiness, but as yr chosen wife—they dare not Sweety mine, you must back me up, for your & Baby's sake." Nicky replied to justify himself for having passed on the letters, insisting that he had not realized their content: "I am really sorry to have disturbed you & made you angry with N's two letters, but in my continual hurry I did not read them, as he spoke so long & fully. But he omitted to speak out about you, dwelling only on the stories about spies, fabrics, workmen, disorders, ministers & the outlook inside the country! Had he said anything about you, do you doubt huzy would not have upstood for you?" If this is true and Nicky really did have no idea of what was in the letters, then this does suggest a high degree of absentmindedness, lack of awareness, and even obtuseness on his part. An alternative interpretation is that he wanted Alix to know what was being said about her, that he wanted to warn her through the medium of his cousin's words, feeling unable to do so directly himself. Lack of awareness of what was being said is, however, the more likely explanation—in which case the Tsar must have been extremely out of touch with current opinion. Had he even an inkling of what Nikolai Mikhailovich's letters contained, he must have realized the likely effect they would have on his highly strung wife.

Even General Hanbury-Williams was on the verge of attempting to warn Alix, during an after-dinner tête-à-tête on one of the occasions she visited Stavka, in mid-November. He had told her he was about to spend a few days in Petrograd, to see the British ambassador and generally catch up with events in the capital. "Well, promise me if you go that you will not believe all the wicked stories that are being gossiped about there," Alix responded. This, recorded Hanbury-Williams, "gave me the opportunity to say something which I had in my mind, and which could not have been said had not the opportunity offered itself." But just as he was about to speak, "the Emperor came up laughing and said: 'What are you two plotting about in the corner?'" That was the end of the conversation, as Nicky and Alix said good night to everyone and left the room. Hanbury-Williams noted: "That was the last occasion upon which I saw the Empress. No doubt if I had spoken, my words would not have had much effect, but I had been urged to do so by someone much concerned, and had never expected to have the chance."

By the final month of 1916, Alix's emotions had reached a pitch of intensity that was not far from madness. She was still convinced, despite all evidence to the contrary, that everything would work out for the best. "But God who is all love & mercy has let the things take a change for the better," she told Nicky on

December 4, "just a little more patience & deepest faith in the prayers & help of our Friend—then all will go well! I am fully convinced that great & beautiful times are coming for yr reign & Russia." Everything anyone said against this rosy picture was to be ignored: "Only keep up your spirits, let no talks or letters pull you down—let them pass by as something unclean & quickly to be forgotten." The victory would be achieved, she insisted, partly by Nicky at last asserting his authority: "Show to all, that you are the Master & your will shall be obeyed—the time of great indulgence & gentleness is over—now comes your reign of will & power, & they shall be made to bow down before you." She lists all those who have opposed her and who are therefore "up to some wrong"—and by now the list has grown to include almost everybody: "the black ones—then Orlov & Drentel'n—Witte—Kokovtsov—Trepov, I feel it too—Makarov—Kaufmann—Sofia Ivanovna—Mary—Sandra Obolensky etc"—in other words, all those who have ever doubted her or, in particular, Rasputin. Everything is black and white to Alix: "The good & bad clergy its all so clear & therefore no more hurts me as when I was younger." No notice should be taken of any criticisms from Maria Fyodorovna either, for "the Michels [that is, the sons of the late Grand Duke Mikhail Alexandrovich—Sandro, Nikolai, Sergei, and Georgy] are behind her." Her conviction that a great fight is now under way, but that the right will triumph, is very striking: "Always near you sharing all—the good is coming, the turn has begun." Just as the opposition to Rasputin is proof in itself for Alix that he is a man of God, so the opposition to herself confirms in her own mind that she is right. "Remember why I am disliked," she writes in one of her many long screeds to Nicky, "—shows it right to be firm & feared & you be the same, you a man,—only believe more in our Friend (instead of Trepov)." In her anxiety to keep her husband up to the mark, she excels herself in bossiness—and confirms what many people had previously thought and said about Nicholas: "Would I write thus, did I not know you so very easily waver & change your mind, & what it costs to keep you stick to Your opinion! I know I may hurt you how I write & that is my pain & sorrow—but you, Baby & Russia are *far too* dear to me." She is still upset and frustrated that Nicky will not listen to Rasputin's advice, preferring instead to heed the words of his official advisers: "I suffer over you as over a tender, softhearted child—wh need giding [sic], but listens to bad advisers whilst a man of God's tells him what to do."

For once Nicky did not entirely bow down under this barrage, and his way of countering it was through humor. (A comment made by General Hanbury-Williams in October suggests a possible reason behind the iron control Nicky usually exercised over himself; the Tsar had been discussing "tempers" with him over dinner, and had said that "he rarely lost his, but when it was bad, 'it was very, very, bad.'") To Alix's letter of December 13, he replied: "Loving thanks for your strong reprimanding letter. I read it with a smile because you speak like to a child . . ." and he signed off: "your poor little huzy with no will." Alix realized that he was taking her less than seriously, and as a result she even—almost—manages to laugh at herself when she writes: "Be Peter the Great, John the Terrible, Emperor Paul—crush them all under you—now don't you laugh, noughty one—but I long to see you so with all those men who try to govern you." She also writes, using words that recalled to them a particular scene in *Through the Postern Gate*: "*It is not necessary* to say poor old huzy with no will, it kills me—forgive me—you understand me I know & my allconsuming love—yes Lovy mine?" But Alix's primary feeling in all this is frustration; why can Nicky not grasp the appropriate way to behave? "It is *war* and at such a time *interior* war is *high treason,*" she protests to him, "why don't you look at it like that, I really cannot understand." And behind it all is her unbending conviction that Russia must be governed autocratically; nothing else will do: "we have been placed by God on a throne & we must keep it firm & give it over to our Son untouched—if you keep that in mind you will remember to be the Sovereign—& how much easier for an autocratic sovereign than one who has sworn the Constitution!" Meanwhile Nicky keeps up his teasing, signing off on December 15: "Ever your very own poor little huzy with a tiny will." Again Alix tells him not to use such words of himself, though she cannot resist adding some criticism: "'One must not speak'—'with tiny will,' but a wee bit weak & not confident in yourself & a bit easily believe bad advices." The next day Nicky continues the joke: "Tenderest love & kisses from your poor little huzy with a bit of will." And then it was nearly time for him and Alexei to return to Tsarskoe Selo for Christmas. "I am so intensely happy to come home & perhaps remain a little while on into the New Year," wrote Nicky on December 17.

His letter crossed with one from Alix that contained dire news: "We are sitting together," she wrote, "—can imagine our feelings—thoughts—our Friend has disappeared." Though she is trying desperately not to believe it, Alix already suspects that Grigory has been killed, and she knows that Felix Yusupov, the young husband of Nicky's niece Irina, and Dmitry Pavlovich, whom she herself had a part in bringing up, who at one time had even been considered as a future fiancé for one of her daughters, are involved. The news was all around the family very quickly, Maria Fyodorovna noting in her diary on December 19: "In the morning Xenia came, we talked only of this unbelievable story. Everyone is rejoicing and praising Felix to the skies for his valiant conquest in the name of the

Fatherland. But I find it terrible how all this was done. Felix and Dm[itry] are now being accused. But I don't believe a word of it. It's an unpleasant situation. The ground is being pulled from under one's feet."

The fact that members of their own family were responsible for perpetrating this greatest outrage, murdering their Friend, their man of God, emphasized in the strongest possible terms for Alix and Nicky, and their children, how isolated they had become, how utterly unsupported by those who should have been their nearest and dearest. It must have been an exceedingly black moment, especially for Alix, for whom there was little or no sympathy from the rest of the family. Her mother-in-law commented on December 20: "Ducky came back for tea, we chatted about everything under the sun, she told me about her last conversation with A[licky], who sees everything very wrongly and with her constant stubbornness and willfulness is only drawing us all into an abyss of misfortune." Alix was now being blamed for the reaction to the murder, particularly for the treatment meted out to Dmitry Pavlovich. "Dm[itry] wanted to let me know that he will never forget how *she* has treated him. He telephoned and asked if he could see *her*. *She* refused and sent Maximovich to him, who announced in *her* name that he was under house arrest. But *she* had no right to do this. It must be that *she* suspects him of involvement in the murder. An absurd idea." Maria Fyodorovna had a tendency to disbelieve stories that disturbed her. When Dmitry was sent off to Persia by the order of the Tsar, who refused to heed the calls for clemency made by many members of the family, Alix again received the lion's share of the blame. "Little Maria [the daughter of the King of Greece] came in the early morning," Maria Fyodorovna wrote on December 31, "gave me a letter from poor Pavel. He is in despair because his son was suddenly sent away to Persia in the night, so that he managed neither to see him nor to bless him. A foul business. My hair stood on end listening to her. Nicky did not even receive Pavel, as he can decide nothing at all on account of *her*, she who hates everyone and dreams of revenge. How will all this end?!"

As Rasputin's murder occurred at precisely the time that Nicky was already preparing to leave Stavka for the Christmas and New Year holidays, and he then stayed for several weeks at Tsarskoe Selo, there is a gap, at this most crucial moment, when one would most like to know the state of Alix's—and indeed Nicky's—mind, in the correspondence between the imperial couple. Thus one can only imagine Alix's inevitable grief and mental collapse, and the support her husband must have given her, requiring all his resources, to enable her to survive intact. When not attending to his wife's needs, he spent the time poring over maps and working on the plans for a spring campaign.

By now Maria Fyodorovna was feeling desperate about the internal state of the country and the role Alix was continuing to play in its governance, despite the loss of her Friend. The belief that Alix was in league with the Germans was so widespread—even though there was no concrete evidence to support such a belief—that probably the only way she could have counteracted it would have been to withdraw to Livadia and stay there, but to Alix herself that would have felt like failure, defeat, and a dereliction of duty. As in a Greek tragedy, no one any longer had any freedom of choice; they each had to play out their part according to their character. No one could any longer hear or understand anyone else's point of view. "If only the Lord would open my poor N[icky]'s eyes," wrote Maria Fyodorovna on January 6, "and that he would stop following her dreadful advice. What despair! All this will lead us to disaster." A week later, she made her own fruitless attempt at intervention: "I talked openly with N[icky], told him the whole truth. But, unfortunately, it didn't help."

In February it was Sandro's turn to make one last attempt to talk frankly with both Nicky and Alix about the parlous state of the country and whether any measures might be taken to save the dynasty. He, like his brother Nikolai and many other members of the old regime, believed that the only chance for survival was for the Tsar to agree to work with ministers approved by the Duma and the Russian people but that Alix was working to frustrate such a scheme, preventing Nicky from hearing the arguments of reasonable people. Sandro told Nicky in a letter, which he handed to him in person: "you cannot govern a country without listening to the voice of the people," but this was not a sentiment acceptable—or even comprehensible—to a confirmed autocrat. Sandro also tried to persuade Nicky of the seriousness of the situation, because he and Alix still seemed oblivious to it, believing that it was only unrepresentative rabble-rousers in St. Petersburg and Moscow who were discontented and that "real Russians" all loved their Tsar and wanted no change in the form of government. This cousin, brother-in-law, and lifelong friend, who signed himself "your devoted Sandro" could not have been clearer in his warning: "Your advisors continue to lead You and Russia towards certain ruin, and in such circumstances it would be a crime to remain silent before both God, You, and Russia. Discontent is growing rapidly and the further it goes, the greater the gap between You and Your People." Alix was in bed when Sandro visited Tsarskoe Selo with his letter (he had been invited to lunch, which he shared with Nicky, the five imperial children—who were all in a happy mood, "totally ignorant of political events"—and an aide-de-camp), and after lunch Nicky took him in to speak to her, as he had requested. He had hoped to speak to her alone, but Nicky decided to stay, sitting impassively on the edge of the bed, smoking.

Sandro gave an account of the conversation in a letter to his brother that he wrote that evening: "I spoke for a long time, an hour and a half, and touched on absolutely all the issues, at each step coming up against [Alix's] objections, which cannot tolerate even the slightest criticism; she is in a state of complete and incurable delusion, her main argument was that everyone needs to be brought to heel, and put in their place, instead of interfering with what does not concern them, that one needs patience to give the present government time, and more in the same vein." Unable to make any headway with either Nicky or Alix, Sandro came to an unpalatable conclusion—that he might have to abandon his loyalty to the Tsar: "for the first time in our lives, we have to ask how far we are bound by the oath given. In all, it's a nightmare, from which I can see no escape." He summed up the situation to his brother in total despair: "The problem of the railways has reached crisis point, we are on the verge of a catastrophe, there is no more coal or food, we are living from day to day, everything is in complete disarray—yet there is no leadership from above, it's enough to drive you mad, up there it's like water off a duck's back, all is blindness and submission to God."

Nicky did not return to Stavka until February 22, and he then went back alone, without Alexei. Alix, Ania, and the children were all at the door of the Alexander Palace to see the Tsar's car drive off, to the usual accompaniment of salutes, flags, and church bells.

By this time Alix has embraced the consoling belief that their Friend Grigory is watching over them from the next world; she misses him enormously, but has convinced herself that his spirit is even closer to them, more protective of them, than when he was alive. Her letter to Nicky on the day of his departure closes in a mixture of love and prayer, in which a kind of resigned desperation mingles with a never-failing hope; she herself seems now to be embarking on her journey into the next world, too, even if she does not yet realize it: "Holy angels guard you, Christ be near you, & the sweet Virgin never fail you—Our Friend left us to her—I bless you, clasp you tightly in my arms & rest yr weary head upon my breast.... Feel my arms encircling you, feel my lips tenderly pressed upon yours—always together, never alone."

While at Tsarskoe Selo Alix was kept busy as her children and Ania succumbed one after the other to measles and the endgame was being played out at Stavka. Nicky was missing Alexei's enlivening company, with nothing to do in his free evenings except play dominoes. But he by no means suspected that the end of his reign was near, remarking to Alix on February 23: "What you write about being firm—the master—is perfectly true. I do not forget it—be sure of that, but I need not bellow at the people right & left every moment. A quiet sharp remark or answer is enough very often to put the one or the other into his place."

Alix was aware of at least some of the disturbances taking place in Petrograd, informing Nicky on February 24: "Yesterday there were rows on the V[asilyevsky] ostrov & Nevsky because the poor people stormed the bread shops—they smashed Filipov['s bakery] completely & the Cossacks were called out against them. All this I know unofficially." But her verdict is that such "rows" and strikes should not be taken seriously, that it was all just "a hooligan movement, young boys & girls running about & screaming that they have no bread, only to excite." She thought that if the weather were colder, they would all stay at home, but that in any event "this will all pass & quieten down—if the Duma wld only behave itself." Her optimism, despite everything, is bolstered by visits to Rasputin's grave, where she "felt such peace & calm on this dear place." Rasputin is now a martyr in her eyes; he has become even more Christlike than when he was alive: "He died to save us," she writes on February 26.

Stavka was kept informed of the revolutionary activity in Petrograd, but it was, writes Allan K. Wildman, "immobilized by the curious behaviour of its pivot, the imperial Commander-in-Chief." General Adjutant D. N. Dubensky kept a detailed diary. He noted toward the end of February that the Tsar "raised no questions about current developments and in general consulted with no one, but pensively strolled along the forest path." When Rodzianko sent an urgent telegram to the Emperor, reporting the disturbances, Nicky merely commented "Some more rubbish from that fat Rodzianko." Dubensky and Professor Fyodorov, the imperial physician, tried to persuade the Tsar to send a punitive expedition to Petrograd under General Ivanov. Nicholas eventually agreed and instructed Ivanov, via Alexeev, to go to Tsarskoe Selo in a command train and set up a headquarters there with two cavalry and two infantry regiments from each of the three fronts, with supporting machine guns and artillery, and the St. George's Cavaliers. But this adventure was ill-fated as the garrison at Tsarskoe Selo had already defected and railway workers prevented the other troops from arriving. In the end the Tsar had to recall the expedition.

Prime Minister Golitsyn now asked Nicholas to form a new government (a "responsible Ministry"), under Rodzianko or Prince Lvov, the Tsar's brother Misha supporting this suggestion. Alexeev urged the Tsar to accept the proffered solution but was cut short, the Tsar announcing his departure for Tsarskoe Selo. Wildman has demonstrated that there was ample evidence that most of the higher officers at Stavka, as well as a number of front and army chiefs and most of the naval commanders, wanted a Duma-based government and were not afraid to force the Tsar's hand. Nicholas departed Stavka on February 28, at five o'clock in the morning. Maria Fyodorovna, who was living in Kiev near Xenia and Sandro (based there as Commander-in-Chief of Russian aviation), had noted in her diary on the previous day: "Very disturbing communications from Pet[rograd]. It's terrible! They say that Nicky is coming back. It must mean it's serious. Despair! In the middle of the war! Bad leaders or bad advisers? Where will all this lead?" The imperial train had no means of communication with the capital or with Stavka. General Ivanov was also out of communication and Alexeev had no authority to make new decisions. He did, however, inform all front commanders of the position in Petrograd, including the possibility that a revolutionary government had been formed. The movement of troops to the capital ceased when Rodzianko wired that a new government had indeed been formed and railway workers must keep supplies moving to the front. Maria Fyodorovna was not alone in continuing to blame Alix for every disastrous development: "Absolutely no news from Peter[sburg]. Very unpleasant . . . The Duma has been closed, why? They say this must definitely be *her* doing. At such a moment another dreadful mistake! One must be really out of one's mind to take such a responsibility on oneself."

Nicky learned of these developments—the setting up of a Provisional Government under Rodzianko, and the taking of the Winter Palace—while on the train. Unable to proceed to Tsarskoe Selo, as the line was reported blocked by revolutionary troops, the imperial train was diverted to Pskov, where General Ruzsky, the commander of the northern front, had his headquarters. Nicholas impressed everyone around him with the calmness of his demeanor during these uncertain few days.

As the situation darkened, the most fearful rumors coming through from Stavka, Alix not knowing Nicky's whereabouts or exactly what was happening to him—in short, as the illusions begin to be stripped away—what remains most clearly is the love these two people had for one another. As hope begins to be lost, so Alix loses her bossy tone, her care and concern for her husband predominating. She will stand by him, whatever happens. "My own beloved, precious angel, light of my life," she begins her letter on March 2, and continues: "My heart breaks thinking of you all alone, going through all this anguish, anxiety & we know nothing of you & you neither of us." After expressing the opinion that, if he is now forced to make concessions such as the granting of a constitution, his promises will not be binding precisely because they are being extracted by force, she tells him: "Yr little family misses its Father. By degrees have told the situation to the older & the Cow—they were far too ill before—a horribly strong measles, such sickness. Pretending in front of them was trying. Baby I say the half . . . Only all wretched you have not come." She has, at least for the time being, given up telling him what to do: "Can advise nothing, be only yr precious self. If you have to give into things, God will help you to get out of them. Ah, my suffering saint, I am one with you, inseparably one, old *Wify*." Maria Fyodorovna was also anxiously waiting for news. "Sandro came to lunch," she wrote on March 2, a Thursday. "It is said that my poor Nicky is in Pskov. Right now this whole nightmare is the only thing I can think and talk about. I received a telegram from Xenia, in which she writes that no one knows where N[icky] is. It is terrifying what's going on. Oh Lord, help us!"

On arrival at Pskov, and on receipt of advice from a number of commanders, including General Brusilov and Grand Duke Nikolai Nikolaevich, Nicky pronounced himself at last prepared to make concessions, to appoint a new government with a leader acceptable to the country—but by now it was too late. After an all-night conversation over the wire with Rodzianko, General Ruzsky informed the Tsar on the morning of March 2 that only his abdication could avert civil war and military defeat. Ruzsky communicated the same opinion to General Alexeev, who then canvassed the opinion of all the army and navy commanders and found they were in agreement. At three o'clock in the afternoon the Tsar signed a telegram to Rodzianko signifying his willingness to abdicate, but when he heard that Alexander Guchkov and Vasily Shulgin (both among the founders of the Progressive Bloc in the Duma) were on their way to Pskov, he asked Ruzsky to delay sending it. The initial plan had been for Nicky to abdicate in favor of his son, but after discussions with Professor Fyodorov, who was not optimistic about Alexei's chances of a long and healthy life, the Tsar decided he could not risk Alexei being separated from himself and Alix, and so he would abdicate on his behalf as well. Shortly after midnight on March 3, Alexeev at Stavka and Rodzianko in Petrograd received word that the act of abdication had been signed.

When Alix received the news of Nicholas's abdication, broken to her by his Uncle Pavel, she thought she understood his motives (though in fact she did not, or not entirely, appearing to believe that he had abdicated—and possibly only temporarily—as an alternative to being forced to grant a constitution) and continued to offer her loving support: "I hold you tight, tight in my arms & will never let them touch your shining soul. I kiss, kiss, kiss & bless you & will always understand you."

Someone else who loved Nicky was his mother, and over the next few days she demonstrated that unconditional love. Sandro came to tell her on March 3 about Nicky's abdication and suggested that Maria Fyodorovna should accompany him to Mogilev (where the imperial train had returned) to see her son. She agreed immediately, and they set off that evening by train. They arrived at Stavka at noon the next day, during freezing and stormy weather. Their train pulled into the "imperial platform"; a moment later Nicky's car drew into the station. "A sorrowful meeting!" wrote his mother. They had lunch together with various members of his retinue and afterward Nicky related what had been going on in the last couple of days—the telegram from Rodzianko advising the formation of a new government and then that he should abdicate in favor of Alexei, Nicky deciding to give the throne to Misha instead, all the generals telegraphing to back the idea of abdication, until at last "*he* gave in and signed the manifesto." "*Nicky* was unprecedentedly calm and majestic in this terribly humiliating situation," wrote his mother. "I felt stunned. I can't understand anything!" That evening at supper Nicky's composure deserted him; "he opened his poor broken heart to me," wrote Maria Fyodorovna, "and we both wept." They spent the evening together in her train carriage, Nicky returning to his quarters at eleven o'clock.

On the next day, Sunday, March 5, Maria Fyodorovna met Nicky at church, where she prayed "first for Russia, then for him, for myself, for the whole family." Nicky was again calm, keeping his pain to himself. On the Monday Maria Fyodorovna spoke to her daughter-in-law by phone; "She is very calm," wrote the Dowager Empress, "but proud and stubborn. What can she be feeling now?" Maria Fyodorovna drew some comfort from a conversation with General Hanbury-Williams, whom she described as "incomparable and moving." She again had lunch with Nicky and his retinue while Nicky returned to the train for supper and stayed for the evening. "Right in front of Nicky's eyes they have raised two enormous red flags above the Town Duma!" commented his mother.

Before joining his mother for supper, Nicky had also asked to see General Hanbury-Williams, who wrote up his account of the meeting:

> I walked down through the gathering darkness and through the gloomy, dirty streets, rendered more sombre by my thoughts as I went along, and there passed through my mind the many happier days when I went to visit the Tsar of all the Russias, who had always received me with that bright and happy smile, which he invariably greeted me with, even when things were not at their best. . . .
>
> Except for a small crowd of loafers outside the entrance gates, there was no one about, and I reached the door of the house, a ray of light from the adjoining General Staff Offices just showing up the muddy path.
>
> At the entrance I was stopped by a sentry with the red band of

revolution round his arm. He at first would not hear of my admission, but I explained who I was, and at the same moment the faithful old body-servant of the Emperor appeared and told the sentry to let me pass unhindered.

Each step I took seemed to bring back some memory to me, the stairs along which the little Tsarevitch used to run to bid us good-bye, the ante-room, which used to be full of officers and ministers on official visits, and where we used to gather daily before lunch and dinner. . . .

I had no time for a set or stilted speech, and all I could say when I saw that familiar face again was: "I am so sorry." . . .

He looked tired and white, with big black lines under his eyes, but smiled as he shook hands with me, and then asked me to come and sit on the sofa where we could talk.

I asked him if he had been able to sleep, and how the children who were ill at Tsarskoe Selo were getting on.

He told me that he had been able to get a certain amount of sleep, and that the news of the invalids was better. An officer had brought him a letter from the Empress hidden in his tunic. This he said had been a great comfort to him in his anxiety for her and the children.

We then talked over plans for his future, as he evidently saw that plans were no longer in his own hands. . . .

He never referred to any anxiety in regard to his own safety, which was typical of him. . . .

As I prepared to leave he asked me for my photograph, which I sent him to-night, and said he would send me one of his.

As I said "good-bye" in anticipation of the more formal farewell to-morrow, he turned to me and added: "Remember, nothing matters but beating Germany."

I went away sad and depressed, fearing that he has still hopes, though I have none.

The next day, snow falling constantly, was again spent quietly. In the evening Nicky and his mother played a short game of bezique. Then news arrived that on the following day Nicky would be allowed to travel.

"Today is one of the most sorrowful days of my life!" Maria Fyodorovna wrote on Wednesday, March 8. "I parted with my beloved *Nicky!*" The ex-Tsar said good-bye to his staff at noon. By eleven o'clock the room was packed, even the staircase and entrance hall being full of people. Sandro was there, along with his brother Grand Duke Sergei Mikhailovich and Grand Duke Boris Vladimirovich. All the generals, officers, and civilian members of staff were present, headed by General Alexeev, along with men belonging to regiments stationed at Mogilev. There was subdued conversation, while everyone kept their eyes on the door through which the Emperor was to appear. Light and rapid steps were heard on the stairs, and everyone fell silent. "Nicky enters," recalled Sandro, "—calm, reserved, bearing the semblance of a smile on his lips. He thanks the staff and begs them to continue their work 'with the same loyalty and in a spirit of self-sacrifice.' He invites them to forget all feuds, to serve Russia and lead our army to victory. Then he says his adieus, in curt soldierlike sentences, avoiding words that could suggest pathos. His modesty makes a tremendous impression. We shout 'hurrah,' as we never had in the last twenty-three years. Elderly generals cry. A moment more, and someone is bound to step forward and implore Nicky to reconsider his decision. Such a move would be useless: the Czar of Russia does not go back on his word. Nicky bows and walks out."

He spent the afternoon, until five o'clock, sitting with his mother. And then, after kissing her repeatedly and embracing Sandro, he left, accompanied in the train by four representatives from the Duma. (The Generals of the allied missions, including General Hanbury-Williams, had offered to accompany him to help ensure his safe passage, but in the end it had been decided, on the advice of Alexeev, that this would constitute an unnecessary provocation to the Provisional Government that had guaranteed his safety.) Nicky, standing at the large window of his carriage, raised his hand in farewell as the train pulled slowly out of the station. His expression, wrote Sandro, was "infinitely sad."

CHAPTER TWELVE

From Ex's to Icons

THERE IS A photograph of Nicholas sitting on a tree stump at Tsarskoe Selo, during the family's confinement there in 1917, three soldier-guards standing to attention in the background, in which his sad and lonely, but dignified and restrained, pose is reminiscent of images of Christ in the garden of Gethsemane before his Passion, the image known as "Christ on the Cold Stone." An example of this was the sixteenth-century Netherlandish sculpture included in the *Seeing Salvation* exhibition at London's National Gallery in 2000, showing Christ seated on a rock awaiting crucifixion, naked and vulnerable. A similar image is *Christ in the Wilderness,* painted by Ivan Kramskoy in 1872, the figure of Christ having appeared to Kramskoy in a vision. He described it as almost like a hallucination, and completed the painting without using a model. "I suddenly saw a seated figure, deep in thought, I started looking at it in great depth (I could) walk around it, and throughout the entire duration of my observations it did not move once . . . it did not notice me. His thoughts were so serious and so deep that I would always come across him in the same position. . . . Here I found that I did not even have to invent anything, I had simply to copy what I had seen. And when I finished, I gave him an audacious name. Was it Christ? I do not know. In the morning, with the rising of the sun, the person vanished." Is it too fanciful to imagine that Kramskoy had had a vision not of Christ, but of the last Tsar? Mark Antokolsky's sculpture *Christ Bound Before the People,* purchased by Tsar Alexander III in 1874 and thus very likely to have been known by Nicky, is another variant on the same theme. In his book *The Avant-Garde Icon,* Andrew

Spira characterizes the narrative of Christ, standing silent before his accusers, as an "ideal vehicle for the profoundly Russian tendency to romanticise and spiritualise—and therefore tolerate rather than conquer—the passive 'victim-disposition.'" Spira argues that this disposition is a peculiarly Russian trait, "a fundamental part of the Russian psyche," linked to climate and landscape. Certainly it was chosen as a theme by a number of nineteenth-century Russian artists belonging to the group known as the Wanderers (favorites of Nicky's, and to which Kramskoy and Antokolsky belonged). "These works" writes Spira, "operate at many levels, in each case sacralising—or *sacrificing* (if one considers the origin of the word: to 'make holy')—the feeling/disposition of endurance and passivity. What was instilled in the Russian soul by long experience of nature was sacralised, or redeemed, by the example of Christ." It is interesting to look at Antokolsky's sculpture in light of these words from Dostoevsky's speech on Pushkin, published in volume 12 of his *Works* in 1905–1906 but delivered during the Pushkin Celebration of June 1880: "I affirm that our peasants were already enlightened a long time ago, by accepting Christ and His teaching . . . his [i.e., the peasant's] chief school of Christianity was the ages of endless suffering he endured in the course of history when, abandoned by all, oppressed by all, working for all, he remained all alone with Christ, the Comforter, whom he received then in his soul and who saved this soul from despair." In her book *The Humiliated Christ in Modern Russian Thought,* Nadejda Gorodetzky claims that this identification of the peasantry with a vision of the humiliated Christ was extended to the rest of the nation, and became the foundation of the belief in "Holy Russia."

In Russian Orthodox spirituality, this attitude toward suffering is included within, but is not entirely synonymous with, the word *smirenie*—which contains the word for peace—*mir*—and carries the sense of being at peace with one's fate. In his provocatively titled book, *The Slave Soul of Russia,* Daniel Rancour-Laferriere quotes an analysis of *smirenie* as the "serene acceptance of one's fate, achieved through moral effort, through suffering, and through realization of one's total dependence on God, an acceptance resulting not only in an attitude of non-resistance to evil but also in profound peace and a loving attitude towards one's fellow human beings." As Rancour-Laferriere points out, this is not the same as passivity or inaction, and *smirenie* is achieved only after great internal effort. This was the state achieved by that Russian saint beloved of Alix and Nicky, Serafim of Sarov.

On the day before the night in which she and all her family were murdered, Alix, together with her daughter Tatiana, who had stayed with her while the rest of the family had gone outside for a little exercise, read two short books from the Old Testament: the Books of the Prophet Amos and the Prophet Obadiah. Some of what they read spoke to their condition exactly.

> *And their king shall go into captivity, he and his princes together, saith the Lord.* [Amos 1:15]

The imperial family had now been in captivity for over fifteen months; this, the Ipatiev House in Ekaterinburg, was their third place of imprisonment. Their "king," the Tsar, seemed in some respects to find his captivity less onerous than the burdens of unlimited power. He had early on joked about being an "ex" (referring to some unpalatable meat served to them as an "ex-ham"), and his innate ability to get on with other people had transferred fairly easily from dealing with courtiers, statesmen, and diplomats to relating to rough soldiers and guards. Only the restriction placed on his physical movements really irked him; he had always needed strenuous physical exercise and now it was largely denied. As ever, he kept most of his feelings hidden, below the surface.

In her memoirs Ania Vyrubova recalls a scene that took place shortly after Nicky's return to Tsarskoe Selo:

> [The Empress] helped me to the window and herself pulled aside the curtain. Never, never while I live shall I forget what we saw, we two, clinging together in shame and sorrow for our disgraced country. Below in the garden of the palace which had been his home for twenty years stood the man who until a few days before had been Tsar of all the Russias. With him was his faithful friend Prince Dolgoruky, and surrounding them were six soldiers, say rather six hooligans, armed with rifles. With their fists and with the butts of their guns they pushed the Emperor this way and that as though he were some wretched vagrant they were baiting in a country road. "You can't go there, Gospodin Polkovnik (Mr. Colonel)." "We don't permit you to walk in that direction, Gospodin Polkovnik." "Stand back when you are commanded, Gospodin Polkovnik."
>
> The Emperor, apparently unmoved, looked from one of these coarse brutes to another and with great dignity turned and walked back towards the palace.

Pierre Gilliard further described the restrictions placed upon the prisoners' use of the grounds at Tsarskoe Selo:

Wednesday, April 18th—Whenever we go out, soldiers, with fixed bayonets and under the command of an officer, surround us and keep pace with us. We look like convicts with their warders. The instructions are changed daily, or perhaps the officers interpret them each in his own way! This afternoon, when we were going back to the palace after our walk, the sentry on duty at the gate stopped the Tsar, saying: "You cannot pass, sir." The officer with us here intervened. Alexei Nikolaevich blushed hotly to see the soldier stop his father.

Friday, April 20th—We now go out regularly twice a day: in the morning from eleven till noon, in the afternoon from half-past two to five. We all collect in the semi-circular hall and wait for the officer commanding the guard to come and open the gates into the park. We go out; the officer on duty and soldiers fall in behind us and take station round the place where we stop to work. The Tsarina and Grand-Duchesses Olga and Marie are still confined to their rooms.

Sunday, April 22nd—We are forbidden to go to the pond; we have to keep near the palace and not go outside the radius which has been fixed for us. In the distance we saw a crowd of several hundred people curious to see us.

The French ambassador, Maurice Paléologue, was one of those who observed Nicholas's calm demeanor in the weeks after his abdication: "The Emperor still presents an extraordinary spectacle of indifference and imperturbability. He spends, in his calm and casual way, his day skimming the papers, smoking cigarettes, doing puzzles, playing with his children, and sweeping up snow in the garden." According to Paléologue, it was Alexandra who more readily interpreted their situation as a spiritual experience, something to be actively endured as Christians—precisely because for her such resignation was harder than for her husband. It took her much longer to adapt to powerlessness. The impression that it was Alix who was behaving in a more "saintly" way than Nicholas is further strengthened by the comments a member of their (much diminished) retinue, Prince Valya Dolgorukov, made in a letter to his mother in December 1917: "She is often depressed, but in a rather gentle mood, and maintains the role she must play, calm, dignified, accepting all news and occurrences with equanimity. He is always the same, suffering morally, expressing himself openly, but has been able to retain his charm and affability." It may be that Nicholas was merely fatalistic, an attitude that was, according to Daniel Rancour-Laferriere, "endemic among the peasant masses in Russia." Fate—the Russian word *sud'ba*—was described by the Russian philosopher Vladimir Solovyov, a slightly older contemporary of Nicholas and Alexandra, as "beyond question." It is unavoidable, and must be accepted with total resignation and passivity. Rancour-Laferriere has pointed out that by personifying *sud'ba* it is easier to lay credit or blame at her door, and consequently evade one's own responsibility.

Nicky's sense of resignation and *smirenie* can, however, be exaggerated. On arrival at what was to be their final place of imprisonment, he was far from resigned to the way he and his family were now being treated, as he recorded in his diary: "The house is pleasant and clean. We have been given four large rooms. We were not able to unpack our things for a long time, as the commissar, the commandant and the guards captain had not had time to inspect our trunks. Then the inspection was like a customs search, just as strict, right down to the last capsule in Alix's travelling medicine kit. This annoyed me so much that I expressed my opinion sharply to the commissar."

The day this entry was made—the day on which Nicky, Alix, and Maria arrived in Ekaterinburg (the rest of the family was to follow later)—happened to be the Tuesday in Passion Week (the Western Church's Holy Week). The inhabitants of the Ipatiev House did what they could to observe Passion Week and Easter, Nicky reading aloud "the appropriate passages from the New Testament, morning and evening, in the bedroom." On the Thursday, he and Dr. Botkin took it in turns to read aloud the twelve Gospel passages set for the day (the readings known as the Twelve Gospels). For the Easter Vigil, a priest and deacon were allowed into the house. "They conducted the service quickly and well," commented Nicky. "It was a great comfort to pray even in such circumstances and to hear: 'Christ is Risen.' "

> *And I will smite the winter house with the summer house; and the houses of ivory shall perish, and the great houses shall have an end, saith the Lord.* [Amos 3:15]

As the senior member of the Provisional Government, Alexander Kerensky took it upon himself to visit the Romanovs at the Alexander Palace. He recalled how the ex-Emperor's remaining staff insisted on adhering to imperial protocol. Arriving at the palace, Kerensky asked Count von Benckendorff to inform the Tsar that he must see him and his wife. "The old count, who sported a monocle, listened to me gravely and answered: 'I shall report to His Majesty.' In a few moments he returned and announced solemnly: 'His Majesty has graciously consented to receive you.' This seemed a trifle ridiculous and out of place, but I did not want to destroy the count's last illusions. He still considered himself first marshal to His Majesty, the Tsar." Benckendorff then escorted Kerensky to the imperial apartments and left him "before the closed door" as he went in to announce him. When Kerensky was finally admitted, he found the imperial family waiting for him. "The whole family was standing huddled in confusion around a small table near a window in the adjoining room. A small man in uniform detached himself from the group and moved forward to meet me, hesitating and smiling weakly. It was Nicholas II. On the threshold of the room in which I awaited him, he stopped as if uncertain what to do next. He did not know what my attitude would be. Was he to receive me as a host or wait for me to greet him first? I sensed his embarrassment at once, as well as the confusion of the whole family left alone with a terrible revolutionary. I quickly went up to Nicholas II, held out my hand with a smile, and said abruptly, 'Kerensky,' as I usually introduce myself. He shook my hand firmly, smiled, seemingly encouraged, and led me at once to his family." Benckendorff remembered the encounter rather differently: "As Kerensky entered he made a sort of bow, and introduced himself as the Procurator-General. He was in a state of feverish agitation; he could not stand still, touched all the objects which were on the table and seemed like a madman." Despite himself, Kerensky warmed to Nicky, but could not feel the same about Alix, who, "stiff, proud and haughty, extended her hand reluctantly, as if under compulsion."

During Holy Week and Easter 1917 the Provisional Government gave permission for the dean of the Fyodorovsky Sobor to stay in the palace, along with a deacon and four singers, in order to conduct services for the imperial family and their servants. In the end they stayed for three weeks. All the liturgy was observed as normal, including, on Good Friday, a procession through the rooms of the palace. On Easter Day the usual festivities were observed, Nicky noting in his diary: "Before lunch I kissed and exchanged greetings with all the servants, while Alix distributed china eggs, which were left over from our previous reserves. In all there were 135 people."

On June 9, Nicky recorded that they had now been held prisoner at Tsarskoe Selo for three months. "It's terribly hard to be without news of dear Mama," he wrote, "but as to the rest, I'm indifferent." At the end of the following month, it was decided by the Provisional Government that the family should be moved away from the capital and farther into Russia. The place chosen for their exile was Tobolsk, seven hundred miles east of Moscow, in western Siberia. The family left Tsarskoe Selo, traveling by train and still with a comparatively large retinue on the day after Alexei's thirteenth birthday. The journey, which took four days, was surrounded by secrecy; the train flew the Japanese flag and bore placards announcing that it was a Japanese Red Cross Mission. It stopped each day in open country to allow Nicky and the children to get out and stretch their legs. The travelers then spent a further two days on a boat before reaching Tobolsk (passing Rasputin's family house in the village of Pokrovskoe during the voyage). On arrival, it was found that the former Governor's House where they were to live was not yet ready for occupancy, so they spent a further week living on the boat, finally moving into the house on August 13. It was still not quite prepared for this influx of people, as is clear from Nicky's diary entry of September 4: "The last few days have brought a lot of unpleasantness in the sense of absence of plumbing. The downstairs w.c. overflowed with waste from the upstairs ones, and we had to stop using them or taking baths; all this because the septic pits are too small, and no one wanted to clean them out." Though Gilliard described the house as "a spacious and comfortable building," it was a far cry from anywhere the imperial family had previously lived. Outdoor exercise had to be taken in a small kitchen garden and a yard.

During the time the family spent in Tobolsk, and later in Ekaterinburg, they were helped to endure their imprisonment by their lifelong habits of discipline and ordering of their days. The younger children continued to have lessons every day, certain hours were allotted for prayers and spiritual reading, they would take such exercise as was possible during the afternoon, and Nicky would read aloud to the family after dinner. One of the main frustrations recorded in Alix's diary is when the family's ordering of their time was disrupted by meals being served later than expected, or by some other intrusion of their keepers into the preferred daily routine.

Sometimes even the calm and phlegmatic Nicky was "deeply upset" by the conditions of their imprisonment, particularly by some of the absurdities of the rules imposed upon them. On November 3, Olga's twenty-second birthday, her father wrote: "I feel sorry for her, poor thing, having to celebrate her birthday in such circumstances." News was eventually received from his mother, who was with his sisters Olga and Xenia in the Crimea. Alix spent much of her time writing letters. One of the people she wrote to was Ania (with whom, in adversity, she had long been completely reconciled), who had been arrested and taken away from Tsarskoe Selo soon after the Revolution. "The spirits of the whole family are good," she told Ania on December 9, 1917. "God is very near us, we feel His support, and are often amazed that we can endure events and separations which once might have killed us. Although we suffer horribly, still there is peace in our souls. I suffer most for Russia, and I suffer for you too, but I know that ultimately all will be for the best. Only I don't understand anything any longer. Everyone seems to have gone mad." A week later she gave Ania more details of the family's condition: "I make everything now. Father's [i.e., Nicky's] trousers are torn and darned, the girls' under-linen in rags. Dreadful, is it not? I have grown quite grey. Anastasia, to her despair, is now very fat, as Maria was, round and fat to the waist, with short legs. I do hope she will grow. Olga and Tatiana are both thin, but their hair grows beautifully so that they can go without scarfs." (The girls had had their heads shaved when they had had measles.) The family endeavored to celebrate Christmas as normally as possible, decorating trees for themselves, their servants, and their guards. By this time Lenin and the Bolsheviks had seized power, overthrowing Kerensky's government. This new regime was far less concerned than Kerensky had been with ensuring the safety of the ex-Emperor and his family, and the new guards assigned to them reflected the harsher spirit taking over in the country. A particularly cruel and pointless privation the family had to endure was the destruction of a toboggan run (a "snow mountain") that they had carefully constructed. "It appears that the idiotic detachment committee decided to do this," Nicky recorded, "in order to stop us climbing up onto it and looking over the fence!"

By the beginning of 1918 even Nicky, who had set himself a project to re-read the entire Bible, along with Maeterlinck's *La sagesse et la destinée*, a collection of reflections on happiness, love, sacrifice, and death, was finding it hard to keep his spirits up, particularly on days when he was deprived of physical activity. "We go into the garden but there's no work to do," he wrote on January 2, "—today I was bored to tears!" He confessed in a letter to his sister Xenia: "For me, the night is the best part of the day, at least you can forget for a while." Alexei captures the sense of boredom in his diary, with its oft-repeated entry of "The whole day was just like yesterday." A particularly bad day for him was January 24, when he wrote: "In the afternoon I twirled a little stick in my hand and watched Papa working up on the roof cleaning snow and how they bring wood in the house. What a bore!!!" The young people tried to stay cheerful by playing games like hide and seek, as well as by staging amateur dramatics on Sunday evenings.

In April Alexei suffered one of his most serious hemophiliac attacks, an internal hemorrhage in the groin that may have stemmed from violent coughing in the aftermath of a cold. The pains were very severe, and the child could neither sleep nor eat for several days. Alix, who sat by him "holding his aching legs" almost round the clock, occasionally relieved by Tatiana or Gilliard, was sustained as ever by her faith: "Well, all is God's will. The deeper you look the more you understand that this is so. All sorrows are sent to free us from our sins or as a test of our faith, an example to others."

Toward the end of the month while Alexei was still recovering and could not yet get out of bed, Alix had to make one of the most difficult decisions of her life. The Bolsheviks decided to move Nicky—no one seemed to be quite clear where he was supposed to be going or for what purpose, there being so many different chains of command in operation at the time—but it was initially thought he might be sent to Moscow. Alix was given the choice of accompanying her husband or staying with her children. After a few agonizing hours of indecision, she chose the former, taking Maria, too. They were taken not to Moscow, but to Ekaterinburg, to the house of the merchant Ipatiev, renamed the "House of Special Purpose." "This is how we installed ourselves," Nicky wrote on April 17/30, "Alix, Maria and I together in the bedroom, sharing the dressing room, Demidova in the dining room, Botkin, Chemodurov and Sednev in the hall. The duty officer's room is by the entrance. In order to go to the bathroom or the W.C., it was necessary to go past the sentry at the door of the duty office. There is a very high wooden palisade built all around the house."

After several weeks of confusion and anguish, the rest of the family arrived in Ekaterinburg on May 10/23; "It was an immense joy to see them again," wrote Nicky, "and to embrace them after four weeks of separation and uncertainty." On arrival, Gilliard and some other faithful retainers were not allowed to join the imperial family. Alexei, who was only just able to walk again after his severe attack of illness, banged his knee getting into bed that first night in Ekaterinburg—"as if on purpose" noted his exasperated father—and was in great pain the whole night, stopping his parents, with whom he was sharing a room, from getting to sleep.

Here the family settled down to further monotony, and ever greater privations. They repeatedly had to beg for permission for even one of the whitewashed windows to be opened during the stiflingly hot summer—a request that was eventually granted, though reluctantly.

Meanwhile, it had been decided to convert the Alexander Palace into a museum, the historical interiors in the central part of the building and the wing inhabited by the Romanovs being opened to the public soon after the family's departure for Tobolsk. The interiors were preserved as closely as possible to how they had been when the Tsar and his family were living there, so that it looked as if they had just left and might return at any moment. The impressions received by visitors tended to be rather more favorable to the memory of the Romanovs than was comfortable to the Bolshevik government, and in 1919 part of the palace was converted into an orphanage named after the "Young Communards." This was not a success, and the rooms concerned were returned to the museum. The Alexander Palace Museum, also thought of as the "Romanov Museum," continued to be very popular with Russians and foreign visitors alike, though some of the contents were sold off to foreigners or taken for the use of Communist Party officials. Despite threats by the government during the 1930s to close the museum, it managed to stay in operation until World War II. The museum's staff packed up and saved what they could of the collection, though thousands of valuable items had to be left behind. The building itself was saved from wholesale destruction by the Germans' decision to convert it into an SS hospital; consequently it was found after the war to be the best preserved of all the suburban palaces that had been behind the German lines, and was subsequently used by the USSR Academy of Sciences for the storage of the collections of its Institute of Russian Literature and to house a display of the All-Union Pushkin Museum. Then, rather than allow the building to be restored as a museum commemorating the Romanovs, it was decided that it should henceforth be used by the navy. But in 1996, after the collapse of the Soviet Union, the World Monuments Fund awarded a grant for the restoration of the palace, and a year later a permanent exhibition entitled *Reminiscences in the Alexander Palace* was created in the wing that had formerly housed Nicky and Alix's private apartments. Restoration began in 2009, when the palace officially recovered its museum status.

The family's final dwelling was also destined for some years to become a tourist attraction, the Ipatiev House being designated a branch of the Ural Revolution Museum in 1927. It then became an agricultural school before being turned into an antireligious museum in 1938, and was taken over by the local Communist Party after the war. It was formally listed as a Historical-Revolutionary Monument in 1974, but was becoming a source of embarrassment to the Soviet government on account of the number of pilgrims visiting it to honor the memory of the imperial family. As a result, the local branch of the Communist Party, whose chairman was one Boris Yeltsin, had the house demolished in July 1977. Nevertheless, pilgrims kept arriving at the site.

> *For, lo, he that formeth the mountains, and createth the wind, and declareth unto man what is his thought, that maketh the morning darkness, and treadeth upon the high places of the earth, the Lord, The God of hosts, is his name.* [Amos 4:13]

Alix had always believed, through all the vicissitudes of her life as Empress and afterward, that God was on her side. During the time of her captivity, she gained some humility, a truer sense of perspective, an ability to admit that she might not always have been absolutely right. Writing to Ania Vyrubova in March 1918, a year after Nicky's abdication, Alix seems to have attained a touching degree of self-knowledge—touching, because it is so unlike her former self. She writes a kind of confession, indicting herself for irritability, especially over trivial matters such as mistakes made by her maid. "It is not difficult to bear great trials," writes the former Empress, "but these little buzzing mosquitoes are so trying." Mentioning that it will soon be the Sunday before Lent, when the Orthodox ask forgiveness for all their faults, she asks her friend: "Forgive the past, and pray for me."

Nicky, recalling his birth on the feast day of Job, the Old Testament character who comes to understand that the ways of God are unfathomable and not to be questioned, and who learns to accept that disaster and suffering are as much, if not more, to be expected by the godly person than joy and triumph, was always less sure that God would vindicate him.

> *Seek good, and not evil, that ye may live: and so the Lord, the God of hosts, shall be with you, as ye have spoken.*
>
> *Hate the evil, and love the good, and establish judgment in the gate: it may be that the Lord God of hosts will be gracious unto the remnant of Joseph.* [Amos 5: 14–15]

Yet the imperial family did not give up hope, at least not until the very end. Seeing themselves as a "remnant," abandoned, isolated, they still believed that God would indeed be gracious. How that grace was perceived by them changed during the months of imprisonment, particularly during the last weeks. The torment of those weeks was increased by the rumor of a plot to rescue them, messages being delivered that may have been no more than a cynical ploy on the part of their captors, a ruse whereby they hoped to prove the family was involved in a conspiracy to escape, which would act as an excuse for their execution. Nicholas seems not to have suspected a plot, but also to have been unsure about the authenticity of the messages. His diary entry for June 14/27, which was his daughter Maria's nineteenth birthday, reads: "The weather was still as tropical, 26 degrees in the shade and 24 in the rooms, almost impossible to bear! We spent an anxious night and stayed awake fully dressed. This was because, a few days ago, we received two letters, one after the other, which informed us that we should prepare to be rescued by some people devoted to us! But the days passed and nothing happened, only the waiting and the uncertainty were torture." Compared with the torment of such false hopes, it must almost have been a relief to interpret the grace of God as a promise to be realized not in this world, but in the world to come. Alix had written in this vein to Ania Vyrubova from Tobolsk in March 1918: "We live here on earth but we are already half gone to the next world."

In a further letter to Ania, written a few weeks later, Alix really does sound like someone who has already "half gone to the next world." There is an elegiac tone here, a mixture of memory and dream, of regret for a life that might have been lived differently, and of sadness rather than anger when confronted with the family's enemies:

> Well, all is God's will. The deeper you look the more you understand that this is so. All sorrows are sent to free us from our sins or as a test of our faith, an example to others.
>
> I should like to be a painter, and make a picture of this beautiful garden and all that grows in it. I remember English gardens, and at Livadia you saw an illustrated book I had of them, so you will understand.
>
> Just now eleven more men have passed on horseback, good faces, mere boys—this I have not seen the like of for a long time. They are the guard of the new Kommissar.
>
> Sometimes we see men with the most awful faces. I would not include them in my garden picture. The only place for them would be outside where the merciful sun could reach them and make them clean from all the dirt and evil with which they are covered.

> *Now therefore hear thou the word of the Lord: Thou sayest, Prophesy not against Israel, and drop not thy word against the house of Isaac.*
>
> *Therefore thus saith the Lord: Thy wife shall be an harlot in the city, and thy sons and thy daughters shall fall by the sword, and thy land shall be divided by line; and thou shalt die in a polluted land: and Israel shall surely go into captivity forth of his land.* [Amos 7: 16–17]

One of the final ironies is that here were Alix and Tatiana reading of catastrophe befalling the ancient Jews, that race they had so often despised in the flesh, and deriving comfort in their own agony from the experiences and the scriptures of the Jewish people. It was with the outcast Jews that they had come to identify themselves, despite the fact that Nicholas was still inclined to blame the Jews for what had happened to them. Among the works that he read aloud to his family during the last weeks of their lives was what he described as "Nilus's book about the Antichrist, to which are appended the 'protocols' of the jews and the masons." "Very topical reading," commented the ex-Tsar. Perhaps he might be excused for holding such prejudiced and ill-informed opinions in 1918, shut away from the outside world as he was and clutching at any possible reason for his downfall (and it is true enough that more than a few Bolshevik revolutionaries happened also to be Jewish). David R. Francis, United States ambassador in Russia, warned in a January 1918 dispatch to Washington: "The Bolshevik leaders here, most of whom are Jews and 90 percent of whom are returned exiles, care little for Russia or any other country but are internationalists and they are trying to start a worldwide social revolution." Nicky may also have been inclined to believe anything written by Sergei Nilus, an apocalyptic thinker and prolific religious writer, and thus to give credence to the so-called *Protocols of the Elders of Zion*, edited and with a commentary by Nilus, because he was connected with Serafim of Sarov. Nilus was supposed to have "discovered," on the eve of the saint's canonization, some apocryphal prophecies made by Serafim about the end of world history and the coming of the Antichrist, his way prepared by revolutionaries and freemasons. The book Nicholas was referring to, to which the *Protocols* were appended, was called *The Great in the Small and the Antichrist, as a close-at-hand political possibility: Notes of an Orthodox believer*. The fourth edition of the book had been published in January 1917 by the famous Trinity-Sergius Monastery, and bore the title: "It is near, even at the doors. About that which people do not want to believe and which is so close." No wonder Nicholas found it "topical reading." He was reading *The Great in the Small* aloud to Alix and Maria during Holy Week and Easter, and finished it on April 29 / May 12.

> *And I will turn your feasts into mourning, and all your songs into lamentation; and I will bring up sackcloth upon all loins, and baldness upon every head; and I will make it as the mourning of an only son, and the end thereof as a bitter day.* [Amos 8: 10]

Though the family could not see all the bitterness that was to come, they had tasted plenty already, with the terms agreed between Germany and Russia by the Treaty of Brest-Litovsk, by which the Russians ceded much territory to the Germans. Nicholas had been led to believe, especially by his generals, that his abdication would further the Russian war effort, that his renunciation was necessary if Russia was to maintain sufficient stability to go on with the war, continue supporting the allies, and ultimately achieve victory over the Germans.

That this did not happen constituted an unbearable disappointment for him, throwing into question his very decision to abdicate. By March 1918, the ex-Tsar was as close to despair and bewilderment as he ever came. "How much longer will our poor Russia be racked and torn apart by external and internal enemies!" he wrote. "Sometimes it seems I no longer have the strength to go on, I don't even know what to pin my hopes on, what to wish for?"

> *And it shall come to pass, if there remain ten men in one house, that they shall die.* [Amos 6: 9]

When Alix and Tatiana read this verse, there remained eleven people captive in the Ipatiev House: the seven members of the imperial family, plus Dr. Botkin, Anna Demidova (Alix's maid), Ivan Kharitonov (the cook), and Alexei Trupp (the footman). They went to bed that night at half past ten.

At about two o'clock in the morning of July 17, 1918, the ex–Emperor Nicholas II, his wife Alexandra Fyodorovna, and their five children—Olga, aged twenty-two; Tatiana, twenty-one; Maria, nineteen; Anastasia, seventeen; and Alexei, just a few weeks short of his fourteenth birthday—with their three servants and their physician, were woken by the commandant Yakov Yurovsky and told to dress and wait in a basement room. Nicky carried Alexei, who was still recovering from having banged his ankle a few weeks previously; Alix protested that there were no chairs in the room where they had been told to wait. Two chairs were brought in. Alix sat on one, Alexei on the other. The four daughters stood near their mother, arranged as for a photograph.

At nearly three o'clock Yurovsky entered the basement room and told Nicky that the Soviet of Workers' Deputies had ordered that they all be shot. The ex-Tsar had only time to exclaim "What?" before he was shot in the head.

> *For thus Amos saith, Jeroboam shall die by the sword, and Israel shall surely be led away captive out of their own land.* [Amos 7: 11]

Nicky died instantly. Alix tried to make the sign of the cross, before she, too, was shot down. Death came more slowly and painfully to their children. The execution squad aimed at their hearts rather than their heads, and the bullets would not pierce the corsets worn by the girls—for the "medicines" so carefully arranged by Alix and her daughters and referred to in her diary were diamonds and other jewels sewn into their underlinen. Intended to be smuggled out in the event of a rescue attempt, the densely packed jewels acted as a form of body armor. When shooting failed to kill the young women, their executioners resorted to stabbing with bayonets—and, again, because of the bulletproof underwear, multiple stab wounds were necessary to complete the task. Alexei, too, protected by his father, had not died in the first hail of bullets. Yurovsky himself finished off the boy with two shots to the head. The doctor, the servants, and Alexei's pet spaniel, Joy, also lay dead.

> *And though they go into captivity before their enemies, thence will I command the sword, and it shall slay them: and I will set mine eyes upon them for evil, and not for good.* [Amos 9: 4]

For decades most traces of the imperial family seemed to have disappeared. The bodies of Nicky, Alix, their children, and their servants had been disposed of in farcelike scenes—trucks breaking down or getting stuck, mine shafts not being where they were expected to be, local peasants appearing at inconvenient times—but sulphuric acid and fire had been employed with the intention that the bodies would never be discovered and identified. Little information was disseminated at the time of the murders, the official Bolshevik papers announcing the execution of the Tsar but claiming that the rest of the family had been removed to a place of safety. Nevertheless, a commission of inquiry into the deaths, conducted over the ensuing months, found plenty of circumstantial evidence in the forest near the village of Koptyaki, including the following objects, enumerated by Gilliard:

> The buckle of the Tsar's belt, a fragment of his cap, the little portable frame containing the portrait of the Tsarina the photograph had disappeared—which the Tsar always carried about him, etc.
>
> The Tsarina's favorite ear-rings (one broken), pieces of her dress, the glass of her spectacles, recognizable by its special shape, etc.
>
> The buckle of the Tsarevich's belt, some buttons, and pieces of his cloak, etc.
>
> A number of small articles belonging to the Grand-Duchesses: fragments of necklaces, shoes, buttons, hooks, press-buttons, etc.
>
> Six metal corset busks. "Six"—a number which speaks for itself when the number of the female victims is remembered: the Tsarina, the four Grand-duchesses, and A. Demidova, the Tsarina's maid.
>
> Dr. Botkin's false teeth, fragments of his eyeglasses, buttons from his clothes, etc.

> Finally charred bones and fragments of bones, partly destroyed by acid and occasionally bearing the mark of a sharp instrument or saw; revolver bullets—doubtless those which had remained embedded in the bodies—and a fairly large quantity of melted lead.

Maria Fyodorovna went on believing that her son and his family were alive, somewhere, for years, her ability to withstand the truth defying all obstacles, including her own sister telling her that she had just returned from a memorial service for Nicky in the Russian Embassy chapel in London's Welbeck Street. George V was there, too: "May and I attended a Service at the Russian Church in Welbeck Street in memory of dear Nicky who I fear was shot last month by the Bolshevists, we can get no details, it was a foul murder, I was devoted to Nicky, who was the kindest of men, a thorough gentleman, loved his Country and his people."

Maria Fyodorovna wrote in her diary for July 30/August 12, 1920: "Today dear little Alexei is 16 years old, and no one knows where they are now! But in any case They are all in God's Hands and under His protection."

> *All the men of thy confederacy have brought thee even to the border: the men that were at peace with thee have deceived thee, and prevailed against thee; they that eat thy bread have laid a wound under thee: there is none understanding in him.* [Obadiah 7]

Fortunately for Nicky and Alix, they never realized the extent to which their cousin George V had joined the ranks of those who "prevailed against" them.

The initial assumption, on the part of both the Provisional Government and the family themselves, was that they were likely to be offered refuge in England, Nicky having noted in his diary on March 23, 1917: "I looked through my books and things, and started to put aside everything that I want to take with me, if we have to go to England."

For many years it was assumed that the British Prime Minister David Lloyd George was behind the rescinding of the invitation, but it is now known that it was the King himself who refused to rescue his cousins, fearing for his own throne if he was seen as sympathetic to the deposed autocrat and his wife, still suspected of German sympathies. In the event, it is unlikely that the imperial family would have been able to leave Russia for England—there having been only a brief window of opportunity for such an escape to be effected—so the English royal family may bear no direct responsibility for the fate of their relatives.

It is nevertheless not a story that does much honor to George V, and it would have appalled his—and Alix's—grandmother, Queen Victoria.

> *Then said the Lord unto me, The end is come upon my people of Israel; I will not again pass by them any more.*
>
> *And the songs of the temple shall be howlings in that day, saith the Lord God: there shall be many dead bodies in every place; they shall cast them forth with silence.* [Amos 8: 2–3]

Few members of the imperial family, in its widest sense, survived the Bolshevik Revolution. Nicky's brother Misha was shot, with his secretary Nicholas Johnson in a forest near Perm, several weeks before the assassination of the ex-Tsar and his family. Alix's sister Ella, along with Grand Duke Sergei Mikhailovich, his secretary, Grand Duke Pavel's son Vladimir, and three of KR's sons were thrown, alive, down a mine shaft near Alapaevsk, grenades being thrown in after them, on the same day as the Ekaterinburg murders. Grand Dukes Pavel Alexandrovich, Nikolai Mikhailovich, Georgy Mikhailovich, and Dmitry Konstantinovich were executed by firing squad in the Peter and Paul Fortress in January 1919.

And that was only the beginning. The Civil War between Reds and Whites resulted in millions of deaths; enforced collectivization and "dekulakisation" in the late 1920s and early 1930s, with its associated famine, killed many millions more. Around a million were executed in Stalin's purges, and throughout the Soviet regime countless others suffered in the labor camps of the Gulag or in exile. Had Nicky and Alix, and their children, seen what was coming to their beloved country and people over the course of the next eighty years, their despair would have been unimaginable. They may have anticipated some of it, but the degree of suffering imposed on the Russian people, and on the other subject peoples of the Soviet Union, could not have been foreseen. "They are mad and have started a fire which will be mighty hard to put out," Sir John Hanbury-Williams had written of the revolutionaries in March 1917, and events proved him right. "Many dead bodies in every place" was no exaggeration.

> *Behold, the days come, saith the Lord God, that I will send a famine in the land, not a famine of bread, nor a thirst for water, but of hearing the words of the Lord:*
>
> *And they shall wander from sea to sea, and from the north even to the east, they shall run to and fro to seek the word of the Lord, and shall not find it.* [Amos 8: 11–12]

Knowledge of the suppression of religion during the Communist era—the closing and desecration of churches; the imprisonment and murder of priests; the setting up of museums of atheism in former cathedrals; the destruction of icons, vessels, and vestments; the persecution of ordinary believers; the replacement of Bibles with Marxist-Leninist textbooks—would also have brought immense, immeasurable grief to Nicholas, Alexandra, and all their children. The fate of two churches in particular—the Church of the Sign (or Znamenskaya) very near the Alexander Palace, and the Fyodorovsky Sobor, consecrated in 1912 and where Alix had her private oratory—would have upset them deeply. The Znamenskaya Church was plundered after the Revolution, and closed after World War II. The Fyodorovsky Sobor was closed in 1934, the sanctuary of the upper church being walled off and turned into a storehouse for the "Lenfilm" studios. The iconostasis, icons, and other ornaments and valuables were scattered, some ending up in various museums, others being lost, sold off, or destroyed. During World War II the church was shelled and became derelict.

Both buildings were returned to the Orthodox Church in 1991, and extensive restoration has been carried out.

> *And I will bring again the captivity of my people of Israel, and they shall build the waste cities, and inhabit them; and they shall plant vineyards, and drink the wine thereof; they shall also make gardens, and eat the fruit of them.* [Amos 9: 14–15]

In the late 1970s remains believed to be those of the imperial family were discovered in a field known as the Porosenkov Ravine, but the discovery was kept secret until the era of "*glasnost.*" The discovery was made official in 1991, when the bones were exhumed, and subsequent DNA testing confirmed the identities of Nicky, Alix, and three of their daughters. In the summer of 2007 a group of amateur archaeologists discovered a collection of remains in a second grave approximately seventy meters away from the larger one, where the first set of remains had been found. Forensic DNA testing has established beyond all reasonable doubt that this second set of remains constitutes what is left of the bodies of the Tsarevich Alexei and one of his sisters—either Maria or Anastasia. Thus all the family, their servants, and their doctor are now accounted for.

After the exhumation and identification of the first set of remains, the then Russian president, Boris Yeltsin, agreed to a state funeral and reburial in the Sts. Peter and Paul Cathedral in St. Petersburg, the ancient burial place of the Romanov tsars, despite the objections of the Patriarch of the Russian Orthodox

Church in Russia, who disputed the authenticity of the bones. At the funeral, held eighty years to the day after the murders, on July 17, 1998, vast numbers of Russians paid their respects. Yeltsin, who attended the funeral in person, gave as a reason for this posthumous reburial "that the current generation of Russians could atone for the sins of their ancestors," and he referred to the murdered Romanovs as "innocent victims of hatred and violence." Dozens of the Tsar's relatives, and diplomats from more than fifty countries, watched the coffin containing the remains being laid to rest as cathedral bells tolled and soldiers gave a nineteen-gun salute.

In his book *In Siberia,* Colin Thubron describes the moment when he first encountered an icon of the imperial family, enshrined in "a sheaf of flickering lights" in a small makeshift chapel in Ekaterinburg. "I examined them in fascination," writes Thubron. "In their icon they had acquired the elongated bodies and court robes of Byzantine saints, and their tapering hands held up white crosses. Crowned and haloed, they seemed to gaze out with a sad foreknowledge of their end. Their features echoed one another's, as in some inbred clan, and they were all washed in the same amber light. All the vitality of remembered photographs—the moods and stains of real life—was emptied and stilled. Sainthood did not allow for them."

Oleg Tarasov has pointed out that the spiritual sense of an icon can be understood not only through the face of the saint depicted but also through the overall contour and pose, gestures, and material attributes of the holy personages. The Holy Royal Passion-Bearers, as Nicky, Alix, and their children in their incarnation as saints are known, are generally shown without specific attributes, and are recognizable largely because of their number and formation. They are a family, and they are grouped as though for a family photograph.

There are now dozens and dozens of icons of the imperial family in existence. In some, the family group wears traditional flowing white robes with gold trim. Others have a more modern feel, such as the 1998 icon "Heavenly Glory," in which the Tsar and Tsarevich wear military uniform while the women are dressed in contemporary clothes. In other icons the Tsar is depicted on his own. The facial features—the famous blue-grey eyes, moustache, and beard—are recognizably those of Nicholas, but he also wears the traditional Muscovite crown, the cap of Monomakh, and the Muscovite court dress of wide, richly colored kaftan. Such icons, argues Wendy Slater in her book *The Many Deaths of Tsar Nicholas II,* create a visual link between Nicholas and his role model, Tsar Alexei Mikhailovich (1645–76), the second Romanov ruler, after whom the Tsarevich Alexei had been named. Such icons are also reminiscent of a photograph of Nicholas widely disseminated during his reign, in which he is dressed as Alexei Mikhailovich for the costume ball of February 1903. Reproductions of this famous photograph have been sold at church stalls as an icon, called the "Tsar-Martyr."

The process leading toward the canonization of the imperial family was not unlike that leading to the glorification of Serafim of Sarov—in that it was inspired to a large extent by popular devotion, with the Russian church authorities seeming to lag behind. The question as to whether Nicholas II should be officially canonized had been under discussion in the Moscow Patriarchate since at least 1990, proponents of the canonization disseminating many stories in which the late Tsar miraculously intervened in people's lives. These stories were broadcast on the conservative religious radio station Radio Radonezh, sold at church kiosks in the form of booklets, and disseminated both electronically and in print. The kinds of problem the miracle narratives address reflect issues in contemporary Russian society—in particular, those concerning housing. Wendy Slater cites the example of a woman who told how she was able to exchange her communal flat for more suitable accommodation after praying to the "Imperial Martyrs." The miracle narratives also include numerous stories in which the Tsar appears in a dream. Slater suggests it may be that the prevalence of physical representations of Nicholas in popular contemporary Russian culture—in icons, photographs, or films—predisposes people to see him in dreams. He always looks like the popular image of him, so that his "kind eyes" make a particular impression on the narrator of the dream.

A particularly appealing narrative has appeared at least three times in collections of miracle stories. In this narrative a woman called Nina Kartashova tells how, when she was ill with pneumonia, she saw a young nurse, aged about seventeen, in her bedroom. The nurse gave her name as "Maria" and spoke with a Petersburg accent. She covered the sick woman with an officer's greatcoat, which she said belonged to her Papa, and remarked: "You'll be quite well today. Papa told me. Today it's his birthday." When Nina Kartashova woke the next morning, she found a branch of fresh lilac in a vase, and a rosary, which had belonged to her late grandmother and was buried with her, hanging on an icon of Christ in her bedroom.

Miracles associated with icons—weeping with a fragrant myrrh or appearing to bleed—also played an important part in the campaign for the family's canonization. Holy Synod deliberated throughout the 1990s—and famously refused to endorse the reburial of the "Ekaterinburg remains" in the Peter and Paul Cathedral in 1998. But finally on August 14, 2000, at a great ceremony in Moscow's newly rebuilt Cathedral of Christ the Saviour, Nicholas, Alexandra, and their five children, along with over a thousand other twentieth-century "new martyrs," who had perished under the Soviets, were canonized.

A particular area of controversy surrounding the canonization concerns the decision not to canonize the imperial family's servants who died with them—the court physician Dr. Evgeny Botkin, Alexandra's maid Anna Demidova, the footman Alexei Trupp, and the cook Ivan Kharitonov. The Synodal Commission on the Canonization had argued that the servants had followed the Tsar into exile out of a sense of duty and therefore did not deserve to be made saints. The émigré historian, Dmitry Pospielovsky, one of the few to write critically of the canonization in the Russian media, found this extraordinary: Surely, he argued, it was the servants who chose to accompany the Tsar to his fate who should be glorified, not the Tsar and his family who had no choice in what happened to them. The fact that Trupp was a Roman Catholic also seems to have presented a problem for the canonization commission.

The Russian Orthodox Church has still not officially recognized the so-called "Ekaterinburg remains," despite almost overwhelming scientific evidence in support of the identification. (The most recent evidence has included samples of DNA taken from the bloodstained shirt Nicky was wearing when he was attacked in Otsu in 1891, which was discovered in the Hermitage Museum in 2008.) The Church's position in 2007 seemed to be that, as nobody prayed in front of the remains and there were no miracles attributed to them, they could not be the relics of saints. It seems to be largely a question of authority, the Church not wanting to lose control of the narrative to the state.

The Orthodox Church has always been at pains to emphasize that the canonization of the imperial family as "Holy Royal Passion-Bearers" is not intended as an endorsement of autocracy or of Nicholas's reign. Rather, it is a recognition of the saintly way in which the individuals concerned conducted themselves in captivity and of the Christian manner of their deaths. Neither are they officially to be regarded as martyrs (though unofficially they frequently are) as they were not killed specifically on account of their faith but for political reasons. By designating them as "passion-bearers," the Church has also placed them in a tradition of holy Russian royals, the first "passion-bearers" having been the first national Russian saints, Princes Boris and Gleb, who died in internecine dynastic conflict in 1015 and were canonized in 1072. As Wendy Slater has pointed out, the medieval hagiographies of Boris and Gleb highlight both their nonresistance to violence and their joyful acceptance of suffering in imitation of Christ—not unlike the idealized versions of Nicholas and Alexandra.

> *In that day will I raise up the tabernacle of David that is fallen, and close up the breaches thereof; and I will raise up his ruins, and I will build it as in the days of old.* [Amos 9: 11]

On the site where the Ipatiev House once stood there is now a magnificent cathedral—the Church on Blood in Honour of All Saints Resplendent in the Russian Land, comprising two churches, a belfry, a patriarchal annex, and a museum dedicated to the imperial family—and at the site where the bodies were disposed of, the Monastery of the Royal Passion-Bearers has been constructed. Part of the monastery complex was destroyed in a fire in September 2010, but restoration is already under way.

> *And saviours shall come up on mount Zion to judge the mount of Esau; and the kingdom shall be the Lord's.* [Obadiah 21]

This is the last verse of The Book of the Prophet Obadiah, the last verse that Alix and Tatiana read together that July morning. It contains a promise, and is reminiscent of the well-known saying attributed to Julian of Norwich—that "all shall be well, and all shall be well, and all manner of thing shall be well." It would have brought comfort to its readers on July 16, 1918, and their faith would have ensured that these words would not have lost their validity, their call to belief, even if Alix and Tatiana could have seen what was to befall them, their family, and faithful servants within a few hours.

A question that inevitably suggests itself, now that the Orthodox Church sees itself as triumphant in Russia, having seen off eighty years of state atheism, and that the late imperial family has become an accepted part of Orthodox devotion, is whether the lives and deaths of Nicholas, Alexandra, Olga, Tatiana, Maria, Anastasia, and Alexei may indeed be interpreted as examples of victory contained in defeat, of the resurrection that first requires a death. In 1981 a special issue of the magazine *Orthodox America* contained the following assertion: "In 1917, Metropolitan Macarius of Moscow saw in a vision the Saviour speaking to Tsar Nicholas: *You see,* said the Lord, *two cups in my hands: one is bitter for your people, and the other is sweet for you.* In the vision the Tsar begged for the bitter cup. The Saviour then took a large glowing coal from the cup and put it in the Tsar's hands. The Tsar's whole body then began to grow light, until he was shining like a radiant spirit. Then the vision changed to a field of flowers, in the middle of which Nicholas was distributing manna to a multitude of people. A voice spoke: *The Tsar has taken the guilt of the Russian people upon himself and the Russian people is forgiven.*" Perhaps it was during his own "passion" that the ex-Tsar came closest to his people. And perhaps through the recollection of this passive suffering those people oppressed by the Soviet system—particularly religious believers—were able to grasp him as an invisible icon, recognizing in the imperial family a quality found in St. Serafim, and in the image of *Christ Bound*

Before the People—an embracing of the role of victim. With all its ambiguities, this, I would suggest, accounts in great part for the strength of devotion to the Holy Royal Passion-Bearers felt by Russian believers who have witnessed the suffering of a persecuted Church and who continue to experience difficulties in their daily lives. And it is perhaps in a sense fitting that Nicholas and Alexandra, who set such store by their belief in the Orthodox "common people," should themselves have become an object of veneration for so many of them. There will be many who conclude that those who see the death of Nicholas II as sacrificial and who venerate the icons of the Holy Royal Passion-Bearers are as deluded as were the figures portrayed on them when they put their faith in a French charlatan and a Siberian peasant. Others will be less sure, having learned at least one thing from the lives of Alix and her beloved Nicky—that simple explanations can be misleading, that human beings are infinitely complex, as is their relation with historical events, and no conclusion can be drawn that is not contingent. The image of Nicholas and his family that the faithful have chosen to remember, to the exclusion of other more ambivalent images, is that encapsulated in the final words of Alix's letter to her husband of March 3, 1917, when she had just learned of his abdication: "I hold you tight, tight in my arms and will never let them touch your shining soul."

ACKNOWLEDGMENTS

A number of organisations and individuals have assisted me in keeping body and soul together during the writing of this book. I am grateful to the Authors' Foundation for the award of the Elizabeth Longford Grant, generously sponsored in affectionate memory of Elizabeth Longford by Flora Fraser and Peter Soros, and to the Trustees of the London Library Trust for subsidising my membership of that wonderful resource. Further financial support came from many of my friends, and I would like to record my thanks to the following (and I hope they will enjoy the result of my labours): Sir Gavyn Arthur, Bibi Basch, Alan Birchenough and Hazel Bartram-Birchenough, Bernard Carey, Geoffrey and Irina Cowley, Monica Darnbrough, Jan Dawson, Martin Dudley, Kelly Freeman and Doug Broom, Andrew Gillett, Mike Granatt, Janis Higgie and John Watson, Francis Ingham, Ian and Kyung Ae Kelly, Nick and Sarah Kelsey, Emma Kirkby, Dominique Lazanski and Marc Sidwell, Dennis and Debbie Lee, Charles Medlam and Ingrid Seifert, Brian and Janet Moore, Una Riley and Doug Milburn, Tony and Anthea Peck, Beatrice and Anthony Perch, Suzanne and Richard Plaskett, Leigh Richards, Timothy Statham, and Alexandre Tissot-Demidov (who also provided me with a photograph of the Tsar from his private collection). I am additionally very grateful to Alexandre Tissot-Demidov and to the British Association, Russian Grand Priory of the Order of St. John of Jerusalem for bearing the reproduction costs of all the other photographs used in the book.

I have benefited from useful conversations with, among others: Professor Simon Dixon of UCL School of Slavonic and East European Studies; Mr Murray

Craig, Clerk of the Chamberlain's Court, City of London Corporation, who supplied me with an account of the resolution for the Lord Mayor to present the Tsar with 'an Address of Welcome in a suitable Gold Box' in 1909; Professor Richard Price of Heythrop College, who gave me a copy of his paper on the canonization of Serafim of Sarov; and Dr Martin Dudley, who carried out some research for me on Tsar Nicholas in his military role.

I have been particularly inspired by many of my students at the Courtauld Institute of Art, where I have been a Royal Literary Fund Fellow over the last three years (and hence throughout the writing of this book). While ostensibly helping them with the writing of their essays and dissertations, I frequently found our conversations of far more help in my own work than they can ever have imagined. So thank you all—and especially Ayla, Wolf, Shir, Liz, Elisabetta, Andrey, Pei-Kuei, Mary, Anita, Chloé, MaryKate, Svetlana, Julia, Ana, Alisa, Tatiana, and Maria.

I also wish to record my thanks to my editor, Charles Spicer; his former assistant, Yaniv Soha; and all the other helpful people at St. Martin's Press, and to my agent, Clare Alexander.

The correspondence of Nicky and Alix is preserved in GARF (the *Gosudarstvennyi Arkhiv Rossiiskoi Federatsii* or State Archive of the Russian Federation). Their wartime correspondence has been collected and published in an edition by Joseph T. Fuhrmann; many letters and diary entries from other periods of their lives are to be found in a collection of materials compiled by Andrei Maylunas and Sergei Mironenko, which includes translations from original documents (such as KR's diary) by Darya Galy. Translations from Alexandre Spiridovitch's *Les Dernières Années de la Cour de Tzarskoïe Selo,* and from Maria Fyodorovna's diary, are my own.

NOTES

1: SETTING THE SCENE: THE ROMANOV TERCENTENARY

1 "The final curtain" Osip Mandelstam, *Stone,* Robert Tracy, tr. and ed., Princeton University Press, Princeton, 1981, 155.

3 "With his usual simplicity . . . Charming" Bernard Pares, *The Fall of the Russian Monarchy: A Study of the Evidence,* Jonathan Cape, London, 1939, 31.

3 "that clear, deep, expressive look" Maylunas, Andrei, and Sergei Mironenko, eds., *A Lifelong Passion: Nicolas and Alexandra, Their Own Story,* Weidenfeld & Nicolson, London, 1996, 106.

3 "large radiant grey eyes" Sergei Oldenburg, *Last Tsar: Nicholas II, His Reign and His Russia,* Mihalap, Leonid I., and Patrick J. Rollins, tr., Patrick J. Rollins, ed., Academic International Press, Florida, 1975–8, Vol. 1, 39.

3 "large grey eyes" Hélène Vacaresco, *Kings and Queens I Have Known,* Harper & Brothers Publishers, New York, London, 1904, 154.

3 "beauty of his frank blue eyes" Pares, *The Fall of the Russian Monarchy,* 31.

3 "usually of a velvety" Vladimir Kokovtsov, *Out Of My Past: The Memoirs of Count Kokovtsov,* H. H. Fisher, ed., L Matveev, tr., Stanford University Press/OUP, Palo Alto, California, and Oxford, UK, 1935, 478.

6 "Once two Ministers" W. T. Stead in Joseph O. Baylen, *The Tsar's "Lecturer-General": W. T. Stead and the Russian Revolution of 1905, with Two Unpublished Memoranda of Audiences with the Dowager Empress Marie Fedorovna and Nicholas II,* Research Paper Number 23, Georgia State College, Atlanta, Georgia, 1969, 39–40.

5 "golden, good, darling Papa" Maylunas and Mironenko, 406.

5 "Love you always" Ibid., 377.

5 "If you happened to be sitting" Alexander Mossolov, *At the Court of the Last Tsar,* Methuen & Co., London, 1935, 64.

5 "extremely idle" Pierre Gilliard, *Thirteen Years at the Russian Court,* Hutchinson & Co., London, 1921, 76.

5 "fat little bowwow" Ibid., 75.

5 "large and beautiful grey eyes" Ibid.

6 "the governess" Alexandre Spiridovitch, *Les Dernières Années de la Cour de Tzarskoïe Selo,* Payot, Paris, 1928–9, Vol. 2, 453.

6 "My children are growing up" H.D.A. Major, *The Life and Letters of William Boyd Carpenter [Bishop of Ripon, Chaplain to Queen Victoria, and Clerk of the Closet to Edward VII, & George V],* John Murray, London, 1925, 264.

6 "Alexei Nikolaevich was the centre" Gillard, 72.

7 "Our faces are like the screech" John E. Bowlt and Olga Matich, eds., *Laboratory of Dreams: The Russian Avant-Garde and Cultural Experiment,* Stanford University Press, Palo Alto, California, 1996, 53.

8 "Some actors spoke" James H. Billington, *The Icon and the Axe: An Interpretive History of Russian Culture,* Weidenfeld & Nicolson, London, 1966, 499.

9 "Give us twenty years" Oldenburg, Vol. 3, 140.

9 "Descriptions of the Tsar's personal life" Richard Wortman "Publicizing the Imperial Image in 1913," in Laura Engelstein and Stephanie Sandler, eds., *Self and Story in Russian History,* Cornell University Press, Ithaca, New York, 2000, 95.

9 "as ugly as possible" quoted in Engelstein and Sandler, 96.

10 "homey grandmotherly character" Ibid., 118.

11 "dark raspberry silk" quoted in Edvard Radzinsky, *Rasputin: The Last Word,* Judson Rosengrant, tr., Weidenfeld & Nicolson, London, 2000, 192.

13 "The Emperor showed" Pares, *The Fall of the Russian Monarchy,* 156.

13 "nerves were tense" Spiridovitch, Vol. 2, 351.

13 "It was magnificent" Maylunas and Mironenko, 377.

13 "Rasputin was standing" Ibid.

14 "Back home, the imperial family" Spiridovitch, Vol. 2, 356.

14 "waving his arms" Maylunas and Mironenko, 379.

15 "nicest of the four" Alexander, Grand Duke of Russia, *Once a Grand Duke,* Cosmopolitan Book Corporation, Farrar & Rinehart, New York, 1932, 140.

15 "What example could we give" Maylunas and Mironenko, 363.

16 "I felt that though" Kokovtsov, 378.

17 "His Majesty never interrupted" Ibid., 456.

2: THE EMPRESS'S ILLNESS, AND HER FRIEND ANIA

19 "quite delightful . . . dropped" Maylunas and Mironenko, 15–6.

19 "that awful pain" Ibid., 31.

19 "those awful pains" Ibid., 81.

19 "we went into the boat . . . swim properly" Ibid. 84.

20 "She has to lie down . . . Her dear father's death" Ibid., 70.

20 "Darling Alixey is" Ibid., 90.

20 "I suffered so" Ibid., 81.

21 "I have just returned" Ibid., 82–3.

21 "This happens to her" Ibid., 103.

21 "Looking at the proud faces" *Once A Grand Duke,* 42.

22 "Dear Alix woke up . . . Dear Alix still has" Maylunas and Mironenko, 123–5.

22 "I was good" Ibid., 209.

22 "my old legs" Ibid., 278.

22 "Doctor just made" Ibid., 307.

23 "the months of physical" *Life and Letters of William Boyd Carpenter,* 263.

23 "For the first time" Maylunas and Mironenko, 351.

23 "Our brief survey" Röhl, John C.G., Martin Warren, and David Hunt, *Purple Secret: Genes, 'Madness' & the Royal Houses of Europe,* Bantam Press, London, 1998, 102–3.

24 "Patients can become hypersensitive" Ibid., 244.

24 "The [Empress] is still feeling weak" Maylunas and Mironenko, 318.

24 "The Tsar said" Ibid., 319.

24–25 "periodic changes . . . mainly by a state" Spiridovitch, Vol. 1, 348–9.

25 "I asked [the Emperor]" Maylunas and Mironenko, 343.

26 "splendid, huge little girl" Maylunas and Mironenko, 154.

27 "of the cardiac muscle" Spiridovich, Vol. 1, 349.

27 "poor Nicky is preoccupied" Ibid., 328.

27 "I am so sorry" Ibid., 364.

27 "In the case of the Empress" Spiridovitch, Vol. 1, 348–9.

28 "The neuro-vascular phenomena" Ibid., 349.

28 "our neurasthenic Empress" Count Witte, *Memoirs,* Sidney Harcave, tr. M. E. Sharpe, London, 1990, 359.

28 "It was this hystero-neurasthenic illness" Spiridovitch, Vol. 1, 349.

28 "The presence of someone" Ibid., 375.

29 "My heart aches" Maylunas and Mironenko, 322.

29 "The last part of our stay" Anna Viroubova, *Memories of the Russian Court,* Macmillan, London, 1923, 40.

29 "I am always . . . Was it nice" Maylunas and Mironenko, 320.

30 "My childish impression" Viroubova, *Memories,* 2.

30 "a lovely contralto voice . . . for some strange reason" Ibid., 28.

30 "charmed all those present . . . It was said" Spiridovitch, Vol. 1, 102.

31 "broken down the wall" Viroubova, *Memories,* 23.

31 "Ania, although she had a sweet" Countess Nostitz, *Romance and Revolutions,* Hutchinson, London, 1937, 87.

32 "signed by important people" Spiridovitch, Vol. 2, 207.

32 "It is a hard thing" Viroubova, *Memories,* 32.

32 "After a year" Ibid., 34.

33 "Positioned in the angle" Spiridovitch, Vol. 2, 207.

3: MYSTICAL CIRCLES, AND THE STRUGGLE TO PRODUCE AN HEIR

34 "A great and unforgettable day" Maylunas and Mironenko, 243.

34 "At about 3 o'clock . . . Luckily Alix felt" Ibid., 206.

35 "Alix feels splendid" Ibid.

35 "May is making" Ibid., 224.

36 House of Romanov album *Rossiiskii imperatorskii dom: [al'bom portretov]*, Petersburg, 1902.

37 "a wonderful few hours" Maylunas and Mironenko, 206.

37 "The Frenchman Philippe" Spiridovitch, Vol. 1, 99.

37 "a man of about fifty" Maylunas and Mironenko, 219.

37 "Immediately after dinner" Ibid., 207.

37 "During his stays in Russia" Spiridovitch, Vol. 1, 101.

38 "One day as my father" Felix Yusupov, *Lost Splendour,* Jonathan Cape, London, 1953.

39 "on the whole a clever man" Witte, 301.

39 "with great sadness" Maylunas and Mironenko, 207.

39 "How rich life is" Ibid., 208.

39 "Our dear Friend" Ibid., 216.

40 "You talk to Mama" Ibid., 214.

40–41 "We drove round . . . I am sure my answers" Ibid., 216–7.

41 "I know by your looks . . . My broad waist" Ibid., 214.

41 "luckily everything internally . . . I can just imagine" Ibid., 217.

41–42 "cried terribly . . . she told him everything" Ibid.

42 "own beloved Wify . . . The first speech" Ibid., 220.

42 "Your precious letter" Ibid., 220–1.

43 "Mama and I talked" Ibid., 218.

43 "My personal opinion" Ibid., 220.

43 "suggestion" Ibid., 221.

44 "a wall . . . smiling sweetly" Ibid.

44 "I can see you" Ibid., 222.

44 "the image of the Virgin" Ibid.

44 "aroused by malice and enmity" quoted in Oleg Tarasov, *Icon and Devotion: Sacred Spaces in Imperial Russia,* Robin Milner-Gulland, tr. and ed., Reaktion Books, London, 2002, 81.

45 "superstitious ignorance" Gregory L. Freeze, "Subversive Piety: Religion & the Political Crisis in Late Imperial Russia" in *The Journal of Modern History,* Vol. 68, No. 2, June 1996, 317.

46 "There was something very special" Maylunas and Mironenko, 229.

46 "It was a very solemn moment" Ibid., 230.

47 "My new country" Major, 262.

47 "bread is nowhere" quoted in Freeze, 326.

47 "One felt an enormous lift" Maylunas and Mironenko, 230.

47 "Then we went in twos" Ibid.

48–49 "She has become terribly thin" Ibid., 232.

49 "soon he will die" Ibid., 219.

49 "wonderfully beautiful" Ibid., 241.

49 "simple men" Ibid.

50 "Contemptuous nicknames" Kokovtsov, 9.

50 "The attitude of almost everybody" Alexandre Benois, *Memoirs,* Vol. 2, Moura Budberg, tr., Chatto & Windus, London, 1964, 214.

50–51 "I have known you . . . not hesitating lest" Kokovtsov, 11–2.

51 "great and unforgettable day" Maylunas and Mironenko, 243.

51 "A band did its best" Lord Brooke, *An Eye-Witness in Manchuria,* Eveleigh Nash, London, 1905, 88.

51 "God never forgets one" Maylunas and Mironenko, 244.

51 "He's an amazingly hefty baby" Ibid., 245.

52 "the terrible illness" Ibid., 240.

52 For more on the Romanov genotype analysis, see M. D. Coble, S. M. Edson, O. M. Loreille, K. Maynard, M. J. Wadhams, et al., *Mystery Solved: The Identification of the Two Missing Romanov Children Using DNA Analysis,* PLoS ONE 4(3):e4838. doi:10.1371/journal.pone.0004838, 2009.

52 "by his healthy appearance" Maylunas and Mironenko, 248.

52 "our dear Friend . . . Thank God" Ibid., 249.

52 "Nobody ever knew" Grand Duchess Marie of Russia, *Education of a Princess,* Blue Ribbon Books Inc., New York, 1930, 61.

53 "It does not require . . . To be called out" *The Times,* October 23, 1904.
53 "A blizzard and intense cold" *The Times,* December 29, 1904.
53 "The disturbance is increasing" Maylunas and Mironenko, 251.

4: AUTOCRACY IN CRISIS

54 "a working man . . . the Tsar was our father" *The Times,* January 25, 1905.
55 "some aspects" Kokovtsov, 35.
56 "when the disturbances" Maylunas and Mironenko, 257.
56 "some priest" Ibid., 256.
56 "that pig Gapon" W. T. Stead in Baylen, 66.
56 "From the conversations" Kokovtsov, 37.
57 "A terrible day!" Maylunas and Mironenko, 256.
57 "he did take their interests" Kokovtsov, 38.
57 "believing that he personally" Ibid., 39.
57 "If this is so" Ibid.
58 "strikes and revolutionary demonstrations . . . pardoned their transgression" *The Times,* February 2, 1905.
58 "The workers expressed" Kokovtsov, 40.
59 "greatly depressed" Ibid., 49.
59 "I am ready" Ibid., 55.
59 "Mama asked Nicky" Maylunas and Mironenko, 280.
60 "And so the Emperor" Ibid.
60 "inconsolable . . . in Moscow" Ibid., 267.
60 "I think that" Ibid.
62 "These rooms, light and spacious" Marie, 34.
64 "from day to day" *The Times,* October 12, 1905.
64 "huge unwieldy machine" Ibid.
65 "still a beautiful woman" Gilliard, 19.
65 "At that time" Spiridovitch, Vol. 1, 43–4.
65 "very fair . . . less transparent" Gilliard, 20.
65 "one of the handsomest . . . a solemn, frightened look" Ibid., 26.
66 "A court valet" Spiridovitch, Vol. 1, 66.
67 "If, despite everything" Ibid., 71.
68 "no untoward incident" Ibid., 196.
69 "The man's an imbecile . . . I myself sat" Ibid., 197.
70 "an irreparable loss" Ibid., 147.
71 "It's terrible, terrible" Maylunas and Mironenko, 277.
72 "Looking back" Alexander, 144.

72 "The welfare of the Russian Sovereign" Oldenburg, Vol. 2, 162.
73 "We call upon" Ibid.
73 "Telegrams are arriving" Maylunas and Mironenko, 283.
73 "At Kherson the mob" *The Times,* November 3, 1905.
73 "in many parts" Ibid.
74 "The disturbances were" *The Times,* November 4, 1905.
74 "The manifesto that I issued" Oldenburg, Vol. 2, 177.
74 "When Nicholas II comes" *The Times,* October 12, 1905.
75 "common sense . . . settle down to work" Kokovtsov, 112.
76 "dressed in a worker's blouse" Ibid., 130.
76 "in a loud steady voice . . . his self-control finally overcome" Maylunas and Mironenko, 293.
77 "unpleasant . . . something about him" Ibid., 272.
77 "taken a personal dislike" Alexandre Benois, Vol. 2, 230.
77 "Nicky was delighted" Maylunas and Mironenko, 293.
78 "I have been forced" Kokovtsov, 77.
78 "When I had explained" Ibid., 75.
78 "I keep trying" quoted in Oldenburg, Vol. 2, 172–3.
78 "an old courtier" Alexander, 227.
79 "He received me" Kokovtsov, 89.
79 "He tries to explain" Ibid., 90.
80 "Despite most convincing arguments" Ibid., 167.
80 "I wish to stand" Ibid., 102.
81 "Russia Revisited" *The Times,* August 18, 1906.
82 "the Duma of national ignorance" quoted in Oldenburg, Vol. 2, 228.
83 "So—it's a coup-d'état" Maylunas and Mironenko, 303.
83 "luminous" Ibid.
83 "generally ill-disposed" Ibid., 282.
83 "I feel with all my being . . . I hardly have the strength" Ibid., 294.
84 "of a far more serious character" Spiridovitch, Vol. 1, 126.
85 "absolutely refused . . . beside herself" Maylunas and Mironenko, 301.
85 "If it's because . . . I have suffered greatly" Ibid., 302.
86 "We had tea" Ibid., 284.
86 "I very much hope" Ibid., 297.
86 "Stana and Militsa came to dinner" Ibid.
86 "the Grand Duke's servants" Spiridovich, Vol. 1, 98.
87 "broken speech" Kokovtsov, 450.
87 "He began to tell her" Ibid.

87 "He openly yet simply" *The Times,* August 18, 1906.

88 "[Karatayev] would often say" Leo Tolstoy, *War and Peace,* Rosemary Edmonds, tr., Penguin Books, Harmondsworth, 1972, 1152.

88 "about Nicholas II do I know" *The Times,* August 29, 1905.

88 "If Count Tolstoy . . . I have no hesitation" *The Times,* October 12, 1905.

90 "ISFJs bring an aura" http://www.personalitypathways.com/type_inventory.html#Inventory.

90 "They feel useful when" Danielle Poirier, Rebel Eagle Productions, www.RebelEagle.com.

90 "They tend to be rather modest" Ibid.

90 "They tend to like to stay" Ibid.

90 "They tend to shy away" Ibid.

90 "primarily toward the inner world" http://www.teamtechnology.co.uk/mmdi/questionnaire/.

90 "They are notoriously bad" Marina Margaret Heiss, www.typelogic.com.

90 "While their work ethic" Ibid.

90 "ISFJs are extremely warm" Ibid.

90 "If any of their nearest" Ibid.

91 "ISFJs have a few, close friends" Ibid.

91 "They hate confrontation" Ibid.

91 "ISFJs make pleasant" Ibid.

91 "ISFJs are traditional" http://sminds.com/cgi-bin/mbti.pl.

5: BEGINNINGS

92 "Sandro, what am I" Alexander, 168–9.

93 "as Papa is still . . . the very best ladies" Maylunas and Mironenko, 43.

93 "I frequently disagreed" Alexander, 25.

93 "deathly pale" Ibid., 59.

94 "the usual fear" Alexandre Benois, Vol. 2, 50.

94 "The glance of a man" Ibid., 52.

95 "the education of a prince . . . Under such circumstances" Gilliard, 86–7.

97 "there is nothing to be anxious about" Maylunas and Mironenko, 91.

97 "I don't know" Ibid.

97 "very nice and comforting" Ibid.

97 "Of course, it is too hard" Ibid., 95–6.

98 "Darling Boysy" Ibid., 98.

99 "I felt as if" Ibid., 99.

99 "a sweet, merry little person" Alice, Grand Duchess of Hesse, *Letters to Her Majesty the Queen,* John Murray, London, 1885, 248.

100 "The horror of my Darling's sudden death" Ibid., 265.
100 "We others quite liked" David Duff, *Hessian Tapestry*, Frederick Muller, London, 1967, 198.
101 "romping . . . pretty little Alix" Maylunas and Mironenko, 10.
101 "The desire to get married" Ibid., 11.
101 "so awfully especially" Ibid., 16.
102 "nobody else will know" Ibid., 17.
102 "My dream" Ibid., 20.
102 "After tea I crept" Ibid., 22.
102 "Would it be right" Ibid.
103 "My trip is senseless" Alexander, 167.
104 "slapped his own forehead" George Alexander Lensen, "The Attempt on the Life of Nicholas II in Japan" in *Russian Review*, Vol. 20, No. 3, 1961, 243–4.
105 "particularly uncomfortable . . . died of heat" Maylunas and Mironenko, 26.
105 "a whole bevy . . . He is very funny" Ibid., 27.
106 "a round ball" Ibid., 28.
106 "I am getting quite tired" Ibid.
106 "so utterly miserable" Ibid., 30.
106 "What happiness can come" Ibid., 32.
107 "I am certain" Ibid., 33.
107 "Yes, it is hard" Ibid.
107 "four-day binge" Ibid.
107 "I could not write . . . Ever your loving and devoted Nicky" Ibid., 34.
108 "life indeed will be" Ibid., 35.
108 "I had a lot of fun" Ibid., 44.
109 "Darling, why did you . . . would only be in their way" Ibid., 45.
109 "There was a whole" Ibid., 46.
109 "My God!" Ibid.
109 "long and extremely difficult" Ibid., 48–9.
109 "with great pomp . . . I am weary" Ibid., 46.
110 "I touched as little" Ibid., 47.
110 "gave a splendid sermon" Ibid.
110 "A wonderful, unforgettable day" Ibid.
110 "she could not say" Ibid., 49.
110 "when it was my good fortune" Ibid., 139.
110 "Wilhelm sat in the next room" Ibid., 47.
110 "I have to say here" Ibid., 49.
111 "They left us alone . . . She has completely changed. . . . Alix is delightful" Ibid. 55–6.
111 "Words cannot express" Ibid., 50.

111 "I have to admit" Ibid., 52.
112 "Oh! it was too awful . . . What a delightful surprise" Ibid., 57.
112 "I feel very deeply" Ibid.
112 "I also feel shy" Ibid., 59.
112 "I must repeat" Ibid., 57.
112 "better not to hurry" Ibid., 63.
113 "with their beautiful big eyes" Ibid., 59.
113 "belly-woman . . . very grand and old-fashioned" Ibid., 67.
113 "I am on duty" Ibid., 68.
113 "While she is here" Ibid., 58–9.
114 "Of course it is in" Ibid., 67.
114 "she was completely transformed" Ibid., 64.
115 "He came quite alone" Duff, 236.
115 "the Windsor tailcoat . . . It seems funny" Maylunas and Mironenko, 78.
115 "sweated a lot" Ibid., 76.
115 "delighted at being in England" Ibid., 78.
115 "that little story . . . My own Boysy" Ibid., 80.
116 "I followed you" Ibid., 81.
116 "all the uncles . . . quite unfitting" Ibid., 100.
117 "My dear Alix" Ibid., 103.
117 "The young Tsar" Ibid.
117 "Nicky has been kindness itself" Ibid., 112.
117 "The crush was tremendous . . . The Empress with heroic courage" Ibid., 105.
118 "I keep feeling" Ibid., 108.
118 "The Emperor" Ibid, 110.
118 "Poor Aunt Minnie" Ibid., 111.
119 "The cheering was most hearty" Ibid., 112.
119 "dear unforgettable Papa . . . no one came" Ibid., 111.
119 "There is very little free time" Ibid., 115.
119 "He is so quiet" Ibid., 114.
119 "I am unbelievably happy" Ibid.
120 "It's inexpressibly wonderful" Ibid., 115.
120 "Read until 7.30" Ibid., 118.
120 "a nice little boy" Ibid., 127.
120 "the most natural" Ibid., 131.
120 "in a state . . . something hard and unpleasant" Ibid., 133.
121 "what a relief" Ibid., 141.
121 "Thank God, Alix coped" Ibid., 138.
121 "I suffered for dear Alix" Ibid.

121 "Alix stood up wonderfully" Ibid., 139.

121 "sweet and friendly" Ibid.

122 "the principles of autocracy" Ibid., 122.

122 "that fatal day" *The Times,* October 12, 1905.

122 "in a terrible state" Maylunas and Mironenko, 122.

123 "In general I am terribly fatigued" Ibid., 141.

123 "It needed no cannon-firing . . . the waving of a handkerchief" *The Times,* May 27, 1896.

125 "The Emperor has not" Ibid.

126 "The demeanour of the multitude" Ibid.

6: AFTER THE CORONATION

128 "It was awful" Maylunas and Mironenko, 145.

129 "about 1300 people . . . They say that by" Ibid.

129 "more than a thousand" Ibid., 147.

129 "I have been tormented" Ibid., 150.

129 "Nicky spent the first" Alexander, 173.

130 "Awoke with the wonderful realization" Maylunas and Mironenko, 150.

131 "easy mastery . . . green velvet mantle" *The Times,* October 10, 1896.

131 "The tsar's visage" Oldenburg, Vol. 1, 69.

131 "Nothing of the kind . . . In future, please spare me" Maylunas and Mironenko, 161.

131 "The uncles always wanted something" Alexander, 173.

132 "even when changing" Maylunas and Mironenko, 160.

133 "second bright happy day" Ibid., 163.

133 "everyone was very disappointed" Ibid.

133 "wonderful . . . just like her mother!" Ibid., 164.

133 "Our little daughters" Ibid., 166.

133 "It's noticeable" Ibid., 172.

134 "irrelevant in themselves . . . resented this malicious matching" Alexander, 169–70.

134 "Fancy Boysy is so sad" Maylunas and Mironenko, 176.

134 "Twice a week" Ibid., 177.

136 "lead inevitably . . . all governments" Oldenburg, Vol. 1, 106.

137 "The Tsar's illness" *The Times,* November 17, 1900.

137–38 "the physical development . . . incited and led astray" Maylunas and Mironenko, 155.

138 "Alix is feeling" Ibid., 184.

138 "A happy day" Ibid., 184–5.

139 "And so, there's no Heir" Ibid., 185.

139 "I am so thankful" Ibid., 186.
139 "Well! There's nothing" Ibid., 188.
140 "I do not want to let . . . three little cherubs" Ibid.
140 "The night was" Ibid., 189.
140 "I cannot describe" Ibid., 196.
142 "It's astounding" Ibid., 201.
142 "there is nothing worse" Ibid.
142 "Thank God" Ibid.
142 "at least the doctors" Ibid.
142 "[The Empress] is looking" Ibid., 204.
143 "in good spirits" Ibid., 209.
143 "flying the French flag . . . escorted by two large cruisers" *The Times,* September 19, 1901.
144 "The Standart, which is almost" Ibid.
144 "astrakhan hats . . . would be frightened" *The Times,* September 14, 1901.
144 "Suddenly to see all this" *The Times,* September 19, 1901.
145 "has been willing" *The Times,* September 23, 1901.
145 "Darling Chicken" Maylunas and Mironenko, 209.
145 "The tsar is benevolent . . . no love for parliaments" quoted in Oldenburg, Vol. 2, 53.
145 *"Yes, divorce"* Maylunas and Mironenko, 209.
146 "I completely agree" Ibid., 210.
146–47 "It is with a very heavy heart . . . It is doubly hard" Ibid.
147–48 "energetic . . . Don't be so gentle" Ibid., 213.
148 "honest" Ibid.
149 "The affair is made more complicated" Ibid., 222.
149–50 "unforgettable Papa . . . good old Imam" Ibid., 223.
150 "that stupid woman" Ibid., 224.
150 "for at least one night" Alexander, 211.

7: FAMILY MATTERS

151 "stupid neck . . . Tenderly and fondly" Maylunas and Mironenko, 304.
151–52 "I feel quite lonely . . . At table, Fredericks" Ibid., 304–5.
152 "continuation of kindred relations . . . the unchangeable friendship" Oldenburg, Vol. 3, 28–9.
152 "There was a tempestuous scene . . . in despair" Maylunas and Mironenko, 306.
152 "What harm our family . . . Where do we have" Ibid., 305.
153–54 "Slender, fragile, self-effacing" Mossolov, 60.
155 "Your turn, Derevenko!" Spiridovitch, Vol. 1, 265.
155 "She always spoke" Ibid., 267.

156 "There had been a particularly agreeable" Ibid., 269.
156 "His majesty has deigned" Ibid., 270.
157 "With all my heart" Maylunas and Mironenko, 315–6.
157 "be an example . . . Above all, learn to love God" Ibid., 318.
157–58 "Girlie mine . . . Now try your best" Ibid., 318–9.
158 "he has a bad leg . . . avoids getting tired" Ibid., 318.
158 "the Empress is very unwilling" Ibid., 319.
158 "When I saw him . . . In Alicky's boudoir" Ibid., 315.
159 "predestined to do something" Spiridovitch, Vol. 1, 290.
159 "How could they not trust" Ibid., 295.
160 "I'm glad you had him" Maylunas and Mironenko, 321.
160 "He is a wily peasant" Spiridovitch, Vol. 1, 296.
161 "We nevertheless greatly desired" Ibid., 298–9.
162 "To the Tsarevich" *The Times,* August 2, 1909.
163 "The treatment of the Empress" Spiridovitch, Vol. 1, 350.
163 "You will read these lines . . . never a word of rebuke" Maylunas and Mironenko, 321–2.
164 "long and lonely journey" Ibid., 322.
164 "I dread the moment . . . It is so hard" Ibid., 322–3.
165 "always to be good . . . I have no secrets" Ibid., 330.
165 "Your letter made me . . . Now do not think" Ibid., 330–1.
165 "Please forgive me . . . Please tell Papa" Ibid., 330.
166 "the attitude of Alix" Ibid., 331.
166 "a sex maniac" quoted in Simon Dixon, "The 'Mad Monk' Iliodor in Tsaritsyn" in *The Slavonic and East-European Review,* Vol. 88, Nos. 1/2, 2010, 397.
166 "He's always there . . . the most terrible rumours" Maylunas and Mironenko, 331.
167 "not all who seem" quoted in Dixon, "The 'Mad Monk' Iliodor in Tsaritsyn," 396.
167 "the pure always attract" Maylunas and Mironenko, 332.
167 "I have no intention" Ibid.
167 "all in white" Ibid., 333
168 "With a last touch" Yusupov, 123.
168 "Yes, dearest Nicky . . . there may be difficulties" Maylunas and Mironenko, 333–4.
168 "It is so sad" Ibid., 335.
169 "My little childy . . . It's not good" Ibid., 335–6.
170 "Loving thanks, Maria Darling" Ibid., 341.
171 "She spoke openly" Ibid., 342–3.
172 "I had not experienced" Ibid., 336.
173 "And what about me?" Spiridovitch, Vol. 2, 68.
174 "I really feel like" Ibid., 71.

174 "It was sufficient" Ibid., 16.
175 "two muffled detonations" Kokovtsov, 271.
175 "I was getting quite tired" Maylunas and Mironenko, 343.
175 "pale and agitated" Kokovtsov, 272.
176 "I returned to Kiev" Maylunas and Mironenko, 344.
177 "the yellow men . . . nature-lovers" Spiridovitch, Vol. 2, 137.
178 "I felt solid ground" Ibid., 138.
178 "The Empress had put" Ibid., 139.
178 "overshadowed his sovereign" Pares, *The Fall of the Russian Monarchy,* 125.
181 "During the years following" Gilliard, 26.
181 "The terrible disease" Spiridovitch, Vol. 1, 405.

8: GRIGORY THE WONDER-WORKER

183 "I went to see Alix" Maylunas and Mironenko, 344.
184 "A motion was tabled" Ibid.
184 "I reminded [Rodzianko]" Kokovtsov, 295.
184 "a great comfort" Maylunas and Mironenko, 344.
184 "In general everything" Ibid., 351.
185 "I made use of a visit" Kokovtsov, 291.
185 "demanding that he" Ibid., 292.
185 "Great was my astonishment" Ibid., 303.
186 "I do not wish" Ibid.
186 "to make it easier" Ibid., 304.
186 "At about five" Ibid.
186 "The Tsar was in his usual" Ibid.
187 "that terrible illness . . . As far as Grigory" Maylunas and Mironenko, 351.
187 "Recently, my wife" Ibid., 352.
187 "Finally, towards the end" Kokovtsov, 317.
187 "I was forced to undertake" Ibid., 317–8.
188 "The reception of the Duma members" Ibid., 318.
189 "This addition made" Ibid., 318–9.
189 "Got up early" Maylunas and Mironenko, 353.
189 "The sun was scorching" Kokovtsov, 321.
190 "The Tsar was in fine spirits" Ibid., 323.
190 "the official communiqué" Oldenburg, Vol. 3, 120.
190 "in pure Russian style" Kokovtsov, 449.
190 "She visited this room" Ibid.
190 "The Empress believed" Ibid.

191 "I told your wife" Maylunas and Mironenko, 353.
191 "The tour of the Borodino field" Ibid., 353–4.
192 "We did not spend" Ibid., 356.
192 "one shooting-party" Gilliard, 29.
192 "One evening after dinner" Ibid., 29–30.
193 "The days from . . . I could hardly bear" Maylunas and Mironenko, 358.
194 "I stayed in Alexei's room . . . On 10th October" Ibid.
194 "The illness does not" Spiridovitch, Vol. 2, 292.
194 "The mother" Ibid., 290.
194 "She withstood it" Maylunas and Mironenko, 358.
195 "There is not a single word" *The Times,* October 28, 1912.
195 "Our wedding took place" Maylunas and Mironenko, 360.
195 "*terrible cruel new blow* . . . I simply can't believe" Ibid., 362.
196 "Yes, dear Mama . . . My first thought" Ibid.
196 "Poor Misha is evidently" Ibid., 363.
197 "Neither the Emperor" Ibid., 366.
197 "Alexei Nikolaevich's condition" Gilliard, 32.
197 "I find it very painful" Spiridovitch, Vol. 2, 295.

9: UPSETS AT HOME, AND THE BEGINNING OF WAR

198 "Vladimir Nikolaevich" Kokovtsov, 418–9.
199 "Then as now" Ibid., 419.
199 "Both of us" Ibid., 422.
199 "Tell me again" Ibid., 425.
199 "I did not press" Ibid., 428.
199 "The Imperial Rescript" *The Times,* February 14, 1914.
200 "stories and love-scenes" Joseph T. Fuhrmann, ed., *The Complete Wartime Correspondence of Tsar Nicholas II and the Empress Alexandra, April 1914–March 1917,* Greenwood Press, Westport, Connecticut, 1999, 73.
200 "*horribly* . . . My heart is heavy" Ibid., 13.
200 "In letters written . . . I have, I think" Viroubova, 346–7.
201 "That season, everything" Spiridovitch, Vol. 2, 451.
201 "mop of badly combed hair" Ibid., 455.
202 "There was great excitement" Gilliard, 97.
202 "as impenetrable and cheerful" Spiridovitch, Vol. 2, 467.
202 "At exactly two o'clock" Maylunas and Mironenko, 392.
202 "I kept an eye" Maurice Paléologue, *An Ambassador's Memoirs,* Hutchinson, London, 1923–5, Vol. 1, 14.

203 "Meanwhile the Czarina" Gilliard, 106.
203 "Went for a walk" Maylunas and Mironenko, 398.
203 "Both you and I" Ibid.
203–04 "his appointment as Commander-in-Chief" Ibid. 394–5.
204 "He looked even worse" Gilliard, 106.
204 "good . . . particularly from" Maylunas and Mironenko, 397.
204 "I signed the manifesto" Ibid.
204–5 "The city was astir . . . was of delicate" Florence Farmborough, *Nurse at the Russian Front,* Futura Publications, London, 1977, 19–20.
205 "When Alexei" Gilliard, 113–14.
205 "The Imperial party" Farmborough, 20.
206 "humble folk . . . The crowd surged" Gilliard, 115.
206 "It was so pleasant . . . for a long time" Maylunas and Mironenko, 401.
206 "And then the shame . . . I must rejoice" Ibid.
207 "the big palace . . . face is tied up" Fuhrmann, 16–7.
207 "Bekker . . . the girlies" Fuhrmann, 18.
208 "so free . . . agoo wee one" Ibid., 20–1.
208 "victory . . . You have to take me" Maylunas and Mironenko, 401–2.
208 "Darling Papa" Ibid., 402.
208 "My brilliant Papa! . . . I don't want to go to bed" Ibid.
209 "Ania was offended" Fuhrmann, 21.
210 "Ania's leg is much better" Ibid., 24.
210 "She is not over amiable . . . She is surrounded" Ibid.
210 "What a curious person . . . No one else ever enters" Paléologue, Vol. 1, 229.
210–11 "Baby sweet . . . Very bad wounds" Fuhrmann, 28.
211 "Now O. & T." Ibid.
211 "bring people more to God . . . With the officers" Ibid., 29.
212 "as he says one must not . . . & give me some sort" Ibid., 35.
212 "grumbling . . . Be nice & firm" Ibid., 37.
213 "our soldier . . . Olga is hitting" Maylunas and Mironenko, 406.
213 "Please forgive me" Ibid.
213 "I am *quite* Russian" Ibid., 407.
213 "My very own boy! . . . You may pray" Ibid.
214 "I take all . . . Its not worth while" Fuhrmann, 41.
214 "This time I managed . . . Believe me, my sweet love" Ibid., 42.
214 "The one serious difficulty" Ibid., 45.
215 "I shall be so shy" Ibid., 41.
215–16 "The Great White Tsar" *The Times,* November 25, 1914.

216–17 "poor boy . . . Yes, God has helped me" Fuhrmann, 44.
217 "first big amputation . . . I had wretched fellows" Ibid., 46.
217 "Ania looked on so coolly . . . Its not a play" Ibid.
218 "When you comfort the wounded . . . So touching" Maylunas and Mironenko, 410.
218 "Hemorrhage" Fuhrmann, 53.
218 "most comforting" Ibid., 54.
218 "we women must all" Fuhrmann, 57.
218–19 "still very much enlarged . . . One says the Synod" Ibid., 62–3.
219 "I feel still not famous" Ibid., 65.
219 "We visited Ania" Maylunas and Mironenko, 416–7.
219–20 "She was nearly dead" Gilliard, 127–8.
220 "You, who know all . . . overtired" Major, 264–5.
220 "A . . . invalid . . . sorely" Fuhrmann, 68.
220 "Baby spent the day . . . must be sure" Ibid., 69.
221 "lovy, fr the very first . . . Ania gets on alright" Ibid., 76.
221–22 "I am so glad" Ibid. 79.
222 "God bless you" Ibid. 82.
222 "which even astonishes me . . . all the free hours pass" Ibid. 83.
223 "What an unexpected joy . . . It reminds one" Ibid., 84.
223 "The palace police" Gilliard, 126.
223 "I have told Vil'chkovsky" Fuhrmann, 85.
224–25 "Wify feels hideously sad . . . I am writing to you now" Ibid., 86.
225 "At the front" Ibid. 87.
225–26 "I met the Emperor . . . He inquired after" Sir John Hanbury-Williams, *The Emperor Nicholas II as I Knew Him,* Arthur L. Humphreys, London, 1922, 40–1.
226 "Yesterday N brought me" Fuhrmann, 88.
226 "I am sure this war" Ibid., 89.
226 "a good deal enlarged . . . I cannot do a thing" Ibid., 89–90.
226–27 "I so well understand . . . We have just returned" Ibid., 92.
227 "She is very put out . . . I was to burn hers" Ibid., 90–1.
227 "Give A my love" Ibid., 93.
227 "I at once sent" Ibid. 96.
227 "Dont you tell N" Ibid., 91.
227–8 "You seem to think" Ibid., 95.
228 "I see now why" Ibid., 96.
228 "I wish I were near you" Ibid., 91.
228 "our first Friend" Ibid., 149.
228–29 "slipped to the right . . . But its very cold" Ibid., 92–3.

229 "You see I am looking . . . Now enough about her" Ibid., 94–5.

230 "I went first" Maylunas and Mironenko, 421.

10: THE GREAT FIGHT

231 "What happiness to know" Fuhrmann, 98.

231–32 "Once more you are . . . Humility is God's greatest gift" Ibid., 100.

232 "It is so hard . . . I shall be careful" Ibid., 101.

232 "I felt very sad" Ibid., 103.

233 "Tatiana and Anastasia . . . This war can mean" Ibid., 102–3.

233 "Only give orders" Ibid., 102.

233 "The Dr. lets me . . . Well, Ania came" Ibid., 104–5.

234 "Au fond, our Friend" Ibid., 105.

234 "Does not like N" Ibid., 106.

234 "Darling mine" Ibid., 107.

234 "Well now all is settled" Ibid. 106.

234 "Have I not also" Ibid., 109.

234 "How the years go by! . . . I am finishing" Ibid., 108.

235 "Gr is rather disturbed . . . 40 days to-day!" Ibid., 111.

235 "Now I have read . . . And you have personally" Ibid., 112.

235 "in old Franz Joseph's bed . . . dug up with" Ibid., 114.

236 "Poor Ania has got again" Ibid., 116.

236 "very dear . . . asked lots" Ibid., 118.

236 "long, dear letter . . . unpleasant" Ibid., 119.

236 "enlarged" Ibid., 124.

236–37 "Yesterday evening Hagentorn" Ibid., 121.

237 "Hard not to be able . . . useful for the train" Ibid., 124.

237 "Slept not famously . . . still God will help" Ibid., 127.

237 "crystals . . . Ortipo climb" Ibid., 129.

237 "in a different tone . . . understand all" Ibid., 130.

237 "With the Emperor" Hanbury-Williams, 44.

237–38 "that is past . . . Poor N cried" Fuhrmann, 131–2.

238 "I have been feeling unwell" Maylunas and Mironenko, 424.

238 "It was sad" Ibid., 425.

239 "It is with a heavy heart . . . Sometimes a word" Fuhrmann, 134.

239–40 "I hope my letter" Ibid., 136.

240 "No, harken unto" Ibid., 135.

240 "turned against a man . . . yesterday it was very hot" Ibid., 138.

240 "He told me he" Ibid. 139.

240 “Thank God N understood . . . Forgive me, but I” Ibid., 141.

241 “Yes, my sweet one” Ibid., 139–40.

241 “I am sad your dear heart . . . walking at the shooting” Ibid., 149.

241 “He begs you most incessantly” Ibid., 141.

242 “I warned him” Ibid., 144.

242 “What concerns Danilov” Ibid., 152.

242 “I send you a stick” Ibid., 144.

242 “Remember to comb” Ibid., 176.

242 “Tho’ other Sovereigns . . . Finds, you ought to” Ibid., 144–5.

243 “During our talks” Ibid., 145–6.

243 “Town is so full . . . you are to pay less” Ibid., 146.

244 “I suffer hideously” Ibid.

244–45 “Yes, Lovy, about Samarin . . . Its not my brain” Ibid., 147.

245–46 “Just a few words . . . Reading this letter” Ibid., 147–9.

246–47 “Now the Duma . . . Do my long, grumbling” Ibid., 153.

247 “dear letters . . . calmed” Ibid., 157.

247–8 “Ah dear, he is not . . . Ah my Love” Ibid., 160–1.

248 “I fear I aggravate . . . Wonder what you have” Ibid., 162–3.

248 “Of course, this is only” Ibid., 163.

248 “Slept little this night” Ibid., 164.

248–9 “Saw Polivanov yesterday . . . bless the troops” Ibid., 165–6.

249–50 “Deary, I heard . . . Please answer me” Ibid., 166–7.

250 “Fear can’t meet you” Ibid., 169.

250 “retreat before the advancing enemy” Hanbury-Williams, 13.

250–51 “You have fought . . . Remember last night” Fuhrmann, 171–3.

252 “I pray for you both dearies” Maylunas and Mironenko, 432.

252 “Be firm to the end . . . the left are furious” Fuhrmann, 172–3.

252–3 “I do hope Gorem . . . I begged him not” Ibid., 177.

253 “I am delighted . . . fond love” Ibid., 182.

253 “Oh Sweetheart, I am so touched” Ibid., 188.

253 “Such calm filled my soul” Ibid., 174.

253 “Thank God it is all over” Ibid., 181.

253–4 “At 3.30 arrived” Maylunas and Mironenko, 435.

254 “N came in . . . Now begins” Fuhrmann, 181–2.

11: FROM COMMAND TO ABDICATION

255 “lives” Fuhrmann, 340.

255 “dares call you” Ibid., 341.

255–6 "I press you" Ibid., 350.
256 "lady thanks" Ibid., 355.
256 "Lovy, you burn" Ibid., 351.
256 "I always tear" Ibid., 357.
256 "queer" Ibid., 341.
256 "clearly and concisely" Ibid., 349.
257 "the cow . . . Goodbye Lovebird" Ibid., 380.
257 "A is sad" Ibid., 395.
257 "The Emperor after an absence" Hanbury-Williams, 83.
257 "cretinised" Fuhrmann, 393.
257 "electrifying" Ibid., 394.
257 "My eye has been hurting" Ibid., 418.
259 "One gets so bitterly disappointed" Ibid., 397.
259 "Sometimes my head" Ibid., 564.
259 "too old" Ibid., 349.
259 "plenty fresh enough" Ibid., 352.
259 "very much values" Ibid.
259 "scream . . . loyal" Ibid., 358.
259 "unlimited confidence" Ibid., 369.
259–60 "Sht[ürmer] has not yet" Ibid., 592.
260 "the red flag" Ibid., 645.
260 "All these days" Ibid., 647.
260 "completely" Ibid., 648.
260–61 "Stürmer being the Minister" Hanbury-Williams, 131.
261 "I remember even Buchanan" Fuhrmann, 648.
261 "so right in that way" Ibid., 649.
261 "good old sort . . . things will be difficult" Ibid.
261 "understand" Ibid.
261 "I am no longer" Ibid., 598.
261 "Lovy, look at their faces" Ibid., 665.
261 "You *know* you are right" Ibid.
262 "Be the *Master*" Ibid.
262 "Trepov flirts with Rodzianko" Ibid.
262–3 "Am so wretched" Ibid., 393.
262 "the devil . . . got hold of" Ibid.
262 "I smiled and thanked him" Ibid., 520.
263 "earnestly" Ibid., 574.
263 "Please, take Protopopov" Ibid., 577.

263 "I must think" Ibid.
263 "All these changes" Ibid.
263 "of the opposite clan" Ibid., 578.
263 "God bless yr new choice" Ibid., 582.
263 "nice, honest people . . . bad ideas" Ibid., 592.
263 "I dont see why" Ibid.
264 "arrange themselves" Ibid., 597.
264 "I don't see another way" Ibid., 593–4.
264 "I am afraid" Hanbury-Williams, 105.
264 "power of will" Fuhrmann, 609.
264 "he has to do" Ibid.
264 "When you get this one" Ibid., 649.
264–5 "Only please don't mix" Ibid., 650.
265 "put me awfully out . . . may not be clever" Ibid., 651.
265 "*Quieten* me, promise" Ibid., 652.
265 "Lovy, my Angel . . . Its difficult writing" Ibid., 653.
266 "Darling, remember that" Ibid., 653–4.
266 "an enemy" Ibid., 667.
266 "bad man . . . sure man" Ibid., 672.
266 "absolutely" Ibid., 409.
266 "simply a revolutionist" Ibid., 411.
266 "in serious times" Alfred Knox, *With the Russian Army 1914–1917,* Vol. 2, Hutchinson, London, 1921, 412.
267 "of a gentleman" Fuhrmann, 412.
267 "most obstinate" Ibid.
267 "a very weak man" Ibid., 560.
267 "exceedingly willing . . . try his best" Ibid., 562.
267 "he is always praying" Ibid., 351.
267 "I beg you not to tell" Ibid., 406.
267 "He begs we should not" Ibid., 488.
267 "A few days ago" Ibid., 491.
267 "I told Alexeev" Ibid., 493.
268 "he invariably met" A. I. Denikin, *The Russian Turmoil,* Hutchinson, London, 1922, 35.
268 "You must not be astonished" Fuhrmann, 493.
268 "Our Friend says about" Ibid., 601.
268 "much put out . . . useless losses" Ibid., 602.
268 "Just got your wire" Ibid., 603.

268 "a second Verdun" Ibid., 604.
268 "In any case our Friend says" Ibid., 612.
268 "an obstinate nuisance" Ibid., 352.
269 "He spoke with Raev" Ibid., 571.
269 "Lovy mine, don't dawdle" Ibid., 411.
269 "living notebook . . . Keep this paper" Ibid., 610.
269 "Tender thanks for your sweet letter" Ibid., 613.
269 "Oh, you precious Sunny" Ibid., 602.
269 "I pray so hard" Ibid., 569.
270 "In December 1916" Maylunas and Mironenko, 489.
271 "During the evening Bible" Fuhrmann, 437.
271 "many wonderful escapes" Ibid., 547.
271 "And the love for Christ" Ibid., 446.
271 "Ah, Lovy, I pray so hard" Ibid., 651.
272 "To follow our Friend's councils . . . if they later on change" Ibid., 658.
272 "Even the Children" Ibid., 678.
272 "Sometimes, swayed by" Maria Rasputin, *My Father,* Cassell & Co., London, 1934, 76.
273 "The stone was very great" Florence L. Barclay, *Through the Postern Gate: A Romance in Seven Days,* G. P. Putnam's Sons, New York, London, 1912, 268.
273 "I don't know why" Fuhrmann, 429.
273 "fancies herself in" Barclay, 86.
273 "upon a comfortable sofa" Ibid., 165.
273 "had a way of keeping" Ibid., 166.
273 "I am afraid" Fuhrmann, 579.
273 "Now a correspondence" Ibid., 589.
273 "help out at the war" Ibid., 595.
273 "more enlarged again" Ibid., 607.
273 "Babykins, you keep him" Ibid., 605.
274 "cups, bread, toast" Hanbury-Williams, 104.
274 "I heard the news" Ibid., 138–9.
274 "The Emperor himself" Ibid., 139.
274 "He dragged some of us" Ibid., 109–10.
275 "cannot simply imagine why . . . he meant & spoke well" Fuhrmann, 463.
275 "led astray by . . . Your first impulses" Reproduced at http://www.alexanderpalace.org/palace/lettersdukes.html.
275 "utterly disgusted" Fuhrmann, 640.
275 "as it becomes next" Ibid.

275 "He has always hated" Ibid.
275–6 "He is the incarnation" Ibid.
276 "He and Nikolasha" Ibid.
276 "I am really sorry" Ibid., 643.
276 "Well, promise me . . . That was the last occasion" Hanbury-Williams, 136.
276–7 "But God who is all love" Fuhrmann, 654.
277 "Only keep up" Ibid.
277 "Show to all" Ibid., 654–5.
277 "up to some wrong . . . the Michels" Ibid., 655.
277 "Always near you" Ibid., 658.
277 "Remember why I am disliked" Ibid., 672.
277 "Would I write thus" Ibid.
277 "I suffer over you" Ibid., 673.
278 "he rarely lost his" Hanbury-Williams, 126.
278 "Loving thanks" Fuhrmann, 676.
278 "your poor little huzy" Ibid., 677.
278 "Be Peter the Great" Ibid., 675.
278 "*It is not necessary*" Ibid., 678.
278 "It is *war*" Ibid., 675.
278 "we have been placed" Ibid., 676.
278 "Ever your very own" Ibid., 680.
278 "One must not speak" Ibid., 681.
278 "Tenderest love & kisses" Ibid., 683.
278 "I am so intensely happy" Ibid., 685.
278 "We are sitting together" Ibid., 683.
278–9 "In the morning Xenia" Maria Fyodorovna, *Dnevniki Imperatritsy Marii Fedorovny (1914–1920, 1923 gody),* Vagrius, Moscow, 2005, 163–4.
279 "Ducky came back" Ibid., 164.
279 "Dm[itry] wanted to let me know" Ibid.
279 "Little Maria came" Ibid., 166.
280 "If only the Lord" Ibid., 169.
280 "I talked openly" Ibid., 171.
280 "you cannot govern" Maylunas and Mironenko, 527.
280 "Your advisors continue" Ibid.
280 "totally ignorant" Alexander, 282.
281 "I spoke for a long time" Maylunas and Mironenko, 531.
281 "for the first time" Ibid., 532.
281 "The problem of the railways" Ibid., 533.

281 "Holy angels guard you" Fuhrmann, 687.

281 "What you write" Ibid., 689.

282 "Yesterday there were rows" Ibid., 690.

282 "a hooligan movement" Ibid., 692.

282 "this will all pass" Ibid.

282 "felt such peace" Ibid., 695.

282 "He died to save us" Ibid.

282 "immobilized by the curious behaviour" Allan K. Wildman, *The End of the Russian Imperial Army,* Princeton University Press, Princeton, New Jersey, 1980, 203.

282 "raised no questions" quoted in Ibid.

282 "Some more rubbish" quoted in Pares, 443.

283 "Very disturbing communications" Maria Fyodorovna, 174.

283 "Absolutely no news" Ibid.

283 "My own beloved" Fuhrmann, 698.

283 "Yr little family" Ibid.

284 "Can advise nothing" Ibid., 699.

284 "Sandro came to lunch" Maria Fyodorovna, 175.

284 "I hold you tight" Fuhrmann, 702.

285 "A sorrowful meeting!" Maria Fyodorovna, 175.

285 "he gave in . . . I felt stunned" Ibid., 176.

285 "he opened his poor" Ibid.

285 "first for Russia" Ibid.

285–6 "She is very calm" Ibid., 177.

285 "incomparable and moving" Ibid.

285 "Right in front of Nicky's eyes" Ibid.

285–6 "I walked down" Hanbury-Williams, 167–70.

286 "Today is one" Maria Fyodorovna, 177.

287 "Nicky enters" Alexander, 290.

287 "infinitely sad" Ibid., 292.

12: FROM EX'S TO ICONS

288 "I suddenly saw" From a letter to V. M. Garshin of 16th February 1878, quoted at http://www.asopa.com/publications/2002december/kramskoy.htm, where the painting can also be seen.

289 "ideal vehicle . . . a fundamental part" Andrew Spira, *The Avant-Garde Icon: Russian Avant-Garde and the Icon Painting Tradition,* Lund Humphries, Aldershot/Burlington, Vermont, 2009, 36.

289 "These works" Ibid., 37.

289 "I affirm that" quoted in Nadejda Gorodetzky, *The Humiliated Christ in Modern Russian Thought,* SPCK, London, 1938, 8.

289 "serene acceptance" Daniel Rancour-Laferriere, *The Slave Soul of Russia: Moral Masochism and the Cult of Suffering,* NYU Press, New York, 1995, 67.

290 "ex-ham" Lili Dehn, *The Real Tsaritsa,* Little, Brown & Co., Boston, 1922, 199.

290 "[The Empress] helped me" Viroubova, 213.

291 "Wednesday, April 18th" Gilliard, 226–7.

291 "The Emperor still presents" Paléologue, *An Ambassador's Memoirs,* Hutchinson, London, 1973, 884

291 "She is often depressed" Maylunas and Mironenko, 595.

291 "endemic among the peasant masses" Rancour-Laferriere, 69.

292 "beyond question" Ibid., 70.

292 "The house is pleasant" Maylunas and Mironenko, 617.

292 "the appropriate passages" Ibid., 618.

292 "They conducted the service" Ibid.

292 "The old count" Kerensky, 328.

293 "before the closed door" Ibid 329.

293 "The whole family" Ibid.

293 "As Kerensky entered" Benckendorff, 59

293 "stiff, proud and haughty" Kerensky, 329.

293 "Before lunch I kissed" Maylunas and Mironenko, 570.

293 "It's terribly hard" Ibid., 576.

294 "The last few days" Ibid., 584.

294 "a spacious and comfortable building" Gilliard, 240.

294 "deeply upset" Maylunas and Mironenko, 584.

294 "I feel sorry for her" Ibid., 588.

294 "The spirits of the whole family" Ibid., 594.

295 "I make everything now." Ibid., 595.

295 "It appears that the idiotic" Ibid., 605.

295 "We go into the garden" Ibid., 600.

295 "For me, the night" Ibid., 601.

295 "The whole day" Ibid.

295 "In the afternoon I twirled" Ibid., 602.

295 "holding his aching legs" Ibid., 610.

295 "Well, all is God's will" Ibid., 611.

296 "This is how we" Ibid., 617.

296 "It was an immense joy" Ibid., 624.

296 "as if on purpose" Ibid.
298 "It is not difficult" Ibid., 606.
298 "Forgive the past" Ibid.
298 "The weather was still" Ibid., 632.
299 "We live here on earth" Ibid., 606.
299 "Well, all is God's will" Ibid., 611.
300 "Nilus's book . . . Very topical reading" Ibid., 610.
300 "The Bolshevik leaders here" David R. Francis, *Russia from the American Embassy,* New York, 1921, 214.
301 "How much longer" Maylunas and Mironenko, 605.
302 "The buckle of the Tsar's belt" Gilliard, 293–4.
303 "May and I attended" Maylunas and Mironenko, 640.
303 "Today dear little Alexei" Maria Fyodorovna, 453.
303 "I looked through my books" Maylunas and Mironenko, 567.
304 "They are mad" Hanbury-Williams, 172.
306 "that the current generation" Boris Yeltsin, quoted at http://www.imperialfamily.me.uk/romanovs_laid_to_rest.htm.
306 "a sheaf of flickering lights" Colin Thubron, *In Siberia,* Vintage Books, London, 2008, 10.
306 "I examined them" Ibid., 10–11.
306 "kind eyes" Wendy Slater, *The Many Deaths of Tsar Nicholas II: relics, remains and the Romanovs,* Routledge, London, 2007, 126.
309 "In 1917, Metropolitan Macarius" *Orthodox America,* Vol 2, No. 4, 1981, see http://www.allsaintsofamerica.org/martyrs/nmrpassn.html.
310 "I hold you tight" Maylunas and Mironenko, 550.

SELECT BIBLIOGRAPHY

Alexander, Grand Duke of Russia, *Once a Grand Duke,* Cosmopolitan Book Corporation, Farrar & Rinehart, New York, 1932.

Alexandra Fyodorovna, *The Last Diary of Tsaritsa Alexandra,* Kozlov, Vladimir A., and Vladimir M. Khrustalev, eds., Yale University Press, New Haven / London, 1997.

Alice, Grand Duchess of Hesse, *Letters to Her Majesty the Queen,* John Murray, London, 1885.

Almedingen, E. M., *An Unbroken Unity: A Memoir of Grand Duchess Serge of Russia,* Bodley Head, London, 1964.

Almedingen, E. M., *The Empress Alexandra, 1872–1918: A Study,* Hutchinson, London, 1961.

Arminius, *From Sarajevo to the Rhine: Generals of the Great War* [translated from the German], Hutchinson, London, 1933.

Arthur, Sir George, *Not Worth Reading,* Longmans, Green & Co., London / New York / Toronto, 1938.

Baring, Maurice, *With the Russians in Manchuria,* Methuen & Co., London, 1906.

Bark, Sir Peter, "The Last Days of the Russian Monarchy—Nicholas II at Army Headquarters" in *Russian Review,* Vol. 16, No. 3, 1957, 35–44.

Basil, John D., "Konstantin Petrovich Pobedonostsev: An Argument for a Russian State Church" in *Church History,* Vol. 64, No. 1, March 1995, 44–61.

Baylen, Joseph O., *The Tsar's "Lecturer-General": W. T. Stead and the Russian Revolution of 1905, with Two Unpublished Memoranda of Audiences with the Dowager Empress Marie Fedorovna and Nicholas II,* Research Paper Number 23, Georgia State College, Atlanta, Georgia, 1969.

Benckendorff, Count Paul, *Last Days at Tsarskoe Selo,* Heineman, London, 1927.

Benois, Alexandre, *Memoirs,* Moura Budberg, tr., 2 vols, Chatto & Windus, London, 1960, 1964.

Benois, A. N., *Moy Dnevnik 1916–1917–1918,* Russkiy Put', Moscow, 2003.

Billington, James H., *The Icon and the Axe: An Interpretive History of Russian Culture,* Weidenfeld & Nicolson, London, 1966.

Bing, Edward J., ed., *The Letters of Tsar Nicholas and Empress Marie,* Ivor Nicholson & Watson, London, 1937.

Blind, Karl, "After the Coronation at Moscow" in *The North American Review,* Vol. 163, No. 476, 1896, 17–27.

Botkin, Gleb, *The Real Romanovs,* Fleming H. Revell, New York, 1931.

Bowlt, John E., *Moscow and St Petersburg in Russia's Silver Age, 1900–1920,* Thames & Hudson, London, 2008.

Bowlt, John E. and Olga Matich, eds., *Laboratory of Dreams: The Russian Avant-Garde and Cultural Experiment,* Stanford University Press, Palo Alto, California, 1996.

Bowlt, John E., ed., tr., *Russian Art of the Avant-Garde: Theory and Criticism 1902–1934,* The Viking Press, New York, 1976.

Bradley, Joseph, "Subjects into Citizens: Civil Society, and Autocracy in Tsarist Russia" in *The American Historical Review,* Vol. 107, No. 4, 2002, 1094–1123.

Brooke, Lord, *An Eye-Witness in Manchuria,* Eveleigh Nash, London, 1905.

Brumfield, William C., "Anti-Modernism and the Neoclassical Revival in Russian Architecture, 1906–1916" in *Journal of the Society of Architectural Historians,* Vol. 48, No. 4, 1989, 371–86.

Buchanan, Sir George, *My Mission to Russia,* 2 vols, Cassell, London, 1923.

Buchanan, Meriel, *The Dissolution of an Empire,* John Murray, London, 1932.

Buxhoeveden, Sophy, *The Life and Tragedy of Alexandra Feodorovna, Empress of Russia,* Longman, London, 1928.

Carlson, Maria, *"No Religion Higher than Truth": A History of the Theosophical Movement in Russia, 1875–1922,* Princeton University Press, Princeton, New Jersey, 1993.

Carter, Miranda, *The Three Emperors: The Last Kaiser, the Last Tsar, the King Who Got Away and the Road to World War I,* Fig Tree, London, 2009.

Chavchavadze, David, *The Grand Dukes,* Atlantic International Publications, New York, 1990.

Chekhov, Anton, *Stories,* Richard Pevear and Larissa Volokhonsky, tr., Bantam Books, New York, 2000.

Chernavin, T., "The Home of the Last Tsar: As Material for a Study of Character," *The Slavonic and East European Review,* Vol. 17, No. 51, 1939, 659–67.

Clark, Katerina, *Petersburg: Crucible of Cultural Revolution,* Harvard University Press, Cambridge, Massachusetts/London, 1996.

Clay, Catrine, *King, Kaiser, Tsar: Three Royal Cousins Who Led the World to War,* Walker & Company, New York, 2007.

Clements, Jonathan, *Mannerheim: President, Soldier, Spy,* Haus, London, 2009.

Clowes, Edith W., Samuel D. Kassow, and James L West, eds., *Between Tsar and People: Educated Society and the Quest for Public Identity in Late Imperial Russia,* Princeton University Press, Princeton, New Jersey, 1991.

Cockfield, Jamie H., *White Crow: The Life and Times of the Grand Duke Nicholas Mikhailovich Romanov, 1859–1919,* Praeger, Westport, Connecticut / London, 2002.

Cornish, Nik, *The Russian Army and the First World War,* Spellmount, Stroud, England, 2006.

Crawford, Rosemary and Donald, *Michael and Natasha: The Life and Love of Michael II, the Last of the Romanov Tsars,* Weidenfeld & Nicolson, London, 1997.

Cunningham, James W., *A Vanquished Hope: The Movement for Church Renewal in Russia, 1905–1906,* St. Vladimir's Seminary Press, Yonkers, New York, 1981.

Daniel, Wallace L., *The Orthodox Church and Civil Society in Russia,* Texas A&M University Press, College Station, Texas, 2006.

Dehn, Lili, *The Real Tsaritsa,* Little, Brown & Co., Boston, 1922.

Denikin, A. I., *The Russian Turmoil,* Hutchinson, London, 1922.

Dixon, Simon, "Archimandrite Mikhail (Semenov) and Russian Christian Socialism" in *The Historical Journal,* Vol. 51, No. 3, Cambridge University Press, Cambridge, England 2008, 689–718.

Dixon, Simon, "The 'Mad Monk' Iliodor in Tsaritsyn" in *The Slavonic and East European Review,* Vol. 88, Nos. 1/2, 2010, 377–415.

Duff, David, *Hessian Tapestry,* Frederick Muller, London, 1967.

Eagar, M., *Six Years at the Russian Court,* Charles I. Bownam & Co., New York, 1906.

Elliott, David, *New Worlds: Russian Art and Society 1900–1937,* Thames & Hudson, London, 1986.

Engelstein, Laura, "Holy Russia in Modern Times: An Essay on Orthodoxy & Cultural Change" in *Past and Present,* No. 173, Oxford University Press, November 2001, 129–56.

Engelstein, Laura, and Stephanie Sandler, eds., *Self and Story in Russian History,* Cornell University Press, Ithaca, New York, 2000.

Erickson, Carolly, *Alexandra: The Last Tsarina,* Constable, London, 2002.

Farmborough, Florence, *Nurse at the Russian Front,* Futura Publications, London, 1977.

Figes, Orlando, *A People's Tragedy: The Russian Revolution, 1891–1924,* Pimlico, London, 1997.

Foley, Robert T., *German Strategy and the Path to Verdun,* Cambridge University Press, Cambridge, 2005.

Francis, David R., *Russia from the American Embassy,* Scribner's, New York, 1921.

Freeze, Gregory L., "Subversive Piety: Religion & the Political Crisis in Late Imperial Russia" in *The Journal of Modern History,* Vol. 68, No. 2, June 1996, 308–50.

Fuhrmann, Joseph T., ed., *The Complete Wartime Correspondence of Tsar Nicholas II and the Empress Alexandra, April 1914–March 1917,* Greenwood Press, Westport, Connecticut, 1999.

Gilliard, Pierre, *Thirteen Years at the Russian Court,* Hutchinson & Co., London, 1921.

Gippius, Zinaida, *Dnevniki 1893–1919 (Collected Works* Vol. 8*),* Russkaya Kniga, Moscow, 2003.

Gippius, Zinaida, *Zhivye Litsa (Collected Works* Vol. 6*),* Russkaya Kniga, Moscow, 2002.

Gorodetzky, Nadejda, *The Humiliated Christ in Modern Russian Thought,* SPCK, London, 1938.

Grabbe, Paul and Beatrice, eds., *The Private World of the Last Tsar,* Collins, London, 1985.

Guins, George C., "The Fateful Days of 1917" in *Russian Review,* Vol. 26, No. 3, 1967, 286–95.

Gurko, V. I., *Features and Figures of the Past: Government and Opinion in the Reign of Nicholas II,* tr. L. Matveev, Russell & Russell, New York, 1967.

Hagemeister, Michael, "Vladimir Solov'ëv and Sergej Nilus: Apocalypticism and Judeophobia," in William Peter van den Bercken, Manon de Courten, and Evert van der Zweerde, eds., *Vladimir Solov'ëv: Reconciler and Polemicist,* Selected Papers of the International Vladimir Solov'ëv Conference held at the University of Nijmegen, the Netherlands, in September 1998, Peeters Publishers, 2000.

Hall, Coryne, *Imperial Dancer,* Sutton, Stroud, England, 2005.

Hamilton, George Heard, *The Art and Architecture of Russia,* Penguin, London, 1990.

Hanbury-Williams, Sir John, *The Emperor Nicholas II as I Knew Him,* Arthur L. Humphreys, London, 1922.

Harcave, Sidney, *Count Sergei Witte and the Twilight of Imperial Russia,* M. E. Sharpe, Armonk, New York/London, 2004.

Harden, Maximilian, *Monarchy and Men,* Eveleigh Nash, London, 1912.

Harrison, William, and Avril Pyman, eds., *Poetry, Prose and Public Opinion: Aspects of Russia 1850–1970: Essays Presented in Memory of Dr N.E. Andreyev,* Avebury Publishing Company, Amersham, England, 1984.

Healey, Dan, "Masculine Purity and 'Gentlemen's Mischief': Sexual Exchange and Prostitution between Russian Men, 1861–1941" in *Slavic Review,* Vol. 60, No. 2, 2001, 233–65.

Hosking, Geoffrey, *Russia: People and Empire, 1552–1917,* Harvard University Press, Cambridge, Massachusetts, 1997.

Iliodor, *The Mad Monk of Russia: Life, Memoirs and Confessions of Sergei Michailovich Trufanoff,* Century Co., New York, 1918.

Iroshnikov, Mikhail, Liudmila Protsai, and Yuri Shelayev, *The Sunset of the Romanov Dynasty,* Terra, Moscow, 1992.

Izvolsky, Count Alexander, *Recollections of a Foreign Minister,* Garden City, New York, 1921.

Jahn, Hubertus F., *Patriotic Culture in Russia During World War I,* U.M.I., Ann Arbor, Michigan, 1991.

Jonge, Alex de, *The Life and Times of Grigorii Rasputin,* Collins, London, 1982.

Joubert, Carl, *The Truth About the Tsar and the Present State of Russia,* Eveleigh Nash, London, 1905.

Kennedy, Janet Elizabeth, *The "Mir iskusstva" Group and Russian Art 1898–1912,* Garland Publishing Inc., New York/London, 1977.

Kerensky, Alexander, *The Kerensky Memoirs: Russia and History's Turning Point,* Cassell, London, 1966.

Kerensky, Alexander, and Paul Bulygin, *The Murder of the Romanovs,* Hutchinson, London, 1935.

King, Greg, *The Court of the Last Tsar: Pomp, Power, and Pageantry in the Reign of Nicholas II,* John Wiley & Sons, Hoboken, New Jersey, 2006.

Kizenko, Nadieszda, *A Prodigal Saint: Father John of Kronstadt and the Russian People,* Pennsylvania State University Press, University Park, Pennsylvania, 2000.

Kizenko, Nadieszda, "Protectors of Women and the Lower Orders: Constructing Sainthood in Modern Russia" in Kivelson, Valerie A. and Robert H. Greene, eds., *Orthodox Russia: Belief and Practice Under the Tsars,* Pennsylvania State University Press, University Park, Pennsylvania, 2003.

Knox, Alfred, *With the Russian Army 1914–1917,* 2 vols., Hutchinson, London, 1921.

Knox, Zoe Katrina, *Russian Society and the Orthodox Church: Religion in Russia After Communism,* Routledge Curzon, London / New York, 2005.

Kokovtsov, Vladimir Nikolaevich, *Out Of My Past: The Memoirs of Count Kokovtsov,* H. H. Fisher, ed., L. Matveev, tr., Stanford University Press/OUP, Palo Alto, California, and Oxford, UK, 1935.

Kondakov, Nikodim Pavlovich, *The Russian Icon,* Ellis H. Minns, tr., Clarendon Press, Oxford, 1927.

Koslof, Edward E., *Red Priests: Renovationism, Russian Orthodoxy, and Revolution, 1905–1946,* Indiana University Press, Bloomington, 2003.

K.R., *Stikhotvorenia,* Petersburg, 1911.

Kschessinska, Mathilde, *Dancing in Petersburg,* Dance Books, London, 2005.

Kuropatkin, A. N., *Dnevnik Generala Kuropatkina,* State Public Historical Library of Russia, Moscow, 2010.

Kurth, Peter, *Tsar: The Lost World of Nicholas and Alexandra,* Little, Brown, Boston, 1995.

Lamsdorff, N., *Dnevnik,* Moscow, 1926.

Lensen, George Alexander, "The Attempt on the Life of Nicholas II in Japan" in *Russian Review,* Vol. 20, No. 3, 1961, 232–53.

Leudet, Maurice, *Nicolas II Intime,* F. Juven, Paris, 1898.

Lieven, Dominic, *Nicholas II, Emperor of All the Russias,* John Murray, London, 1993.

Löwe, Heinz-Dietrich, "Political Symbols and Rituals of the Russian-Radical Right, 1900–1914" in *The Slavonic and East European Review,* Vol. 76, No. 3, 1998, 441–66.

Major, H. D. A., *The Life and Letters of William Boyd Carpenter [Bishop of Ripon, Chaplain to Queen Victoria, and Clerk of the Closet to Edward VII, and George V],* John Murray, London, 1925.

Maria Fyodorovna, *Dnevniki Imperatritsy Marii Fedorovny (1914–1920, 1923 gody),* Vagrius, Moscow, 2005.

Marie, Grand Duchess of Russia, *Education of a Princess,* Blue Ribbon Books Inc., New York, 1930.

Markov, Vladimir, *Russian Futurism: A History,* Macgibbon and Kee Ltd., London, 1969.

Marks, Steven G., *How Russia Shaped the Modern World: From Art to Anti-Semitism, Ballet to Bolshevism,* Princeton University Press, Princeton/Oxford, 2004.

Massie, Robert K., *Nicholas and Alexandra,* Gollancz, London, 1967.

Massie, Robert K., *The Romanovs: The Final Chapter,* Cape, London, 1995.

Matonina, Ella, and Edward Govorushko, *K.R.*, Molodaya Gvardiya, Moscow, 2008.

Maud, Renée Elton, *One Year at the Russian Court: 1904–1905,* John Lane, London/New York, 1918.

Maylunas, Andrei, and Sergei Mironenko, eds., *A Lifelong Passion: Nicholas and Alexandra, Their Own Story,* Weidenfeld & Nicolson, London, 1996.

McKenzie, Frederick Arthur, *From Tokyo to Tiflis: Uncensored Letters from the War,* Hurst & Blackett Ltd., London, 1905.

Mirsky, D. S., *A History of Russian Literature,* Routledge & Kegan Paul, London, 1968.

Morrill, Dan L., "Nicholas II and the Call for the First Hague Conference" in *The Journal of Modern History,* Vol. 46, No. 2, 1974, 296–313.

Mossolov, A. A., *At the Court of the Last Tsar,* E. W. Dickes, tr., Methuen & Co., London, 1935.

Neilson, Keith, *Britain and the Last Tsar,* Clarendon Press, London, 1995.

Newmarch, Rosa, *The Devout Russian: A Book of Thoughts and Counsels Gathered from the Saints and Fathers of the Eastern Church and Modern Russian Authors,* Herbert Jenkins, London, 1918.

Nicholas and Alexandra: The Family Albums, text and captions by Prince Michael of Greece, conceived and compiled by Andrei Maylunas, Catherine O'Keeffe, tr., Tauris Parke Books, London, 1992

Nicholas II, *Dnevnik [1913–1918],* Zakharov, Moscow, 2007.

Nicholas II, *Journal Intime de Nicholas II,* A. Pierre Agrege, tr., Payot, Paris, 1925.

Nichols, Robert L., and Theofanis George Stavrou, eds., *Russian Orthodoxy under the Old Regime,* University of Minnesota Press, Minneapolis, 1978.

Noel, Gerard, *Princess Alice: Queen Victoria's Forgotten Daughter,* Constable, London, 1974.

Norman, Geraldine, *The Hermitage: The Biography of a Great Museum,* Jonathan Cape, London, 1997.

Nostitz, Countess, *Romance and Revolutions,* Hutchinson, London, 1937.

Oldenburg, Sergei S., *Last Tsar: Nicholas II, His Reign and His Russia,* 4 vols., Patrick J. Rollins, ed., Leonid I. Mihalap and Patrick J. Rollins, tr., Academic International Press, Florida, 1975–8.

Paléologue, Maurice, *An Ambassador's Memoirs,* Hutchinson, London, 1973.

Pares, Bernard, *The Fall of the Russian Monarchy: A Study of the Evidence,* Jonathan Cape, London, 1939.

Pares, Bernard, "Sir George Buchanan in Russia" in *The Slavonic Review,* Vol. 3, No. 9, 1925, 576–86.

Pipes, Richard, *Russia Under the Old Regime,* Penguin, London, 1982.

Pipes, Richard, *The Russian Revolution, 1899–1924,* Penguin, London, 1994.

Podbolotov, Sergei, "'. . . and the Entire Mass of Loyal People leapt up': The Attitude of Nicholas II Towards the Pogroms" in *Cahiers du Monde Russe,* Vol. 45, No1/2, 2004, 193–207.

Presto, Jenifer, "Unbearable Burdens: Aleksandr Blok and the Modernist Resistance to Progeny and Domesticity" in *Slavic Review,* Vol. 63, No. 1, 2004, 6–25.

Radzinsky, Edvard, *Rasputin: The Last Word,* Judson Rosengrant, tr., Weidenfeld & Nicolson, London, 2000.

Radzinsky, Edvard, *The Last Tsar: The Life and Death of Nicholas II,* Hodder, London, 1992.

Radziwill, Princess Catherine, *The Intimate Life of the Last Tsarina,* Cassell, London, 1927.

Rancour-Laferriere, Daniel, *The Slave Soul of Russia: Moral Masochism and the Cult of Suffering,* NYU Press, New York, 1995.

Rappaport, Helen, *Ekaterinburg: The Last Days of the Romanovs,* Hutchinson, London, 2008.

Rasputin, Grigory: *Dnevnik Rasputina,* Olma Media Group, Moscow, 2008.

Rasputin, Maria: *My Father,* Cassell & Co., London, 1934.

Rawson, Don C., *Russian Rightists and the Revolution of 1905,* Cambridge University Press, Cambridge, 1995.

Rodzianko, M., *The Reign of Rasputin: An Empire's Collapse,* Philpot, London, 1927.

Rogger, Hans, "The Beilis Case: Anti-Semitism and Politics in the Reign of Nicholas II" in *Slavic Review,* Vol. 25, No. 4, 1966, 615–29.

Röhl, John C.G., Martin Warren, and David Hunt, *Purple Secret: Genes, "Madness" and the Royal Houses of Europe,* Bantam Press, London, 1998.

Rossiiskii imperatorskii dom: [al'bom portretov], Petersburg, 1902.

Russia's Golden Map: Masterpieces of Russian Art, from the collections of the State Tretyakov Gallery and Russian Art Museums, Scanrus, Moscow, 2003.

Sazonov, Sergei, *Fateful Years,* Stokes, New York, 1928.

Schelking, Eugène de, *Recollections of a Russian Diplomat,* Macmillan, New York, 1918.

Sciacca, Franklin A., "In Imitation of Christ: Boris and Gleb and the Ritual Consecration of the Russian Land" in *Slavic Review,* Vol. 49, No. 2, 1990, 253–60.

Screen, J. E. O., *Mannerheim: The Years of Preparation,* Hurst, London, 1970.

Shevzov, Vera, *Russian Orthodoxy on the Eve of Revolution,* Oxford University Press, New York, 2004.

Shulgin, Vasily, *Poslednii Ochevidets: Memuary, Ocherki, Sny,* Olma-Press, Moscow, 2002.

Sinyavsky, Andrei, *Ivan the Fool: Russian Folk Belief,* Joanne Turnbull and Nikolai Formozov, tr., Glas, Moscow, 2007.

Slater, Wendy, *The Many Deaths of Tsar Nicholas II: Relics, Remains and the Romanovs,* Routledge, London, 2007.

Spira, Andrew, *The Avant-Garde Icon: Russian Avant-Garde and the Icon Painting Tradition,* Lund Humphries, Aldershot/Burlington, Vermont, 2009.

Spiridovitch, Alexandre, *Les Dernières Années de la Cour de Tzarskoïe Selo,* 2 vols., Payot, Paris, 1928–9.

Steinberg, John W., *All the Tsar's Men: Russia's General Staff and the Fate of the Empire, 1898–1914,* Woodrow Wilson Center Press, Washington D.C., 2010.

Steinberg, Mark D., and Heather J. Coleman, eds., *Sacred Stories: Religion and Spirituality in Modern Russia,* Indiana University Press, Bloomington, Indiana, 2007.

Steinberg, Mark D., and Vladimir M. Khrustalëv, *The Fall of the Romanovs: Political Dreams and Personal Struggles in a Time of Revolution,* Yale University Press, New Haven/London, 1995.

Surh, Gerald D., *1905 in St. Petersburg: Labor, Society, and Revolution,* Stanford University Press, Stanford, California, 1989.

Sworakowski, Witold S., "The Authorship of the Abdication Document of Nicholas II" in *Russian Review,* Vol. 30, No. 3, 1971, 277–86.

Tarasov, Oleg, *Icon and Devotion: Sacred Spaces in Imperial Russia,* Robin Milner-Gulland, tr. and ed., Reaktion Books, London, 2002.

Thubron, Colin, *In Siberia,* Vintage Books, London, 2008.

Thyret, Isolde, " 'Blessed Is the Tsaritsa's Womb': The Myth of Miraculous Birth and Royal Motherhood in Muscovite Russia" in *Russian Review,* Vol. 53, No. 4, 1994, 479–96.

Tikhmenev, N. M, *Iz vospominanii o poslednikh dnyakh prebyvania Imperatora Nikolaia II v Stavke,* Izdanie Kruzhka Revnitelei Russkogo Proshlogo, Nice, 1925.

Timberlake, Charles E., ed., *Religious and Secular Forces in Late Tsarist Russia: Essays in Honor of Donald W. Treadgold,* University of Washington Press, Seattle/London, 1992.

Tuchman, Barbara W., *The Guns of August,* Presidio Press, New York, 1962.

Vacaresco, H., *Kings and Queens I Have Known,* Harper & Brothers Publishers, New York/London, 1904.

Van der Kiste, John, and Coryne Hall, *Once a Grand Duchess: Xenia, Sister of Nicholas II,* Sutton Publishing, Stroud, England, 2002.

Varlamov, Aleksei, *Grigorii Rasputin-Novyi,* Molodaya Gvardia, Moscow, 2007.

Vassili, Count Paul, *Behind the Veil at the Russian Court,* Cassell & Co. Ltd., London/New York/Toronto/Melbourne, 1913.

Veresaev, V., *In the War,* Leo Wiener, tr., Mitchell Kennerley, New York, 1917.

Viroubova, Anna, *Memories of the Russian Court,* Macmillan, London, 1923.

Vyrubova, Anna, *Vospominania,* Zakharov, Moscow, 2009.

Waldron, Peter, *Governing Tsarist Russia,* Palgrave Macmillan, New York, 2007.

Ware, Timothy, *The Orthodox Church,* Penguin, Harmondsworth, England, 1967.

Warwick, Christopher, *Ella: Princess, Saint and Martyr,* Wiley, Chichester, England, 2006.

Weber, Mark, "The Jewish Role in the Bolshevik Revolution and Russia's Early Soviet Regime" in *The Journal of Historical Review,* Vol. 14, No. 1, 1994, 4–22.

Wildman, Allan K., *The End of the Russian Imperial Army,* Princeton University Press, Princeton, New Jersey, 1980.

Wilton, Robert, *The Last Days of the Romanovs,* Thornton Butterworth Ltd., London, 1920.

Witte, Count, *Memoirs,* Sidney Harcave, tr., M. E. Sharpe, London, 1990.

Wortman, Richard, *Scenarios of Power: From Alexander II to the Abdication of Nicholas II,* Princeton University Press, Princeton, New Jersey, 2000.

Yusupov, Felix, *Lost Splendour,* Jonathan Cape, London, 1953.

Zernov, Nicolas, *The Russian Religious Renaissance of the Twentieth Century,* Darton, Longman & Todd, London, 1963.

WEB SITES

http://www.alexanderpalace.org/palace/index.html (See, in particular, extracts from Nicky's diaries, translated by Jsenya Dyakova.)

http://www.kingandwilson.com/AtlantisArticles/Inheritance.htm (Greg King and Penny Wilson: Official Anti-Semitism and the Last of the Romanovs)

http://www.kingandwilson.com/AtlantisArticles/SummerSkerries.htm (Greg King: Summers in the Finnish Skerries: Life Aboard the Russian Imperial Yachts)

INDEX

1. Various reasons have been suggested for Alix's constant ill health, ranging from the purely psychosomatic to genuine heart problems. Why do you think she took to her bed so often, and could her illness, whatever it was, have been cured?

2. Is it fair to suggest that Queen Victoria exercised a rather negative influence over her granddaughter Alix?

3. The conventional wisdom has been that Nicholas II was a weak Tsar, constantly swayed by the opinions of others and unable, or unwilling, to assert himself. Do you think this judgment is accurate, or has he been treated unfairly by history?

4. How do you think Alix and Nicky measured up as parents?

5. How responsible was the Tsar for the events of "Bloody Sunday" in 1905, when many demonstrators were killed in St. Petersburg's Palace Square?

6. What was the nature of Alix and Nicky's relationship with Ania Vyrubova? Was she just Alix's close friend, or something more sinister?

7. Why were Alix and Nicky so drawn to mysterious "mystical" characters?—first Monsieur Philippe, and later Grigory Rasputin? Were they fooled by these characters, or was there some justification for the confidence the Tsar and Tsarina placed in them?

8. To Alix and Nicky's horror, many of their close relatives experienced matrimonial disasters and were frequently involved in scandal. Can you identify any particular reasons for this, or were these just cases of bad luck?

9. Both Alix and Nicky often prayed for wisdom, and yet they frequently seemed to act very unwisely. Did they receive no answer to their prayers, or were they incapable of hearing the answer?

St. Martin's Griffin

10. Given the characters of everyone involved, could the events of 1917 and 1918 have turned out any differently?

11. Would it have made any difference if the Tsarevich Alexei had not been a hemophiliac?

12. How responsible was King George V for the assassination of his Romanov cousins? Could anything have been done to save them?

13. The Russian Orthodox Church has beatified Alix, Nicky, and their children as "Holy Royal Passion-Bearers." Can this be justified?

For more reading group suggestions, visit www.readinggroupgold.com.